Also by Stuart Sillars

ND SURVIVAL IN FIRST WORLD WAR BRITAIN

**Also published by Macmillan*

£25

CW01623663

BRITISH ROM/
AND THE SECONI

*ART

Ihr naht euch wieder, schwankende Gestalten!
Die früh sich einst dem trüben Blick gezeigt.
Versuch' ich wohl, euch diesmal festzuhalten?
Fühl' ich mein Herz noch jenem Wahn geneigt?
Ihr drängt euch zu! nu gut, so mögt ihr walten,
Wie ihr aus Dunst und Nebel um mich steigt;
Mein Busen fühlt sich jugendlich erschüttert
Vom Zauberhauch, der euren Zug umwittert.

J. von Goethe, *Faust*, Dedication

DMS
1904–1990

Contents

List of Illustrations

Acknowledgements

Any book of this sort is to some degree a collaborative effort and I am glad to thank many people for their help in its writing. The staff of the University Library, Cambridge were as always patient and encyclopaedic. The Rev Brian Ruddock provided much helpful advice about the painting by Cecil Collins discussed in Chapter 5; Carol C. Abdo, of Clare Hall, Cambridge, read parts of the text in early draft and offered much help and support. Jenny Wood, of the Department of Art, Imperial War Museum, answered many specific queries and gave invaluable assistance with the illustrations. The staffs of the South London Art Gallery, London Borough of Southwark, and the City of Bristol Museum and Art Gallery, helped in the reproduction of pictures by Frank Dobson and Henry Carr respectively. Sarah Dann and Margaret Cannon of the Macmillan Press gave encouragement and practical help in no small measure; Anthony Grahame edited the text with great accuracy and tact.

Despite this plethora of assistance, those errors, omissions and examples of wilful perversity which remain are my sole responsibility.

March, Cambridgeshire, 1990

STUART SILLARS

1

Some Versions of Romanticism

I

Entrance to a Lane[1] is a painting that impresses us at once with its immediacy. We are drawn into the pool of light of the lane itself by a composition which has all the clarity of Turner's vortices yet none of their frenzy. A series of roughly ovoid forms linked to stems in the top quarter of the foreground tell us that we are standing beneath a tree; the balance of deep, cool greens and rich, hot ochres not only reveals the landscape before us but presents the still air through which it is seen. A white rectangle receding in the centre is the lane itself; to its right a further wall of ochre sharply defines the 'entrance' and then, further back, melts with a sombre grey as the lane recedes. Alive with experience, the image is no less essentially a painting: the bird suggested at eye-height is a *trompe l'oeil* impasto streak, the changing textures of path and foliage are rough stipple work, the heat between us and the land is the medium brushed porcelain-smooth. The painting's rhythms are at once those of a fragment of experience – 'where you lean against a bank while the van passes',[2] perhaps – and those of an abstract pattern, circling yet static, recessive yet of one surface. It is, in short, a painting which embodies and revitalises attitudes and techniques which are the essence of English Romanticism; and it was painted in 1939.

Graham Sutherland's painting is one of the finest, as well as one of the earliest, examples of something which for a while accounted for a dominant tradition in British painting and writing in the central decades of this century. It is something which has recently become known as 'neo-Romanticism', and those who worked within its shores regarded as a school of 'neo-Romantics'. This is not a term which is helpful; it has a tone of dismissiveness which suggests a second-handedness of approach which implies a lack of direction, much as 'neo-Georgian' is used to describe unimaginative housing estates of the sixties and seventies. It seems to me that there is more a sense of continuing and extending an earlier approach than the kind of refuge-taking the term implies, and for this reason I shall use 'Romantic' as a general label for the work to be discussed here. Even this is misleading: the artists and writers were not a school or a movement – English art does not have such careful organisation, preferring to be gloriously disruptive of the best laid schemes of art-historians. Perhaps the best way to regard them is as a series of separate strands – now intersecting, now diverging – to produce the fabric of the art of the decades. Sutherland's painting is in a sense representative, in being a landscape. There is more to what the artists and writers of the time produced than a vision of the landscape; yet the land, and the vision, are twin forces which are rarely absent from the fabric, in varying proportions, in differing intensities, and in changing forms.

Looking at Sutherland's painting raises a number of questions about Romanticism in the forties. At the simplest level, we are prompted to discover how typical this painting is – what facets and features of its style and stance may be found in other work of this painter, let alone that of others working at around the same time. And that begs a larger question: how far is forties Romanticism something that can be reduced to a similarity of styles, and how far, like Romanticism in the eighteenth and early nineteenth centuries, is it a matter of stance and approach rather than likeness of subject and form? If the later upsurge takes many forms, what are they? How may they be defined and clarified, in both form and philosophy? Underlying all these there is a larger question: what is it that binds together forms and styles which are apparently so diverse in their visual identity?

Once we have moved towards answers to these questions, we must address others. Where does Romantic art fit within the longer stream of British art during the century – a stream which, even in the thirties, included tributaries as diverse as Euston Road documentary, the formalism of the 7 & 5 and Unit One, and a Surrealist tide which, to judge from the evidence of the 1936 exhibition, was in itself a flowing together of several separate currents. Within this large question is contained a more specific one: how is it possible for artists who were formerly adherents of the most rigid theories of abstraction to become followers of something which appears to revert to the practice of representational art?

It is not only change within visual art that we must consider. What is the nature of Romanticism in literary art? How is it related to painting? Even those with the most limited acquaintance with English painting will suspect that Romanticism of the mid-century is strongly literary; but what is the precise nature of the links? We need, too, to spread our view still further, and ask about the links with more popular art of the time – film, illustration, poster design, photography. In the mass communication age few artists can be impervious to the existence, if not the influence, of such forms.

The final question is perhaps the hardest. What is the relation between these Romantic artists and their environment, social, political, human and natural? No art can exist in a vacuum and, as the title of this book implies, Romantic art of the forties is firmly and deeply a response to the brutality and suffering it finds all around it. As George Orwell had made clear in the thirties,[3] all art is political, even if it seems consciously to avoid making a political statement. Much of the finest Romantic art of the time, as well as a fair amount of the worst, reveals deep commitment of a kind which is political because of the human values it represents, not through adherence to a more limited stance, and stating a creed, not a manifesto: the nature of that creed and its role and value at the time is something which we cannot ignore.

II

The thirties were, artistically as well as politically, an immensely crowded decade. English art was as splendidly various as it had ever been. Ben Nicholson was producing abstract constructions, the series of white reliefs which reduce proportion to essential elements and yet make profoundly witty comments on depth and recession. Naum Gabo and Barbara Hepworth were experimenting with sculptural forms and textures of similar purity, while Henry Moore moved on from his studies of Toltec-Mayan forms to explore the massiveness of the human figure within genres that were still broadly traditional. Paul Nash was exploring idioms that brought together continental Surrealism, a Celtic concern for prehistory and the English landscape tradition; John Piper was developing a personal abstract style and experimenting with collage, while

Graham Sutherland was moving from etching to the broad landscape compositions created from his encounter with the Welsh landscape. Depending on your point of view, it was all either a vast confusion of styles – showing a bewilderment in the face of the European avant-garde or making testimony to the diversity of the English genius – or a melting pot waiting for the mould. It is tempting for the art historian to take the latter view, and see all the separate elements as waiting for the various rallying-cries (which Chapter 2 will chronicle) and, once having heard them, to develop with the more coherent diversity of different kinds of representationalism.

English art in the thirties has been fully and ably discussed elsewhere[4] and it is not my intention to cover the ground again here. The point I wish to make is that the period was one of very great diversity, and that seeing in it an abrupt switch from Abstraction to Romanticism is to simplify it in at least two ways. First, there is no gathering together under the banner of Romanticism, since the art of the forties is in its own way markedly disparate in styles and stances; secondly, abstraction does not die at the birth of Romanticism, but rather the two are different facets of the same philosophy, the newer Romanticism growing in part from the purity of vision that abstraction has achieved and giving to it, in return, a sense of direction which perhaps before it lacked. It is a coming together of what at first and superficial sight might seem to be opposites but which are in fact not so very far distant: the union is one that is richly productive, as Chapter 2 will reveal.

If we cannot see in visual art a sudden change of direction, what may be said of literary movements? In his incisive study *Reading the Thirties*, Bernard Bergonzi remarks:

> This, indeed, is a common assumption of literary history, where the 'social realist' poetry of the thirties disappears and is replaced overnight by the 'neo-Romanticism' of the forties.[5]

As Bergonzi goes on to make clear, this has enough truth about it to make it attractive yet too little to be convincing. The thirties were a decade when writers were concerned with social conditions, but not to the exclusion of all else; and, in any case, to think of Romanticism as the antithesis of social concerns is to betray a limited grasp of what it is. English Romanticism has at its roots a deep concern with social realism, evidenced in Byron's involvement in Greece, Shelley's concern with English political reform, Blake's passionate anger at the literal satanic mills of the Midlands and the intellectual ones of the academic establishment. Whatever we may say about Wordsworth's movement from lukewarm revolutionary to tepid Tory, at the essence of his writing is a concern for individual experience which argues in itself for an interest in the place of the individual, whatever his or her origin, within the larger social structure. Similarly, a very large part of Constable's interest in landscape is taken up with a concern for the relationship between the individual and the natural setting, to suggest a structure of harmonious stewardship. The idea that Romanticism is a state of refuge from reality is a later nineteenth-century coining, perhaps the result of post-Tennysonian mediaevalism and the art-and-craft withdrawal of some of Morris's followers, but not Morris himself.

It is the same for the writers of the thirties. Auden not only wrote a *Letter to Lord Byron*,[6] but couched it in a fine imitation of the earlier poet's style, with a directness of address to individual mores that is a twentieth-century equivalent of *Don Juan*.[7] His early political plays are in many senses a return to the artistic and moral dilemmas of Byron and Shelley: the hero of *Paid on Both Sides*[8] is in many ways a descendant of *Manfred*,[9] and the concerns he and his fellows show are not too far removed from that of the adolescent Wordsworth in coming to terms with the world in which he finds himself. MacNeice's *Autumn Journal*[10] is a tentative, personal version of *The Prelude*,[11] observing contemporary reality and commenting upon it with the psychological apparatus of its day as Wordworth did with that of his own age.

The concern for the spirtual well-being of the people apparent in Day Lewis, Auden and Spender again has its basis in the Romantics' feeling that all should be able to share the experience of individual development, which was generally restricted to the few; and it is striking that, for example, 'An Elementary School Class Room in a Slum' ends with an idealised vision of the liberating power of literacy and education in terms of a direct sensory experience of nature, exhorting the windows which contain the children in the school to

> Break, O break open, till they break the town
> And show the children to the fields and all their world
> Azure on their sands, to let their tongues
> Run naked into books, the white and green leaves open

> The history theirs whose language is the sun.[12]

The equation between the natural world and literary or aesthetic endeavour as forces of moral nurture is one that is frequent in forties Romanticism, as will become clear in the later chapters of this book; it is also one that has clear origins in the outlook of the first Romantics.

Social concerns are not always so controlled. When Day Lewis warns us to take heed of the warplanes in 'Newsreel', his passionate irony and anger seem direct linear descendants of Shelley's in *The Mask of Anarchy*[13] – though even here the natural world provides a fundamental source of imagery:

> See the big guns, rising, groping, erected
> To plant death in your world's soft womb.
> Fire-bud, smoke-blossom, iron seed projected –
> Are these exotics? They will grow nearer home[14]

It is not only the poets who continue the passion. George Orwell's Gordon Comstock,[15] failed poet and inadequate lover, rails against the economic system and the social constraints on human relationships with an interconnectedness and force that suggests the Blake of the *Visions of the Daughters of Albion*[16] as well as the economic diatribes of the *Songs of Innocence and Experience*.[17]

Even the diction of so many thirties writers, in consciously adopting the idiom of the people, owes much to the precedent of Wordsworth and Coleridge in the *Lyrical Ballads*:[18] the fact that Auden and others move away from it to something highly personal is not perhaps so very different from the later shifts in style of those earlier advocates of poetic democracy. There is even a parallel in the political stance: despite the sense of involvement cultivated by Auden, Spender, Day Lewis, their work remains aloof, so that they take on the stature of the Bard so revered by the early Romantics, speaking in a voice which, although struggling to make itself heard by the people, is essentially separate from them.

There is a similar paradox behind other movements of the time. In the cinema, the most significant achievements in Britain lay in the field of the documentary, in the guiding hands of John Grierson. Yet social observation was not all it seemed; Grierson himself revealed that his aim was to influence rather than to inform when he remarked 'I look upon cinema as a pulpit'.[19] *Night Mail*[20] had music by Benjamin Britten and a text in part by W. H. Auden; *Coalface*,[21] produced by Grierson, had the same combination and was edited by the painter William Coldstream. The camerawork was free and subjective, giving an intensely-felt presentation of the work and the workers, who emerged as heroic figures, either battling against nature in the manner of Flaherty's *Man of Aran*[22] or against mechanical forces in *Night Mail*. In *Housing Problems*,[23] a film revealing the conditions of slums, there is still a desire to show things in an imaginative way: cockroaches are shown silhouetted against peeling wallpaper behind a brass and iron bedstead, and the slum-dwellers again emerge as heroes of Romantic individualism. The whole is summed up by A. Vesselo, a leading critic of the day, in a review of *Out to Play*:[24]

> Mr Lowenstein's attitude towards the slum children whom he photographs at play in the streets and in the parks is frankly romantic; as is indicated by the forgiving smiles of his householders on discovering that urchins have tampered with their door-knockers, and, in the final playground sequence, by the interjected heads-against-the-sky shots that we know so well.[25]

This shows very clearly that the presentation of Romantic individualism is not inimical to realism of a sort, and that the two co-habited as easily in the films of the decade as in its poetry. It is all a kind of preparation for perhaps the most Romantic film image of the war years: the sequence showing a Spitfire gleaming in the sun as it shoots over a field of ripened corn which waves in its slipstream, showing a unity between the Romantic hero, the machine and the natural world that typifies this kind of Romantic realism.[26]

The documentary urge did not only affect film-makers. The thirties saw the expansion of radio programmes into similar territory. A series of talks titled *The Day's Work* brought people of all backgrounds – a steeplejack, a postman, a Covent Garden porter – to the microphone to describe their jobs; more controversial ground was occupied by the *Whither Britain?* series of talks begun in 1934. Lance Sieveking began to develop 'radio features', helped by new outside broadcast techniques: *Gale Warning* and *Scotland Yard* were popular in this genre. Enquiries of a different but related kind were carried out by Mass-Observation, the organisation founded in 1936 by Charles Madge and Tom Harrisson whose voluntary 'observers' recorded the behaviour of local people as well as their own experiences.[27] In the thirties they recorded the events of coronation day, *May 12th*,[28] and, amongst other things, discussed the social importance of 'Doin' the Lambeth Walk', reactions to the threat of war, and the courtship habits of working-class couples on the beach at Blackpool.[29] In a sense it was part amateur sociology and part voyeurism, but it also evidences an interest in the common person as Romantic hero which descends directly from Wordsworth and Coleridge, and was part of the general setting from which grew the Romantic realist tradition of the forties.

Much the same is true of contemporary photo-journalism. Stefan Lorant founded the magazines *Lilliput*[30] and *Picture Post*[31] in the thirties, both of which combined factual record with a passionate concern for the rights of the individual. *Picture Post*'s articles on unemployment explored the territory of the film documentary, and its treatment of anti-semitism in Nazi Germany was the most outspoken of its time, having a profound effect, as Chapter 6 will show, on the young Michael Tippett.

All of these share a further element which we may associate with earlier Romanticism; an intrinsic and passionate political commitment, whether it be found in Auden's early socialist poetry or the faith in the individual working-man in the films of Grierson and others. Throughout forties Romanticism, this commitment to the individual remains strong, whether it lie in voicing the confusion of personal experience, or simply in revealing a strongly individual vision.

When all of these forces are considered, the sudden disappearance of social realism and its replacement by Romanticism in the poetry of the very end of the decade is revealed as nothing more than a convenient fiction for the literary historian. The most celebrated poems of this time have a quality which makes them part of the immediate, sensual tradition of Romanticism while losing none of their human or political commitment. It is as if the general passion, the wide-angle admonition, the vision of the common man as hero of the earlier years, are all brought into a close focus which is intensely personal and expresses itself through an awareness of just how precious everyday human experience is, most particularly so when it is shared.

This is most particularly true of poems written near the end of the decade. MacNeice's 'The Sunlight on the Garden',[32] with its wonderfully taut, involuted structure, has a valedictory richness which suggests the damascene texture of Keats' experience seen through a gauze of twentieth-century disillusion. Auden's love-lyrics, especially 'Lullaby',[33] show the power of the totalitarian state to threaten human love but not to destroy it; feelings are hedged about with all sorts of qualifications, but they endure. The Romantic sense of doom, perhaps self-inflicted and self-indulgent in earlier ages, has been given literal truth and urgency by the events around us.

These thoughts all come together most completely in Auden's 'September 1, 1939'.[34] The 'points of light' shown in a world seeming to await its destruction are 'ironic'; the realism of the thirties means that they could be nothing else. But the compassion of the thirties, born of the Romantic tradition, also ensures that they remain, and are not extinguished quite by refined despair or aristocratic cynicism. The fact that Auden later disowned the line 'We must love one another or die' does not negate it; it becomes an immediate personal response in time of war which reveals a tentative advancing of opinion, a lack of confidence in idea and structure which crops up repeatedly in the writing and painting of the time. Not only does this reflect the fragmentary nature of experience – a time of momentary gaps in bombing, snatched leaves and essentially temporary relationships: it seems also to echo the fragmentary, unfinished or revised state of a great deal of earlier Romantic poetry and painting. That which deals with feeling is, after all, necessarily fragile.

Out of all this emerge two key points. First, that the poetry of the thirties is not anti-Romantic because it is social realist; the two are not mutually exclusive, and indeed are often much too close even to be called different sides of the same coin. Second, that the poetry of the forties which is more obviously Romantic is only so because of the experience of the thirties. The cause has defined itself; the primacy of the individual *in tempore bello*. Now that it is too late for warnings, it is time for nurture; and the nurture is the richer for being limited and qualified by the unease and uncertainty of the situation, and the astringent, chastening force of twentieth-century modernism. In the same way, forties Romanticism in painting grew out of the purifying influence of abstraction and the liberating force of Surrealism, alongside the visual influence of film and photography. In both forms, it is the control of its antecendence which makes it a modified and socially involved form of Romanticism; it is a confrontation with reality, not a retreat from it.

III

This book does not set out to chronicle a revival of Romanticism. It is too early for that; and, in any case, inclusivity is perhaps something temperamentally opposed to the nature of Romanticism, which deals with the intensely-felt moment rather than the ordered continuum. Instead, it sets out to suggest ways in which the nature of high Romanticism – the Romanticism of Turner and Constable, but also of Cotman and Palmer – is philosophically continued, extended and rekindled in the work of the generation that reached artistic maturity during the Second World War. I have chosen to restrict the scope of the book to the years of the war because this concentration demonstrates, if anything can, the ways in which Romanticism may be used directly to address the most urgent of human needs, to show once more that Romanticism is not a retreat from reality but a direct psychological engagement with it, often with the help of an official organisation such as the War Artists' Advisory Committee which directly commissioned work from artists as a record of and comment on contemporary events and circumstances. These things apart, the war years are a natural subject of study because they saw the production of much of the finest work of the Romantic sort: if apology is needed for selectivity on this basis, I offer it here.

Even within these limits, the discussion is selective. Apart from the limitations of space, it is not the intention to be inclusive, since the presentation of a mere chronicle would suggest a uniformity which the work of the period does not possess. Instead, it looks in some measure of detail at work which seems important because it represents a particular kind of Romanticism, or because it is splendidly unrepresentative in its Romantic nature. Many aspects of the subject have been covered in detail elsewhere; many are omitted with regret. Stanley Spencer's contribution to Romanticism is not covered here because his genius lies in uniting the strand of emblematic detail most often found in the European Catholic tradition with the broader sweeps of English Romanticism; neither is Ivon Hitchens', because his landscape vision stands in a line of descent so direct that there seems little to say about it. Leslie Hurry's personal re-creation of Romanticism, at times very direct, for example in his reworking of Delacroix's *Liberty at the Barricades*[35] in *This Extraordinary Year, 1945,*[36] has a Gothic intensity which places it alongside the main stream of forties Romanticism rather than within it. David Jones receives less substance than I would wish because of the very personal nature of his writing and painting within a tradition as much Celtic as Romantic. The work of Gerald Wilde, Robert Colquhoun and Robert MacBryde seems to pursue directions of Romanticism different enough from those discussed here for it to be seen as the subject of a study of rather a different kind. The influence of the theories of Wyndham Lewis is a further specialised topic which deserves separate detailed study. I hope it will be possible at some later date to correct some of these imbalances.

It would also have been possible to discuss some of the ways in which Romanticism manifested itself in other, more popular art forms of the forties. The anthologies of poetry produced at the time, such as *Poems from the Forces*,[37] and those which were published later, such as the Oasis anthologies[38] and Catherine W. Reilly's *Chaos of the Night*,[39] are a rich vein; so, too, are the anthologies of earlier writing, pre-eminent among which are those published by Frederick Muller,[40] and the popular series of books such as Collins' *Britain in Pictures*[41] under the general editorship of W. J. Turner. These are dealt with only in passing when they could easily have been the basis of a whole chapter. A separate book could be written about wartime periodicals, pre-eminent among which should rank *Penguin New Writing*[42] and *Horizon*:[43] a cursory glance at the contents pages of any number of either will reveal the range of contributions and contributors, including as they do articles about politics, literary and art criticism, short stories, poems, film reviews and reproductions of paintings, drawings and theatre designs; these are the work of writers in the forces – miners, train-drivers and seamen as well as professional artists and critics.

Important in a different way are the volumes produced by the Ministry of Information about various facets and fronts of wartime activity, and the immense number of posters and other materials we might loosely but not dismissively call 'propaganda ephemera'. These and the treatment of contemporary events in the press are a worthy subject of study in themselves, to examine and evaluate the degree to which they might be seen within the stream of contemporary Romanticism in the attitudes they adopt and techniques they employ.

Those who wish to remedy some of these deficiencies are recommended to look at some of the many other books on the period. Robert Hewison's *Under Siege: Literary Life in London 1939–1945*[44] discusses not only writing of all kinds of the war years, but also touches on aspects of visual art and gives an account of the circumstances of production of art of all kinds. Malcolm Yorke gives a biographical introduction to the work of key artists in his *The Spirit of Place: Nine Neo-Romantic Artists*.[45] The work of individual poets of the war years has been well and extensively covered; mention here of individual studies would be invidious. Film is treated by Nicholas Pronay and Jeremy Croft in 'British Film censorship and Propaganda Policy During the Second World War',[46] Frances Thorpe and Nicholas Pronay in *British Official Films on the Second World War: A Descriptive Catalogue*[47] and Anthony Aldgate in *Britain Can Take It*.[48] Ian McLaine's *Ministry of Morale*[49] discusses the work of the Ministry of Information; R. M. Titmuss, in *Problems of Social Policy*,[50] provides an incisive and compassionate study of the human issues of war. Two exhibition catalogues also offer introductions to the visual art of the time in ways which will appeal to different readers: *The Neo-Romantics: Drawings and Watercolours*[51] accompanied an exhibition at the Imperial War Museum; *A Paradise Lost*,[52] one at the Barbican. A fuller list is provided in the Select Bibliography.

Even allowing for this book's selectivity and omissions, the 'versions of Romanticism' we may encounter in the forties are diverse: some, in fact, may not appear at first glance to have anything to do with Romanticism, while others seem to stray far beyond it into depositions of faith founded on things as various as Anglo-Catholic iconography and the nitrogen cycle.

There is that kind of Romanticism which is concerned with what is ostensibly realism; a recording of events which is, despite appearances, a Romantic rekindling of experience, which may be used for any kind of purpose from the statement of political order to the sharing of personal bewilderment. There is a reworking of the Romantic notion of the Sublime, that state of perception in which fear offers us a purification of the vision and understanding, to suggest some kind of moral path through circumstances which on the face of it appear to be apocalyptic. There is an extension of earlier Romantic views of the natural world, apparently in an effort to show its accessibility to all and build an equivalent of the relation of stewardship between human and vegetative creation of the first Romantics. And there is a further vision of the land which sees, in its processes of destruction, change and renewal, something of sombre splendour and exultant hope, in which the heightened awareness and intensified emotions of the experience of living through devastation and loss are directed into affirmations of faith which are full of risk but full, too, of great spiritual power.

These and other strands are all part of the fabric of Romanticism of the war years. They are held together by a single key relationship, that of the external world and the inner, organising and refining sense of the artist, which in various kinds and orders is apparent in every kind of Romanticism. In an article published in 1942, Graham Sutherland described the equation which lay beneath his paintings of the Welsh countryside, *Entrance to a Lane* included. In so doing he drew together the theoretical and practical developments of the preceding fifteen years which saw the growth of forties Romanticism, and which are the subject of Chapter 2:

> It was in this country that I began to learn painting. It seemed impossible here for me to sit down and make finished paintings 'from nature'. Indeed, there were no 'ready made' subjects to paint. The spaces and concentrations of this clearly constructed land were stuff for storing in the mind. Their essence was intellectual and emotional, if I may say so. I found that I could express what I felt only by paraphrasing what I saw. Moreover, such country did not seem to make man appear little as does some country of the grander sort. I felt just as much part of the earth as my features were part of me. I did not feel that my imagination was in conflict with the real, but that reality was a dispersed and disintegrated form of imagination.[53]

2

The Romantic Continuity

I

> We know very little of English artists. Few have been studied. We have still only the beginnings of an art history. Books on English painting are mostly of individual taste, category books (animal painters, watercolour painters, portrait painters, genre painters), and books which, whether 'histories' or picture galleries, repeat an arbitrary reading of artists made first of all round about 1850.[1]

Geoffrey Grigson's assertion makes salutary reading in an age when it is easy to assume that the artists of the thirties and forties had the kind of ready acquaintance with the major figures of English art that an intelligent and well-travelled sixteen-year-old can have today. It reminds us that, at the period of the revival of interest in Romanticism, the awareness of the painting of the past was severely limited. This puts the rediscovery of the first Romantic painters into rather a different light and, as we shall see, has consequent effects on our ideas of how some artists of the thirties and forties saw themselves in relation to the tradition; how the notion of what we might loosely call a Romantic continuity came to develop; and how this actually worked in practice.

Before looking at this rediscovery of English art – the archaeological aspect, if you like, of a Romantic revival – it is worth staying with Grigson's paragraph: it reveals other stances and assumptions in the growing awareness of the presence of the past in English art in the thirties and forties.

The first point that is striking is that Grigson is talking at all about 'English artists'. At least since the Post-Impressionist exhibitions of 1910 it had been the accepted theology amongst intellectuals and art-critics (the two terms are not interchangeable) that all that was soundest in ideology and finest in practice came from continental

Europe. Cubism, Fauvism, Constructivism, Surrealism, significant form-ism – all these sprang directly from European models even if at times, as at the Surrealist Exhibition of 1936, they seemed to be convenient banners under which to display a more indigenous kind of art. Yet Grigson is now talking about English art and admitting that 'we know very little' about it. Here, then, is evidence of a shift, of a reaction against prevailing Francophilia: English art is worth talking about, even if we have to admit significant ignorance of it.

Grigson's second sentence reinforces this, in accepting that English art is worthy of study, even though little has as yet been done. The mention of the word 'studied' is in itself important, in accepting 'art' as an academic discipline rather than as part of a tradition of 'connoisseurship' at one extreme or a training in draughtsmanship at another. Later in the article Grigson goes on to say 'We know much, though, of English poets'; another revealing remark. It shows how closely the study of art was linked to the study of literature, and suggests that it is to become part of a legitimate field of intellectual enquiry for the literary historian and critic as much as for the collector or practising artist. This leads us to another key notion: 'Romanticism' is a topic which cannot for long be separated into 'art' and 'literature'.

It is also significant that Grigson talks of 'English artists' and 'English poets', not of 'English art' and 'English poetry'. This reveals a tendency still strong in the approach to art and letters: a view which sees it very much within a biographical context, made up of significant individuals rather than a larger current of ideas and styles. Perhaps this is better than the obsession with 'movements' which we have still not outgrown; but it does show a stance towards art and its creation which has at its root the idea of the creative individual artist, to which the English liberal humanist tradition, itself born of Romantic individualism, is fundamental. This reveals the prevalence of a 'Romantic' stance within Grigson's critical method and, by extension, the glimpse of contemporary aesthetics this affords cautions us against any grouping of 'Romantic' or 'neo-Romantic' artists of the forties. Similarity of outlook does not in itself create a school and, though many of the painters of this time shared ideals (and in some cases studios), we need to remember that there was no declared intent of a movement behind what they were doing.

This is reflected, too, in Grigson's comments on 'the beginnings of an art history'. He is writing at a time when only very recently had the traditional approach to art been that of the connoisseur, so that – with a few significant exceptions – English art history in the thirties was dominated by books which took what we would now call a thematic approach – sporting-prints, landscape, drawings and other generic histories. The ostensibly impartial, scholarly 'histories' which much of this chapter will suggest are in many ways a major, if not the dominant, voice of aesthetic theory and practice of the thirties, are of comparatively recent descent. Grigson's article is typical of them in considering 'The Politics of an Artist' and relating the philosophy of the artist to predominant social and historical movements of his time.

The very newness of this approach reveals something else that is important in the idea of a Romantic continuity in the thirties and forties: at several – though not all – of its levels it is bound up with a delight in the rediscovery of earlier art and the discovery of the fact that it can be studied seriously. Grigson is one of the first if not the first to use the term 'art history' when talking in English about the study of English art: the joy in finding a new endeavour which is both intellectually rigorous and aesthetically satisfying is never far away in writings of this sort in the thirties and early forties. This explains the word 'ostensibly' in the preceding paragraph: although many of the books and articles which share in the rediscovery of Romanticism show scholarship of a high order, they are reflections of the aesthetics of their own times as much as explications of those of an earlier age. When many of the writers are also artists of international significance, this is not surprising; the thirties were a rare period when writing about art was something engaged in by 'those who can' and not 'those who can't'. It is in this sense that the Romantic rediscovery most valuably becomes a 'literary' activity. The activity is undertaken by writers and artists whose individuality is never in question, and in this Grigson's style and stance is again representative simply because of its own highly individual nature.

Grigson concludes by looking, with a polemicist's disdain, at the 'arbitrary ranking of artists first made in the 1850s'. He is talking here about Samuel Palmer, an artist who died in 1881. It is all very recent, especially when we remember that Stanley Spencer and Paul Nash were both born in 1889, Graham Sutherland and John Piper in 1903. To some extent what we are witnessing in the thirties is the first attempt to come to terms in a dispassionate – as well as an intellectually rigorous – way with the art that was still a dominant taste a generation ago, much as, *mutatis mutandis*, a generation in the seventies and eighties strove to come to terms with the Romantic art of the thirties and forties which had been forcefully rejected by its forebears in the fifties and sixties.

Grigson's single paragraph thus gives us a kind of test bore through some of the strata of thinking about English Romanticism, and indeed English art in general, that were present in the thirties. Neither should we overlook its subject: the study and discussion of Samuel Palmer's work is a topic of no little significance in the thirties and forties even though, as I hope to establish, his direct influence has been distorted and over-emphasised. This topic, and the series of ideas raised by Grigson's paragraph, needs to be seen within the larger stream of developments of art history and art practice which constitutes the literary and philosophical basis of British Romanticism in the second quarter of the century, in the great blossoming of books and articles, reproductions and exhibitions concerning works of earlier Romantic art.

II

Of the books which contributed to the growing awareness of Romanticism in the twenties and thirties, the first was in many ways the finest: Christopher Hussey's *The Picturesque*.[2] Not only does it provide information of an archaeological nature about the important artists and theorists of the Picturesque; it establishes the fact that the way of seeing represented by the new ideals of the mid-eighteenth century is something which is both radical and irreversible.

The essence of the Picturesque Hussey defines as the immediate, emotional perception of those qualities in physical landscape which are the most perfect in a painted picture – composition, colour, proportion – without the intermediate filter of the reason or notions of taste and decorum. Once this is accepted, the whole basis of the relationship between the external world and the vision of the painter changes, and the doors to all kinds of stylised depiction are unlocked: as Hussey says, 'The picturesque can thus be seen to provide the first step in the movement towards abstract aesthetic values'.[3] More particularly, we may see in this the force which holds together the separate strands of British art in the thirties – Surrealism, Constructionalism, Abstraction, and more traditional landscape: all are in some measure an emotional or subjective response to the external world, a recreation of reality and experience in painterly terms, the reason by-passed in the drive towards experiential expression. Hussey makes two related points. First, he establishes that this kind of seeing, once established, becomes instinctive:

> The recognition of the picturesque had become as instinctive as that of day and night. Only when the eye has learnt to see the qualities stressed by painters with other conventions, whether Giotto or Cézanne, are we jogged out of the picturesque habit and allowed to view it as a phase.[4]

We can go further than this, I think, and say that even the vision of Cézanne depends on the instinctuality of the Picturesque vision: it is rather a rearrangement of the balance between inner and external realities, the painted and the observed world, than a complete rejection of the subjective equation between them which the Picturesque, for the first time, postulates and celebrates. The pervasiveness of the Picturesque, most particularly through development into the full-blooded Romantic notion of the artist's eye creating as much as perceiving what it experiences, is something fundamental to British Romantic art of the forties, holding together work as diverse as images by Charles Cundall and Graham Sutherland, Ethel Gabain and Henry Moore, as later chapters will argue.

The second point that Hussey makes is that, without the kind of aesthetic development given to it by those who seek to extend the visual vocabulary, the Picturesque becomes ossified. Taken to its extreme conclusion, this gives rise to that view of art which regards Constable as the patron saint of table mats and nice country walks in its refusal to grasp the revolutionary nature of *how* he perceives the landscape. Talking of the development of the Picturesque in the Barbizon school in France and the work of Turner and Constable in England, he concludes:

> There it should have rested, after a century's hard work in the bosoms of poets and gardeners, travellers, architects, and painters. But no. It is still in request to write for the newspapers, and to sit on the Council for the Preservation of Rural England.[5]

Writing in 1927, Hussey could not have known that the basis of Romantic perception of which he was writing would soon be radically intensified and given new worth by a blood transfusion from European abstraction; for all that, his comment is still strikingly relevant to much of the paint and ink expended in the forties in work that is avowedly popular in destination. Chapter 3 will show how this instinctive belief in Picturesque perception as the only kind of truth in painting was used – almost certainly in an unconscious way – by artists to convey messages which are nationalistic, revisionist and simplistic but still, in a curious way, emotionally nourishing.[6]

Hussey's book is significant in one further dimension – in making clear the ideas of the early Romantics concerning the value of terror as part of the true Sublime, and in this showing once again the primacy of the emotions, untramelled by the intellect, in the act of aesthetic perception or creation. Hussey provides the first clear modern account of the ideas of Edmund Burke on the aesthetically invigorating and morally purifying nature of pure terror. After lucid vignettes of the philosophies of Shaftesbury, Hutcheson and Hogarth, Hussey concludes thus:

> But it was Burke who sponsored passion and emotion as the products of aesthetic perception. It was this substitution of emotion for reason, and of passion for decorum that made possible the great poetry and the vile architecture of the nineteenth century. He loosed emotion from the corsets of the intellect.[7]

He goes on to list the qualities of the Sublime – obscurity, power, privations, vastness, infinity, succession and uniformity – and to place the Picturesque usefully between beauty and sublimity by attributing it to objects which 'had neither the smoothness of the beautiful nor the overwhelmingness of the sublime'.[8] Thus not only does he provide a brief guide to the aesthetic categories of early Romantic perception, but also introduces a term which is to be of basic importance in aesthetic debate of the next decade: the 'object'. And he concludes his discussion of the Sublime by showing how Burke had, in company with Uvedale Price – who, like Payne Knight, was a progenitor of Picturesque theory – 'mistook subjective associations for objective qualities'.[9] In so doing he points towards a further key development in British theorising of the thirties which is another shift in the balance of existing terms rather than a move to wholly new ideas: that the landscape created by an artist is an expression of his own inner mental furniture, expressed in shapes which may be loosely based on outer landforms, so finishing the process begun by those earlier theorists in establishing that the outward structures are symbols of inner thought, not tangible entities of their own. Hussey's book is of considerable importance in reviving, clarifying and criticising these earlier ideas; it deserves to be given more prominence in the vortex of aesthetic theory and practice with Romanticism at its centre which took place in the second quarter of the century in Britain.

In this respect it is more important and certainly more far-reaching in its analysis than Kenneth Clark's *Gothic Revival*,[10] important though this is in making available a great deal of information and offering a reappraisal of the taste of an earlier generation. It is a pity that Hussey's book, bearing as it does the title of a movement generally associated – in the author's own words – with 'gardeners' and 'travellers', is often seen as chronicling the more superficial, landscape-gardeny part of Romanticism rather than directly confronting the genuine perceptual revolution of Romanticism, since it contains far more thorough-going intellectual analysis of this revolution than does Clark's better-known work. Clark's book is of major importance in a different way: it provides an account of the earliest elements of Picturesque Romanticism in Scott and Chatterton, and is the first modern work to take seriously the motives behind Beckford's Fonthill and offer a critique of Walpole's *Description of Strawberry Hill*.[11] But for all this it remains an historical account rather than a document which seems to underlie future debate about the relation between artist and landscape: perhaps this is inevitable in the critic who on his own admission 'can't understand'[12] the abstract paintings of Paul Nash. It is to the backward-looking picturesqueness of Betjeman's Victorian revivalism that this book ultimately belongs, not to the forward-looking reinvention of Romanticism in Sutherland, Nash, and so many others, whose work is discussed in later chapters.

After Hussey, the next art historian to engage with Romanticism as a force for the present is Laurence Binyon. In a lecture given in 1935[13] he offered a reappraisal of what he called 'the Romantic Movement or Romantic Revival',[14] interestingly using the terminology of the earliest appearances of the word 'Romantic' in the seventeenth century[15] as referring to the interests and values of the writers of early romances, such as Spenser. Yet he goes on from an account of the more recent rejection of Romanticism as being 'not sufficiently concerned with actual life'[16] to see in high Romantic painting a direct confrontation between the painter's spirit and the force of external creation. Talking of the Yorkshire Moors, the Cumberland fells and the Welsh mountains and the way in which Girtin saw them before he painted them, he says:

> They were no longer scenery, chosen for picturesqueness; they were elemental presences, to be portrayed in their majestic bareness, which the human spirit could confront without fear because it was conscious of an equal loftiness of itself.[17]

And later, he says of Constable:

> without a trace of mystical feeling, what he felt was so genuine and profound that his art is quite distinct from that of a mere realist.[18]

Both of these passages reveal something important about the way Romantic art was being seen: its resemblance to external, physical reality is no longer important. Girtin is painting a spiritual confrontation, Constable a feeling of oneness with surrounding reality that is so deeply real that any suggestion that it is simply 'mystical' can be rapidly dispensed with. Binyon here is offering another version of what Hussey has established; that Romanticism is an equation between inner and outer reality founded on a spiritual or intellectual experience within the artist. The implication that it is neither a retreat from reality nor a feat of simple topographical illustration is implicit within this: Romanticism emerges from Binyon's reconsideration as something of considerable philosophical import and the idea of the balance between internal and external forces, symbolic, imaginative, creative, spiritual or whatever else, is further expanded by it.

By 1939, Binyon had developed further his idea of the inner-outer balance of Romantic art. In his introduction to a collection of watercolours reproduced by what is still a very fine process, but which then must have been breathtaking,[19] he talks of Cotman's main concern as being 'to persuade the material given him by Nature into a rhythmical design' and says that in *Greta Bridge*[20] the artist seizes on the sharpness and squareness of rock formations almost with the *parti pris* of a Cubist'.[21] Here is the vital link between critical reading of earlier Romantic landscape and present-day landscape painting: Binyon makes clear the way in which Romantic artists seem to recreate their landscapes by following visual principles which depend on abstract qualities of rhythm and form, at the same time as depicting recognisable external features. This is a key extension of the idea of inner-outer balance implicit within all Romantic art: that Binyon has expressed it here, most likely for the first time in British art-historical criticism, is not only a very perceptive act in itself, but also a statement of great import about the direction of much contemporary British art and its relationship to earlier Romanticism – a relationship which is no mere historical reference or retreat but instead a genuine development and extension of its tenets in conjunction with the theory and practice of art of the recent past and the present.

Binyon is not alone in this drawing together of abstraction and Romanticism. Three years earlier, Grigson and Piper had got together to produce their controversial article in *Axis*,[22] which is seen by many as the turning point in British Romantic art of the decade. That is to overstate its importance; but nevertheless it is a striking piece of writing when seen in the context of what was going on in the studios of Nash, Piper, Hepworth and Nicholson, seeming as it did to reject the whole theory of abstraction in an attempt to return to some referential, external subject-matter in painting. Seeming is not being, however. What Piper and Grigson are saying is that abstraction and representation can come together; and the fact that they say this with frequent illustration from the English Romantics demonstrates again that the relation between inner idea and external form which is fundamental to Romanticism can find expression anew in the idioms of a later generation which has gone through the intellectual labyrinths of abstraction but has now returned to the need for some external reference. Piper puts the idea early in the article:

> The point is fullness, completeness: the abstract qualities of all good painting together with the symbolism (at least) of life itself.[23]

At a stroke this brings together the idea of the abstractness of Romantic painting, the relationship between inner and outer reality it contains, and the deep need for these two to be combined in contemporary British art. What is also striking is a burgeoning social awareness, not in any overt political dimension but in the sense that art should reflect life. It is stated diffidently in this passage in the parenthetical 'at least' before 'life itself'; it is made more explicit at the end of the article which asserts that 'our job is to feel history, to feel art and life';[24] in the claim that 'There is only a human instant, a *being*';[25] and, most passionately, in the last paragraph:

> The fiends are busy, desperate and fierce, but outside ourselves, we can at last allow our common humanity to rule us, or give us advice. Great art comes from great living; great living comes from our common humanity promising or filling out or still defining a high social shape to which each peculiar person can decently relate himself. I believe that men may have to wait a hundred years before such a shape is renewed.[26]

What Grigson seems to be saying here is that the vision of the Romantics is the proper vehicle through which the artists of his own generation may make their comment on the social nature of their times, by absorbing its reality into the abstract nature of their own art and re-presenting it in the equation between individual and external worlds which is at the heart of English Romanticism. The autumn of 1936 was, of course, a suitable year for declarations of political position; the war in Spain had caused polarisation in worlds far wider than the artistic community. Yet the statement is important: reading it we should not be surprised that the ideological commitment present in the work of artists during the war years very often goes alongside an aesthetic which rests on an earlier British tradition. The ideas voiced in this article are amplified and extended in a collection of writings by artists and critics, *The Painter's Object*,[27] which appeared in the following year. It is curious how the word 'object' surfaces again: Burke uses it in his *Philosophical Enquiry*[28] to refer to the external feature which produces an emotional response of terror in the onlooker and, as has been noted, Hussey points out that this involves mistakenly attributing the emotions of the beholder to the item being beheld. Yet the word is ideal for its purpose: the painter's object is in one sense the thing that he or she paints, objective reality or subject matter, and in another his or her aim or intention – objective – in painting. By the very title of the collection we are brought back to the duality that lies at the heart of Romanticism – of the forties as well as of the preceding century's opening decades. John Piper's insistence on the renewed importance of the external object makes this duality clear:

> But the object must grow again; must reappear as the 'country' that inspires painting. (It may, at the worst, turn out to be a night-bomber, or reappear in a birth-control poster – but it will grow again, somehow.)[29]

Outward land forms are taken in by the artist and mixed with his or her ideas, feelings and responses to them and the world of which they are a part. The resultant images and shapes are then figured forth in the paintings; they have become both a representation of the original forms and a re-presentation of them, symbolising in an untranslatable fashion the emotions, desires and anxieties of the artist within his or her experience of them. This is less than literal reality since it is no photograph; it is more than literal reality since it attempts to re-create the whole experience of the moment. In this, despite the stylistic differences and the greater psychological awareness of the later period, we are set firmly in the stance of the high Romantics.

Myfanwy Evans' introduction makes clear the use to which external reality, now expanded from landscape to everyday life, should be put by the artist. The artist must 'use it, squeeze it, purge it and convert it into shrines for all who want it to enjoy'.[30] A little further on she talks of Picasso, in *Guernica*, 'purging into formality'[31] his experience and feeling at the devastation of the Basque capital. Once again the mind filters and changes, but the stress on a social or moral standpoint is greater here; abstraction has been modified not only in form but also in content and context.

Elsewhere in *The Painter's Object*, there are references to the ancient stone circles,[32] the oldest sculptures of England,[33] and the surreal nature of everyday objects.[34] All of these are to become important in various strands of later Romantic art. Yet what binds them together is the idea of the artist's modifying vision, and it is this outlook which seems to underlie the great majority of significant paintings of the forties, even though it finds outlets in great range of different structures and styles.

Once this statement of intent and stance has been made, the feeling of kinship with earlier Romantic artists and writers grows considerably. Doubtless the revival of interest was also helped in the war years by a concern to revisit the national heritage for which battle was being fought and a delight in the natural world amid the image and the reality of urban desolation: yet the influence of the earlier progression of ideas must surely have been strong in the production of two important books during the war years, since they were written severally by the joint authors of the *Axis* article of 1936. John Piper's *British Romantic Artists*[35] appeared in the Collins *Britain in Pictures* series – short, well-illustrated books which are in themselves essential reading for anyone trying to recreate a very specific area of the intellectual climate of the war years. Piper is concerned throughout to show the ways in which British artists have used external forms as a symbolic statement of inner feeling. The distinction between Romantic and earlier painting is established thus:

> Till then, sentiment had only been an ingredient of painting. Pictures had been flavoured by a general sentiment – a Claude-like contemplation or a Salvator Rosa-like melodrama – but it had never occurred to anyone to make an effect of weather or season carry the whole weight . . . But Girtin and Turner set out to discover a pictorial shape for the urge that had possessed Wordsworth: the urge to make a particular effect of sun or rain, calm or storm, light or shadow, gloom or gaiety, stand as symbol for something universal. They wanted to make landscape a means of reporting and recording, not places and things, but life.[36]

This is a simplified, popularised account of the arguments advanced in *Axis* and *The Painter's Object*, almost to the extent of losing an awareness of the validity of the paintings described as paintings, so intent is it on stressing their symbolic significance. Yet the importance of uniting outer and inner worlds is again made clear, and the paragraph is a key utterance of contemporary critical thinking as well as perhaps the most important first point of entry to most British painting of the time.

The rest of the book explores the truth of this statement with reference to other artists. In Gainsborough's *Landscape with a Bridge*,[37] 'the form perfectly embodies the feeling';[38] in Girtin's *The White House, Chelsea*,[39] 'the atmosphere, the time of day, has created the whole mood of the picture; and with the mood, the form'.[40] Sometimes one feels that this becomes a little excessive: I am not sure I can agree that Bewick, in his 'spontaneous overflow of powerful feelings, could see all human experience in a bird's nest'.[41] But the point is clear: nature is a symbol of feeling. Not only this; it is also a consolation, if not a religion: Turner and

Girtin 'saw the need for a religion of nature that would supersede the image-worship of earlier romanticism'.[42] If we read 'the Picturesque' for 'earlier romanticism' and consider the Romantic landscape which involves us in a moment of heightened spiritual unity with the perceived natural world, as opposed to that which offers us merely an attractive composition, we can understand the distinction. More than this, we can also understand the modified forms of this experience in many contemporary British paintings: Piper is once again commenting on the art of his own age as well as that of an earlier one. This he does explicitly at the end of the book, discussing Paul Nash, Frances Hodgkins and Graham Sutherland as genuinely Romantic contemporary painters. And, perhaps most important of all, his book made available the texts of Romantic paintings at a time when the originals were buried in Welsh hillsides or concealed in private basements; for the generation of artists growing up at the time this was of major significance.

The other major work of the war years is Geoffrey Grigson's anthology of Romantic writing,[43] which appeared in the same year as Piper's book. The collection includes substantial passages from Blake, Wordsworth, Keats, Coleridge, Clare, with smaller contributions from Crabbe and Shelley and only three items by Byron. It begins with excerpts from Boehme and his English disciple William Law on the spiritual character of the natural world and the immanence of God within it; it refers to Milton as 'the great goldfield, the Klondike of the Romantic Miners'.[44] All of this suggests that its view of Romanticism sees it firmly in the valley of earthly delights envisaged by Milton as evidence of God's love for prelapsarian humankind, with humanity placed in a position of stewardship over nature and capable of seeing God through its circumambient beauty. That three of the four sections of the anthology are titled in strongly visual, if not visionary, terms completes this: 'The Morning Redness'; 'The Peak'; 'the Sensual Valley'. Grigson's anthology fulfils not only the invaluable role of making texts available in a book-hungry society, it also shows that the Romantic idea of external reality as an image of inner state has merged with a view of Romanticism which sees earthly sensuality as part of an English tradition deeply rooted in Milton's biblical sensuality, and in that it reflects, insofar as any single volume can, one important characteristic of much British art of the time: its sensual immediacy and involvement with the natural world.

The re-creation of Romanticism in practice takes on a great range of forms, as the succeeding chapters seek to explore. Some artists use Romantic experiential landscape to record and comment on events; some use distorted natural forms as ironic comment on contemporary reality; some see the natural world as the only source of dynamic continuity in a world of destruction. To all of them, and to many others, the Romantic equation between inner and outer reality is fundamental; the experience Graham Sutherland recorded in Pembrokeshire early in the forties, quoted at the end of Chapter 1, is but one expression of this. The tradition of Romanticism is continued and expanded with a range that is the logical product of such an aesthetic and with a human richness that is the inevitable result of its closeness to its own times. Within the chaos of apocalypse, the artist has again found his object; the dangers as well as the opportunities of it all are summarised by Keith Vaughan:

> Freud has said: 'Only for the most select and most balanced minds does it seem possible to guard the perceived picture of external reality against the distortion to which it is otherwise subjected in its transit through the psychic individuality of the one perceiving it.' It is unlikely that any artist could fulfil such strict requirements as these, but it is the problem forever facing the Romantic artist. Any hypothetical absolute reality is likely to be transformed in its passage through the human consciousness. The point of value lies in whether our own experience is enlarged by the distortion.[45]

III

John Piper, we have seen, was a central figure in the revival of interest in Romanticism. His book *British Romantic Artists*, appearing as it did in the central year of the war, in a popular series of easily available and relatively cheap volumes, not only made Romanticism available to a wide reading public, but also acted as a kind of summary of the story so far, bringing together historical interpretation and painterly criticism in a statement of the main stream of current thinking about Romantic art. Yet this function as a chronicler is only one aspect of his contribution to the continuity of Romanticism; Piper is primarily a painter, and as well as his writing we must confront the question of the nature and degree to which his own work may be called Romantic.

The answer to this question is, I think, contained to some extent within his approach to earlier art as well as to his own, and his stance towards ancient buildings: the notion of extracting the essence of a tradition and continuing it is never far away from all of these aspects of the artist. In his concern for the architecture of the past, most notably in conjunction with John Betjeman, there is a sense that his concern lies with seeing the present through the past and the past through the present. This is revealed in his *Axis* discussion with Geoffrey Grigson. He talks of artists having to 'rediscover a technique',[46] not having to develop one; he talks of Picasso as 'a painter who has invented, by rediscovery and hard work, a complete professional equipment', who has 'never denied the tradition of painting'.[47] At the same time – perhaps it is the other side of the same coin – he is concerned that art should represent not a retreat from life but a part of it. A key word here is 'completeness',[48] suggesting that a painting should be both an abstract arrangement of colour and shape and part of life itself, this last both because it takes from life and gives to it a kind of fixity: hence, a Samuel Palmer 'fixes the whole passion of his age'.[49] But for the contemporary artist Piper feels this is a problem. It seems Piper feels that the sheer newness of the Romantics' discovery of experience and individuality gave their paintings a life which later works lack – 'buoyant' is the word he uses in this context. At the time when Romanticism was at its greatest, the novelty of recasting external events through the filter of inner perception allowed the artist to produce something of far greater vitality – ' a gay medium'[50] – than we may produce now. The reason is simple: we have become so preoccupied by experience, so encapsulated within the perils of the psyche, that experience 'tends to sink *our* expression in the form from the first, making it heavy and soggy, without wings or breath'.[51] The two strands come together to point the way forward: 'life in painting . . . is re-born from the material – paint and canvas, wood and stone – instead of being sunk in it to be lost'.[52]

Piper is arguing here for a new lightness of expression, drawing on the tradition of the past but uniting abstract and representational through the newly-discovered personal experience of the Romantics and a delight in the materials of the artist. It is a retreat from the weight of the unconscious, the psychobabble of introverted expressionism which, in 1936, was much in evidence in Abstraction, Constructivism, Dadaism, Surrealism and the whole couchfull of psychoanalytic concerns of the artist,[53] and an advance towards the immediacy of statement made possible by the losing of experience in the physicality of paint which was possible for Turner, Cotman, Girtin, Palmer.

This is a very important concept because it helps us to understand exactly what Piper is doing in his painting of the thirties and forties. And this in turn provides an answer to the many problems which Piper's work presents for anyone wishing to place it within a period which includes work by Moore and Sutherland, against which it can very easily appear lightweight or lacking in emotional depth. It is very different from the works of such artists in the way it approaches the reality it presents: but it is not trying to do the same things. It is not enough simply to dismiss Piper's work of the time as 'neo-Picturesque' – not, at least, without close study of what this actually signifies. At risk of setting up a new intentional fallacy with which to defeat a well established one, it is important to try to make clear the nature and extent of Piper's achievement in the Romantic continuity of the forties.

Piper began his career with painting that was firmly in the main stream of European abstractionism, helped by his membership of the 7 & 5 group and inclusion in the 'Abstract and Concrete' exhibition of 1936. Yet even within some of the work produced at this time there seems to be a leaning towards a kind of rhythm and depth which is not wholly abstract: *Painting*[54] suggests a depth and interaction of planes which has to do with objects and not the pure space of Nicholson's white reliefs, and his early figure paintings suggest more a re-working of established forms in the manner of Cézanne and Matisse than a wholesale rejection of them in the manner of the 'purest' abstract artists of the time. This is important; it suggests that Piper's abstraction was in need of some kind of external correlative to give it the 'completeness' of which he was later to speak, and that an interest in planes of pure colour, while an essential ingredient of his work, was not in itself enough.

The change to a more directly representational art is not something which comes about overnight. Nor does it grow wholly from his more commercial work of the thirties in the recording of landscape; the beach collages of the same decade show a move towards a kind of representationalism which strives for a balance between abstract and referential, in which again the concern for planes of colour is dominant but extended by its referential element. The same is true of paintings such as *Forms Against a Sky*,[55] which further merges abstract and representational, exploring the rhythm of planes yet still suggesting a figurative representation of forms half-human against the horizon.

By the later thirties, the first *Shell Guide*[56] completed, the crawls around Brighton and ancient churches with Betjeman accomplished, the personal declarations of *Axis* and *The Painter's Object* made, the true nature of Piper's work within a Romantic strain is established. It may be seen, for example, in an oil such as *Italian Cheltenham*.[57] Here a rather Italianate church is reduced to a series of touching and overlapping planes which, mostly rectangular and lacking surface detail, give it a strong likeness to the earlier abstracts. At the left of the building a campanile-like structure is pierced by two round-arched windows, and this provides the main motif of detail in the work, taken up by the windows in the end of the church which is presented parallel to the picture's plane in characteristic Piper fashion. The whole is embraced by a semi-circular line where the building meets the ground, which moves to a diagonal at the right-hand side as the building recedes. The scene is reduced to a series of planes of simplified texture; if *Forms Against a Sky* is the abstract leaning towards the representational, this is most certainly the representational leaning towards the abstract. Similar techniques are developed in *Autumn at Stourhead*.[58] This shows, from a realistically low viewpoint, a vista across the lake towards the Pantheon, with the Bristol cross to the left of the painting's centre and the famed Palladian bridge just out of sight behind it. The composition is in Piper's familiar reductive style, a series of planes and textures, although there is a little more sense of surface interest than in earlier paintings where all is brought down to a series of flat colours.

What is happening in this painting is that Piper is seeking to re-establish the reality that he sees through the simplifying filter of abstractionism, reducing it to a series of separate planes and colours which alternate between the purity of flat tones familiar from European formalism at its most refined in Mondrian and Nicholson, and areas of simple texture which reflect not so much the feel of the object being presented but that texture transformed into something which might represent it in a collage – as, say, a type of coarse wollen cloth might represent grass. If we take these together with his ideas of earlier art as expressed in the *Axis* article, what Piper is doing becomes clear: he is taking the element of abstract rhythm in a Cotman or a Girtin and applying this, in an updated fashion, to a scene which might well have been included on an eighteenth-century sketching trip, thus unifying contemporary abstraction and earlier Picturesque. This approach presents the scene in a way which is much simplified, ascetic almost, rarefying and refining shape and texture so that we see the hidden rhythms of the buildings and garden as much as the things themselves. Piper's own experience of seeing it is represented not by the heavy psychological burdens which have threatened to 'sink' our vision, but in a way which allows colour and texture – the raw materials of the painter to which he argued a return – to predominate in the reworking of the form that is presented. In this lies the element of the Romantic in his work; the act of intrepretive vision is still there, in this reworking as a simplified pattern. Because it looks simple and straightforward – lightweight, almost – it is easy to overlook the Romantic changing that it contains; because it has the simple rhythmic quality of earlier Picturesque painting without the heavier emotional overtones of high Romanticism – because it resembles Cotman at his purest rather than Turner or Constable at their most intense – it is easy to call it neo-Picturesque. Certainly it does not present us with an emotional or spiritual statement of great depth and complexity, but it still uses the Romantic vision, the re-creation of the outer landscape through the refining process of the inner vision, and it is thus a continuation of the Romantic tradition. We may not find it as powerful as a Sutherland; but that is because of a difference in the nature of the change wrought on external forms by the governing sensibility, not because the change is not there: the difference is one of degree, not kind.

There is also another sense in which *Autumn at Stourhead* is a continuation of the Picturesque, one which is perhaps responsible in no small measure for the confusion which it might arouse in contemporary onlookers. It is a presentation of one of the 'incidents' in the garden of Stourhead, attractive views planned by Henry Hoare and Colen Campbell[59] to delight the eye of the visitor following one of the walks around the estate. We are thus subsumed not only into the surroundings of Stourhead, but into the position of an aristocratic visitor, almost like being given the role of an extra in *Mansfield Park*. Unless we know about the way in which Stourhead was intended to be seen, and relate this to the simplification of forms that Piper is carrying out within it, we cannot fully appreciate the painting. When we are aware of this, it becomes a witty and elegant allusion to and extension of a tradition. But it remains aristocratic and referential, couched in what socio-linguists would call a restricted code. This as much as anything else marks off Piper's work from other manifestations of Romanticism which we shall consider in the remaining chapters; it is defined very much by the tradition it continues, and must be seen as part of that, otherwise it will remain apparently nothing more than 'neo-Picturesque' and, in the words of a recent and distinguished critic, full of 'suggestions of vacant stage sets'.[60]

The problem with Piper's work arises most acutely in a discussion of the wartime paintings and drawings. Several of these continue the line of thought begun with the architectural paintings of the thirties, with the more urgent purpose of placing on record historic country houses under threat from bombing. Yet the paintings of Renishaw and the royal estate at Windsor continue the Picturesque tradition more in what they do than how they do it, presenting topographical views of great houses rather than simplifying the formal structures of, say, Cotman or Girtin in the manner adopted in *Autumn at Stourhead. The Gothic Archway, Renishaw*,[61] for example, shows a Gothic folly from a high, detached viewpoint, not part of any contemporary or later visitor's view, and in a loose, bravura watercolour style. In the freedom of its brushwork it builds on the technical foundations of Romantic watercolourists, but in all other senses it remains a contemporary watercolour rather than a comment on any earlier tradition. Here Piper is fulfilling the role of a recorder, rather than genuinely extending a convention – and in this, of course, he is precisely fulfilling the terms of his commission.

Piper's treatments of bombed buildings are the essence of the problem. Take *Lansdown Crescent, Bath*.[62] To the right of the centre stands the ruined tower of the chapel, behind a pile of rubble and next to a tree still growing in its grounds. At the left, the end of the crescent is seen in silhouette, while the crescent itself curves around in the background, holding the composition together and also uniting the rectangular and curved forms of the walls and arches of the remains of the tower. Piper's familiar technique of simplified planes is again apparent, and the whole is presented with the same lightness of touch apparent in *Italian Cheltenham*. The figures 'JR 1794' incised on the ruined tower wall add to the impression of a picturesque view and, in all, it is as if the convention of Picturesque classical ruins from the eighteenth century has been revisited. We are not given any moral response to the scene; there is no sense of outrage, compassion, or even loss behind the elegant poise. It is instead a scene presented in simplified terms which move towards abstraction. The same is true of other paintings. In *House of Commons, Aye Lobby*[63] the ruined building is seen through a gothic arch, the square forms of the panelling to the left echoed in the square tower at the rear and the square tunnel effect of the receding form. The doorway to the left foreground and that in the centre of the middle ground continue the form of the arch which frames the composition and offset the otherwise heavily rectilinear forms of the painting, and these are further broken by the wreckage in the foreground and the jagged edges of the receding wall to the left. This rhythmic balance is aided by the use of colour; the deep red of the door at the left, the gold of the panelling and the deep blue square of steel mesh in the distance form patterns to define the composition, and the strokes of red in the foreground give it a further dynamism. It is a painting which reduces the events almost to abstract terms, but which again makes no reference to suffering; once more it is a kind of reductive Picturesque. An early commentator on Piper's work saw his achievement in revealing the 'accidental romance in and beyond the horror';[64] certainly it does not offer us any direct involvement in the horror itself. Even in the baldest compositions, such as *Interior of Coventry Cathedral, Nov 15 1940*,[65] which shows the bare walls of the cathedral standing screen-like against the night sky, there is a feeling of detachment; the process which has reduced the composition to a series of abstract shapes has also reduced it to a state of dispassionate observation.

What is happening here is clearly some form of Romantic reinvention of the scenes depicted; yet for many onlookers these paintings will fail because this essentially human process of reinvention seems to lack humanity. The issue is well expressed in far more general terms, with no specific mention of Piper, in a radio discussion of 1941 between Clive Bell, Herbert Read and V. S. Pritchett. Asked by Bell what he looks for in a picture of the ruins of Bristol, Pritchett replies 'a statement of the essence of the scene, in which I include the human experience which belongs to it, the suffering and the courage which were endured and the horror and pity of the surrounding context'. Bell counters, as a kind of last stand of the Francophile moderns against the insular Romanticists:

> If only Canaletto had painted the ruins of Bristol he would have expressed exclusively an emotion for what he saw. He would have cared no more whether the ruin was made in the year 1941 than whether it was made 2000 years ago. Now your romantic

> artist is so much concerned with the circumstances in which the ruins were created that he may be distracted from the proper artistic purpose of expressing a visual experience.[66]

A classical purity would seem to be Bell's ideal here, something which clearly alarmed Pritchett: he begins the next talk in the series by saying he is 'rather bothered' by Bell's seeming 'longing for an artist to paint air-raid damage without expressing any human emotion'.[67] He goes on to ask Graham Sutherland if he approaches his painting in this way and is told that 'it's the force of the emotion in the presence of the subject which determines and moulds the pictorial form that one chooses', a true statement of the Romantic principle in operation.

It is not, of course, the simple Classic-Romantic antithesis a superficial reading of this exchange would suggest. Indeed, Bell continues after the passage quoted above by admitting that 'unfortunately for my argument, it is quite possible that the romantic artist may produce as good a work of art as anyone else'. Indeed, his opening sentence about Canaletto's expressing 'exclusively an emotion for what he saw' implies a Romantic stance in the sense defined by Sutherland and so many others in the aesthetic of the time. What seems to be the case is that we are talking again of two different sorts or degrees of Romantic filtering of external reality, one which stresses experiential emotion, one a more purely visual conversion of reality into a rhythmic series of near-abstract forms.

At root it is perhaps a personal issue of moral outlook; I have to confess that looking at Piper's paintings of blitzed buildings I do not feel moved as I do when looking at Sutherland's treatments of similar subjects, regardless of the fact that a Romantic filtering of a similar kind has taken place – it is the result of this filtering that matters. To me – and presumably also to Bell – the most successful of Piper's wartime paintings is *Passage to the Control Room*,[68] which shows an underground passage reduced to a series of clinical planes, against which roof beams, pipes on the ceiling and arrows on the floor form a contrapuntal movement, and a series of numbers serve to define the recession of the corridor. It is clinical, classical and (in the literal sense) inhuman; for these reasons it seems an appropriate reflection of the reality it records, a control room set apart from the realities of suffering. It has a congruence of form and treatment which the paintings of bombed buildings lack; we cannot help feeling that there is an incongruity between the desolation of the subject matter and the simplicity of form and purity of texture. The distortion wrought by the observing artist is not enough adequately to represent the desolation of the scenes; there seems to be an emotional mismatch between the two.

It may be that Piper's vision is one of extreme remoteness which, given time, will come to be valued as one of almost classical detachment, seeing in the bombed buildings a new arrangement of colour and form that is significant only because of its visual and spatial nature, not as something representative of human suffering. There may even be some irony contained within this, a brutal presentation of the futility of human endeavour and frailty: this is something that future generations will have to decide. It may be, too, that the fault lies in the onlooker: perhaps we should not, like Pritchett, automatically expect an emotional statement in response to ruins caused by bombing and instead look for the kind of chaste arrangement prized by Bell. Perhaps, ironically, Piper sees the buildings as only the true abstract artist can, as a series of shapes; perhaps he sees them as an eighteenth-century painter would see classical ruins, with a visual curiosity but a human impartiality. What is not in doubt is his Romantic rearrangement of what he sees: but at the moment it seems that the emotional detachment is too great and, by his own terms, Piper has failed to fix the life of his times by providing an emotional response of a quality to match the displacement of the events he records. This is one version of forties Romanticism, but it is not that which is closest to the temper of the time.

IV

Alongside the revival of interest in the general theory and practice of the Picturesque and Romantic ran a stream of writing about individual figures in English art of the preceding hundred years. Constable had been the subject of a study by E. V. Lucas[69] in 1924, and two years later a volume of reproductions of his work had appeared in the series *Portfolios of the Great Masters*.[70] Another study appeared in 1927,[71] and in 1931 the letters to Leslie appeared,[72] to be followed in 1937 by Leslie's *Memoirs* of the artist in revised and enlarged form.[73] In 1939 the National Gallery bought the painting still known as the 'sketch' for *Hadleigh Castle*,[74] in which the artist's mood glooms magnificently through the whole composition.

Critical awareness of Constable's achievement follows swiftly. John Piper praises Constable's ability 'to see a landscape whole, as a picture'[75] and stresses both the abstract quality and the experiential intensity of his finest painting. By 1946, with the artist's works once more on display after wartime storage, the anonymous writer of 'From a Painter's Note-Book' could point to the popularity of Constable that was at once his salvation and his destruction:

> Then there is the national Constable, the patron saint of the Englishman's claustrophobia. And the printed calendar Constable, the four-colour process Constable. We all know enough to leave them in their poker-work shrine. The attachments have been a sad burden for Constable to bear.[76]

Not only is the popular incarnation of Constable rejected: so, too, is the painter-as-rebel whose sketches of the six-foot canvases represent his real self, the final versions the respectable tamings-down forced on him by an uncomprehending art-market. Constable can now be seen as both a Romantic in the sense of expressing his experience through and within his landscape and a Romantic in the sense of the soft-toned composer in the manner of the great Claude whom, in company with Turner, he revered beyond all other. A similar insight is shown by Keith Vaughan in the outstanding *Penguin New Writing*[77] article which has already been quoted, when he dismisses the facile claim that Constable was the forerunner of Impressionism by saying that his strength lies elsewhere, in providing 'a hint of that power of organization that is not seen again until Cézanne' to 'relate the parts to the whole both psychologically and plastically'.[78] The process of rehabilitation and understanding seems to have reached completion, with Constable recognised as an artist of great Romantic stature and an example for contemporary painters to follow in the immediacy of that experiential relation to landscape which is inseparable from his sense of composition and feeling for the textures of paint.

The same is true of Turner. The *Liber Studiorum* had appeared in facsimile in 1899 and 1904, and in the latter year a collection of watercolours appeared.[79] Three further collections of watercolours appeared in reproduction in the twenties, to be followed by many more in the thirties and A. J. Finberg's life of the painter in 1939.[80] But the great event was the rediscovery of many of the late canvases in the basement of the National Gallery and their exhibition to the public for the first time. Graham Sutherland singled out two canvases for mention in his discussion of the inner-outer dichotomy in English painting, and we can feel his excitement in the discovery that he shares the earlier artist's delight in re-forming external shapes so that they become part of a personal vision:

> In his Petworth Interior in the National Gallery, and his 'Sunrise and Sea Monster' in the Tate Gallery, we recognize the quality of that excitement which their remote and intangible ecstasies arouse in our minds.[81]

As for Turner and Constable, so for other Romantic artists. Gainsborough's *Morning Walk*[82] was first exhibited to the public in 1936; John Piper, ever the archaeologist, produced an early article on Fuseli in 1938.[83] Blake, too, began to attract more serious critical attention than before. Sutherland, for example, takes as the starting point of his article a quotation from Blake's *Marriage of Heaven and Hell*, and discusses through the visionary work of that artist the problem of unifying inner and outer vision – that same glorious problem for Romantic theorists of the 1930s as for those of the 1800s. The real impetus to Blake studies was the publication of the three-volume illustrated Nonesuch edition in 1925[84] which made available the full dual text of word and image, and the appearance in the following year of Laurence Binyon's edition of the engravings.[85] Yet the reassessment if not quite the rediscovery of Blake in the inter-war years is not only important because it reveals aspects of the aesthetic of thirties Romanticism, but also because of its influence on a group of artists of that time.

It is possible to trace a very clear and very specific line of descent from Blake through his immediate disciples Calvert and Palmer to later artists, first and perhaps most particularly Graham Sutherland and then in the later generation John Craxton and John Minton. The influence is one that is much remarked in accounts of forties Romanticism,[86] but it deserves deeper exploration than it usually receives not only because it shows the close links between the art-historical rediscovery of the earlier Romantics and the contemporary practice of art, but also to establish the exact nature of what is one of the closest links, if not influences, of style and stance between the two periods.

The middle twenties were a time of much importance in this movement. Almost at the same time as the Nonesuch Blake appeared,

Laurence Binyon published his study of the artist's 'followers',[87] in so doing not only bringing to light the work of Calvert and Palmer but also branding them with the marks of discipleship which on the one hand establishes a tradition but on the other at times blinds us to their true individuality as artists and thinkers. With his characteristic *hauteur* Grigson was later to dismiss this as 'a picture book',[88] thus apparently refusing to recognise its chief glory, which lies in presenting the works of these artists in reproductions of outstanding quality. That of Calvert's tiny watercolour *The Primitive City*[89] is still the finest coloured reproduction of the painting to be found, and the wood and line engravings have a depth and clarity remarkable in modern photographic process-plates.

The second illustrations[90] in Binyon's book are a series of eight of the seventeen produced by Blake as illustrations to *The Pastorals of Virgil* edited by R. J. Thornton from Ambrose Philips' translation in *Imitations of the Eclogues* published as a schools' edition in 1821.[91] These extraordinary images, Blake's first and only venture into the territory of the wood-engraving newly charted by Thomas Bewick,[92] show the figures of Colinet and Thenot within familiar Blakeian landscapes, enfolded by nurturing trees while tending sheep, leading bullocks or engaged in harvest revelries. Of them, Binyon perceptively observes:

> To Calvert and Palmer Blake's woodcuts to Virgil's *Eclogues* revealed a path which they could follow in freedom, each pursuing his own end.[93]

Binyon goes on to illustrate the major wood- and line-engravings of Calvert and Palmer, from which it becomes apparent that his judgement is quite valid; both artists do indeed extend and develop the genre begun by Blake.

Seeing such work must have had a very great effect on young artists in the twenties. Here was a whole new tradition, almost completely unknown hitherto, and discovered at a time when other forces were working to move artists in the direction of the pastoral drypoint. There was considerable demand in the international art-market for such work, particularly in the USA, where the etchings of Whistler were much collected and had created interest in similar work. The tradition of English book-illustration was also strong, helped by a resurgence of interest in the English countryside after the desolation and depredation of the First World War. Although the last anthology of Georgian poetry[94] had appeared in 1922 – Georgian from Virgil's *Georgics*, not the reigns of the Georges – the Georgian poets' interest in the land, combining as it did practical earthiness with mystical vision, was still strong. Added to this were the beginnings of the rejection of European art as the universal arbiter of contemporary aesthetics. All of these practical, philosophical and aesthetic strands wove together in Binyon's volume and what it presented. Here was a tradition which showed dazzling mastery of its form, developed the idea of closeness to the land with a sensuality which at times became openly erotic, and was also wholly English.

Binyon's book was followed by a series of other events which allowed the work of Blake's so-called 'followers' to gain greater exposure, both revealing and extending the appeal it held for contemporary artists and collectors. In 1926 Martin Hardie and James Laver mounted for the Victoria and Albert Museum 'an Exhibition of Drawings, Etchings and Woodcuts by Samuel Palmer and other Disciples of William Blake'. The next year, Hardie gave a lecture to the Print Collectors' Club, whose members included Graham Sutherland, the popular engraver F. L. Griggs and Paul Drury; he quoted Palmer's ecstatic comment in the *Sketchbook* on Blake's Thornton wood-engravings: 'There is in all such a mystic and dreamy glimmer as penetrates and kindles the inmost soul.'[95] Hardie's comments reveal one of the achievements of Palmer's work that was valued most highly at the time: that same unity between inner vision and outer reality that came to be fundamental in other treatments of Romanticism. Palmer, he claims, 'was working at this period with the inward eye as well as the outward gaze . . . he is telling you, as only the great artist can, not about what he has seen, but about his thoughts – his thoughts about the glory of the sun, the magic of moonlight, the mystery of the stars.'[96] Heady stuff; but we should not allow the purple mist to obscure the truth of the point Hardie is making and the aesthetic which it reveals – that landscape is to the artist of the modern period a series of forms to be reinvented as symbolic representation of individual, psychological truth.

Later in the lecture, Hardie is much more explicit in seeing Palmer as in some way embodying the needs of the contemporary artist by readjusting landscape to fit mindscape. *In a Shoreham Garden*[97] he says is

> singularly modern in its outlook, in the stark directness of its

> methods, in its 'arbitrary schematisation', and even in its use of the bare toned paper. There is no attempt at literal representation . . . that scented wealth of old blossom in an old garden embodies all the sunshine and magic of the countryside, and is more real than literal realism could have made it.[98]

Here, the external world is sifted and rearranged into an abstract, sensual pattern making daring use of colour, light and texture: the process described is almost exactly that gone through by Graham Sutherland when seeking to paint the Welsh landscapes, as described in his *Horizon* article.[99]

Some years later, Geoffrey Grigson was to write an article for *Signature* on Samuel Palmer,[100] the first fruits of researches which were to lead to his full-length study *Samuel Palmer: the Visionary Years*.[101] This is often seen as the key document in the revival of interest in Palmer, which may be the case from a biographical and art-historical standpoint. Yet it is clear that the *Signature* article continues in the vein first mined by Hardie, in – amongst many other things of value, including large quotation from Palmer's writing and reproduction of some key images – stressing the nature of his art as a balance of inner and outer visions. He talks of the 'dramatic lighting', 'glow' and 'romantic mystery of the exaggerated dark descents' as an entity which 'comes out of the peculiarity of Palmer';[102] of the way in which his paintings contain 'a disinterested as well as a psychically interested concern'.[103] The final paragraph of the article includes the same passage from Freud used by Keith Vaughan in the article quoted on page 27, and concludes with an apposite comment from someone who it comes as a shock to realise was Palmer's contemporary – Gerard Manley Hopkins:

> 'A kind of touchstone of the highest of most living art is seriousness; not gravity, but the being in earnest with your subject – reality'. Apply that to the visions of Palmer.[104]

From all this it is quite clear that the critics of the thirties saw in Palmer – in the etchings but also the watercolours – a quality of passionate rearrangement of reality which, in its philosophy rather than its style, was something they were courting in the art of their own age. Other writings about Palmer of the time – a complete catalogue of the etchings,[105] an article on his place in English etching,[106] reproductions of his Virgil etchings,[107] Grigson's article on his 'politics' with which this chapter began – certainly extend the currency of his work; but they do not add significantly to this essential reason why it was valued at the time, which tells us much about the nature of contemporary Romanticism and hints at the nature of the influence of Palmer's work on contemporary art practice.

It is not only Palmer who is regarded in this way, and whose work is made available to a wider audience. Binyon's volume of 1925 probably still contains more reproductions of Calvert's work than any other book;[108] and an article by A. J. Finberg on 'Edward Calvert's Engravings'[109] offered a complete catalogue as well as further reproductions. Nowhere is there a statement as complete as those of Hardie and Grigson about the ways in which Calvert's work represents an ideal of contemporary Romanticism, but the fact of its reproduction vouches for the fact that it appeals to similar tastes, and that the line through represented by Blake and Palmer is continued in the exquisite blend of linearity and texture of work such as *The Ploughman*.[110]

All of this should leave little doubt about the nature of interest in this particular strand of late Romantic art in the theory and criticism of the inter-war years, but its significance is more than that of an embodiment of contemporary taste and values. It is almost a commonplace that Palmer's influence on Sutherland was one of the starting points of thirties Romanticism, and we need now to examine just how far, and in what ways, the line that we have traced and the values that it represents had an influence upon the paintings of the later Romantic artists.

V

Graham Sutherland later recalled the effect of his first sight of Palmer's work:

> I was amazed at its completeness, both emotional and technical. It was unheard of at the school to cover the plate almost completely with work, and quite new to us that the complex variety of the multiplicity of lines could form a tone of such luminosity.[111]

Sutherland's stress on 'emotional and technical completeness' is revealing: it suggests both a craving for the balance between inner and outer landscape so much a part of the revival of interest in Romantic art and a concern for the technical means of achieving it. Spirituality and technique thus come together; but the latter seems to predominate, since Sutherland's recollection continues:

> as we became familiar with Palmer's later etchings, we 'bit' our plates deeper. We had always been warned against 'over biting'. But we did 'over-bite', and we burnished our way through innumerable states, quite unrepentant at the way we punished and maltreated the copper.[112]

What we have here is a fascination with the technical embodiment of the transforming power of the imaginative vision: it is not simply the fact that spirituality alters external reality that strikes Sutherland, but the technical methods by which such imagery can be made real. This is worth stressing because it shows a concern to make Palmer's technical quality a real presence in his own work, instead of either a vague influence of what is generally and loosely called the 'visionary' quality of that artist's work or a direct stylistic impetus. What we are dealing with here is a desire to make the imaginative and the technical qualities of a Romantic artist fuse together and provide a single potent force in the work of a contemporary one, and this explains both the elements of visual similarity to Palmer in much of Sutherland's early work and his movement away from it soon afterwards, in an effort both to define his own imaginative vision and find ways of showing it which are technically and spiritually fitting.

In practical terms, the likeness between Sutherland and Palmer is very apparent in the former's etchings of the middle twenties. Even before Sutherland's encounter with Palmer, his etching shows an immense technical skill with the medium, works such as *The Black Rabbit*[113] revealing great dexterity in the control of gradations of line and texture to create recessive movement of much rhythmic subtlety. Yet for all that they are largely in the descriptive and evocative tradition of Seymour Haden, Frank Short and many lesser figures who produced detailed yet atmospheric images of the English countryside, both to illustrate topographical books and to satisfy the growing print market. Sutherland's etchings of this period are 'Romantic' inasmuch as they reflect a gently Georgian love of the countryside developed into what amounts to a rather sentimental urban eye's love of its abandoned places, and a skilful use of the medium to present its charmingly shaggy textures in, say, *Warning Camp*[114]. There is almost the feeling that the technique is in danger of being swamped by the presiding fashion of decorative prettiness.

This changes dramatically in the first work produced after Sutherland had seen Palmer's work. *Cray Fields*[115] is striking in this respect. A very low sun, encircled by rays of light, shines through a group of hop poles above heavily textured earth. A plough lies at the right foreground, balanced to the left by ears of corn circling across to echo the curve of the plough's handles. In the middle ground at the left two figures are reaping; in the distance may be seen a cottage and some apple trees. Above them a very literal, child-like star of David sheds rays which imitate palely those of the sun. In the sixth state of the etching – that from which most impressions were taken – the light from the dying sun is made to appear greater by the omission of the outline of the sun itself, the handles of the plough are lightened, and the corn stalks in the foreground are omitted. The cumulative effect of these changes is to increase the sense of depth in the etching, so that we have the sense of standing almost within reach of the plough, and also to add to the sense of the passing moment, that fragmentary instant between daylight and dark which so fascinated the Victorians. The influence of Palmer is apparent here both in the subject matter and the style. The transient light of evening over a harvest scene is the essence of his oil *The Gleaning Field*,[116] and light shining through trees is a frequent motif in the later etchings illustrating Milton and Virgil. The foreground plough recalls the farming implements which Palmer delighted in leaving apparently strewn in the foregrounds of his composition, where they seem natural outcrops of the nurtured landscape rather than the clumsy *repoussoir* devices they would remain in less skilled hands. The textures, too, have the kind of knobbly immediacy in which Palmer delighted, aided by the exaggerated *chiaroscuro* which arises naturally from the time of day. As yet the etching does not show the kind of obsessive, all-over working characteristic of Palmer's later work to which Sutherland himself draws our attention, but in all other respects the influence of Palmer is very clear.

Much the same is true of *Michaelmas*.[117] A child-woman figure stands before the gable-end of a house, with the familiar child's stars illumining the dark sky. The composition is framed on the left by a tall, full tree and on the right by the end of a wall on which flowers are growing, and the ground has the furrowed, mottled character of *Cray Fields*. The whole allows Sutherland great scope for the rich textural variation which is by now habitual, and the influence of Palmer is revealed in this and in the compositional placing of the figure and the high, thin building which, in simplified form, recalls the church in *Coming from Evening Church*.[118] The movement is continued in *St Mary's Hatch*[119] and *Lammas*,[120] both of which show figures in a furrowed foreground before a low-eaved cottage. In the former they carry sheaves of corn in front of a high-walled graveyard in which a massive tree overshadows the gravestones and an old, pierced Gothic porch; in the latter they stand before small apple trees and a background of another cottage and more trees, with a wheeled plough in the right foreground. All is Palmeresque in texture and subject.

If we move to *Pecken Wood*,[121] however, a change is apparent. Textures are still of great importance, but in a different way: the etiolated figures of the earlier engravings have been replaced by a central figure almost obliterated by the faggots on his back: it is as if he has been absorbed into the woody essence of the scene. At the rear there is another dying sun shining through trees, but the texture is thinner, the composition more linear; these trees grow straight up and have only a little foliage at their height. The shift is towards a rather more chaste use of Palmer's delight in texture, with rather fewer overtones of spirituality, a move assisted by the absence of the children's star. *The Village*,[122] roughly contemporary with the most Palmeresque of the etchings, also shows a growing individuality: not only is it set in full daylight, lit by streams of light from the right, but it has a breadth of composition, what Wölfflin would call an 'open' form, in which the landscape flows out of the boundaries of the print instead of stopping with them as it does in the other images. Textures abound, as before, and there are decaying fences and an uncertain barn: but the openness shows a quality of vision which is quite Sutherland's own.

By the end of the decade, in *Wood Interior*,[123] the individuality is clear. The delight in texture has become simplified and stylised, and the rather static quality of *Cray Fields* gives way to a sensual, linear dance in the contrasting forms of the trees: the rather coy stars are replaced by a flight of birds in the far distance and a white bird in the middle ground, which between them do much to define the inner recession of the image. *Pastoral*[124] takes the process of simplification a stage further: texture is still important but the range limited and controlled to give a further chastening of effect, and the forms of the trees and the alternation of light and shadow create a rhythm which is much more abstract than hitherto. When we come to *The Garden*,[125] Sutherland's mature individuality is quite beyond question. The central motif is an abstracted, stylised representation of tree, flower and fern; the walls and houses are reduced to their bare, formal minimum; the background trees and their circular beds form a rhythmic echo of the central figure; and these and the tree shapes move in counterpoint to the homophony of the buildings. Sutherland's vision has transformed the tangible, natural scene which may or may not have been the external 'original' of the image.

What has happened in this movement is quite clear. At first, Sutherland's etchings are virtuosic but lacking in personality; under the influence of Palmer, he at first copies both the earlier artist's style along with his intensity; then, as his strength in this grows, his own vision begins to assert itself. Finally, the power of his imaginative vision to create a landscape of a quite individual order, and to subordinate his technical dexterity to its needs, is apparent in *The Garden*. This growth towards individuality reaches its fulfilment in work such as *Entrance to a Lane* discussed in Chapter 1 and the 'biomorphic' paintings of the very late thirties and forties which will be discussed later on.

The growth of Sutherland's etchings in the twenties has been examined in detail because their development allows us to grasp the exact nature of Palmer's influence on Sutherland, and this in turn is revealing about the precise importance of Palmer in the evolution of Romanticism in the thirties and forties. The initial stylistic imitation is of only passing importance: what matters is that Palmer's power emotionally to transform and elevate external forms in accord with his own mental powers – in his case an essentially spiritual process – has allowed Sutherland to develop a similar transformation in his own work. Chapter 7 will show that this is something he uses to very different ends from Palmer: but it is clear that, as the likeness of image diminishes, the influence of Palmer's stance towards landscape increases. What began as imitation has become an immensely liberating force in allowing the personal vision to develop: Sutherland has absorbed a Romantic aesthetic and made it part of his own process of image-making to enable the production of what are, as we shall see, among the most important paintings of the war years. It is in this sense that Palmer's influence is most important, and in this sense too that Sutherland is a deeply

Romantic artist. The Romantic nature of his art is not in its stylistic likeness to Palmer, but in the philosophy which underlies it.

Sutherland was not the only artist whose work shows the mark of Palmer. John Craxton was born in 1922 and thus not influenced by the revival of the twenties; when he began to produce work that was noticed, Palmer was firmly established as a major figure of English Romanticism. Grigson's 1941 *Horizon* article contained reproductions of Palmer's *Early Morning*[126] and *The Valley Thick with Corn*:[127] Craxton was enthralled by them, and several of his early works reveal the influence.

Poet in a Landscape[128] shows a seated figure, reading, at the right of the composition, beneath a tree whose branches curl down and around while thinner shoots reach out to form curious forms like distant birds. A large tree thrusts horizontally along the ground to terminate in angular horns at the front of the picture's plane, and the rest of the foreground is filled with large, drooping leaves and vegetative blades terminating in enlarged seed-pods. In the distance there is a tree in a fold of rounded, swelling hills, and a crescent moon whose shape is echoed in similar forms within the vegetation. The tonality is dark and intense, and the swirling, twisted forms give the image an air of disturbing intensity within which the poet sits in an air of taut calm.

The influence of Palmer which is often seen in this work is hard precisely to define. The dark tonalities, rapidly receding perspective and low view point are all typical of his work, as is the central motif of the tree folded within hills and the moon which is almost a caricature. The horn shapes in the tree's branches are also suggestive of Palmer's more bravura work. Yet there is a freedom of movement which is far removed from Palmer, and the textural interest, although clear, lacks the variety, tension and depth of that artist's vegetation. The distortion is something which might be regarded as an extension of the kind of planar simplification apparent in, say, *The Valley Thick with Corn* and, overall, the forms of Palmer's watercolours and gouaches are more apparent than those of his etchings in Craxton's work. Perhaps, too, there is something of the sensuality of Calvert in Craxton's work of this period. It is as if the line from Blake's Thornton wood-engravings has been continued in a very personal way by Craxton, for very personal reasons. The same qualities are found, in slightly differing proportions, in other works of the time: *Dreamer in a Landscape*,[129] *Poet and Birdcatcher in a Landscape*,[130] *Shepherd in a Moonlit Landscape*[131] and *Reaper with*

Mushroom[132] all share the turbulent lines and elephantine vegetative forms which threaten to engulf the figures at their cores. Writing of these early paintings in the 1960s, Craxton himself commented that the figures were derived from the shepherds of Blake and Palmer and added significantly that they were 'my means of escape and a sort of self-protection'.[133] At the time, however, he pointed to other influences:

> Palmer goes with Rimbaud in the sense that both had that incredible unconscious poetic gift that only had to be stimulated – but it never goes on for long . . . It is not the leaves in Palmer I like but the leafy *ness*, that essence of leaf that presses against my senses. Take away the poetry and you're left with Pre-Raphaelitism at its dullest.[134]

Once again it is the element of the reinvention of a landscape in personal terms which is the most apparent feature in Craxton's debt to Palmer – a debt which, as Craxton himself accepted, is mixed with aesthetic parallels with Rimbaud and, as Grigson suggested, with 'arrangements and vegetation out of Rousseau'.[135]

A few years later, Craxton was producing work of a very different kind, and it seems that, for him as for Sutherland, the idea that landscape could be transformed by the imagination into something rich, luxurious and not always in close contact with reality was the liberating force needed to release the full creative impulse within himself. There are some fine illustrations to those anthologies of earlier poetry which contributed so much to the revival of interest in earlier Romanticism; and there are paintings which, as Chapter 7 will show, re-create a Romantic relationship with the land in a genuinely contemporary manner. It is in providing this release, and not in offering a stylistic model, that the major significance of Palmer's work is to be found in the work of Craxton. This is given further force by the fact that the stylistic similarity between Craxton's work and Palmer's has, it seems to me, been overrated. There is one very straightforward practical reason for this: Craxton's first two works in this form, *Poet in a Landscape* and *Dreamer in a Landscape*, were reproduced in *Horizon*,[136] and remained in private ownership rather than public display. This meant that they were most remembered as small monochrome images of a size similar to the reproductions of Palmer etchings and watercolours in the same journal and elsewhere. This is important during the war years, when few actual paintings were available for examination, as it were, in the pigment: reduced in size, Craxton's paintings look darker and more intense, much closer to the intensity of Palmer and Calvert. Added to this are the references to Rimbaud and Rousseau, which suggest the more cosmopolitan nature of Craxton's aesthetic outlook, something found far less in Sutherland before the thirties. Taken together, it all leads to the conclusion that Craxton's Palmer was an entity very different from Sutherland's: it was certainly a way of grasping the principle of the transforming effects of the subconscious within an ostensibly representational vocabulary, but one tangibly moderated by continental European influences and exaggerated by the forms of reproduction in which his work was most seen at the time of its execution. And, like Sutherland, Craxton was to use the experience of this discovery a little later on to produce work which is his own genuine contribution to the continuation and extension of Romantic art.

John Minton absorbs and uses Palmer's art in a third manner. For him, too, it is a revelation of the liberating effect of the personal vision, the directly perceived scene; yet, because he combines his own style without elements of Palmer's in a more truly eclectic fashion, he is able to extend it more fully and thus create a development of of earlier Romantic style in a wholly contemporary manner – something which is not so with the works of Craxton and Sutherland of this sort. *Dark Wood, Evening*[137] takes the rich, encrusted textures of Palmer's work at its most characteristic and offers a new simplicity: it is as if we are being offered a reinvention of Palmer through post-Impressionist eyes. The same is true of *Landscape with Harvester Resting*:[138] Minton is extending the stylistic possibilities of the earlier artist in a clear, personal way. But the most important work within this tradition is *Recollections of Wales*.[139] Rolling back in a series of crisp undulations through the centre of this composition is a road or path that seems to recall the roads of Sutherland's Welsh landscapes of the thirties. On either side, intricate vegetation gives way in the middle ground to hollows scooped out of the land; on the right, a pair of gnarled tree trunks stand in balance to the main element of the composition. This is a tree which, though apparently barren at its trunk, bursts into riotous yet delicate leaf just above head height, and then sweeps across the landscape like an erratic parody of a classical festoon. Beneath this, wrapped in fabric which seems to combine classical drapery and winding sheet, is the figure of a woman. One leg is bared, recalling the half-naked figure of the soldier in the frontispiece to David Jones' *In Parenthesis* (1937), and the head is turned inwards to follow the path of the tree bough, another echo being provided in the hair which blows freely above it. The whole is an intricate balance of line and mass, the complex turns of the road mirroring in another dimension the twists of the tree, while the tree and figure in the foreground balance each other and are reflected in the two dead trees of the right. Variation of texture is considerable, the smooth scoops of land contrasting with the intricate working of the leaves, and the whole held together by the movement of the light which provides further variations of intensity.

What does the image mean? Just as the spirituality of Palmer's work is diminished by precise explication, so Minton's image suffers in transliteration, but its main direction is clear. The presence of the female figure and the bounding vegetation balances and offsets the arid forms of the dead trees and the stony surface of the road to suggest regeneration in a natural cycle, with associations of Celtic fertility implied in the title. The female figure is vulnerable too; this is no simple statement of an assured regenerative principle. But even the limitation is important; this is a twentieth-century reinvention of the Romantic idea of growth and renewal through the earth, tentative rather than complete, its faith lying in organic cycles rather than presenting – as Palmer does – earthly riches as image of celestial splendour. Palmer's intensity is taken and seen through the filter of both contemporary styles and contemporary preoccupations. Nature is still central to the redemptive process, but it is a tentative hope of renewal that we are offered here, not a sure embodiment, and in this Minton's image is totally a reflection of the times. This is the difference between Minton's use of Palmer, and Craxton's and Sutherland's. They use Palmer as a means of self-discovery; Minton enfolds elements of the earlier artist's visual world within his own mature style.

In using and developing the earlier tradition, Minton's painting is representative, while losing nothing of its individuality, of the finest sort of Romantic art of the war years. As earlier parts of this chapter have made clear, Romanticism became a living force again in the twenties and thirties through the work of a number of art historians, its principles informing the work of a number of artists in different ways. This is no sterile refuge from the perils of modernism; the succeeding chapters will show that, like Minton and Sutherland, artists of the war years were to use the philosophy and the outlook of the earlier Romantics fully to confront the aesthetic and moral issues of their own day.

3

Romantic Realism

I

One manifestation of the equation between inner and outer reality in high Romantic art in Britain is something now so commonplace that few would regard it as anything other than inevitable. Described in the simplest terms, it is the use of a series of external features to re-create an experience, in which they act as a trigger to recall a moment of existence in a particular place and time. That is not, of course, the whole story, nor is it the sole source of the greatness of the finest work of this kind; but it is a feature which had not existed before the immense shift of perception of the late eighteenth and early nineteenth centuries, and one which has since become so much a part of everyday visual depiction, from holiday snaps to advertising copy, that it requires a major effort of dissociation for us even to become aware of it at any conscious level. It is this feature, strong in both painting and literature, which is the conceptual source of a major strand of Romanticism in English art of the Second World War.

The exact nature of this feature has been well defined elsewhere, most notably – though with slightly different conclusions – by Karl Kroeber,[1] with reference to the mature paintings of John Constable. *The Haywain*,[2] more properly *Landscape: Noon*, allows us not only to witness a moment in the passage of the cart through the stream but, because of the use of landscape, sky and weather as a re-creation of an emotional state, directly to share the artist's experience of the moment. This, and the tradition of like works for which it stands as representative, is unlike any earlier use of landscape. There is no moral or iconographical force behind this scene; no suggestion that it is the landscape of heaven as in Van Eyck, a garden of earthly delights as in Bosch, or a collection of emblems of ownership as in Gainsborough and earlier eighteenth-century portraiture. It is, despite its meticulously ordered composition and wonderful immediacy in the use of paint, a moment of the painter's experience, ordinary yet extraordinary, and this allows it to act as a trigger to make real that experience for us, too, as we look on. To this revolutionary principle is added another; this experience is available to all, to any individual regardless of social rank or creed, unlike the restricted code of the Picturesque and, as we have seen, in Piper's revisiting it. It is this aspect of the lone, individual experience, the interchange between outer and inner worlds where each becomes symbol of the other, that is central to the finest and most typical of English Romantic paintings of landscape. It is also – because of its stress on individuality and accessibility before hierarchy – something which has very strong and, to some establishment eyes, very subversive political overtones. Experiential, aesthetic and political are drawn together; and this is no less true in the 1940s than in the 1820s.

The experience does not end here. A conceptual extension of it is found most precisely in Wordsworth, in the stance which underlies the whole of *The Prelude* and *The Excursion*, but is most clearly stated in a passage from Book 11 of the former. It is worth quoting at some length – from the 1805 version which, perhaps ironically in view of the passage's argument, is far clearer in its final lines:

> There are in our existence spots of time
> Which with distinct pre-eminence retain
> A renovating virtue, whence, depressed
> By false opinion and contentious thought,
> Or ought of heavier or more deadly weight
> In trivial occupations and the round
> Of ordinary intercourse, our minds
> Are nourished and invisibly repaired –
> A virtue, by which pleasure is enhanced,
> That penetrates, enables us to mount
> When high, more high, and lifts us up when fallen.
> This efficacious spirit chiefly lurks
> Among those passages of life in which
> We have had deepest feeling that the mind
> Is lord and master, and that outward sense
> Is but the obedient servant of her will.[3]

This makes clear what we might call the other half of the significance of experiential landscape, which complements the onlooker's ability to impose a mood upon it. Moments of acute perception can exert a benign moral restorative force on us when they are recalled at a later date. The word 'renovating' is striking here. In the two-part *Prelude* of 1799 Wordsworth uses 'fructifying';[4] in a draft of the 1805, 'vivifying'.[5] Neither has the force or exact significance of word finally chosen, and the fact that the poet had difficulty in finding the precise term perhaps suggests its crucial importance to the concept involved. The earlier terms suggest the power of generation and kindling of the spirit, but it is only 'renovating' which adds to this the sense of repeating the freshness of earlier times, carrying with it the idea that moral renewal rests on the recollection of the first experience, the 'spot of time', where outward experience is a symbol for inner feeling. This use of landscape is an inevitable extension of the Romantic idea that it is not the external landscape itself which is of greatest importance, but our experience of it.

This approach to landscape, as an external trigger to recall earlier experiences of which it is part and draw moral sustenance from them, has become so deeply entrenched in our culture that we do not realise its revolutionary newness in terms of the perception, creation and moral use of visual images, and the shift it marks from a hieratic and iconographic use of landscape to one that is individual, classless and immediate. Yet the use of images, verbal or visual, to stimulate memory and rekindle experience – often to 'renovate' a higher emotional state or feeling to which they are linked – is common in nineteenth-century art and almost inescapable in the age of celluloid and the snapshot. The war years are no exception: during them, it is clear that this stance towards visual images is of major significance in presenting a version of contemporary reality and an attitude towards it. In different circumstances this can involve the use of images for what may be called propaganda, at one end of a notional scale of attitudes, and at the other end their use to convey more personal, compassionate or even dissident responses to the events they portray. I do not suggest any conscious imitation of this approach by artists at this time – there is no explicit reference to this approach in the critical studies of Romanticism which appeared in the years between the wars. Rather I would argue that the stance so briefly outlined in the last few paragraphs had become such a fundamental element in the workings of perception, visual imagination and memory in the post-Romantic generations that it is quite inevitably a part of the attempts to record reality fostered by various agencies from the beginning of the war.

For this reason, this kind of Romanticism – which often arises in works which, in the common sense of the word, do not appear in the least Romantic – is every bit as important as the more obviously Romantic art of the time. Work of this sort covers an immense range, from painting which is visually unexciting, politically quiescent and socially limited to painting and writing which is intimate and deeply compassionate. Although it is less familiar than the more overt kinds of Romanticism it is nonetheless a central strand of British Romantic art of its day.

II

In order to make the work of artists commissioned by the War Artists Advisory Committee available to as many people as possible, and so justify the scheme in offical circles, a series of slim volumes of plates was issued, under crown copyright, by Oxford University Press in 1942. The general title of the volumes was *War Pictures by British Artists*, and the first series contained four volumes: *I War at Sea; II Blitz; III R.A.F*; and *IV Army*. They contained images by some of the most important artists of the day, including major works by Moore, Sutherland and Piper. It is not these which are the main concern here, but some of the more directly representational paintings and drawings which use external reality to recreate earlier experience and direct our stance towards it in the manner which may most accurately be called Romantic realism.

Some idea of the reasons why those in authority thought the use of artists to record events would be of value may be gained from the paragraph which appeared inside the front cover of each book. The main aim is that advanced by Marshal Haig in equivalent publications of the First World War[6] – to provide a record of events for future generations. Yet the assumptions about the nature of this record, and the place of the artist in providing it, are very clearly Romantic in nature.

The paragraph begins by rejecting both verbal accounts of war and 'big, formal compositions like the battle pictures which hang in palaces' – an interestingly Romantic notion in turning away from formality and order towards immediacy and accessibility to the common man which, as we shall see, is not always borne out by the images themselves. It continues in a way which reveals a clear Romantic stance:

> even photographs, which tell us so much, will leave out the colour and the peculiar feeling of events in these extraordinary years. Only the artist with his heightened powers of perception can recognise which elements in a scene can be pickled for posterity in the magical essence of style.[7]

The first sentence makes quite explicit the idea that the artist is recording the emotions of the event as well as the reality; and the second, in an essentially Romantic view of the artist as hero, makes clear that only he or she may first select the key elements of the event and secondly find appropriate expression for them 'in the magical essence of style'. The statement that the artist is ordering the reality by selecting items most typical of its nature, and then expressing them in his or her own style, is very close indeed to the idea that the external events become a reflection of the artist's own feelings or response to them – and so we have a statement about the nature of these paintings which seems uncannily close to the ideas of the presentation of reality in art which we have distilled from Constable and Wordsworth.

This attitude is also clear in the preface to the second series of books of paintings,[8] which concludes with this sentence:

> Many of their new paintings, because they are created out of an experience common to us all, speak with the immediate appeal of popular art.[9]

What is being said here comes even closer to the idea of images as triggers of experience: because the images are born of common experience, they are genuinely popular because all of those who lived through similar moments can share them – a view of the role of painting which has far more to do with the idea of placing some kind of order or understanding on the flux of life than with the idea of creating purely aesthetic forms and structures.

How does this work in practice, when we look at the paintings? It all depends, as is the case with all Romantic art, on the nature of the individual artist and the individual painting.

A key painting in the popular and official art of the war years is *The Withdrawal from Dunkirk* by Charles Cundall.[10] The painting was completed in June 1940 and submitted for purchase to the War Artists Advisory Committee next month. At this time Cundall already had a strong reputation as a painter of national ceremonies, and the submission led to the purchase of the painting and Cundall's appointment as a salaried war artist, first with the Admiralty to record the work of the Merchant Navy and, from February 1941, to take the place of Paul Nash with the RAF. The painting rapidly became one of the most famous representations of major events of the war, after being displayed at the National Gallery.

Recent commentators have seen this painting as an example of the 'documentary realism'[11] which is so frequent in the war, produced by 'a conscientious, accurate and accomplished recorder',[12] and we may assume that its popularity when first exhibited was due largely to the apparent accuracy with which it recreates events. Certainly it is a clear, representational painting of the retreat. It depicts the evacuation of troops from the Dunkirk beaches, on the left of the painting, by ships and boats of all kinds and sizes to the right. The top half of the composition is dominated by a large pall of smoke, flanked by two smaller ones, which drift diagonally across from left to right, spreading and merging as they do so to occupy almost the whole top left quarter of the canvas. Aircraft, mainly RAF Hudsons, fly in the right-hand upper quarter, giving depth and aerial perspective to the scene. The main detail of the painting takes place in the lower left hand quarter, which shows troops waiting to be removed by sea, having wounds dressed, and in some cases sheltering from air attack. The middle ground is dominated by a horizontal line of troops wading out to a waiting transport ship, and in the foreground small boats carry men off the beaches. To the right, at the very edge of the canvas, is the stern of a ship, in the lee of which two small boats are riding while the soldiers in them wait to scramble up ropes. The tonality throughout is restrained, using a palette largely composed of sepias and ochres, which merge with the grey-black of the dominating pall of smoke at the left and the purer grey-blue of sky and sea at the right. All of this presents the scene with what seems to be photographic realism, so that the painting is at first examination a vivid and almsot documentary recreation of the events.

Yet the painting is not what it seems: in many ways it exemplifies a kind of Romantic reorganisation of experience which is far from uncommon in apparently dispassionate records of the events of the war. First there is its selection of one particular aspect of the subject that it presents – the removal of Allied troops from the Dunkirk beaches rather than the harbour mole. During the nine days of the evacuation, from 27 May to 4 June 1940, a total of

338,226 British and allied troops were brought from Dunkirk. Of these, 239,555 came from the mole and the relatively much smaller figure of 98,671 from the beaches.[13] Simply in selecting the scene on the beaches rather than that on the mole, Cundall is making a Romantic choice in preferring the improvised to the formal, the unexpected to the expected. He is not alone in this; the whole legend of Dunkirk rests on the triumphant improvisation of the voyages of the little ships to snatch the troops from the beaches and victory from defeat.[14] In this simple act of selection, then, Cundall is both adopting a Romantic stance and using it as a kind of instrument of psychological survival, in making a military reverse appear as a triumph of national character. But the essential Romanticism of this painting goes far deeper than its selection of a subject.

The key to this is the viewpoint. The events are shown from a high vantage point of considerable distance from what is happening on shore. This may be from the superstructure of a ship equivalent in size to the one at the extreme right-hand of the canvas. Yet this is unlikely: it cannot be the same ship, as close examination of the painting reveals that it is facing diagonally forward and to the right of the frame; and it is unlikely to be another ship of similar size, since such a vessel would be unlikely to be able to get so close inshore. Is it, perhaps, from a low-flying aircraft? This is certainly a possibility, as Cundall may well have witnessed the event himself in such a way. Yet again this seems unlikely, as the aircraft is significantly lower than the Hudson shown in the middle ground to the right, and indeed would be in serious danger of flying into the masts of the ship at the right. The height above the shore seems too great for a groyne or harbour wall. In short, it is very hard to account for a naturalistic viewpoint from which the action is being observed and presented.

The conclusion to which we are drawn is that the viewpoint is unreal and impossible, conceived by the artist to show the scene in the most complete way and give us the illusion of sharing in the experience of seeing it, but ultimately failing in this because we could not possibly have seen it from this angle. The painting has that strange mixture of apparent authenticity and underlying falsity common in much film and television fiction; it tempts us to share the action and its emotions, yet bases this on a false premise by showing it to us from a vantage point that we cannot possibly adopt.

How, then, can we call the painting Romantic? To understand

this we must be aware of a paradox which lies at the root of the kind of perception revealed in this painting and many others. To all intents and purposes, the painting is a Romantic recreation of the events it shows – with, perhaps, the addition of an element of the anecdotal realism of Frith. We are invited by the painter to take the image as real, and to re-live the experience of it in all its horror and heroism. Yet we cannot share the experience with the immediacy with which we share *Landscape: Noon*. There, we know exactly where we are standing in relation to the scene, and know that it is physically – mathematically, even – possible to work out our position within the valley. The same is true not only of countless other Romantic landscapes but also of other images of the withdrawal from Dunkirk including the celebrated newsreel footage of troops wading from the shore on to a ship, seen from behind the guns and rigging of the vessel. Here a photographic image – despite the haughty rejection of such things in the preface to *War Pictures* – seems to give us a fuller and more real share of the experience than a painting which supposedly presents it more intensely. With both Constable's landscape and the newsreel images we know just where we are; this physical rooting allows us to share the experience of the artist or photographer and re-live the experience in true Romantic fashion. In Cundall's painting there is no such location – we are cast adrift in space and experience events as no one could have experienced them at the time.

The spatial uncertainty also has other effects: it creates a moral distance between us and the events, a re-ordering which surely has much to do with the painting's original popularity in official circles and its frequency of reproduction in official media. The point is that distance adds order and pattern. The events have been re-ordered by Cundall just as those in the river near Flatford have been re-ordered by Constable – but with a very different result on the onlooker. In Cundall's painting we are allowed to share what we are encouraged to think is the artist's experience, but at the same time we are held at a distance from the experience of those on the beaches. This seems to have been apparent even to some contemporary viewers, regardless of the painting's great popularity. Stephen Spender seems to be aware of it when he complains of the failure of paintings to convey anything to suggest the actual experience of the soldiers involved in the fighting:

> The retreat from Dunkirk is one of the few episodes in the fighting of this war which we can see: but the picture of the men standing on the beaches and in the sea, being taken off in a stream of frail-looking little boats, does not show us, behind that vast cloud of overhanging smoke coming from the shore, what the German attack looked like.[15]

Every detail of this description relates to some aspect of Cundall's composition, and so it seems clear that Spender singled it out as an example of that kind of painting that is unsatisfactory because, although it appears to offer us an experience of the events it depicts, it really holds us off from them because of the stance it adopts.

Yet, even though it does not allow us to share the soldiers' experience, the painting *is* Romantic in the way that it shows things. It presents a view which is carefully ordered by the beholding spirit – the mind being once again 'lord and master' of what it sees in true Wordsworthian manner. But it is *not* Romantic in that it does not present us with an experience of someone actually involved in the events. It is a trigger to recall a series of emotions surrounding an event, but a trigger in a heavily modified way: image and experience, vision and reality are modified to present things in a very particular manner.

The question 'why?' now surfaces. Why does Cundall present the scene with physical and moral distance? For each soldier on the beach, the experience must have been disconcerting, shocking and isolated – if not as an individual, as part of a small group of people sheltering, queueing, wading. An experience of this sort is not 'more real' than the view of events shown by Cundall, but it is more particularly that of the people actually involved in them. In shifting the viewpoint from the personal and immediate to the general and distant, Cundall has made an important human and political shift – and this accounts , I think, for the popularity of the painting at its first exhibition. We see things not as a confused individual but rather as a detached generality. This shift entails a movement up the hierarchy, from those who are there to those who are nominally in control: we can see things as a pattern, with men moving to safety in an orderly, disciplined way. Cundall has used the Romantic device of experiential landscape to make us feel that we see things as they are, but he has really presented them as they appeared only to the politician or historian, as the saving of several thousand souls from the jaws of defeat, at a period of intense discomfort and danger. And so the artist, in presenting what appears to be a simple, realist record, has in fact adopted, almost certainly at a subconscious level, a major device of Romantic painting and turned it to the service of national survival – a sort of instinctive, experiential propaganda. Doubtless the work gave comfort to many who had relatives involved in the evacuation and who needed to see the event in terms of a national heroic myth, since it allowed them apparently to share the experience. But the painting does not allow the onlooker to share the experience of those who were on the beaches: it is an adaptation – or a perversion, depending on one's political stance – of the Romantic experiential stance for nationalistic purposes.

Muirhead Bone's treatment of the same theme, *The Return from Dunkirk*[16] offers another variant of the Romantic experiential landscape turned to official purpose. Subtitled 'Arrival at Dover', it shows troops disembarking from a small boat onto the quayside at Dover. In the foreground, soldiers are climbing up a steep gangplank and then turning to walk towards the onlooker. At the left several small boats of various kinds are coming into harbour; to the right, behind the quayside crammed with soldiers, four large steamers lie berthed while the disembarkation continues. The quay curves round to end in a lighthouse which provides a formal vanishing point. Structurally the composition is strong, with two recessive lines of ships, one static and continuous, the other dynamic and irregular – respectively the moored craft and those still arriving. These are balanced and offset by the two lines of troops, one rising diagonally up and across the foreground parallel with the plane of the picture, its movement echoed by the slanting smoke from the ships in the middle ground, and the other moving at an angle towards the onlooker.

The composition conveys intense activity and movement within a structure of formal control, presumably intended to give rise to a tension between these two elements; yet the tension is conspicuously lacking, perhaps because the soldiers themselves have a strangely wooden, unreal appearance. This is not the woodenness of exhaustion. In the nearest boat all the figures are standing; none is discernibly wounded, and those who are moving are doing so with strong gestures – look, for example, at the shoulders and upper arms of those marching up the gangplank. All seem, too, to be in possession of rifles, helmets and other equipment. Just how unlike the reality of the situation this is may be seen by considering the following account of the troops as they crossed the channel, written from personal experience by a pilot who flew regularly over the 'little ships':

> We saw a grimmer picture than most in England at that time as we flew day after day down the Solent into the Channel. We saw the remains of what had been a proud fighting unit, now scattered with only the uniforms they stood up in, bloodied and torn as they slumped on the decks of British ships of all types. These limped into Southampton Water, some with their superstructure damaged, some with shellholes down to the waterline and one, a destroyer with its propeller shot away, being towed in by another damaged ship. In they all crawled at what seemed to me from the air to be a snail's pace. Troops were everywhere and the wounded were quickly and quietly loaded onto trains.[17]

It should perhaps be pointed out that the writer's commitment to the war effort is nowhere in doubt in the book from which this passage comes: it is a clear, dispassionate record of events made from immediate personal observation, similar to those seen by Bone but presented without the modifying filter of that artist's stance towards them.

As with Cundall's painting, the viewpoint in Bone's wash drawing is distant and elevated, though not quite to the same degree, so that here we may feel genuinely a part of the scene – presumably standing on an elevated section of the quayside looking down on the men as they disembark. Yet despite the involvement, we remain onlookers rather than participants. Once again the event has been recreated as an historical happening, modified to suit a particular view of the withdrawal – in, for example, the healthy men carrying full kit – rather than giving us an experiential sharing in the Romantic fashion which the drawing seems, at first glance, to offer us. Both Cundall and Bone, in their different ways, use experiential Romanticism to present a very clearly ordered, and some would say distortive, image of the experience of Dunkirk.

This use of Romantic re-ordering to stress a hieratic order and national purpose stands at the opposite end of the scale to the Romantic stances and attitudes which we find elsewhere in writing and painting of the war years, which stresses in its forms and techniques the sanctity and equality of all kinds of individual experience. It is tempting, but fallacious, to see these images as the beginning of a linear progression towards more individual and more compassionate uses of Romanticism in a social context. There is no clear line of development; but, as later chapters will show, there are many instances later of Romanticism playing a role in revealing a social outlook, perhaps even in revealing a social policy, diametrically opposed to that of these paintings, with their paradoxical simultaneous use and undermining of the Romantic convention of landscape in recalling and re-presenting a shared experience.

III

The images of Cundall and Bone are the kind of formal representation of events habitually seized on by the military historian and the contemporary chronicler as the basis of myths essential for survival, either psychological or political. The very scale of their subjects perhaps leads them towards distortion. What artistic treatments are there of the more personal and immediate aspects of the war years – the experience, for example, of people who lived in London and the other cities which suffered bombing from 1940 onwards? Subject matter is no guide to treatment, of course, but it is interesting to examine how the kind of Romantic realism we are here concerned with was employed by artists treating more personal, more fragmentary aspects of experience.

Depictions of shelter life during the Blitz are quite rightly dominated by the sketchbooks and drawings of Henry Moore. These will be discussed later; for the moment we should do well to remember that, at the time, other treatments were thought to be more accurate representations of reality and thus, in the opinion of many, 'better' works of art. The wash drawings of Feliks Topolski and Edward Ardizzone were often seen in this way and, as attempts at representation within the genre of Romantic realism, they deserve close study to define the degree and direction to which Romantic re-ordering of events is present within them, and their significance both artistically and socially.

Topolski's *The Tube; October 1940*[18] is dominated by the receding line of the tube rails to the left, which disappear into the tunnel mouth at the top. To the right, shelterers are shown in varying detail along the platform. In the middle ground two tin-hatted figures, presumably air-raid wardens, stand talking beneath a large 'WAY OUT' notice; next to them a woman is standing holding a baby just in the exit. Between these figures and the onlooker are a number of other shelterers. Those furthest back are sleeping peacefully at right angles to the platform, their shoulders resting on the base of the curving tunnel wall. Closer, a woman sits with her head bent forward on a bench under an 'Underground' symbol containing the words 'LEICESTER SQUARE'. Bundles of clothes and other figures occupy the foreground, with a woman lying open-mouthed next to a child, a tiny baby beside them; they face directly towards us, stretched supine along the platform. The main interest of the foreground is provided by the very stout figure of a man who sits, hands defiantly on his knees, smoking a pipe. The whole is held together by the circular washes representing the tunnel walls and ceiling.

Topolski's image is one which, within the style of a rapid pen, ink and wash sketch, sets out to be representational – the clearly legible signs and the anatomically accurate, if sketchy, forms of the shelterers all make this clear. Any suggestion of the kind of transformation of sleeping figures into complex human and landscape forms in the manner of Henry Moore – a very different and much more complex form of Romanticism – is quite absent. Yet, just like the Cundall and Bone images, the work displays a Romantic stance in the filtering and re-ordering of the subject it presents, like them subtly changing the nature of the experience it invites us to share.

This is apparent in the depiction of the figures. Most are rigid and orderly: it is as if the two near the exit are lying to attention. The woman comforting her baby by the exit is formal to the point of being derivative, a catalogue figure, almost; and the two wardens have a taut alertness beneath their apparently casual stance. The figures sleeping with bowed heads seem more in prayer than asleep; they are in the awkward compromise between sitting and kneeling usually known as the Anglican squat. Most noticeably, the two figures in the foreground are painted with a kind of comic tenderness. There is no sense of vulnerability about the supine woman whose mouth has fallen open; she is more a figure of fun than a representative of suffering. Clearest of all is the artist's attitude to the large man who sits right of centre in the foreground. J. B. Morton – author of the comic 'Beachcomber' column in the *Daily Telegraph* – defines this very precisely in his introduction to the volume where the drawing is reproduced. After drawing our attention to the figure as 'the disgruntled pipe-smoker' he continues:

> We recognise that man at once. We know what he is thinking, and what he is about to say. I served with him in the last war, and often heard him say it. He was younger and slimmer then – a grousing infantryman. Anybody may meet him in any London street to-day.[19]

Here, once again, is evidence of the tradition of the anecdotal beloved in popular painting of the Victorians – the desire to identify and give narrative substance to any human figure depicted which so exasperated Whistler. But as well as revealing a popular attitude towards painting in England this paragraph shows the stance of the artist to his subject – the mood or feeling which the ordering intellect has imposed upon the experience and wishes to re-create in the image, in a manner totally fitting both to Romantic precedent and, in its nature, to the thinking and needs of the times. The approach to the people presented is one of kindly, tolerant patronage; here are the comic Cockneys we all know and love from the music hall, but who have suddenly become tough and unbeatable in moments of stress, thrusting aside all discomfort with their indefatigable sense of humour. The figures sleeping to attention, the Anglican squatters, the woman comforting her baby in popular parody of religious icon, the comic sprawl of the woman in the foreground and the imperturbably disgruntled pipe-smoker – all are presented to us in a recreation of the experience which is quite typical of the official 'London can take it' stance of the time, and which uses the Romantic projection of mood upon scene to make its point. There is even an element of the hieratic, the two wardens apparently there to preserve the old class structure and order as much as to protect and rescue those injured by falling bombs.

Events were often rather different. The files of Mass-Observation, then working for the government to collect information on morale, suggest that the kind of bonhomie and social unity beloved of official recorders of the Blitz was often more imagined than real.[20] But this is not the place to further or destroy actualities or myths of national unity: my point is rather that Topolski's image uses a Romantic approach to convey a particular attitude towards an experience, which happens to be quite in accord with that which the establishment wished to promulgate at the time.

Morton's introduction dwells at some length on the kind of people presented in the paintings and drawings the collection reproduces – the 'commonplace men and women who, were they not so familiar to us, would already have assumed epic stature'.[21] This is another fine Romantic sentiment, the elevation of the everyday into the epic being a fundamental principle of *The Prelude* and the *Lyrical Ballads*; and the claim is to some extent borne out by the most intense images of the time, those of Moore and Sutherland. Yet it is worth considering some images other than these to show how the same Romantic projection of mood and attitude onto the object represented may reveal an approach to these 'commonplace men and women' which is far less egalitarian in nature than its Wordsworthian precursor and equivalent. Forties Romanticism can ally itself to reactionary, as well as revolutionary, causes.

In the Autumn of 1940 Edward Ardizzone completed a series of images of people in and around the shelters in the East End of London, seven of which are reproduced in the *Blitz* collection. All show figures with the characteristic rounded, almost bloated forms familiar from the artist's pre-war work, which consisted largely of children's book illustrations. The couple in *The Trek to the Shelter – Silvertown, September 1940*,[22] for example, look more as if they are setting out for a picnic than going to the shelter, despite the landscape of rubble and sandbags through which they are walking. There is a similar feeling in *Off to the Shelter*,[23] in which a group if women and children – pompously otiose in the Ardizzone fashion – walk from a dark alley into a brilliantly-lighted shelter while a pair of men look on from the left-hand foreground, for all the world like a pair of second-rate Cockney music-hall comedians. Only in *Sleeping in a Shelter*[24] do we find any suggestion of the sheer exhaustion of the Blitz victims, but even here this is offset by the sheer comfortable bulk of the figures. The shelter is dry, well-lit and, to judge from the absence of blankets, warm – a far cry from the cold, overcrowded and insaniatary conditions of the larger public shelters such as 'the Tilbury'[25] in the earlier years of the war. The note accompanying these images furthers this attitude:

> The first of the six pictures shows the Cockney spirit undismayed and undefeated. In the second and third East Enders hurry with their bedding to reach a place of safety before nightfall.[26]

Here and in the images themselves it is as if another species is being described. Both see the shelterers as stereotype Cockneys, comic yet indefatigable, as an example of how the nation is pulling together to survive the Blitz – the attitude which was certainly shared by many, but which is distortive of the experience of those who actually lived in Silvertown and went to the shelters every night, often walking several miles and setting off at midday to reach safety because of the meagre provision of shelters in their own neighbourhood. The Romantic projection of attitude upon image is clear and, in this instance, damning.[27]

We should not assume that all depictions of suffering humanity from this period betray such a use of Romantic mood-portrayal to convey official attitudes or simplified, mythic stances. Although they are fewer in number and were certainly less celebrated at the time of their completion, some strive to record an experience with greater immediacy and less order, both allowing us to share the fragments of life which they depict and inculcating a nurturing compassion towards the people and subjects they present. One such image is *Bombed out, Bermondsey*,[28] by Ethel Gabain. A group of four women, with haggard faces and wearying postures, stand in a circle before a row of tenement houses destroyed by a bomb. In the very foreground, partially cropped by the picture's edge, two schoolboys are standing, one talking, the other facing away from us and looking at the ground with hands thrust deep in trouser pockets. None of the figures is desolate or abandoned; instead, each seems disturbed but 'carrying on' under great stress. The intensity of these figures is balanced by others – a woman at the left gazes with a kind of unseeing concentration at the razed houses, while the young child she holds in her arms stares straight out at us with a look almost of accusation. Opposite her, a group of older boys stand amongst the wreckage, not in postures of heroic rescue but simply resigned, bewildered by the task of sorting through the rubbish.

It is a striking composition: in purely aesthetic terms, there is a rhythmic quality to the balance of the groups of figures, a kind of stunned, static dance, that recalls the abstract qualities we can see in many of the finest Romantic paintings – the dynamic friezes of Stubbs, say, or the taut exchanges of Wright of Derby. Nowhere in the other images discussed in this chapter is there such a balance of literal and abstract qualities. Yet at the same time, there is a compassion towards the figures. These are no stereotypes or parodies, like the patronising, comic figures of Ardizzone: they are real people trying to make sense of their lives and continue with them in some semblance of dignity, the women intent on material survival, the boys as if suddenly made aware that the business of being bombed is no playground game. They are depicted in an almost literal way, yet there is a sense of respect in their portrayal which is a thousand miles from the approach of the more official stance of Cundall and Bone; they are real people, confused, uncertain, yet trying to carry on, the women with their daily rituals of shopping and washing, the schoolboys with theirs of play and rites of passage to manhood.

In this balance lies the true Romanticism of the painting. Constable rearranges his landscapes so that they take on an almost abstract pattern in the arrangement of shapes and forms; the eye looking at *Landscape: Noon* is led in a circle around the cart, the meadows, the cottage, the foreground dog. In *Bombed out*, we are led around the four groups of people in a similar way. Yet both convey the feeling, the experience of the moment. There is no rhetoric or reorganisation which distances or makes sense of things in the Gabain as there is in the Cundall; that artist would have painted the scene from a far greater distance, imposing an order by showing heavy rescue squads at work and a pattern of life emerging. Gabain is immediate, compassionate, respectful and involved: she offers no easy answers, no mythic force. We are simply allowed to share the moment, with its pain and confusion. This, and the formal rhythm of the image, make it deeply Romantic in the complex philosophical sense of presenting a landscape and an attitude towards it, and also in the political sense of the overwhelming respect for the individual and the flux of his or her daily life which characterises all Romanticism from Rousseau onwards. It is also Romantic in the sense that it offers just the hint of continuity and survival of the individual human spirit amidst the desolation brought about by Governments: the woman at the left gazing at the rubble is pregnant. I find this a powerful, moving yet wholly unsentimental image, philosophically Romantic yet quite un-romanticised in presenting the experience of ordinary people searching quietly and with dignity for a way through.

Gabain's work is not alone in showing this kind of stance. Four paintings by Keith Vaughan were reproduced as the first photogravure supplement to *Penguin New Writing*.[29] The first of these is *Camp Construction – The start of a new day*.[30] A figure stands in a small, square enclosure to one end of a series of semi-circular steel hoops erected as the framework of a Nissen hut. In the background a further set of hoops is in place, next to another hut which appears complete; further metal hoops and sheets of corrugated iron cladding lie in the right foreground. The scene is sombre and overcast, heavy washes dominating the sky just before dawn, but the solitary figure is dramatically lit from the front of the picture.

This contrast gives the composition its impact, which is considerable: with his back turned on us and a sheet of corrugated iron between him and the skeletal hut, the figure is completely isolated. His depiction has a fragile grace about it which gives him a vulnerability to match his isolation, surrounded as he is by inorganic, unfeeling metal forms. He is quite astray, both in the bleak setting and in his task of camp construction. The viewpoint, on a level with the eyes of a spectator, lets us become part of the scene; the approach, conveyed in the contrast between dark skies and graceful yet vulnerable figure, makes us share the artist's compassion for the man at odds with this bleak military place. The dark washes and splashes of light are used in a manner as thoroughly Romantic as Constable's to show the artist's mood and attitude to what is shown; the result is something of great compassion which is quite characteristic of what one writer has seen as the major achievement of Vaughan's painting: its ability to convey 'something of the sense of loss and displacement that was common to civilians in uniform'.[31] Romantic ordering of experience to guide the response of the onlooker is used here just as it is with Cundall, but for a wholly different spiritual purpose. Like the Gabain, it is personal and uncertain, not ordered and mythic.

Reading at Night[32] has the same compassionate experience of sharing in the isolation of someone caught up with the dehumanising effects of war. A single figure lies reading in a tent, a candle at his side throwing a circle of light over his face, chest and arms; the rest of the composition – the man's body, a companion in the next bed, and the walls of the tent – is in heavy darkness. There is a tenderness in the line of the body which once more moulds our response to compassion; once more the Romantic stance has been used to convey genuine human, individual sharing of the complex isolation caused not by the horrors of war but by its material and psychological dislocation. Other images have the same effect. *Breakfast in a Marquee*[33] places us opposite two soldiers at a table in a tent. Neither looks at the other, and we share the isolation of the nearest figure whose sunken eyes and small head on a large, greatcoat-bloated body again suggest a soul astray in someone else's military life. *Recreation Room, Sunday Afternoon*[34] shows a group of men writing letters, reading or sleeping; individual activites in which there is no contact. Each figure faces almost studiedly away from the others. The soft outlines and gentle washes help in conveying an attitude of tenderness to these men drawn up in conflict of someone else's making.

It is not only the form, composition and tonal qualities of these watercolours that are striking: it is their selection of subject matter. Instead of the large, national epic of Dunkirk, seen from a distance which allows order to emerge or be imposed, and a national myth to be reinforced – or incidents in and around shelters which allow a stereotype of survival to be stressed – we have in the work of Gabain and Vaughan fragments of experience in confusion and uncertainty. Yet there also exists an innate dignity and endurance, shown with genuine compassion. Romanticism reorders and colours all of these works, but in these more intimate images we see it as an assertion of tenderness and understanding for the suffering of what Rayner Heppenstall calls 'The patient Khaki beast'.[35] It is a part of forties Romanticism which deserves to be better known.

IV

Visual treatments of fragments of reality are complemented throughout the war by written ones. These too reflect a Wordsworthian stance – the recording of an isolated, and in some cases apparently insignificant, moment of experience in the flux of time and events. The booklets issued by the Ministry of Information[36] represent one level of this, if a very formal and public one, an effort to make sense of things blunted and redirected by the need to see them within a very large, general context – though they do not reflect as overtly a propagandist stance as might be thought. Some of them move towards a record of individual experience: two booklets were published of broadcasts by members of the RAF recording their experiences, *We Speak from the Air*[37] and *Over to You*,[38] some of which have much personal immediacy. Yet the nature of their origins, and of the experiences they record, which inevitably are the dangerous and the heroic, place them far more in the convention of earlier officially-inspired anthologies of battle recollections, like the volume of *Somme Battle Stories*[39] published soon after the opening of the offensive in 1916. Yet there is a difference: whereas those were 'recorded' by Capt A. J. Dawson and illustrated by Bruce Bairnsfather, creator of 'ole bill', these accounts were delivered at the microphone by the individuals to whom they occurred and, even allowing for the fact that they must have been very carefully vetted in the selection and supervised in the execution, the stories do move towards a representation of individual experience of a sort not encountered in the First World War. Depending on one's point of view this is either an index of the greater social equality of the forties, or an indication of the official need to stress the involvement of every individual – 'chaps like us' – in the war effort.

We might also consider that the short stories of H. E. Bates fall into the mould of Romantic realism. Bates was commissioned by the RAF to produce a series of short stories which were published as *The Greatest People in the World* by 'Flying Officer X' in 1942. The degree to which these represent an official and therefore censored view of the events of the war is a detailed and complex study which falls beyond the limits of this book; but it is certainly true that Bates succeeded in conveying a sense of the involvement of a series of individuals within an official structure and events of great danger, so that the element of Romantic realism is certainly one of the foundations of his writing.

No writing published during the forties will be completely free of official influence in some respect: the laws and conventions of peacetime expression were still in force, and added to them were the controls administered by bodies as various as the Ministry of Information and the Ministry of Supply, which controlled the issue of newsprint to magazine publishers and which thus had a fast remedy for those who overstepped the limits. Despite all these limitations a tradition developed which saw the experience of the individual as its essence. It drew on many origins. There was the recent example of documentary film, now flourishing in the war years in the work of Humphrey Jennings and others at the Crown Film Unit, ostensibly recording and presenting the actuality of the times while – with different degrees of intention and of success – reflecting the preoccupations and ideals of the film-makers to create a further kind of Romantic fixing of experience.[40] There was the photo-journalism of *Picture Post*, recording the responses of 'ordinary people' to events such as the Oxford by-election,[41] or trying to show how it felt to be unemployed.[42] Perhaps there was also a streak of latter-day Bloomsburyism, having trickled out of the squares to influence more popular writers towards prizing the individual and his or her feelings.

Despite these other influences the roots of this kind of writing at the most fundamental level remain essentially Romantic in a very specific way. Writing of the Romantic realist genre of the forties is definitely outside the tradition which, created by Scott, is still the basis of a lot of popular fiction. Here a normal person – it helps if the person is of the same class and gender as the intended reader – is caught up in world events, so that the reader can vicariously re-live tumult and passion both personal and global. There clearly were and still are novels written about the forties which work in this way, but their rhetorical stance towards both subject and reader is far distant from those of the Romantic realist writing of the time. This is instead concerned with recording the flux of daily life, either uneventful or momentous but very often the former. The writer is in all instances the person to whom the events have occurred, the intention sometimes to clarify and contextualise, but more frequently simply to try to relate inner and outer reality and so bring some sense of order and resolution. Sometimes this leads to an awareness of a larger pattern or purpose, a deeper significance within the daily round; more often it does not, instead simply providing a clarification if the minutiae of the everyday and perhaps allowing us to see their ritualistic importance in everyone's life.

These elements taken together provide us with almost all the key ingredients, style and setting left aside, of *The Prelude.* The only element lacking is the notion of developmental growth, the strand of the *Bildungsroman* in Wordsworth which these later fragments of autobiography lack. This is part of the fragmentary nature of the life that they record, the tentative quality we shall see emerging quite often in Romantic art of the forties as one response to a decidedly fragmentary existence: Romanticism has been modified to fit the times and the situations, but in other senses the stream continues.

The most complete collection of Romantic realism can be found in the series of articles published under the general title 'The Way we Live Now' in *Penguin New Writing* beginning with its second issue in January 1941. Writing in that issue's foreword the editor John Lehmann described this as 'a feature . . . in which each month a different worker, a soldier, or someone "in the thick of it" will describe and discuss his (or her) recent experiences'.[43] Lehmann here reveals his political stance in the assumed equality between worker and soldier and their shared position 'in the thick of it'. This is more likely the lasting convictions of thirties ideology than the more transient 'war socialism' but, whatever its origins it reveals the key feature of Romantic realist writing of this sort: the primacy and equality of all kinds of experience, whatever their origin, nature or degree of lasting significance. In this he is nailing not only his politics but his Wordsworthian ethics to the *Penguin New Writing* masthead. There is also a larger aim:

> I should like to think, however, that it was helping towards a reaffirmation of human values, in a world suffering from the triumph of inhuman ideas and the pursuit of values which are unreal and destructive.[44]

It is an aim which hovers unspoken above a very great deal of the Romantic art and writing of the forties: and, after all, there are many worse things for an artist to aim for.

These qualities are continued in the first article of the series, called simply 'The Way we Live Now – I' by B. L. Coombes.[45] The son of a Herefordshire farmer, Coombes became a miner in South Wales – that in itself is enough of an emblem of the industrial despoliation of Wordsworthian innocence. He came to prominence in left-wing journalism in the thirties with articles such as the *Picture Post* study of unemployment mentioned above and his autobiography – titled, with finely-judged ambiguity, *These Poor Hands* – published in 1939. He was thus the ideal choice for the first article of the series. It describes the arrival and descent of a pit-shift during an air-raid, balancing in a very restrained way darkness above and within the earth, and the two versions of moral eclipse these represent.

> Men find their mates by calling with subdued voices as if sound, too, was forbidden. They are doubtful of a shadow near their shoulder until the voice reassures them. Finally they merge together, a black army in the complete darkness, and start to tramp upwards along a narrow lane to the colliery.
>
> On the right, far below them, a flooded river hisses and splashes. The sound of huge stones being rolled along by the water echoes up to the men. A line of whitened posts mark the danger edge of the ravine, but the coal dust that spreads from the trains passing during one day spoils the work of 'the whitewash bloke'.[46]

There is a simplicity and lack of comment here which gives the writing great dignity and depth. The uncertainty of the men's movement seems to imply a larger lack of direction, and their anonymity a sense of shared suffering. The description of the river is similarly restrained, but the idea of despoliation of nature is hard to avoid, echoed as it is in the strictly literal reference to the lost labour of 'the whitewash bloke'. This is experiential writing which both conveys the immediate events and hints at their larger significance, which is made explicit later in the article:

> Surrounded by coal, people must starve for heat. With abundant harvests we must go short of food. To me it seems all wrong; so needless – so futile.[47]

Later, at the end of the article, Coombes adds this:

> We are not spectators looking on at the battle of life; we are in it and so what we write is true and sincere. If our methods are sometimes crude and unpolished it is the conditions, not ourselves, that are to blame. We plead for a better life and security for all.[48]

It is the true Wordsworthian model; an experience deeply felt which prompts a deeper reflection on the nature of existence, here added to the ideal expressed in the *Lyrical Ballads* that the 'simple and unelaborated expressions'[49] are fundamentally most strong. There is no sense of Romantic escape here, though: it is a confrontation with difficulties and inequities Coombes sees all around him, welded into the social structure just as strongly as coal dust and grime is subsumed into the valley air. Coombes does not use metaphors like this, and his writing is the stronger for it; the point makes itself by implication, so that experience, landscape and political stance are inseparably fused, just as they are, each in different ways with different effects, in the painting of Cundall and Vaughan.

Willy Goldman contributed the second article to the *Penguin New Writing* series. Born in Stepney, Goldman left school at fourteen and worked in the docks, engineering and the East End sweatshops. His article is one of the few accounts of the blitz on the East End written by those who were born and brought up there and as a result it lacks the whiff of sociological enbalming fluid which is often present in studies by outsiders. Thus he is able to make clear some of the effects of the blitz which other writers miss:

> the housework has to be rushed through in a race against 'given' time. It has to be completed, in other words, not only before dark, but *well before dark* – for the night's 'lodging' is not 'booked', but has to be competed for.[50]

This captures something which Ardizzone's patronising sketches of comic Cockney stereotypes trekking to shelter could never grasp; that the ritual of ordering the house, so important a part of the everyday lives of so many London women, must be kept going amid all the dislocation of the blitz, and the only way for this to happen in the limited time is by frenzied hurry. The paragraph tells us a good deal about the strain of wartime life which no amount of sociological enquiry can; it is Romantic in recording the everyday experience of ordinary people in their own language, not in seeking a romanticised retreat from intrusive reality. This is true elsewhere in the article:

> There is something very sad about these back-streets. (A stranger might well believe he had stumbled into a partly sacked city.) The silence does not suit them as it does the widely terraced and richly foliaged suburb. It is the gossiping, the street cries, the children, the dogs that give a slum the 'life' it has. Without these manifestations it might well be a desert.[51]

We are back to Wordsworth's notion of the primacy of ordinary speech, which has become something quite precious since its disruption by the bombing. This has far more than merely literary implications; how many post-war planners, I wonder, grew up in such streets and realised the importance of noise instead of prim suburban silence in the new estates of the fifties and sixties intended to re-house those bombed out in the blitz? Romanticism is here revealed as a social attitude far more than an aesthetic stance. Goldman goes on to say how the blitz revealed the 'inflexibility' of the class system, but with greater percipience than many chroniclers: he refers to its 'discovery' which came about because 'many people have the notion that a large-scale catastrophe falls on everyone with equally crushing force'. It is clear that it did not: Goldman swiftly dispels the fiction of rich and poor sharing shelters by saying that the 'better-class' shelterers go off and eat good meals in 'electrically equipped "better-class" restaurants'[52] whereas the inhabitants of the tenements go back to find that they cannot cook because of burst gas-mains. The Romantic experiential record presents us with a viewpoint just as precise here as Ardizzone's sketches, albeit one that is diametrically opposed.

Other articles in the series show similar uses of the technique. Gordon Jeffery writes about an early-morning train journey from his billet to the shipyard where he works;[53] Leonard York tells of driving a train during night raids.[54] Both use the language of their situation with the kind of spontaneity which is the intellectual foundation of the *Lyrical Ballads*. Others use the Romantic tradition in different ways. Donald Swanson gives an account of a voyage on a coastal steamer[55] which is at first uneventful except that they are followed by an albatross. Twice it is seen and on each occasion it is described not as a friendly omen but as 'a bloody great Heinkel'.[56] They have dinner – 'tell the cook I've —— better dinners'[57] – and then they are attacked by a bomber, which is described as 'a bloody great albatross'.[58] The interplay between animal and mechanical, benevolent and destructive, is subtle and deliberate; Coleridge's imagery of unity with and rejection of the natural world is extended in a truly contemporary manner, showing how the habit of destruction makes the writer think even of the natural world in terms of annihilation. The lack of any final resolution or unity is yet another image of impermanence and the lack of a solution – this mariner does not bless them unawares, nor does he receive any redemption, but is instead grateful simply to escape death in the bombing attack. Romanticism continues, moderated and tempered by the limitations of the times.

A rather more self-conscious piece is Louis MacNeice's record of returning by sea from New York to London,[59] commenting on the way the city has changed:

> London since the blitz has become more comprehensible. Because this great dirty, slovenly, sprawling city is a visible and tangible symbol of freedom; it has not been centralised, organised, rationalised, dehumanised into a streamlined ad. for the cult of the State.[60]

MacNeice is here continuing the Romantic tradition of seeing London as a symbolic entity: for Wordsworth it was a spiritual entity, for Blake an emblem as well as a very tangible essence of institutional evil, and for MacNeice it becomes, in the renewed human contact of the blitz, a breeding ground for genuine human contact and nurture.

From No. 13, *Penguin New Writing* expanded its 'Way we Live Now' article into a whole section, 'Report on Today',[61] which continued to develop Romantic experiential writing. Taken together, the pieces discussed here constitute one of the most important threads of Romantic realism of the period; it is regrettable that space does not permit its further consideration. But the last of the original series of articles is too important to be left out – Keith Vaughan's account of the arrival by train of the first casualties from France.[62]

> Three tiers of bunks lined the white walls, each with a face that stared out quietly and expressionless, like the eyes of an animal caught for a moment in a car's headlights. We felt strange and helpless and remote from us in experience. Some turned to look at us, visitors out of the night, from another planet. Others were still locked in their prisons of pain, where we had no admittance. No one spoke. We drew on our stretchers and began the routine of unloading, glad of the work that would let us forget our awkwardness.
>
> The stretchers were held up level against the bunks and the men coaxed, like animals, to brave the crossing onto their steel meshes. They dragged across those parts of their bodies they were able, the rest we carried for them, grotesque shapes of wool and splint and bandage, joined to them only by pain.[63]

Experience is here reduced to the essential elements of existence – pain, compassion and the animal impossibility of sharing someone else's feelings. It is completely self-sustaining, with no attempt to contextualise, justify or explain; the last sentence is the climax of this intensity. For a moment we are as involved with Vaughan's experience as we are with Wordsworth's fear on the lake or his ecstasy when skating. As there is no contextualising so there is no attempt at distortion; Cundall and Bone would have made this heroic and general, Ardizzone comic and bundled. In Vaughan's writing, as in his painting, we are given confusion, exclusion, separateness, recreating the experience just as it was. The account is immediate, involving and compassionate, modifying its concern for the natural world by using imagery – the car's headlights – of its own age, seeking not to find order in events but merely to record them. In its immediacy and its tentativeness it offers us no solution but the human compassion which is the essence of its experience: it is forties Romantic realism at its finest.

The final paragraph of Vaughan's article describes the ambulances moving away from the stations, continuing the tense compassion of the helpers in their awkward desire to help the wounded, still with no sense of context or resolution. But at the very end, as the ambulances move out of the town, there is just a hint of consolation and renewal, something that is to be a major element of forties Romanticism as those who are there seek to make sense of their experience not in the hectoring claims of nationalism but in the instinctive, renewing processes of the natural world.

> The drivers sweated with anxiety at each scar on the tarmac that might hold a fresh pocket of agony for the men behind. We left the town and moved on into the country; beneath the mounting sun, between fields heavy and still with the green abundance of summer.[64]

4

Blitz Sublime

I

> A mode of terror, or of pain, is always the cause of the sublime.[1]

This short sentence from Edmund Burke expresses one of the key notions from one of the key documents of early English Romanticism. In establishing the Sublime as a state of feeling higher than beauty, Burke not only foresaw – if not quite invented – the whole idea of Romantic *angst* and the *frissson* as ultimate experience, but also stressed that feature which marks out Romantic aesthetics from all that had gone before: now it is the feelings which are the subjective judge in matters of art, not any apparently objective canons of taste. He continues:

> Whatever is fitted in any sort to excite the ideas of pain, and danger, that is to say, whatever is in any sort terrible, or is conversant about terrible objects, or operates in a manner analogous to terror, is a source of the *sublime*; that is, it is productive of the strongest emotion of which the mind is capable of feeling.[2]

Earlier, Burke has defined the effects created by the Sublime in the responsive sensibility, saying that, as long as the terror is not 'actually noxious', it has a kind of purifying effect on the onlooker, and is 'capable of producing delight'

> not pleasure, but a sort of delightful horror, a sort of tranquillity tinged with terror; which as it belongs to self-preservation is one of the strongest of all the passions.[3]

Terrifying objects, whether an avalanche in the Grisons or the eruption of Vesuvius, have a purifying and revivifying effect on us:

they clear away any trivial concern and leave us with a passion for self-preservation which is strong, unalloyed and thus the progenitor of a kind of delight through its pure intensity. And thus we have the origin of some of the most striking work of the Romantics, from the paintings of awesome natural scenes[4] or passages from older literature chosen for their power to terrify,[5] to poems of contemporary personal experience such as Coleridge's 'Hymn before Sun-rise, in the vale of Chamounix'[6] and Wordsworth's confrontation with the 'huge peak, craggy and huge' in the celebrated stolen boat episode.[7]

This is all an accepted part of the history of Romanticism itself, but it also has a lot to offer in clarification of a certain kind of painting and writing of the 1940s. To say that the influence of the earlier movement was conscious or the resemblance recognised would, I think, be tendentious and, in any case, irrelevant; I have no wish to play the game musicologists call *Reminiscenzjagd*. Certainly, Christopher Hussey had discussed Burke's ideas in his book on the Picturesque, as Chapter 2 has made clear, but whether or not the artists of the forties whose work seems to develop his ideas in a contemporary setting had read this is not of immediate interest. The presence of the idea of fear and its effects in work of the forties is perhaps a demonstration of another way in which the perceptual approaches of the Romantics had become so much part of the artistic consciousness of the time that they were adopted almost instinctively as a response to the events of the time. There is another reading which on the surface is less likely but which becomes more persuasive after detailed study of important works in their historical contexts; perhaps the similarity shows an instinctive recourse to approaches like those of Burke which is revealing about mental attitudes and strategies to ensure survival when death and destruction are all around us.

In many of the paintings of events of the blitz which were most celebrated at the time, there is an element of the pure terror which is familiar from high Romantic paintings of great natural disasters. In important prose writing of the time, too, there is an approach familiar from the Gothic novel and the poetry of personal growth and salvation of the high Romantics. Yet neither form stops at the mere desire for what Samuel Butler calls 'conventional ecstasy',[8] a thrill of pain to satisfy a dulled aesthetic sense. It goes beyond this as a way first of recording the experience of fear – sometimes modified, as in Burke, so that the danger is not quite immediate and personal

– and then changing it into something which has a deep power to move. This kind of sublimity is similar to the Romantic idea of beauty but is very different in subject from the conventionally beautiful. At the same time it has a kind of tranquillity which seems to record the feelings of the beholder – the artist involved in the blitz, recording experience and feeling as much as external, objective reality.

The Romantics exploited the Sublime as one facet of the thrillingly new idea of inner, personal experience; the artists and writers of the forties used it as an unwitting response to events which at the time were genuinely apocalyptic, both recording and reacting to them. In this they instinctively modified the Romantic stance to fit the exigencies of the age and the nature of their own mental needs; here as elsewhere Romanticism is not merely a movement of archaic escape, but a response of mind and spirit modified by current needs and contemporary attitudes to them. This is a response of the artist which uses the trappings and the idioms of a kind of Romanticism to come to terms with the arbitrary yet visually glorious, terrifying yet aesthetically uplifting, circumstances of daily and nightly life in Bristol, Bath, Coventry in the early forties: the Sublime has become, quite instinctively, a mode of survival.

II

From the autumn of 1940 onwards, there was no shortage of what Burke would have called objects of the Sublime, as first London and then important provincial cities became the targets of Nazi bombing raids. Many painters of the time were involved in recording aspects of the blitz, either under the auspices of the WAAC or from more personal drives. Some painted buildings which it was feared would be destroyed, some the effects of the desolation, and some the actual process of destruction. Of this last subject, many painters produced work which can clearly be seen within the tradition of the Sublime. Some of their work today seems to do little more than sensationalise – to continue, in fact, the purest form of the Sublime in its painterly manifestations. Other paintings do more, developing and extending a tradition in various significant directions.

One painter who seems to continue the simpler notions of the Sublime is Henry Carr, who was employed as an honorary captain in the public relations division of the War Office. His work includes wash drawings of the subterranean communities in the Chislehurst caves set up by refugees from air raids, portraits of leading civil servants and war correspondents, and scenes from the actions in Italy and Tunisia. In the present context his paintings *St. Clement Dane's Church on Fire after being Bombed*[9] is of particular interest.

The church is shown silhouetted against the night sky. Beside it can be seen on the left the Law Courts and on the right a group of office buildings standing on the Strand and backing onto the Temple. The famous 'wedding cake' tower of the church is lit from behind by flames which leap from the roof of the nave and shine brightly through the windows of the west wall. Firefighters stand before the building dwarfed by both it and the erupting flames. The viewpoint is low, and we see the church from directly before the west end, roughly at the intersection of Aldwych and the Strand. The blazing church is shown from the viewpoint of someone present at the scene so that we are involved in the destruction; it is indeed a vision of the Sublime in the destruction of an aged, classical building.

Despite all this, the link with the tradition of the Sublime is perhaps too strong in this case for us to feel personally involved, personally threatened. The destruction of the church is terrible and appalling, but this is largely because of the event itself, not the depiction. The figures are too small and distant for us to share their suffering, the space around the church – mostly between us and the building – is so great as to remove any feeling of enclosure or threat. We are left with the feeling that this does indeed produce the kind of response that Burke had in mind – 'a sort of delightful horror'. It is a painting directly in the Sublime tradition of Turner's *Burning of the Houses of Parliament*:[10] we see the event and response with a *frisson* of fear which is kept securely under restraint by the controlled distancing. Ironically, the interpretive powers of the artist here seem less effective in drawing us into the event than the sheer immediacy of many of thr finest photographs of the blitz, paramount among which are those taken by Bert Hardy for *Picture Post*:[11] these thrust us into the actuality they present so that we experience fear with no apparent filter or distance. In Carr's painting, by contrast, any larger feelings we might have are the product of our own response to the event, not the result of the painting's evocative or emotional impact; those who lived through the blitz will respond with far greater intensity to such a painting, one feels, than those who come later and see it with greater detachment. There is little to suggest that the imitation of the earlier practice of the Sublime is conscious; but it is suggestive that, when in Italy, Carr painted *Vesuvius in Eruption*,[12] the subject beloved of Wright of Derby and a frequent source of fashionable terror on the Grand Tour.

Other paintings present versions of sublimity which involve us more completely. Frank Dobson, an artist who had been officially employed in the First World War,[13] was commissioned to produce a number of paintings of the home front. His *Bristol, November 24th, 1940*[14] records the effects of the first raid on the city, ten days after the devastation of Coventry. It shows a terrace of shops, the Georgian proportion of their windows reduced to bare holes revealing interiors which are nothing but flame; an unnatural brightness is cast over the foreground, while the further distance is obscured by a cloud of luminous smoke. The façade of one of the buildings has almost completely collapsed; the others have a semi-abstract quality caused by the lack of mullions and transoms in the windows and the sharp contrasts of colour and tonality between the black brickwork and the glaring flame.

Once again the desolation is made forcefully clear and we respond with the degree of awe familiar from earlier notions of the Sublime. Yet the effect is different from that of Carr's painting; these are familiar provincial houses, the Georgian façades of a once-fashionable street turned into shops by a later generation which could be found in any English city between the wars. Carr's painting, however familiar its subject to contemporary Londoners, depicts an architectural monument of a different sort; the tower by Joshua Marshall in 1670 and the nave by Wren in 1682 are classical structures designed for a formal purpose, not vernacular buildings familiar from daily, personal use like the Georgian shop-fronts of Dobson's Bristol. As a result we are far more closely involved, and the feeling of awe and terror that Dobson inspires is much more immediate than any fashionable feeling of Romantic Sublime: the distance is less, the experience correspondingly more real.

Dobson also draws us into the painting by his choice of viewpoint. We see the street as from an upper window of one of the shops on a road at the foot of the hill, perhaps one which crosses at right angles the road of burning buildings. So we see things from a familiar viewpoint, the window of a bedroom perhaps, or the first-floor flat above a shop. In normal times, the street scene of dingy respectability would have greeted the occupant every day, standing for order and continuity in a shabby kind of way; now it is transformed into a frenzy of fire and destruction. It is almost a parody of *Alice Through the Looking Glass*; we look through the window to see not the familiar, safe street but a vision of chaos come again made the more terrible because the buildings are still recognisable in outline.

It is this combination of the familiar and the terribly new that gives the painting its force, and through which it endows the tradition of the Sublime with something forcefully contemporary. This scene is not something merely aesthetic and so divorced from real experience; the same quality is apparent in these lines from the diary of a Bristol woman which record the same November raid:

> . . . went to the sitting-room. We didn't need any light for the room was lit up with the glare of the fires . . . Our sitting-room window woodwork is so hot you can hardly bear your hand on it. The house rocks as the bombs drop. It is like a 'Wellsonian drama' come true.[15]

Dobson is not painting a modern version of the fashionable detached *frisson* caused by the eighteenth-century Sublime: he is presenting us with a view of twentieth-century destruction which draws on the paradoxically surreal elements of actual experience both to record the events of the night and to make us share the fear of those who lived through them. His painting veers towards abstraction because the events themselves move a similar distance away from what hitherto had been reality; a similar movement is shown in the above paragraph, which refers to 'Wellsonian drama', most probably the elaborate air-raid scenes of the film *Things to Come*,[16] based on a book by H. G. Wells. The Sublime has been wrenched out of the Grand Tour and the Gothic ruin and thrust into contemporary reality to be made terribly familiar yet fearsomely new, and in this Dobson's painting succeeds in reinventing a version of Romanticism which rests fully on the experience and the needs of its own time.

Carr's view of the blitz carries on the Sublime *frisson*; Dobson's rekindles the surreal terror created by the bombing. Is there a depiction which uses the Sublime to bring any suggestion of something positive from the surrounding destruction? This must depend very much on the stance of the onlooker and in this we must be aware that the view of the 1990s and beyond is very different from that of the forties. Yet there does seem to be at least one painting which takes elements of a Romantic technique, most particularly the Sublime depiction of an event to create fear, and modifies and extends them to produce a response which can be seen as reassuring and nurturing: Leonard Rosoman's *A House Collapsing on Two Firemen, Shoe Lane, London EC4.*[17] One of the best-known and most widely-reproduced paintings of the blitz, it was completed in August 1941 while the artist was working as a fireman with the National Fire Service at Maresfield Gardens, London, a short distance away from stations where William Sansom and Stephen Spender worked.[18] This painting represents very well a particular approach to the blitz, and a series of conundra which face the present-day onlooker trying to evaluate within an historical context paintings of that period and subject. It is a fine example of the latter-day Sublime, modified and developed in subtle and complex ways to meet contemporary needs, but it also carries with it a series of insistent moral and aesthetic questions.

The canvas depicts the falling wall of a house frozen in the instant before it crashes to the ground. The street is narrow, and the wall has already struck the front of a row of houses opposite. Bricks and debris are flung back by the force of the impact, and the impression of dynamism and energy is created by these objects and fragments of wood and masonry thrown up by the force of the collapse. The whole of the painting is in a single tonality which ranges from the blood-orange, flame-lit foreground to more distant shadows of sombre brown, giving it both the emotional impact of this very rich colouration and a concentration of tone usually found only in monochrome photographs. The 'photographic' element is enhanced by the depiction of the house-fronts still standing at the right of the composition, which are shown much foreshortened and in the blurred, unfocused manner of a rapid documentary photograph.[19] In the dark triangle between falling wall, street and standing houses are silhouetted two firemen, still holding a hose but being bent towards the house-fronts on the right by the force of the collapsing wall. It is a freeze-frame in a dynamic continuity, suggesting immense power in the collapsing building and a heroic vulnerability in the two firemen.

It is this that gives it the quality of the Sublime: there is little doubt that we are instilled with the 'mode of terror, or of pain' familiar from Burke and his followers. To those who lived through the blitz, the immediacy must have been grave; it is, in a fearsome way, a recollection of experience of the kind which is basic to Romantic landscape and which, as we have already seen, is common among even the most detached or politically distorted images of the day. Yet in this it is much more powerful than those earlier Romantic paintings which seek to instil the Burkeian terror. The figures in de Loutherbourg's *An Avalanche in the Alps*,[20] perhaps the best-known Romantic embodiment of the Sublime, recoil from the falling rocks which are about to engulf them, but they do so in the stylised emotional poses made popular by Charles Lebrun and his followers.[21] And these are conventional Italian peasants, not travellers on the Grand Tour, whereas Rosoman's firemen are real contemporary people, Londoners like those who will look at the painting. These two distancing forces are enhanced by the viewpoint: de Loutherbourg places us high above the threatened peasants and apparently out of danger; the eyeline in Rosoman's canvas is dangerously low, quite clearly that of someone standing on the same level, in the same street, as the engulfed firemen. Our fear as onlookers is real; that of the painting's first viewers must have been magnified by the painting's effect in triggering recollections of their own recent experience, the 'my bomb' story which every city-dweller had in 1940.

Rosoman's painting can therefore be seen to out-Sublime the Sublime itself; but where does this leave us in terms of its aesthetic or moral value? We know that it was painted from direct personal experience, recording a raid in which he was involved as a firefighter; we know, too, that the two figures shown are actual firemen, both of whom were killed by the falling house. Rosoman himself was later to find the picture 'sentimental and superficial',[22] and it is certainly a long way away from the stylistically sparse studies of men and machines which he produced when attached to the Royal Navy in the Far East as a war artist in the later years of the war.[23] For us, there is discomfort in the way the painting makes dramatic capital out of suffering in arresting a moment in the death of the two firemen; yet for those who were there the experiential quality of the painting, both in recording an actual incident and in triggering memories of similar ones in their own lives, very probably had an effect of no little cathartic value. The popularity of the painting suggests that it perhaps went further than representing shared experience, to give dignity and heroic stature to the ordinary fighting men of the time. The note accompanying the image when it was reproduced in *War Pictures by British Artists* seems to suggest that the aspects Rosoman himself now finds displeasing were the very ones which gave it validity and force to its contemporary viewers:

> This dramatic incident, in which two members of London Fire Force were killed in action, was witnessed by the artist, who is himself a fireman and saw much service in London during the heaviest raids.[24]

This sentences is intriguingly revealing about the contemporary response. First, there is no mention of the painting as a painting; the comment is concerned solely with the incident depicted and might equally be describing a photograph or episode from a film. This suggests the wide appeal of the canvas – it is not significant only to those concerned with 'art', but is relevant to the general experience of those living through the blitz. In this, the painting is commendably living up to the aims of the War Artists' Advisory Committee in providing a documentary record of the events of the times. But the art historical significance is that experience and art-work are fused into one here; it makes the kind of comment on reality which could only be possible at a time when the Romantic ethic of experiential painting has become an unthinking part of the outlook not only of the artist but also of the common man. Sentimental and superficial it may now be to the artist's sensibilities; to those who were there, it is simply real.

The comment is also important in stressing that the artist 'is himself a fireman'. Just as the painting makes us share the reality of its experience, so the artist shares the reality of ours: this is no piece of highfalutin studio invention by an 'Artist' who has never strayed beyond Hampstead or Chelsea. The biographical information gives the painting validity and reinforces the idea of shared suffering. The references to the two firemen continue this; they were 'killed in action', a term used before the Second World War exclusively of soldiers on a military fighting front, never of those employed in a technically 'civilian' role. The same emphasis is shown in the comment that Rosoman 'saw much service' in the London raids. The blitz put everyone into the front line; the idea of shared struggle is strong here and, even discounting the establishment intent to make all pull together which inevitably underlies the note because of its place of publication, there is in this something which again unites artist, onlooker and dying firemen.

It is almost a Marxian paradigm of shared experience in art, and in this lies its importance as a piece of contemporary Sublime. The terror it depicts is real, and shared – by viewpoint, by experience, by consent in the accompanying note. The firemen and the artist are heroes, and so too by implication are all those who live through such happenings, who share the 'dramatic' events of the sort the painting records. The painting's original viewers look on it with a *frisson* of fear that is genuine and based on recollections of direct involvement, not on aristocratic theorising and detachment enriched by literary *sensibilité*. The fear is accompanied by a feeling of heroism and endurance in the firemen, in the artist and in themselves; it is a genuinely demotic painting both in style and in the response it generates, and this heroic fortitude is a kind of catharsis, a way of enduring. Once more an element of Romanticism has been espoused, by instinct and because it has been assumed into the common way of seeing, and extended in the circumstances of the forties to meet contemporary demands, here of psychological survival more than of aesthetic stance. An earlier outlook has spread out to embrace a greater need; emotionally the Sublime has come of age.

III

It is not only in visual treatments of the blitz that aspects of the Sublime may be seen. There is a whole covention of writing which, taking as its basis the experience of intensive air raids, sees its visual nature as something of great and paradoxical beauty and goes on to employ this in a variety of ways to offer some kind of spiritual and emotional nurture.[25] At a simple level there is the popular literature of blitz-romance,[26] seen in popular novels and also in entertainment films such as *I Live in Grosvenor Square*.[27] More serious writing for patriotic and political purposes sometimes shares this outlook: a semi-documentary novel dealing with the experiences of ambulance crews in the blitz, *The Squad Goes Out*,[28] makes frequent reference to the dark beauty of the London nights and the extraordinary effects of lighting caused by blazing buildings; and Humphrey Jennings' *London Can Take It*,[29] with commentary by Quentin Reynolds, employs similar effects to stress the tenacity and endurance of the population of London in the autumn of 1940 and influence public opinion in the USA towards support of the British cause. But there are more complex uses of the landscape and experience of the burning city, and one of the most significant is Graham Greene's novel *The Ministry of Fear*.[30]

In the winter of 1941–2, Graham Greene found himself in Sierra Leone, working for the secret service.[31] Despite the separation, his impressions of blitzed London remained strong, and these and the influence of a thriller by Michael Innes led him to write an 'entertainment' which blends actual and surreal, eighteenth-century Sublime and twentieth-century outrage, in a manner which allows genuine compassion and comfort to emerge from what, on the surface, is closer to a contemporary re-working of the Gothic than a serious psychological novel.

The plot of *The Ministry of Fear* revolves around the character of Arthur Rowe who has recently stood trial for the mercy killing of his terminally-ill wife. By unknowingly giving a coded signal at a 'guess the weight of the cake' stall at a charity fête he wins a cake which contains a microfilm, and so enters a process of intrigue which involves his being visited by a mysterious figure whom he only escapes when his house is destroyed in an air raid; a fake murder at a séance; his confinement in a bogus nursing-home; and his eventual escape to some hope of contentment. Along the way he encounters Willi and Anna Hilfe, the former a Nazi agent, his sister Anna a figure who becomes the focus for Rowe's displaced love and pity. This bare outline is enough to reveal the themes of the outsider and the corrosive effects of pity already characteristic of Greene's work and so make clear that this is more than just a thriller; but it is the way that the effects of the blitz, both visual and psychological, are used which makes of it something akin to a contemporary version of the Sublime, and the depiction of both the external events and Rowe's own inner attitudes and reactions to them that makes the novel important in a more general manner as a piece of mid-century Romanticism.

There is a hint in much of the book of a longing to recapture a Wordsworthian childhood, free and instinctively in touch with the natural world. This is clear in the opening scene, where Rowe finds himself outside the fête in a London square:

> The fête called him like innocence: it was entangled in childhood, the vicarage gardens and the girls in white summer frocks and the smell of herbaceous borders and security.[32]

As he entered the fête:

> Arthur Rowe stepped joyfully backward into adolescence, into childhood. There had always been a fête about this time of year in the vicarage garden, a little way off the Trumpington Road, with the flat Cambridgeshire field beyond the extemporised bandstand, and at the end of the fields the pollarded willows by the stickleback stream and the chalk-pit on the slopes of what in Cambridgeshire they call a hill.[33]

This is Wordsworthian Romanticism tempered by all kinds of twentieth-century experience. To begin with, it is an adult longing to enter childhood again, something not present in Wordsworth. Rowe steps back not into childhood but into adolescence, a time of greater uncertainty; and the whole event is hedged around by contemporary limitations – the fête will have to end soon because of the blackout, the quality of items for sale is so much poorer than before the war, the cake of so much importance is a great rarity in being made with real eggs. Underlying all of this is the dominant fact of Rowe's life, as yet not stated openly but revealed in several small hints, of his having killed his wife, an act revealing both the fallen state of experience and the ideal state of hope. This gives Rowe something of the quality of a present-day Manfred, with a sense of guilt inseparable from his own feelings of love and nurture for others and little sense of his own worth. The quality is strengthened by the psychological intensity added to the novel's central passage where Rowe is 'treated' by Dr Forester. To make the point more incisive still, the opening section of Book Two of the novel has the ironic title 'Conversations in Arcady'; the nursing home is a parody of the country house 'improved' in the eighteenth century to follow the ponderous doctrines of the Picturesque.

As the novel develops there is less concern with aspirations and parodies of recapturing an ideal past, yet there are other elements which show just as strongly Romantic ideals tempered by present-day attitudes and experience. The whole of Rowe's relationship with Anna Hilfe exemplifies this. On the surface it supplies the conventional 'love interest' when the book is seen as a popular novel, part thriller, part 'romance'. At a deeper level there are more important significances. If Rowe represents a post-Freudian embodiment of the Romantic outsider, we might hope that Anna Hilfe represents a kind of redemption, almost an earth-mother or eternal feminine. Her name – Hilfe – would lead us to suppose this, and that she is someone who can 'help' Rowe. In a practical sense she does this to some extent, but things are not so simple or positive, and there is certainly no comfortable nineteenth-century movement towards the altar. Anna is herself doubly a displaced person, in being a refugee from central Europe and in knowing that her brother is a traitor; she is another Romantic outsider.

Greene uses the balance between Rowe's longing for resolution and his awareness of its impossibility – itself an updating of a Romantic yearning for the unattainable – in a way that is both ironic and dynamic. At the end of the novel, on his way to meet Anna, Rowe confronts both the hope and the reality:

> He had hoped that wherever Anna was there would be peace; coming up the stairs a second time he knew that there would never be peace again while they lived.[34]

The declaration of shared love with which the book ends is similarly tense and halting: she has 'the air of someone perpetually on guard to shield him', he is aware that he is 'pledging them both to a lifetime of lies'.[35] Yet there is a sense in which the ending is positive:

> It occurred to him that perhaps after all one could atone even to the dead if one suffered enough for the living.[36]

A little later, the book ends with Rowe thinking that 'after all one could exaggerate the value of happiness . . .'[37]

All of this shows the book as a direct descendant of the Romantic novel in its structure and its themes, yet one which uses current ideas of psychological processes and Greene's own response to contemporary reality to temper and modify them according to mid-twentieth-century needs. This is true, too, of its use of images of the blitz itself, which forms the setting of the novel – a setting which is closer to what Henry James referred to as an 'envelope' than the usual idea of 'background', since the emotionally heightened atmosphere of the novel results very largely from the abnormal and seemingly apocalyptic events of the bombing of London. Instead of the windswept moors of *Wuthering Heights*[38] or Gothic labyrinths of *The Mysteries of Udolpho*,[39] we have the strange beauty of the night sky and the arbitrary destruction of houses and office-blocks as an external correlative to the strained emotions and displaced lives of the characters. It is in this that the novel becomes a contemporary version of the Sublime.

This is seen explicitly in several places and also in the underlying movement towards the novel's conclusion which is – despite its severe qualifications – ultimately hopeful. We are first aware of the combination of beauty and fear of the blitz, seen through Rowe's eyes, in the third section of the opening chapter:

> Three flares came sailing slowly, beautifully down, clusters of spangles off a Christmas tree: his shadow shot out in front of him and he felt exposed, like a gaolbreaker caught in a searchlight beam. The awful thing about a raid is that it goes on: your own private disaster may happen early, but the raid doesn't stop. They were machine-gunning the flares: two broke with a sound like cracking plates and the third came to earth in Russell Square; the darkness returned coldly and comfortingly.[40]

Here there is the element of strange, unexpected beauty in the falling flares, at first distant and harmless like Christmas decorations, now nearer and threatening as they are machine-gunned. What is also striking is Rowe's response; we realise from his fear of exposure that the fear is genuine and by no means Sublime or redemptive. It is intriguing at a surface level that this exposure comes about through rapid changes of light, as his shadow leaps forward in the light of the falling flares: such exaggerations of *chiaroscuro* are a feature of earlier Romantic paintings of the Sublime and also, as we have seen, of those of Dobson and Rosoman. When the dark returns, it brings comfort; as elsewhere, extremes of light are used to show an extreme of emotion, and the return to normality is signalled by the coming of the dark.

Elsewhere in the novel aspects of the bombing are described in terms suited to the intense, heightened awareness which characterises the onlooker's response to the Sublime – the quality of spirituality which Burke describes as a 'delight' which is 'a sort of tranquillity tinged with terror' and which often reveals itself as 'awe, reverence and respect'.[41] The raid is seen, the morning after, as a kind of religious ritual, whose final act is the publication of casualties in the papers as a sort of 'Ite Missa Est';[42] bombed London is seen in terms of the ruins of Pompeii or a vision of Jerusalem laid waste: 'Jerusalem must have looked something like this in the mind's eye of Christ when he wept . . .'.[43] The mood is expressed most explicitly late in the novel when Rowe is driven through the city by Mr Prentice from the Special Branch:

> It was a long and gloomy ride, but all the time Rowe repressed for the sake of his companion a sense of exhilaration: he was happily drunk with danger and action.[44]

These references and the frequent other allusions to the taut mood of Londoners before, during and after bombing raids convey strongly the state of psychological intensity which has much to do with the response induced by the earlier Sublime, modified by twentieth-century psychology and concentrated by the immediacy of the experience.

The most significant development of the idea of the Sublime is found jointly in the movement of the novel and the way this is reflected in the title. Writing thirty years after the book's publication, Greene had this to say of it:

> The title *The Ministry of Fear* I took from a poem by Wordsworth (Arnold's selection of poems was one of the volumes I had brought with me from England), and the novel was bought unseen by an American film company on the strength of Wordsworth's title.[45]

This is not as helpful as it might at first sight seem in providing a source in a high Romantic work for the book's predominant voice. The edition of Wordworth by Matthew Arnold to which Greene refers is that published in *The World's Classics* in 1879: it does not contain a poem with the title 'The Ministry of Fear'. Nor does any other edition of Wordsworth; and neither does the phrase appear in any of his poems. Casual readers of the novel might well suppose that the title refers to a government department of the kind now familiar from Orwell's *1984*[46] – Ministry of Truth, Ministry of Love – concerned with various acts of institutional blackmail and betrayal; and indeed one of the characters in Greene's novel refers to a Nazi archive in which every potential blackmail victim in an enemy country is card-indexed to produce what amounts to 'a kind of Ministry of Fear'.[47] Where, then, is the link with Wordsworth?

One can never fathom the workings of the memory, especially

in connection with the creative impulse; but it seems not unlikely that Greene subtly changed some lines of Wordsworth's which were familiar to him from an earlier reading so that they provided a title fitting to the moral and psychological nature of the novel – serious enough, despite its being an 'entertainment' – rather than finding an exact quotation as he later suggested. In so doing, he reveals a great deal about his own response to the physical and moral disruption of the blitz by seeing it within the context of a Romantic worldview. In short, Greene is reinventing and remoulding Romanticism to suit the exigencies of the day, just as Rosoman subtly develops the Sublime or, as later chapters will show, Moore and Nash took what they needed from conventions of Romantic landscape.

Seen in a context both of Wordsworthian Romanticism and of Greene's own Catholic philosophy of sin and redemption, the novel's title refers not to a government department but to the theological notion of ministry – the redemptive power of anguish and suffering. While Wordsworth never explicitly refers to the ministering power of fear in this way, he does on occasion come close to it. The idea of ministry is stated clearly in 'Dion', where the speaker addresses 'Ye Gods' and continues:

> Your Minister would wash away
> The spots that to my soul adhere;
> But should she labour night and day,
> They will not, cannot disappear[48]

This, however, has no suggestion of the benevolent ministrations of fear. In *The White Doe of Rylstone* there is a passage where the narrator appeals to the 'Mute Spirit of maternal love', which had once before appeared to him 'Sent upon embassies of fear', to descend to the character Francis 'in radiant ministry' and say:

> "If hope be a rejected stay
> Do thou, my Christian Son, beware
> Of that most lamentable snare,
> The self-reliance of despair!"[49]

Here, in a passage of a little over a dozen lines, there is a reference to ministry, a reference to fear, and a statement of the idea of the isolation of despair. Of these the first two are not only the basic linguistic elements of the title of Greene's novel but also underlie its larger movement; and the last is fundamental to the psychological state of Arthur Rowe at the start of the novel, where he is locked away in his own guilt and despair brought on by the mercy-killing of his wife. This is not to suggest direct reference: perhaps Greene had read these lines, perhaps not. But it certainly makes clear that the kind of psychological states and processes in his novel have much to do with similar states in the poems of Wordsworth.

The passage in Wordsworth's poetry which is most closely related to the title and movement of Greene's novel comes in *The Borderers*:

> Benevolence, that hast not heart to use
> The wholesome ministry of pain and evil,
> Becomes at last weak and contemptible.[50]

This is an idea fundamental not only to *The Ministry of Fear* but also to a lot of Greene's other writing: that goodness can be deeply corrosive if it is unable to learn from suffering. It is through enduring 'pain and evil' as much as through enduring fear that Arthur Rowe reaches the end of his journey towards the redemption, qualified though it be, that he finds with Anna.

Greene's half-remembered reference to a title in Wordsworth is ultimately far more revealing than a simple, accurate allusion to a poem from which the title was taken. It suggests that the whole of the redemptive process of the novel is rooted in the ideas of earlier Romanticism, in which fear and other extreme states of experience such as pain and evil can exercise a benevolent and curative influence upon the individual. Wordsworth's approach here is at least a first cousin to the ideas of Burke about the restorative powers of fear in the earlier theory of the Sublime. Greene's use of similar ideas does not show either a direct influence or a conscious re-working; the most we can say is that he may have read the lines and then wrongly recollected their exact content when giving a title to the novel. That does not matter: what does is that a novelist of the forties, in writing an avowedly more popular work which takes contemporary circumstances as its setting, should have as its basis a series of ideas and approaches towards the nature of our experience of fear and threat which are fundamentally similar to those of an earlier Romantic, modified and amplified by the addition of twentieth-century ideas of experience, disillusion and the nature of psychology. This makes the novel, just as much as Rosoman's painting, a cornerstone of forties Romanticism.

IV

Seen in the context of art-history and the growth of literary styles, the versions of the Sublime developed by Rosoman and the rest have much to say about the deepening of the idea of 'Romanticism' in British art of the war years. It also has a wider significance.

The various pre-war committees which had been set up to plan for the treatment of the civilian population in time of war were unanimous in two things: first, the casualties in the first weeks would be apocalyptic in scale and, secondly, the psychiatric dislocation caused would be even greater. The Mental Health Emergency Committee adopted a tentative estimate that mental disorders would be three times as great as physical injuries, and another that there would be four million mental cases in the first six months of bombing.[51] The expectation of disorder and consequent panic, which would clog the streets and render impossible troop movements by rail, was also the major impulse behind the planning of evacuation:

> It was regarded simply and solely as a military expedient, a counter-move to the enemy's objective of attacking and demoralising the civilian population. The Government thought that a large exodus from London and other cities was inevitable; panic would send the people out and unless the Government took firm control chaos and confusion were bound to ensue.[52]

All of this makes quite clear the expectation that those of the population who were physically unharmed by the bombing would very rapidly be in a state of mental collapse. The truth is rather different. First, it is clear that the number fleeing from the cities at the height of the blitz was smaller than expected: in the official history, R. M. Titmuss establishes that '500,000 fewer people left Greater London during the bombing of 1940–1 than at the outbreak of war'.[53] There are, certainly, records of those taking rapid and near-panic flight;[54] yet, in sheer statistical terms, it would appear that, after the first and the most savage bombardments, most people preferred to stay where they were than to flee to unknown areas – something confirmed by the continual numbers of those drifting back from the safety of the country to the familiarity, albeit a dangerous one, of the towns.

Secondly, not only was the number of psychiatric casualties far smaller than had been expected, but admissions to psychiatric wards actually fell after the initial increase caused by the influx of people who, on the outbreak of war, it was felt could no longer be looked after at home. The official figures for admissions drop from just under 28,000 in 1939 to 25,200 in 1940 and fractionally over 24,000 the following year. Though the figure rises steadily to 29,576 in 1945, the greatest rise comes in the first complete war of peace, when the figure jumps by just over 6,000, to continue by nearly 4,000 in 1947.[55] Contemporary records reported that 1.4 per cent of those treated in London shelters showed evidence of any mental disorders;[56] and cases of attempted suicide among women notified to the police in England and Wales were 32 per cent lower in 1941 than the average of the pre-war years.[57]

Various reasons have been advanced for this. Titmuss suggests[58] that the war brought to many a degree of financial security unknown in the thirties, and that this, coupled with the sense of social importance and personal worth many were given by air raid duties, had a powerful curative effect on neuroses. There was also the sense of traditional responsibilities and patterns having been laid aside, and of being placed in a new world which, whatever else it lacked, certainly was not short of excitement.

For those who might otherwise have suffered from depression or anxiety, the blitz offered an external correlative to the familiar state of inner turmoil: external and internal worlds came together to produce a curious and unwonted harmony, and it is perhaps this as much as anything else which explains the ability of those who habitually suffered from minor psychiatric disorders to adapt most readily to the circumstances of destruction in which they found themselves. Thus Graham Greene's Arthur Rowe, his life knocked askew by the combination of guilt and tenderness which he feels for his dead wife, may look on the devastation in the streets with equanimity; it reflects his own spiritual turmoil.

For those not habitually haunted by mental disorder, too, the blitz had external compensations. It would be absurd to discuss the experience of being bombed out as something exciting or exhilarating, and only the most superficial popular literature written at the time or later attempts to do so. Yet the most complete collection of personal experiences of the time, the archives of Mass-Observation, suggests that an element of exhilaration is very common. A report prepared for the government by this organisation talks of the 'intense excitement'[59] people feel when telling others of their experiences. Other accounts prepared by individual M-O 'reporters' talk of initial fear giving way to an awareness of the beauty of the night sky lanced through by searchlight beams, and also the sense of personal achievement in having kept control of anxiety.[60] Published recollections tell the same story, and of these the most striking comes in Charlotte Haldane's *Truth Will Out*:[61] the sheer beauty of the scene of bombardment creates a feeling which removes all fear. Here is the curative force of Burke's ideas made plain, but in a way which goes even further than his own assertions: his Sublime, it seems, is based on real feelings and responses to beauty, but instead of giving a self-indulgent and rather artificial *frisson* it acts to control and overcome terror.

For both those used to suffering mental illness and those generally categorised as 'normal', the experience of bombing is one related to a heightened state of awareness: the new sights and sounds of the blitz, the suspension of the usual order, the sheer risk and closeness of death or injury, gave the experience of living a fresh intensity. This intensity is in no small measure founded on fear, this fear derived in part from the visually spectacular. In this sense, then, the paintings of the Sublime have a real psychological function to perform, in presenting the state of heightened awareness compounded of fear, risk and freedom from everyday responsibility and order; they offer the contemporary onlooker a record of his or her own endurance as well as recreating the exhilaration of the event. Greene's novel takes the process a stage further, by offering a longer-term pattern of the curative power of fear as a kind of redemptive ministry.

It is this sense of exhilaration provided by the experience of the blitz which provides the link between the painting and writing discussed earlier in this chapter and the psychological states of those living through it. The Sublime was part of reality for city-dwellers of the early forties; the art which recreates it is offering a very real psychological service. Perhaps Burke and his followers knew more than we imagine about the workings of terrifying objects on the mind of the onlooker; the instinctive return to his ideas in an important strand of the painting and writing of the time is not only aesthetically striking, but also has much to tell us about the mechanics of human survival and the place of art within it. The ministry of pain and evil is apparent, alongside the ministry of fear.

5

The Nurturing Earth

I

Fundamental to English Romanticism is a notion of the land. The earliest writers who can be called Romantics bemoan the change in traditional patterns of ownership and cultivation, Goldsmith deploring the land 'where wealth accumulates and men decay',[1] Gray using the land around Stoke Poges churchyard as a symbol of unrewarded toil in generations of those who have tilled its soil.[2] The early watercolourists discover in the land something of new interest in terms which are at first merely topographical[3] and then move on towards an aristocratic sense of novelty in finding pleasure in newly-fashionable vistas.[4]

Shortly afterwards, the real revolution begins with the development of the whole sequence of experiential relationships with the land. Instead of the genteel Platonism of 'improvement', the Picturesque suggests an emotional response of amusement and involvement with the shaggy and disproportionate;[5] the Beautiful engenders calm through appealing to a sense of order;[6] and the Sublime gives us delight through a *frisson* of fear in, say, de Loutherbourg's *Travellers attacked by Banditti*.[7] All these prepare the way for the great emotional exchange between land and beholder essential in high Romanticism, be it Wordsworth seeing 'into the life of things'[8] and being morally regenerated by the influence of landscape, or the recreation of an experience of nature, fusing intellect and emotion with external forms which both create and symbolise them, in Constable[9] and Turner.[10]

Within much, if not all, of the mature Romantic concern for landscape is the awareness of its function as external symbol of internal state, the rediscovery of which was so important in the thirties and forties. Constable's radically new use of skies and clouds as the emotional touchstone of a painting, instead of a mere shadowing of the tree-line in earlier landscape,[11] is a very strong example of this; Keats's 'vale of soul-making'[12] is defined with a sombre yet glowing visual acuity which shows a greater understanding of Claudian Romanticism than any other poet of his generation. For all his rejection of Wordsworthian mysticism, Blake frequently employs the surrounding totality of the natural world as a symbol of the creative, poetic force within humankind;[13] and Crabbe plays virtuosic variations on Romantic symbolic landscape in the diverse ways of seeing in 'The Lover's Journey'.[14]

Landscape is not limited to human symbolic meanings. In another tradition it is both terrestrially real, as a late outcrop of Puritan thinking which sees earthly bounty as an expression of divine love, and prophetic of a celestial fullness which is both material and spiritual. Samuel Palmer's *The Harvest Moon*[15] seemingly shows both an earthly and a heavenly harvest, and throughout Palmer's work there is the feeling that the landscape is not so much of the here as of the hereafter; and Calvert's visions such as *The Bride*[16] return us to a perfect prelapsarian world.

This last trend can be seen as part of a long line of English art and literature which presents the here and the hereafter in precisely the same terms – those of the contemporary landscape. The *Revelation*[17] of Dame Julian of Norwich; the 'lily crucifix' of Holy Trinity, Long Melford;[18] the *Dream of the Rood;*[19] Piers Plowman's vision;[20] the poetry of Vaughan[21] and the meditations of Traherne[22] – these are simply the outstanding countours of a body of writing in which, through a glowing diversity of symbolic techniques and significances, the landscapes of heaven and earth merge. This tradition shares an impulse with Romantic landscape: the need to make sense of humanity's place within a created world, and to offer a way through the complexities of existence. Philosophically, both this need and the means of satisfying it take a great number of different forms, but it is always there. It is there, too, in a bewildering diversity of forms in a great deal of the painting and writing of the forties: the land, literal and symbolic, is at its philosophical and stylistic heart, and is used by the artist to address the spiritual and aesthetic demands of the time just as, in different ways, it was used in earlier times. It is this which marks out so much of the art of the forties as a deeply serious continuation of the English Romantic tradition and a contribution to the spiritual and political temper of the nation. Its various forms are the subject of the remaining chapters.

II

The relationship between humankind and the landscape postulated by Romantic writers in the eighteenth and early nineteenth centuries was, as even the foregoing sketch has suggested, something of considerable moral and philosophical complexity. By the nineteen-twenties and thirties it had become much simplified. Later nineteenth-century industrialisation and rapid urban growth had led to a widespread assumption – in literature, in painting and in many aspects of suburban building and planning – that the countryside and its values were physically, morally and spiritually somehow 'better' than those of the town. The Garden Suburb movement, Bedales School, the rural craftsmen's guilds, suburban architecture based on Voysey's reinvention of Tudor principles, excursion trips by buses and trains into the rural hinterland of many cities – all of these developments of the turning years of the century had given expression to this idea and had impinged themselves in various degrees on the national consciousness.

To all this was added the physical and moral devastation of the First World War. Not only did the destruction of nature in the fighting itself lead to a greater sensitivity to the landscape in painters and writers of the time, but the years after the war saw a desire in many to live away from centres of population in rural settings or, if this were not possible, to visit the country as a relief from the pressure of the town. The setting up of the Land Settlement Association, which encouraged ex-soldiers to start farming on smallholdings, was one aspect of this; another was the way in which, helped by the rapid spread of public transport, the availability of cheaper, mass-produced cars and the growth of suburban sprawl, the countryside began to be seen as a recreational area for the urban classes. In literary and visual terms, this is reflected in the large number of very fine illustrated books about the English countryside, often combining eulogistic prose with idealised line-drawings and finely-lit monochrome photographs.[23] It is a broad stream, including and uniting forms as apparently diverse as landscape by John and Paul Nash[24] posters by Graham Sutherland[25] and guide books by John Betjeman.[26] The tradition embraces a genuine awareness of the nature and growth of the English countryside[27] as well as a more basic desire to see in it a place of safety and refuge from urban ugliness. It is a strand of art and life which is pervasively important in a view of inter-war Britain, which has not as yet received the attention it deserves.

This tradition was solidly established at the coming of war in 1939. During the war years the skein which had brought together leading artists and advertising executives began to unravel, the separate strands pursuing different courses. Piper recorded aspects of landscape and heritage in paintings of national monuments, as Chapter 2 has shown; Ceri Richards and many other of the finest artists of the generation saw in the fecundity of the land the only chance of renewal and survival in the waste of war, as Chapter 7 will make clear. Pursuing a direction which was both more limited philosophically and much more general politically was the thread of imagery which sought to present the beauty of the English countryside as both an aesthetic object and a set of moral values for which battle was being joined.

During the First World War there was a strong tradition of depicting an ideal pastoral England, a kind of village Eden with its own divinely-ordained social structure and natural justice which was a latter-day incarnation of the kind of High Toryism which made Constable and Palmer bitterly resentful of the 1832 Reform Act.[28] It presented visions of village greens, country churches and a society which was as safe as it was squirearchical – in other words, it represented a consciously retrospective and much simplified version of a Romantic vision of England, with neither the revolutionary zeal nor the moral and philosophical intensity of the early Romantics.[29] Much the same may be said of one kind of visual and verbal imagery of the forties.

A good deal has been written elsewhere on the nature and effect of this kind of imagery.[30] It is perhaps at its most familiar in popular literature and illustration, and in films which present the English countryside as an emblem of the birthright of the English in a kind of popularised nature-mysticism. In popular film, for example, the landscape is used to convey a vision of English traditions of freedom, justice and closeness to the land. The wartime films of Powell and Pressburger, most notably *A Canterbury Tale*,[31] do this quite explicitly, using a modern progress to Canterbury as a means of uniting the present with the past and the religious with the natural. The use of images of the English countryside in more straightforwardly propagandist films such as *The Lion has Wings*[32] and *If War Should Come*[33] are more direct appeals to a desire to protect England, home and beauty. Often the countryside is seen through a literary filter. The allusion in *A Canterbury Tale* is obvious; other versions of the approach may be seen in popular anthologies such as Collie Knox's *For Ever England*,[34] a collection of poetry and prose about the English spirit and its values through the ages. Large numbers of books were published during the war about the English countryside, English architecture, traditions and customs,[35] so that the view of the nation as a latter-day Eden is very common in imagery of all kinds which, in its own, if rather limited way, waters down the ideology and imagery of Romanticism to serve the needs of the moment.

There are also more progressive uses of this imagery. Notable among them is the series of four posters designed by Frank Newbould for the Army Bureau of Current Affairs and issued in 1942, bearing the slogan 'your Britain – fight for it now'. Of these the best known is *The South Downs*.[36] It is an ideal vision of Britain, not in any way related to actual wartime conditions. Against a background of rolling downland depicted in lush greens, a shepherd is seen driving his flock towards a farmhouse which is nestling in a valley, surrounded by protective trees. An old tree stands at the right foreground, suggesting the age-old quality of the landscape; directly above it an ancient castle may be seen on the horizon.

All this creates an image of unity between man and the natural world which is simple and direct, deliberately creating thoughts of Britain at its most pastoral and ideal. There is no hint of the scars of war, nor is there any suggestion of building a better Britain – an idea which, even in 1942, was beginning to have considerable currency and whose discussion the ABCA itself was to do much to encourage.[37] Before the war, Newbould designed posters for the Great Western Railway; this later vision of the countryside is in many ways a development of that style, with its flat colours and lack of detail encouraged by contemporary lithographic processes as much as by the influence of European modernism. There are also similarities to the book-jackets and illustrations of Brian Cook for the highly successful Batsford series on the English countryside and its institutions.[38] Taken together, this derivativeness is almost a kind of security, implying as it does the continuity of pre-war traditions. Instead of encouraging city-dwellers to visit actual places it aims to encourage people in the forces to carry with them an ideal concept of 'your Britain', and feed on it to find energy and conviction in battle. No matter that the view is idealised, or that the Britain shown is not immediately a part of the pre-war world of most servicemen; it is the ideal icon which is presented, appealing to feelings of patriotism and the national heritage of beauty in landscape.

Despite all the apparent continuity, the poster does however move away from earlier pastoral visions of the nation in one important respect: the slogan. In stressing that this is '*your* Britain' it subtly inculcates feelings of possession as well as of duty, implying that fighting for the country will in some way reap the reward of becoming a part of this ideal. This is significant. Earlier images of the nation carry with them a patrician feel, suggesting that the Britain depicted belongs to the gentleman farmer or the hereditary landowner; here, it becomes the spiritual possession, the birthright almost, of everyone who reads the poster. Perhaps this reflects in small measure the 'war socialism' which was to lead to the founding of the Welfare State.[39] In a more specific way it shows a move away from the clumsiness of the earliest posters of the war. The most notorious of these, issued in September 1939,[40] bore simply a crown and the following legend in white on a black ground:

YOUR COURAGE
YOUR CHEERFULNESS
YOUR RESOLUTION
WILL BRING
US VICTORY

The divisiveness is clear: *you* do the work, *we* will reap the benefits. It suggested the kind of rigid class-structure so prevalent between the wars, and was the subject of outraged protest: even *The Times* called it 'insipid and patronising'.[41] Newbould's poster may present an idealised view of Britain; at least it suggests that the ideal is there for all to share.

This is true in larger measure in the other posters of the series. The untitled one generally referred to as *Village Green*[42] shows a typical English village, the composition dominated by a large, ancient elm or oak. Beneath its branches on one side three young cyclists are picnicking, balanced on the other by three ducks. To the right a couple of village elders drink leisurely outside the half-timbered pub; to the left a row of ancient cottages stretches to the frame of the poster but curves in the centre towards the village church, whose square tower is pierced by Gothic windows and surmounted by a flag of St George, and whose churchyard is entered through a lych-gate. All is quiet and contentment, another ideal vision. It is very similar to George Clausen's poster *A Wish*[43] produced for display in YMCA huts behind the front line during the First World War: this shares the ancient church and cottages but replaces the single tree by two smaller ones which frame the composition. There is no pub, and the only figures are a mother and child, two older people talking at the lych-gate and a man sitting beneath the tree to the right. At first sight Newbould's poster is an direct continuation of the tradition, yet there is one addition which is socially very significant: the cyclists. These are not members of the village community, but tourists, city-dwellers who have come out into the country. It is they who give validity to the poster's slogan, 'your Britain'; in showing them, Newbould makes the ideal pastoral accessible to all, foreshadowing the greater egalitarianism to come. It is a small but valuable shift which reflects the changing approach to the countryside in the inter-war years; it is now accessible to all, a source of regeneration and delight.

The approach continues in the two remaining posters of the set. *Alfriston Fair*[44] shows swings, roundabouts and sideshows in the shadow of large, old trees, with the spire of a village church in the middle distance. Here the old heritage is being modified and made accessible to all in a contemporary form of amusement. One of the tents has a legend which can just be made out to read 'Jarley's television centre'; this is no fake re-creation of a nineteenth-century hiring fair, no mock-Hardyesque; it is a fair for the contemporary masses. The last poster of the set[45] shows Salisbury Cathedral across the meadows from the river. Here Newbould's earlier work for the GWR is important; we are being shown the Cathedral as eager tourists are shown it on a railway poster, or as it is shown in, for example, the GWR's pre-war *Holiday Haunts*[46] book which lists places to visit and trains to take in the railway's territory. Newbould's Britain is again accessible to all: it is more than just a reworking of the ideal pastoral. The choice of Salisbury Cathedral is of further significance in extending Romanticism: the building is seen between trees from a low viewpoint across meadows, almost from the viewpoint in Constable's paintings. Stylistically it is far simpler; but again we are given a kind of re-working of a Romantic image which is almost self-consciously assertive both of its tradition and of the new elements it brings to it. Important in these is the simplified style of flat colours and limited detail, but so, too, is the idea of the cathedral being a shared property of all the onlookers, part of 'your Britain', just as Canterbury Cathedral is the shared destination and source of spiritual comfort and poise for a telling diversity of characters in Powell and Pressburger's film.

Newbould's posters are important as a contemporary development of Romantic attitudes in one further way, which follows from their presenting the countryside as a place of common resource. In 'Tintern Abbey', Wordsworth stresses the role of remembered 'forms of landscape':

> oft in lonely rooms, and 'mid the din
> Of towns and cities, I have owed to them,
> In hours of weariness, sensations sweet,
> Felt in the blood, and felt along the heart;
> And passing even into the purer mind,
> With tranquil restoration: feelings too
> Of unremember'd pleasure; such, perhaps,
> As may have had no trivial influence
> On that best portion of a good man's life,
> His little, nameless, unremember'd acts
> Of kindness and of love.[47]

The landscape of the banks of the Wye has come to be, for Wordsworth, an icon of tranquillity; by thinking of it he can recall the peace he found when visiting it. This approach to landscape and experience has become so much a part of later existence that we tend to forget the newness of Wordsworth's idea, and the newness of the Romantic linking of landscape with psychological state which makes such ideas possible. Newbould's posters, like almost every poster or photograph which depicts the countryside, aims at evoking an emotional response in us. Here it is one of involvement with the landscape – made accessible to all by Newbould's subtle changes to traditional stances – which gives us not 'tranquil restoration', but a sense of belonging which will in theory give us courage to fight and protect it. Such a nationalistic and belligerent use of pastoral imagery may not be something with which we may now sympathise; but it is one which, we cannot deny, has its origins in Romanticism and develops its stance to confront head-on the practical needs of its day.

III

Those visions of the countryside which present it as an ideal pastoral, the Englishman's birthright for which he is fighting, undoubtedly served some function for the establishment in promoting patriotic zeal – however falsely based – and for the individual in suggesting both national identity and personal haven. Yet they are really rather superficial uses of the image of the countryside, which bear little relation either to the original vision of the land of the first Romantics or to a view of it which incorporates the deeper realities and needs of the contemporary situation. For a view which does this, and also prepares us for the greater emotional and visionary intensity of the finest work of the period, we need to turn to what may seem an unlikely source: the illustrated booklet *Land at War* produced anonymously for the Ministry of Information and published in 1945.

The book takes as its basic subject the way in which the need to produce food at home, instead of relying on imports made precarious by the blockade, resulted in a great renaissance of agriculture throughout Britain. This eminently practical basis marks off the book from those writings and images concerned with looser, more general or more visionary concepts of the land: it is concerned with a very specific and very arduous relationship between humankind and the earth. In one sense it concerns the problems which always crowd in on those who make a living from the land; in another it is quite contemporary. This duality gives the book its unique nature and importance within the whole spread of writing and painting which explores the relationship with the land. It is also a duality which shows it – however unlikely this may seem, given the nature and purpose of the publication – to be a direct development of earlier Romantic notions as a response to the exigencies of the mid-century.

In some ways this continuation is fairly straightforward, appearing in a form familiar from other treatments. Near the beginning, for example, there is a passage which stresses the richness of the English soil and the closeness of the English people to it:

> There are few farmlands in the world more lush, more responsive, or able to bear a greater variety of crops than those in these islands; there are few men with a better natural feeling for the land than that which our farmers and farm workers possess.[48]

This seems only just over the horizon from the golden fields of Samuel Palmer and the visionary landscapes of Powell and Pressburger; although there is no mention of a mystical link, the sense is still of an ideal richness which is by implication celestial in the 'natural feeling for the land'.

Added to this feeling in the book is the kind of general historical awareness seen in the simpler visions of the countryside for patriotic or nurturing purposes. The need to cultivate the land in the face of a naval blockade and threatened invasion is compared with that felt in the time of the Armada:

> Queen Elizabeth, gazing upon the quiet sheepwalks of the countryside, knew the danger in their idleness and persuaded the farmer, by forcible methods, to bring out his plough and look to his land again.[49]

The historical context is also made clear by references to the National Farm Survey which recorded available land in 1940, in comparison to the Domesday Book of 1066 'in which William the Conqueror reviewed the wealth of his new kingdom'.[50] The point is given visual force by a page opening which presents part of the Domesday Book opposite a page from the Survey:[51] the past is still a powerful presence, the sense of continuity strong.

Although the continuing context of the past is made quite clear in these fairly simple ways familiar from other popular texts, *Land at War* uses more subtle techniques to present the idea of genuine change and growth within tradition. One of these is apparent very near the start, in a passage lamenting the state of much British agriculture during the slump of the thirties – 'a process of neglect and deterioration began, and it was not a happy story'.[52] At the same time, the book's illustrations make clear the process of decay. The upper photograph on page 10 shows a derelict barn. It is salutary to compare this photograph with some of Graham Sutherland's early etchings, in particular *Number Forty-Nine*[53] and *Warning Camp*[54].

Sutherland dwells lovingly on the textures of decay, the wild flowers and long grasses surrounding the buildings and the play of light and shade caused by the uneven roof and missing tiles; in this early stage it is for the artist a source of delight such as that found by earlier Picturesque painters in shaggy, overgrown lanes and old, collapsing buildings. This was a phase Sutherland was soon to grow out of, predating as it does even the intensity of his Palmer-inspired etchings of a year or two later, discussed in Chapter 2; but it shows a stance towards the countryside which is 'romantic' in the popular and perhaps the worst sense, seeing it as a repository of pretty decay and pleasing texture which the town-dweller can use as a way of escape from smoke and toil.[55]

By contrast the photograph is sharp and forthright; the textures are exposed, not caressed. The caption also makes clear the approach:

> Tumbledown buildings, idle tools, fields strangled by weed and flood – these were the legacies of ill luck, bad markets, slump. This had to be made good.[56]

This is genuinely contemporary, urgent even: the economic jargon of 'bad markets' and 'slump' reminds us that this countryside is not a retreat from the real modern world of trade but a central part of it. Here it is worth recalling that none of the high Romantic artists and writers who dealt with the countryside could afford to ignore this either; they may have allotted to the country worker a dignity beyond his and her natural quality, but certainly they did not, like some Arcadians of all periods – Hayman[57] and Leslie,[58] say – endow it with a Parnassian quality where every shepherd is a prince in exile, every shepherdess a lady-in-waiting. Here the land is real not idealised, the need to cultivate pressing, and the attitude a development of key elements of earlier Romanticism in response to genuine contemporary circumstance.

Another way in which the book presents a recension of Romantic outlook is in the continuation and extension of a Wordsworthian concept about the nature of language used by those who work on the land. In the Preface to *Lyrical Ballads*, Wordsworth makes the celebrated claim that those who live a 'low and rustic life' have more fully-grown feelings than those who endure 'the encreasing accumulation of men in cities' and speak 'a plainer and more emphatic language' because they 'hourly communicate with the best objects from which the best part of language is originally derived'.[59] Something very close to this theory seems to underlie the later writer's approach to the language of those who dwell in the land. This is true not so much of the frequent passages where particularly significant acts of reclamation or harvest are told in the words of farmers themselves; these more probably rest on the sound journalistic principle of telling a story in the words of the person most closely involved. Towards the end of the book, however, there is a passage which clearly suggests that the words of the countryman are of greater validity and value than those of the town dweller.

> As these men talk, you find their phrases short, to the point, falling on the ear like proverbs or blank-verse quotations, exceedingly simple and memorable:
>
> "Never touch that field after Christmas."
> "Ground's too cold."
> "Cold as my grandmother."[60]

– and so on for another dozen or so lines. Yet this is neither a collection of quaint countryisms to amuse the town-dwelling reader nor an anthology of ancient wisdom. The passage goes on:

> They talk with new words, too, though delivered with the same sure sense of truth:
>
> "What d'you balance your mangolds with?"
> "Super and sulphate of ammonia."
> "Two hundredweight sulphate to four of super."

Once again the simplicity of diction is being revealed, but the new is being absorbed into the traditional: the language is the same but not the same, and the attitude towards it shows once more a contemporary development of Romantic ideology.

This is a theme that continues throughout the text – both verbal and visual – of *Land at War*. Older patterns and skills are stressed as being combined with new ones. Writing of the need to plough every available piece of land including those hitherto thought too steep or inaccessible, the author points out that 'the horse and the tractor are not enemies',[61] the former reaching into difficult corners, gradients and hollows while the latter can tackle ground that is very rough or full of stones. One of the most remarkable ways in which the closeness of humankind to the land is described in contemporary terms comes in an account of the use of heavy machinery by women.

> A group of Land Girls arrive, laughing and chattering. They start

> up their tractors, mount them and drive away, one after the other, each with a train of rattling equipment hooked on behind. One is going out to the lower hills to plant potatoes. Two others, dressed in oil-black overalls and mounted on a strange-looking machine with crawler tracks, are bound for the wet valley to work on a drainage job. This machine is a Cub excavator; it has a terrific, lurching power and a long snout armed with jaws and teeth of steel. It is astonishing that a machine of such size could be operated by girls at all. But these are chosen for their mechanical aptitude . . .[62]

This is something which goes right against two important and linked traditions: the role of women and the place of machinery on the land. Given the contemporary stance towards the employment of women it is not surprising that the writer should voice astonishment at the Land Girls' ability to control farm machinery; yet there is more to it than this. The whole tradition of nature mysticism associates women with generation and fertility, linking the gender to the submissive yet fecund role of the earth. Yet here they are given a strikingly active role, totally in accord with the pressing needs of the moment.

The second element is the presence of heavy machinery in the landscape. For the first Romantics this was not a major issue in itself – the antithesis was between machinery in the new industrial communities and habitual, age-old patterns of work in the agricultural villages. Two or three generations later, the first presence of mechanical farm implements was seen as something deeply destructive. Hardy's stance is both typical and outstanding in its vehemence: in the celebrated threshing scene from *Tess of the d'Urbervilles* the machine is operated by a man who is not named, and is excluded from the mysterious relationship with the land which dominates so much of the novel:

> He was in the agricultural world, but not of it. He served fire and smoke; these denizens of the field served vegetation, weather, frost, and sun . . . He spoke in a strange northern accent; his thoughts being turned inwards upon himself, his eye on his iron charge, hardly perceiving the scenes around him and caring for them not at all; holding only strictly necessary intercourse with the natives, as if some ancient doom compelled him to wander against his will in the service of his Plutonic master. The long

> strap which ran from the driving-wheel of his engine to the red thresher under the rick was the sole tie-line between agriculture and him.[63]

Later on, when Tess is forced to work on the shaking platform of the machine, her yoking to the device prefigures her despoliation by d'Urberville as much as the presence of the machine in the field images the ruin of the natural world. Hardy is no idealist: in all his novels the work in the fields is back-breaking and long-lasting. Yet the pain and exhaustion is a natural process, whereas the machine is a metallic, inorganic interloper which is deeply unnatural. That it offends both against the country and against Tess as a woman is a further reflection of the traditional image of woman as generative, natural force; that the scene is subsequently described in terms of the Vale of Tophet, the 'place of burning' where children were sacrificed by fire to Moloch, king of the Ammonites, shows how clearly the machine is regarded as something destructive of the created world.

This is, of course, an extreme example of the attitude towards mechanised agriculture, and we should be aware that, for many farmers, the coming of steam traction and later the Fordson Tractor was a blessed release from long, hard labour. The passage from *Land at War* was, it must be remembered, written at least in part to proselytise the new approach to agriculture of which the use of machines and women was a major part. Yet these qualifications admitted, the difference between it and the Hardy is no less striking. Woman and machine are now willing partners in the cultivation process, working with the land rather than despoiling and being despoiled.

This idea of harmony with the land is perhaps the most significant aspect of the book as a latter-day development of a Romantic idea. The speed of gathering arable crops with combine-harvesters; the work of the Plant Breeding Station in developing new strains of grass; the use of artificial fertilisers and artificial insemination; the development of new breeds of cattle by scientific stock-control are all described with enthusiasm and delight. All these new elements are absorbed into the landscape instead of being seen as threats to it, or simply ignored in the desire to present an idyllic pastoral. In this, the text represents a very striking development of the notion of humankind working in conjunction with the natural world which is crucial to much Romantic thinking. All of Constable's landscapes are worked landscapes in which a perfect, ordered balance between humanity and nature is presented. *Boatbuilding near Flatford Mill*[64] is a good example. The barge in the foreground is being built from wood sawn in a nearby saw-pit from the trunk of a tree which grew locally; when it is complete it will be floated out onto the Stour by the simple expedient of removing the neck of land which separates its staithe from the river. There it will be steered by a local oarsman, as the barge already on the river is being steered. Trees and river are being brought together and used naturally by man; it is part of the process of stewardship of the natural world which goes back to Eden. The irony here is that Constable's vision is a retrospective one; already when it was painted there were newer ways of building barges and the new industrial processes had caused a migration to the cities which meant that the organic links between humankind and the natural world which paintings like this present were no longer holding. By contrast, the link suggested in *Land at War* is actual and contemporary.

The vision of the natural world presented in *Land at War* is an extension of Constable's inclusiveness to embrace the mechanical forces developed by humankind – and, as we have seen, it now embraces woman as well as man in this new pattern of cultivation. The land which is just as recalcitrant, just as nurturing as it ever was, is now nourished by new mechanical and chemical forms just as, in the vision of Constable, it was nourished and extended by human and organic ones. And there is, of course, a further parallel. The ideal relationship seen by Constable had already disappeared, with the growth of industrial communities which uprooted villagers from their birthplace and broke the cycle of continuity represented by barge, river, tree and earth. The ideal had long gone by the 1940s; yet the war offered a chance for the bond between humankind and the natural world to grow again, in the return of so many city dwellers to the country through evacuation, or through working on the land, either as a Land Girl or as a temporary worker helping to get in the harvest. This is reflected in the very closing paragraph of *Land at War*:

> Surely the gulf that has hitherto existed between the two communities, town and country, could be bridged in no better way than this?[65]

Land at War is a public information booklet written for a large and predominantly urban readership. It is perhaps asking too much for it to reflect every aspect of an updated Romanticism which has been argued for it in the preceding paragraphs. Nonetheless, it is a demonstration of the degree to which attitudes of Romanticism are so basic to the contemporary outlook that so many such ideas can be clearly seen within it. For contemporary readers, it might perhaps have presented a vision of a better future made possible by the war, in which a greater closeness with the natural world and a recapturing of an ideal Britain might be possible, and mechanical and chemical inventiveness is absorbed into the ancient cycle of sowing and harvest, an almost Blakeian coming together of opposites. Today, we know that this is not possible, that such extensive use of chemical fertilizers destroys the richness it seems to create and offers only an illusory prosperity. The ideals of *Land at War* were credible only at that moment of equipoise when intensive farming seemed a way of recapturing the ideal relationship with nature as well as offering plenty for all. It is not the first Romantic prophecy to be deeply undercut by subsequent reality; but for its moment it is a vigorous and brave vision.

IV

Although the countryside is fundamental to most versions of forties Romanticism which take the land as their central symbol, it is not so in every case. One way in which the tradition of exchanges with the land is modified in the art of the time is the inclusion of the city in a peculiarly contemporary version of Romanticism. It is the city which is seen as an object of beauty, revealed as it is in the new circumstances of war, and which offers the involved onlooker a wholly new range of experience which is re-created in word or image. In its most extreme manifestations this forms the 'Blitz Sublime' of Chapter 4; yet it is not only a relationship of fear which is involved in this strand of Romanticism. There is a gentler and more tentative approach which, while lacking the completeness and purification of the high Romantic exchange with nature, nonetheless reveals a development of that earlier clutch of responses in an attempt to deal with contemporary reality.

At the most direct level this takes the form of a simple awareness of the new beauty of the city. Stephen Spender, writing a war diary for *Horizon*, makes this very clear.

> . . . the weather has been particularly fine lately, the streets glitter a biscuit yellow all day, the crowds waiting at the bus stops for the few buses give the town an air of festivity, the sand bags on the side walks, the strips of paper on the windows, the balloons in the sky, are all sufficiently new in the bright sunshine to be interesting and almost gay.[66]

What gives this writing its particular quality is its immediacy, created in large measure by the loose punctuation so that each element is presented with equal weight and the whole appears to be a spontaneous response which stresses the transformation of the familiar into something strange and new.

This makes it very different from earlier Romantic views of a city. Wordsworth's view from Westminster Bridge[67] sees London as a sleeping unity, a kind of glorious piece of kinetic scupture bathed in early morning sunlight, the physical distance and separation of the viewpoint – on a bridge, for a moment apart from both banks of the city – providing the key to the poem's whole attitude. We might expect in Spender a greater sense of anger at the city, or rather the City – the economic system on which the urban organism rests – in the manner of Blake's 'London'.[68] But this would be to forget the key element in Spender's outlook – the fact that all the familiar relationships and systems have been laid aside in the newness of war. Their newness is what gives the sandbags, the paper on the windows, the barrage balloons, their great atttaction for Spender. There is no permanence, no depth, no philosophical answer, in this vision, but it is precisely this deficiency, this temporary nature which provides its essence as a piece of genuine contemporary experience: all the usual patterns have been laid aside and what is left is just as fresh and strange as the experience of beholding it is transient and uncertain, hedged about as it is by the feeling that all will shortly vanish.

Related to this at one level is the sense of release from everyday concerns that has been remarked in Chapter 4. A further kind of release of more immediate relevance to the changing visual nature of the city is provided by the way in which the cities were constantly offering themselves up to new analysis and interpretation from new angles as buildings were destroyed in successive raids. The effect of this is noted elsewhere by Spender:

> There is something of release in the destruction of the greatest monuments, and what is released is the spirit which they enshrined. At the same time there is something that is dead and inhibiting about a tradition that lives on without being appreciated. It is right that Londoners should have derived a sense of the greatness of Wren's architecture from the destruction of the city churches.[69]

The awareness of newly-revealed beauty when the demolition of neighbouring structures allows a building to be seen from an unfamiliar angle generates a new kind of aesthetic sensitivity in the city-dweller, sharpening the awareness of the visual environment. And, whether or not Spender's idea of the release of the spirit enshrined in an old building has any validity, it is certainly a version of the exchange between viewer and view that is a most practical development of the inherited Romantic outlook on the landscape. The new scene is recorded with a fascination which is directly in the tradition of the early painters of the Picturesque by Humphrey Jennings, in *London Can Take It*;[70] by photographers in *Lilliput*;[71] and by many of the less celebrated war artists and writers,[72] all of whom have diverted the tradition to produce images of the city, not the country. But this recording is supplanted by more subtle stances towards the built and destroyed environment which show a more striking reworking of the Romantic precedent.

The city at night is the basis for the most significant of these. Here moonlight, perhaps the most transient of all experiences of nature, becomes even more fleeting because it is associated with searchlights, bombing, suffering and the possibility of immediate death; the transience of the moonlight becomes an image of the feelings of life being strictly temporary which underlay all wartime urban experience. It thus becomes a further reworking of the Romantic use of landscape as emotional symbol. Another passage from Spender shows this clearly:

> The world appears a desert. There is no woman, there are no children, there is no faith, there is no cause. The moon shines above the London streets during the blackouts like an island in the sky. The streets become rivers of light. The houses become

> feathery, soft, undefined, aspiring, so that any part of this town might be the most beautiful city in the world, sleeping amongst silk and water. And the moon takes a farewell look at our civilization everywhere. I have seen it as an omen in Valencia, Barcelona and Madrid, also. Only the houses were not plumed, feathery, soft, there: the moon was brighter, and they seemed made of white bone.[73]

This is a very striking piece of symbolic writing, projecting feelings and fears onto the landscape in a manner which is wholly Romantic, yet doing it to the city, not the country. The symbolic force only becomes truly apparent at the end, with the reference to Spain, yet even here the description is still apparently quite literal. It is only the reference to the houses' being made of white bone that reminds us of what happened in Spain, the urban annihilation that when Spender was writing was hourly expected to descend on London. This is made explicit in the 'farewell look' the moon is taking, but it underlies the rest of the passage, which sees the scene with the sharpness of someone taking in external sensations as if for the last time, at a moment when the empty city stands as an emblem of hope deserted and faith betrayed. It is a view of the city markedly different from that advanced by Louis MacNeice in the *Penguin New Writing* article quoted in Chapter 3: for Spender there is no distance to lend symbolic hope to the desolate townscape. True, he is writing before the desolation, in apprehensive expectation rather than immediate confrontation; the difference is still striking, though, as an illustration of the different ways the Romantic stance is used as a means of coming to terms with destruction, real or expected.

The peculiar, temporary beauty of the city, both real and symbolic, is given the most extended statement in Elizabeth Bowen's short story 'Mysterious Kôr',[74] where incompleteness is stated on a deliberately bewildering range of levels to enable us to share the mood of setting and events. The fundamental tone of the story is the subtle yet precise sensation of unfulfilment experienced by Arthur and Pepita who, on the one night of his leave, must stay at the flat she shares with the homely yet uncomprehending Callie. This engenders a sense of separation and incompleteness which in turn creates a vulnerability in the two characters. All of these qualities are reflected in the references to moonlight and its subtle visual effects which dominate the mood and movement of the story, giving the city a transient, incomplete beauty and making it seem helplessly vulnerable to aerial attack. This is apparent right from the first paragraph:

> Full moonlight drenched the city and searched it; there was not a niche left to stand in. The effect was remorseless: London looked like the moon's capital – shallow, cratered, extinct. It was late, but not yet midnight; now the buses had stopped the polished roads and streets in this region sent for minutes together a ghostly unbroken reflection up. The soaring new flats and the crouching old shops and houses looked equally brittle under the moon, which blazed in windows that looked its way. The futility of the black-out became laughable: from the sky, presumably, you could see every slate in the roofs, every whited curb, every contour of the naked winter flower-beds in the park; and the lake, with its shining twists and tree-darkened islands would be a landmark for miles, yes, miles, overhead.[75]

The effect here is one of strange beauty, but also of defencelessness under the moon's light – the moon is 'remorseless', the buildings 'brittle', the blackout 'futile', the flower-beds 'naked'. This is both a literal effect and an outward symbol of the main characters' feelings of vulnerability and unfulfilment. The technique is familiarly Romantic but its use for an urban setting is as radically new as the peculiar mood of transience and uncertainty it creates. There are references to natural objects – the flower-beds and the lake in the park, the trees on its islands – but these come after the references to wholly urban things – 'soaring flats', 'crouching shops', 'polished roads' and 'buses'. The use of moonlight almost makes the landscape recall those in paintings by Friedrich,[76] with the signal difference that here it is a town, and a town under threat from twentieth-century desolation, that is being illumined, not a visionary rural or mountainous scene.

The tone set by the opening continues throughout the story. On the next page, for example, there are references to bird song subsiding while people emerge from the underground 'around the anti-panic brick wall', hurrying to get out of the moonlight 'as though dissolved in the street by some white acid.' The natural world gives way to the urban. Within this landscape emerge the figures of a man and a woman, 'blotted into one shadow', on their way to the park. By creating the moonlight scene before the appearance of the two main characters, Bowen has established that it is the reality of which they are a part, and not simply a reflection of their mood. Thus we, the onlookers, accept their discussion of the strange unreality of the city as quite accurate since it coincides with what we have already seen. Our vision and the vision of the central characters are the same, intensifying our experience of the landscape and situation by making us feel that we share it with them.

The significance of the story is enriched by the frequent references to the 'Mysterious Kôr' of the title. This is the title of a poem by Andrew Lang which is in its turn a reference to a deserted city which appears in the novel *She* by H. Rider Haggard. The novel was immensely popular when it appeared in 1877. It was hailed as a resurgence of romance, and sold a thousand copies a week. Praised by J. M. Barrie and Edmund Gosse, it subsequently enjoyed six film adaptations and treatment as a stage play and a ballet by the time of the outbreak of war.[77] There were also seven book-length sequels or parodies in the year of the novel's publication; *He*,[78] by Andrew Lang and W. H. Pollock, dates from some years later and contains the poem which is the basic allusion of Bowen's story. Lang wrote to Haggard calling *She* 'one of the most astonishing romances I have ever read'[79] and, even if regarded as a bibliographical freak, it is certainly outstanding, containing as it does passages of hieroglyphs, black-letter Gothic and various other passages from runic texts associated with the discovery of a secret land ruled over by the formidable 'She-who-must-be-obeyed' or 'Ayesha'. In appreciation of Lang's sentiments Haggard used the poem, without acknowledgement, as an epigram in subsequent editions of the book.

The Romantic creation of a lost world, once flourishing but now laid waste, is an extension of Shelley's 'Ozymandias'[80] and the whole Romantic fascination with exotic communities and doomed peoples. Simply making a reference to such a community adds considerable Romantic continuity to Bowen's story; it makes the ironic suggestion that London, like Kôr, will one day vanish. This adds a further layer of meaning to the transience created by the moonlight, and has obvious import in terms of the city's vulnerability to bombing. Yet the significance of the reference goes far deeper than that, as the text of the poem makes clear. It is worth quoting in full since it is not easily available today.

Not in the waste beyond the swamp and sand,
The fever-haunted forest and lagoon,
Mysterious Kôr, thy fanes forsaken stand,

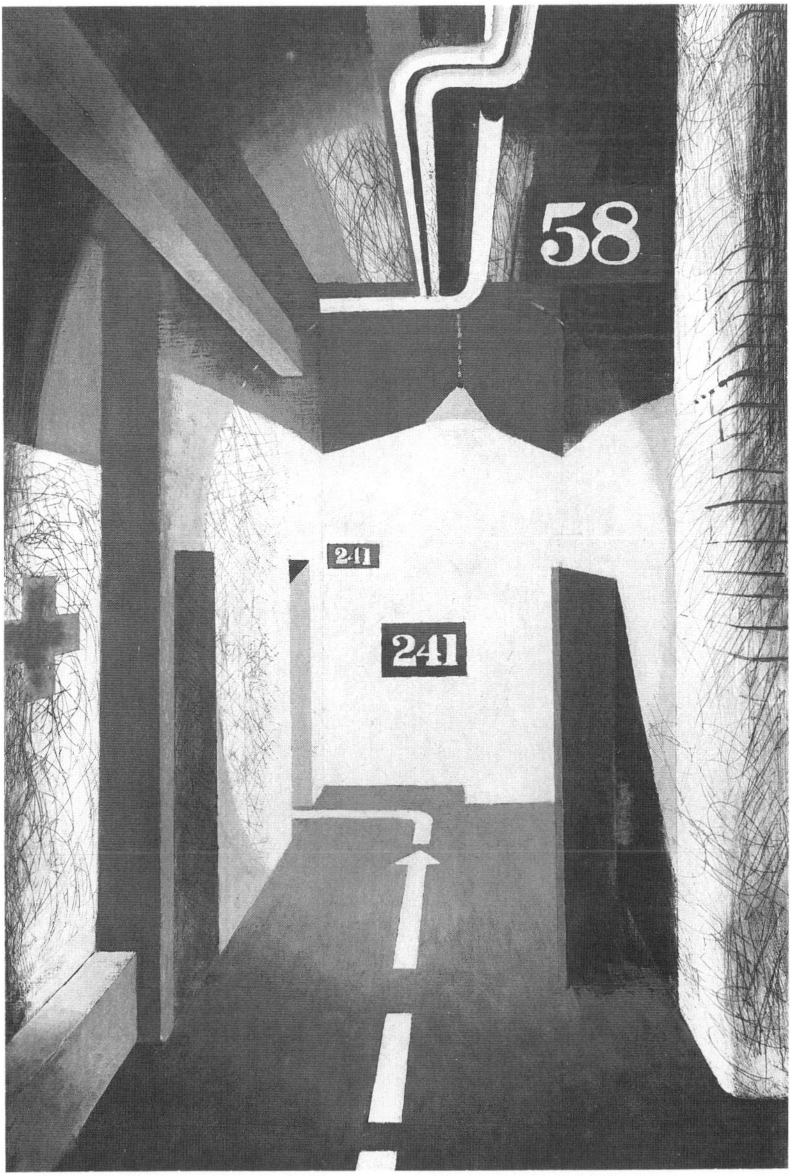

1 *The Passage to the Control Room at S. W. Regional Headquarters*, by John Piper.

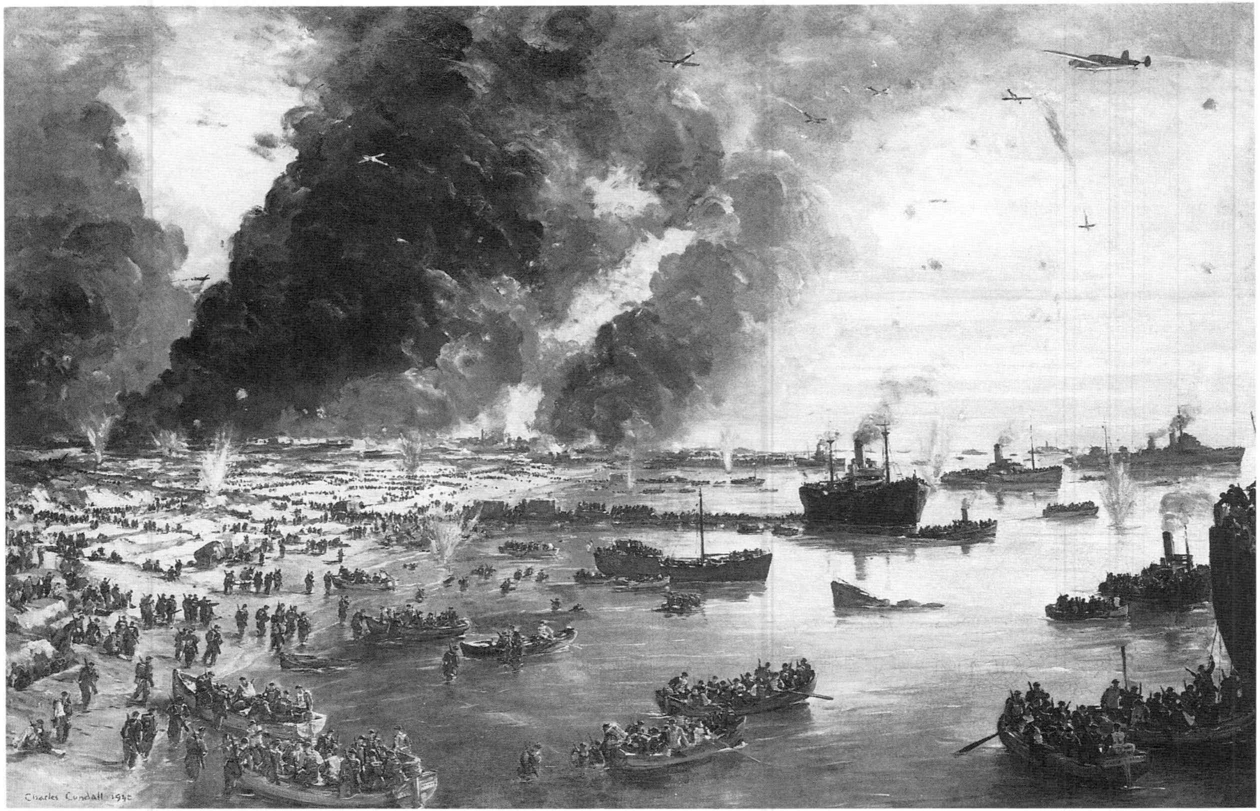

2 *The Withdrawal from Dunkirk*, by Charles Cundall.

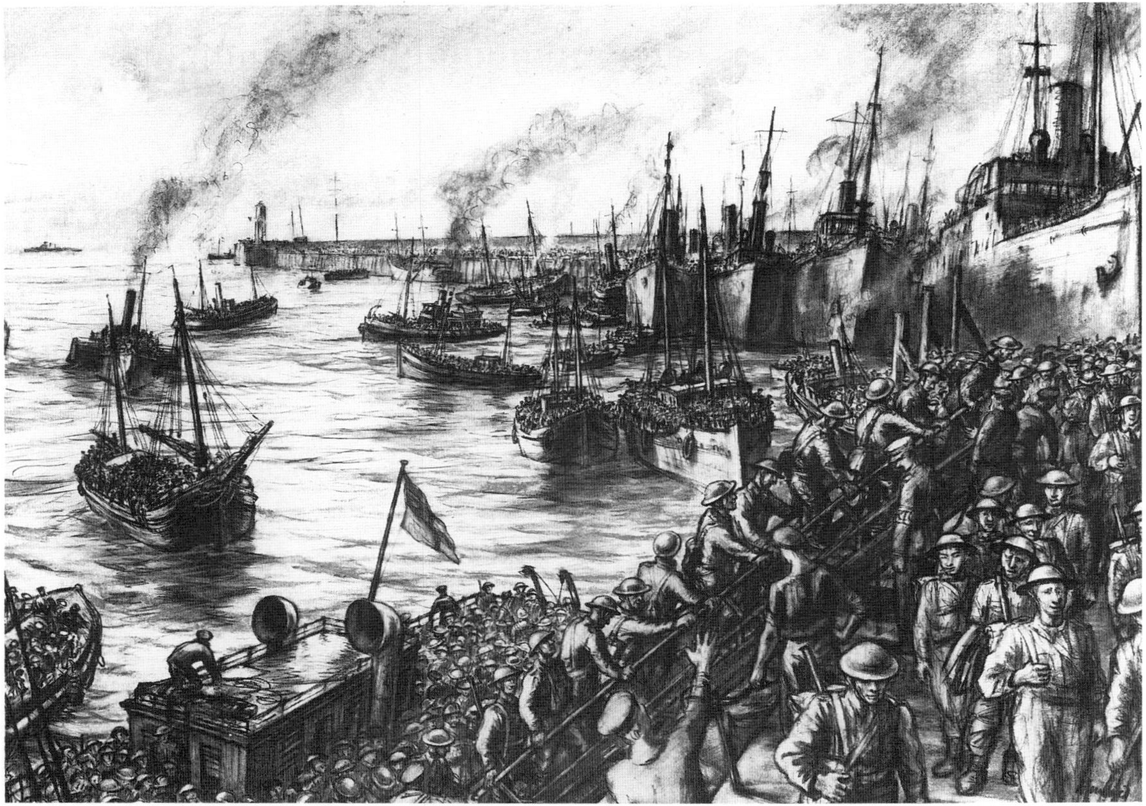

3 *The Return from Dunkirk*, by Muirhead Bone.

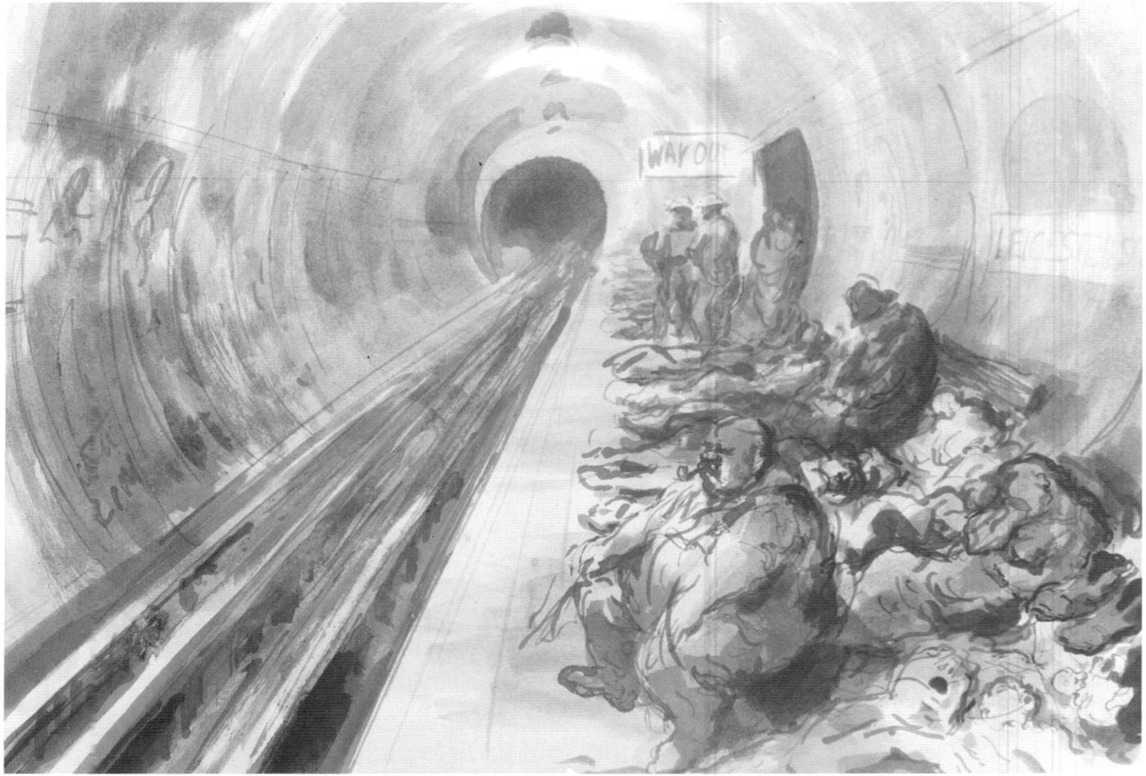

4 *The Tube, October, 1940*, by Feliks Topolski.

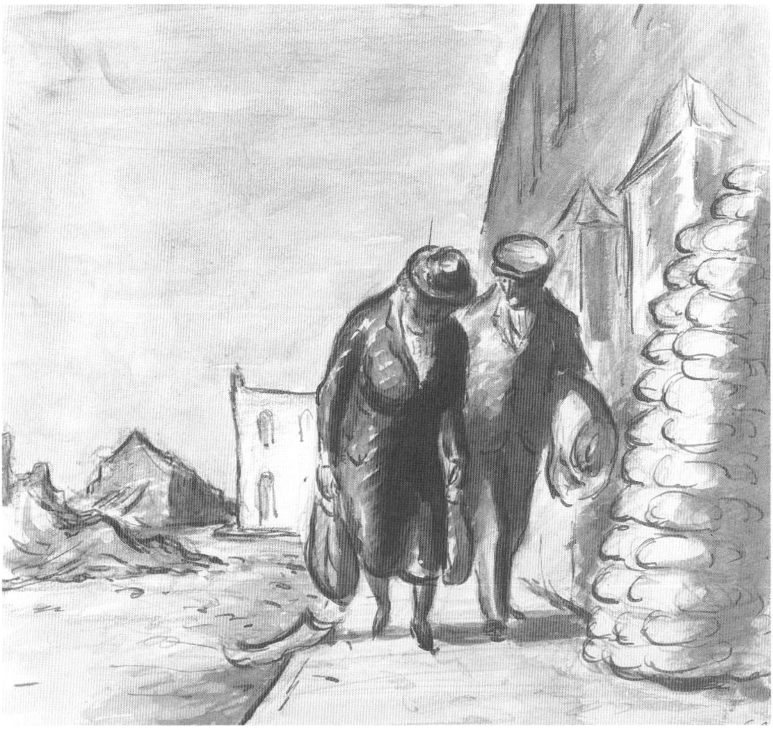

5 *The Trek to the shelter–Silvertown, September 1940*, by Edward Ardizzone.

6 *Bombed out, Bermondsey*, by Ethel Gabain.

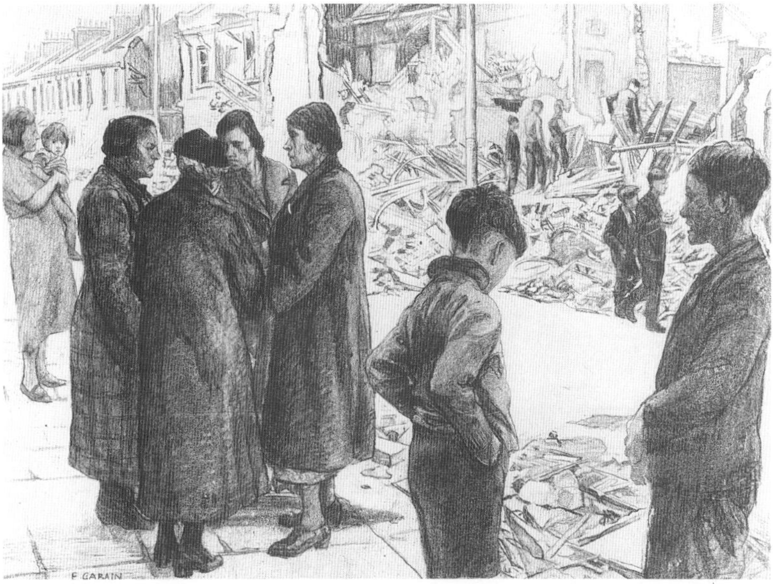

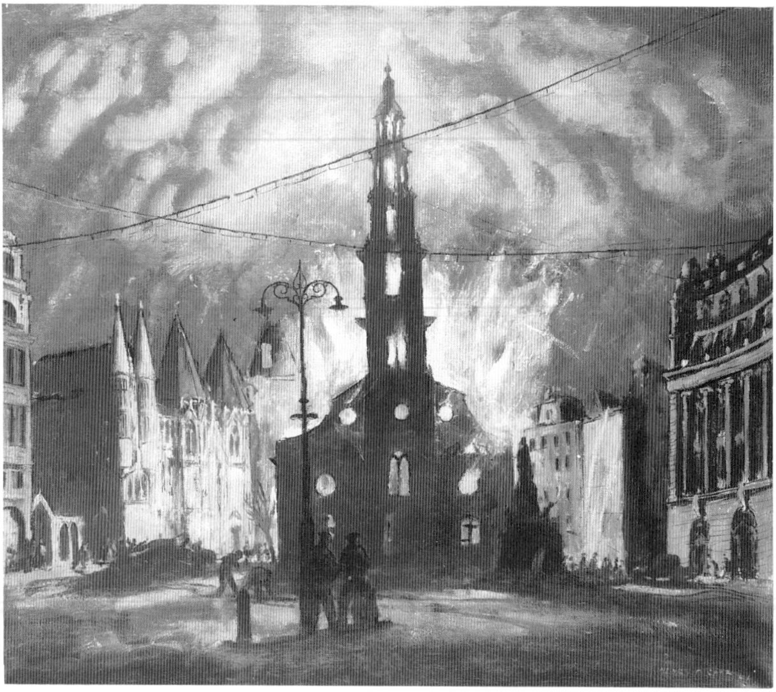

7 *St. Clement Dane's Church on Fire after being Bombed*, by Henry Carr.

8 *Bristol, November 24th, 1940*, by Frank Dobson.

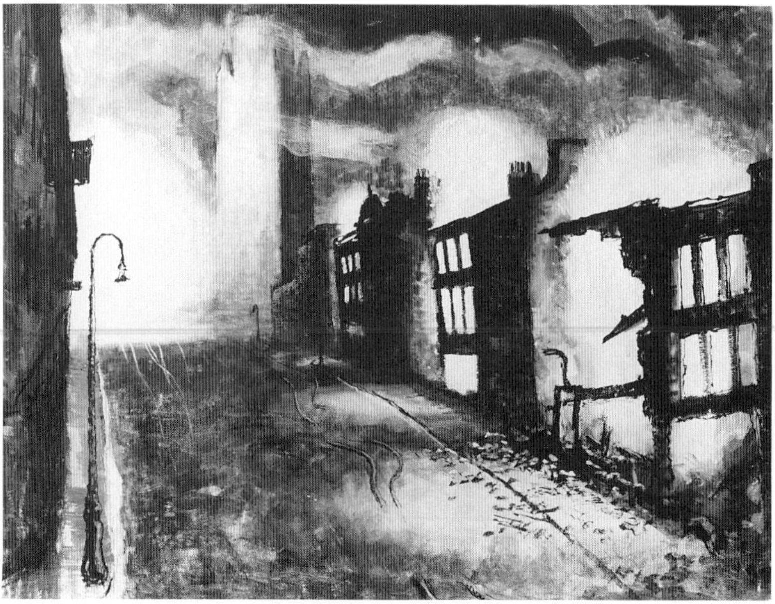

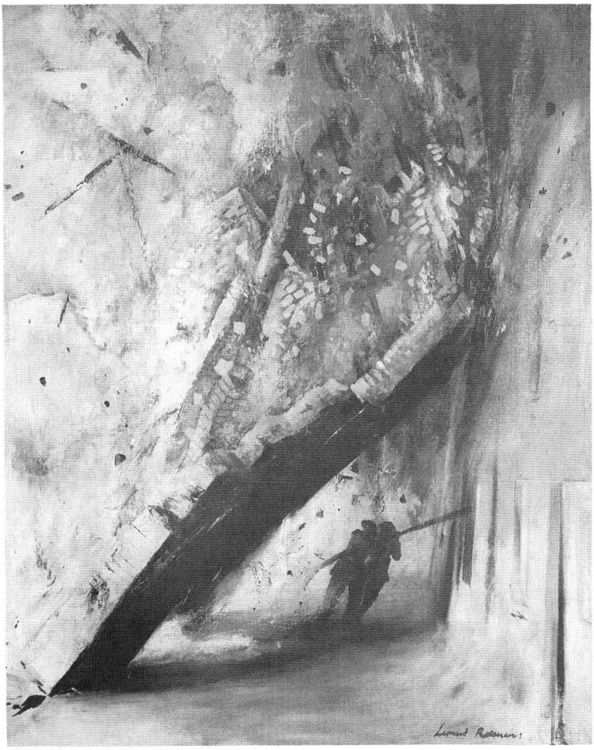

9 *A House Collapsing on two Firemen, Shoe Lane, London EC4*, by Leonard Rosoman.

10 *Your Britain–Fight for it Now* series: Village Green, by Frank Newbould.

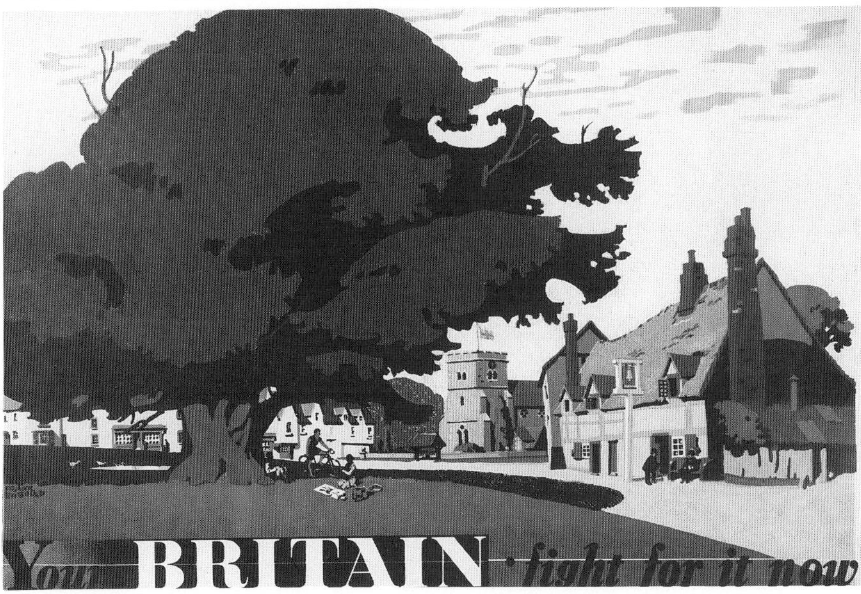

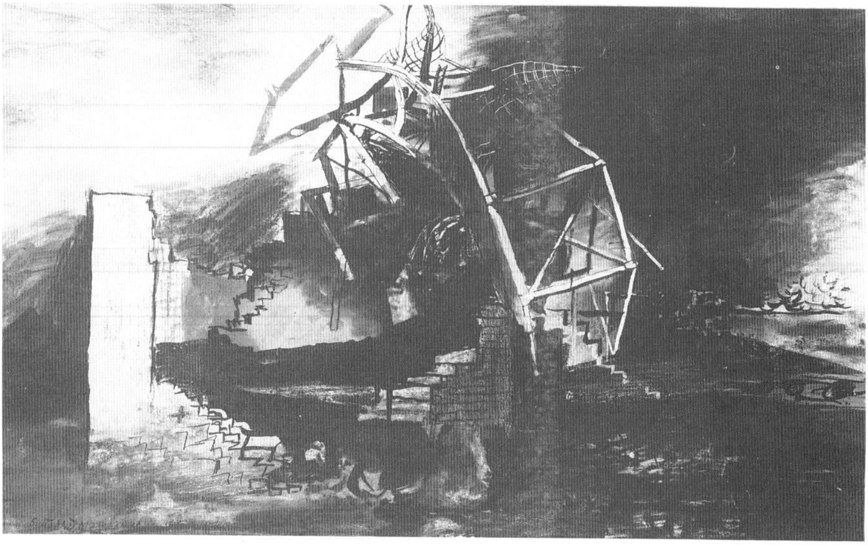

11 *Devastation, 1941, City: Fallen Lift Shaft*, by Graham Sutherland.

12 *Your Britain–Fight for it Now* series: 'Clean, airy and well-planned dwellings', by Abram Games.

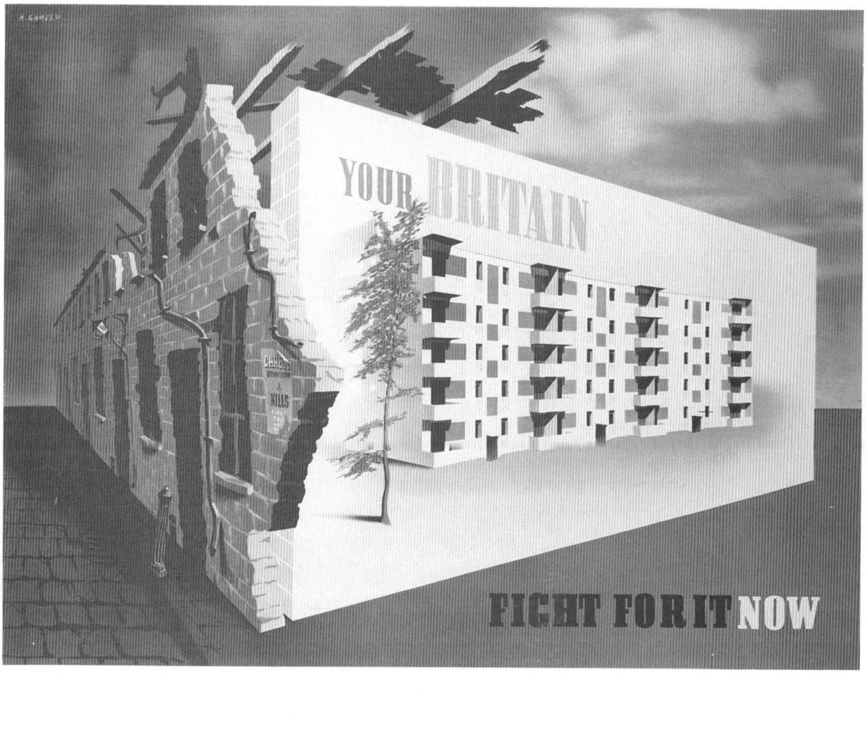

With lonely towers beneath the lonely moon!
  Not there doth Ayesha linger, – rune by rune

Spelling the scriptures of a people banned, –
The world is disenchanted! oversoon
Shall Europe send her spies through all the land!
Nay, not in Kôr, but in whatever spot,
In fields, or towns, or by the insatiate sea,
Hearts brood o'er buried loves and unforgot,
Or wreck themselves on some Divine decree,
Or would o'er leap the limits of our lot,
There in the Tombs and deathless, dwelleth SHE.[81]

The poem is quoted from memory by the two characters, adding a further level of distance; it is a half-recollected poem about a novel which describes a ruined city. This is the kind of palimpsest of allusion and reference which delighted the early Romantics, seen in Chatterton's Rowley poems,[82] for instance, or Fuseli's paintings based on Milton's reworkings of old English fairy myths.[83] In Bowen's story it adds still further to the sense of the unattainable. This is helped by a knowledge of the full text, with its stress on the fact that SHE dwells not in Kôr itself but wherever forlorn hope abides – 'buried loves and unforgot', and 'the Tombs and deathless'. Thus the unattainable is not in the distant past but forcefully alive, in the mind of those who refuse to abandon an illusion. Transience, yearning, desolation – all of these combine to add greatly to the patina of insubstantiality created by the moonlit distance of the lovers in 'Mysterious Kôr'.

The London that the story creates is real, yet still forsaken, changed as it is by the moonlight: the people are real too, yet changed by their inability to direct their lives towards the fulfilment they crave. Seen in the context of Kôr, they achieve a timelessness, and are almost presented as Romantic doomed lovers. Pepita goes so far as to embrace Kôr in preference to the real world round about her, as she shows in this exchange with Arthur:

> *The world is disenchanted,* it goes on. That was what set me off hating civilization.'
> 'Well, cheer up,' he said; 'there isn't much of it left.'[84]

Pepita wants to take refuge from something incomplete in something unreal and desolate, yet Romantically attractive: the lack of fulfilment and yearning for completion is like a set of Russian dolls each of which open to reveal another concealed within it, except that all the levels are apparent simultaneously in the story.

The incompleteness continues when the two lovers arrive at the flat; the presence of Callie is intrusive and, as the two women sleep in one bed while Arthur has the divan in the living room, 'slivers of moonlight' disturb their sleep. There is no need for Bowen to make references to the moon as the goddess of chastity; though the lack of physical union for the lovers is important enough, the unfulfilment works on a far greater level. It is shown repeatedly: 'If there'd been more time, we might have gone to the country, though I don't see where we'd have gone there,'[85] says Arthur, suggesting the more conventional Romantic notion of the country as place of fulfilment. They are denied even the scene of refuge of screen lovers – an idyllic country cottage with oak beams, reached with the help of a Singer Roadster and some scrounged petrol coupons.

The appeal of Kôr, and of the moonlight which recalls it, is not wholly irresistible for Callie. Near the end of the story, she turns to the window and finds that 'the moon's power over London and the imagination had now declined',[86] and a little later in the same paragraph we are told 'on the whole she felt this was for the best'. There is no permanence to this Romantic illusion; but it still exerts a great pull over her at the end of the story. Pepita is dreaming of walking with Arthur in a city of 'void, pure streets', yet he is the start of the dream, not the finish, 'the password, but not the answer.' And then: 'it was to Kôr's finality that she turned'.[87] All that is true to Pepita is the finality present in a poem about a Romantically desolate city; there is no permanence in the moonlit streets, or with Arthur, but only with a poem – and, we must remember, a poem recalled in a dream where it is linked with her earlier walk with Arthur through the moonlit streets, and their talk about Kôr. Ultimately it is unreality which has more appeal – the Romantic unreality and yearning of Kôr, not the contemporary unreality and all too real transience of the moonlight and the vulnerable city.

In 'Mysterious Kôr', the moonlit city and a network of allusion to a poem is used to create a mood, but it achieves more than that: it creates a psychological state of deep disquiet because of its unfulfilment on many levels. The city is real, yet compared to an imaginary, poetic landscape which is just as disturbing, just as incomplete: here there is no sense of refuge in landscape in the manner of so much popular romance of the time. The landscape is symbolic of a mental state, but it is also a tangible entity, both literally and symbolically fleeting. The transient and unreal is more atttactive for Pepita than the transient and actual; the landscape stands, ultimately, for her own feelings of wishing to withdraw from a world where nothing reaches completion to one which, even if unreal and desolate, has at least the appeal of mysterious, Romantic finality. In using such a landscape in such a manner, Elizabeth Bowen is extending and radically adapting the Romantic use of setting to show the tentative, transient landscape – both external and psychological – that is characteristic of the moment. In making the landscape urban rather than rural she is further extending it to provide a genuine response to the time. Literally and psychologically, in 'Mysterious Kôr' we have no abiding city.

V

The progress from a simple view of consolation in the beauty of the countryside to an awareness of fragility and transience in the appearance of the town is a rapid and a radical move in the art of the war. It is not, of course, a regular or a consistent progression; but it does show a remoulding of earlier conventions and stances to fit and in some measure express the feeling of the time.

Why should an awareness of this sort come about at this time? One of the reasons, I think, has been made clear by Spender: that the bombing gave city-dwellers a new awareness of their environment by presenting buildings seen from new angles and, by placing the whole setting under threat, making the onlooker more aware of its beauty. Another is offered by the idea that the boundaries between city and country were eroded. Graham Greene records in his fragmentary diary of September 1940 that 'In those days London had been a collection of villages':[88] the division of the city into small areas perhaps did something to the idea of community which earlier the separating, centrifugal impulses of city-dwelling had tended to destroy. In a more literal way, the use of areas of waste land for the cultivation of food and the return to uncultivated growth in other places blurred the boundaries still further:

> Endless allotments – beds of potatoes, onions and lettuces in parks, in the new open spaces from bombing, tomatoes climbing up ruins – trees and shrubs overgrowing evacuated and

> empty houses and gardens; in some places shells of eighteenth century cottages with black windows and Rousseau-like forest enveloping them, straying out over the road – no railings – climbing in windows.[89]

One might almost consider the growth of Rousseau-like 'natural' communities, like those in the Chislehurst caves and others in Epping Forest,[90] as a recourse to earlier modes of living, a dreadfully literal embodiment of earlier theory: what had been in part an aristocratic fashion now became a frightening and dislocating reality for many. And to Jennings' list of rural elements now visible in the cities must be added the eruptive growth of wild flowers on the bombsites, and the creation of habitats for all kinds of migrant birds not normally found in urban settings, to be reflected in turn in artistic statements such as Walter Spradbery's poster in *The Proud City* series showing the Tower of London while wild flowers bloom richly in the foreground,[91] C. Eliot Hodgkin's painting *The Haberdasher's Hall*[92] which shows wild flowers in bloom before a landscape of devastated buildings, and photographs of similar scenes in *The Illustrated London News*.[93]

This has to do with what is probably the most significant aspect of the new Romanticism of the war years; the idea of regeneration and rebirth in the natural world, which we may find in many forms and degrees of intensity in the finest work of the time. It grows from a simple awareness of the countryside which abounded early in the war, yet it also includes ideas of moral and political regeneration – as Chapter 8 will make clear. In 1942, Alberto Cavalcanti made a film based on a short story by Graham Greene, called *Went the Day Well.*[94] It tells the story of the capture of an English village – teashops, thatched cottages, village green and all – by German troops disguised as English soldiers. They are defeated and put to rout, but not by the traditional forces: it is the squire who is the Quisling, the local poacher who sounds the alarm, and a Cockney evacuee who gets through to bring help. The old England of cottages is still there as an object of beauty, but now it is not merely accessible to the city dweller but depends upon him for its continuity: city and country are interdependent, in a symbiotic relationship which – at last, long years after the industrial revolution has set up the fatal distance between the two – the people are beginning to understand. The image of unity between country and city is as yet tentative, the awareness of the beauty of the city unsure and transient; its fruition glorious yet short-lived. But, for a little while, it is there, and its importance both in aesthetic history and in the political life of the nation[95] is something which will grow and develop as surely, to be cut down as swiftly, as the wild flowers on Tower Hill and the arable crops on reclaimed fens.

6
A Child of Our Time

I

It is not only in the painting and writing of the forties that a continuity and development of Romanticism is clear; it is apparent too in music. In a sense it is impossible to compare English music of the twentieth century with earlier English Romantic music since, at the time of the great explosion of Romanticism in European music, England still had few composers of stature. Yet in another sense the tradition of English music that developed in the present century is rooted very firmly in a longer tradition of English art and thought which may be termed Romantic, concerned as it is with fundamental relationships between humanity and the natural world, either through a modal style which is drawn from the idioms of folk music or through settings of texts which stress this relationship.

The setting of texts from an earlier period is perhaps one more facet of the upsurge of interest in earlier art which has been explored in Chapter 2. This is something which marks the period off from earlier ages since, apart from the Bible and other liturgical texts, it is unusual in any historical period for composers to set texts from a period significantly earlier than their own. Purcell sets Dryden[1] and Tate;[2] Handel, the work of whatever craftsman-librettist is to hand,[3] not infrequently setting texts he adapted and assembled himself;[4] Elgar, Cardinal Newman;[5] Delius, Nietzsche;[6] the early Vaughan Williams, Walt Whitman.[7] But then, suddenly, it all changes and the great texts of the past become suitable for English composers to set – perhaps because of a greater confidence in their notes matching the earlier words, perhaps as part of a general longing for the past in the early years of the century, perhaps as a genuine concern to extend and continue tradition, as an adjunct to the folk-song movement, perhaps in a desire to recapture visionary moments of an earlier age, perhaps through nothing more complicated than the easy availability of texts in the popular standard library editions which flourished after the coming of mass literacy and public libraries.

Whatever the cause, the move to set texts by older poets is strong. It is almost a parallel with the first Romantics' urge to return to older legends and images – with Fuseli's illustrations of the Bible[8] and Shakespeare,[9] Blake's of Milton[10] and Dante,[11] for instance. A little earlier, the great revival of English folk-song had taken place, first in the process of their collection by enthusiasts like Sabine Baring-Gould[12] and Cecil Sharp,[13] then in their absorption into the melodic outlines and musical fabric of composers such as Vaughan Williams,[14] Holst[15] and Grainger.[16] The parallel here with the first Romantics' use of the idiom and heritage of the common man is close, along with the rejection of industrial society and its idioms of speech and song which is one impetus behind the *Lyrical Ballads*. Often folk-song and reference to texts from earlier ages come together: Vaughan Williams' *Job, A Masque for Dancing*[17] is a complex unity of the folk idiom of modal melodic structures and the high art of Blake's idiosyncratic illustrations, added to the notion of an emblematic Jacobethan masque, as various a blending of folk, historical and contemporary idioms and ideas as anything produced by a high Romantic illustrator.

By the time of the later generation, coming to artistic maturity at the start of the war in 1939, the pattern of such reference was firmly set. Vaughan Williams' *Five Tudor Portraits*,[18] settings of poems by John Skelton,[19] is one example of the tradition. Another is Gerald Finzi's *Dies Natalis*,[20] a setting of ecstatic passages from Traherne's *Centuries of Meditation*, inspired by seeing the angel roof of St Wendreda's March, and couched in a very personal modal folk-idiom – a piece which shows well the desire to return to the ecstatic mode of sacramental unity with the natural world which is a recurrent strand in English poetry and an underlying element of much native Romanticism.

At the same time, overshadowing all else except possibly Vaughan Williams of the old school, is Benjamin Britten. An intensely literary composer, it seems clear that Britten had absorbed a great deal of the current climate of interest in Romanticism in the 1940s, yet combined it with his own compositional styles to arrive at settings of earlier English texts which avoid completely the hint of modal archaism so often present in the less complete works of his predecessors. Often the choice of text is extremely original: Christopher Smart's *Jubilate Agno*,[21] set as the result of a commission from St Matthew's,

Northampton and first performed in 1943; the collection of poems in the *Serenade for Tenor, Horn and Strings*,[22] which includes a setting of Blake's 'Sick Rose' which captures the sinister sensuality of the poem's symbol and texture in its thick, dragging string sonorities and piercing natural horn solo; the adaptation of one of the most haunting of Crabbe's tales from *The Borough*[23] to form a libretto of disturbing simplicity and directness in *Peter Grimes*.[24] In all of these, the text is set in a directly contemporary manner, its own nature clarified and underlined through the eyes of the present. And there is awareness, too, of the visual tradition as it is currently regarded: the cover of the first edition of the *Serenade* bears a reproduction of Samuel Palmer's *Harvest Moon*.

But it is not these works, celebrated though they be, and important in reworking Romantic texts to provide a new element of contemporary sensuality and intellectual comment, that are the most striking in showing the Romantic continuation at work. It is to a work which is at first sight part of a different style and stance altogether that we must turn to find the most complete statement and use of the Romantic ethos in present-day clothing, as a contemporary statement of endurance and renewal: Michael Tippett's oratorio *A Child of Our Time*.[25] More than any other composition of the forties it demonstrates a search for an idiom which is both universal and personal, part of a tradition and yet representative of its own times, related to contemporary issues yet offering a spiritual hope that transcends them. Above all, it demonstrates the way in which Romantic aesthetics and images are inseparable from human compassion and political convictions, so that the continuation of an earlier world view becomes a way of confronting, and not retreating from, desperately urgent contemporary problems.

Since the early thirties the fusion between Tippett's artistic personality and his human and political outlook had been clear. He had acted as musical director for a scheme providing work-camps for unemployed miners, and written a folk-song opera *Robin Hood*,[26] both the musical idiom and the subject of which revealed a commitment to the people's cause. He had organised and conducted an orchestra of out-of-work cinema musicians, and written *War Ramp*,[27] a play which exposed the capitalist basis of the First World War.[28] All of this demonstrates not only a commitment to the theory of socialism, but a strong practical desire to relate his music and music-making to the needs of the people, a feeling of oneness with the common outlook and idiom which extends and develops the political aesthetic of Romanticism way beyond anything thought of by Wordsworth and Coleridge but which nevertheless shares its original basis.

In the thirties Tippett had also produced a setting of *A Song of Liberty*, the final section of Blake's *Marriage of Heaven and Hell*, which begins with these lines:

1. The Eternal Female groan'd! It was heard all over the Earth.
2. Albion's coast is sick silent; the American meadows faint!
3. Shadows of Prophecy shiver along by the lakes and the rivers and mutter across the ocean: France, rend down thy dungeon.[29]

Although Tippett later disowned the setting, the text seems to have made a lasting impression. As will later emerge, Blake's larger ideas of progress as well as the specific images of water and the natural world used in this passage are important in the moral and narrative progression of the text of *A Child of Our Time*. Although Blake's poem is intensely topical, it is also expressed darkly through his private mythology: Tippett shares this Romantic commitment with Blake, but alters it by making his expression far more accessible, voicing his outrage at contemporary wrong in terms which are universally applicable. In a series of articles[30] about the oratorio, Tippett makes clear its importance in both his musical development and the statement of his political objectives, which rest on deep personal commitment to humanity. The oratorio, its context, its relation to contemporary political journalism, and Tippett's own writings about all these things together constitute a 'text' of great significance in contemporary Romanticism.

Seeing the responses to the threat – and, after 1936, the reality – of war in Europe from Auden, Isherwood and other writers and artists, Tippett was striving for a way to express his own abhorrence of war which would also allow him to continue the development of his own musical language. For a time he thought of giving these feelings expression through an operatic treatment of the Dublin Easter rising of 1916, something which would have been deeply radical, if not outrageous, in the musical and political climate of the day. But nothing came of this. Instead, the external stimulus was provided by an incident in 1938 which was widely reported in the English press, most particularly in *Picture Post*.[31] A 17-year-old Polish Jew, Herschel Grynsban, whose parents had been deported from Germany, had shot and killed vom Rath, an official at the German embassy in Paris. The action unleashed the most savage of the Nazi Pogroms, with 50, 000 Jews arrested amid countless acts of brutality. The same year, the German writer Ödön von Horváth published his novel *Ein Kind unserer Zeit*[32] which discussed the dilemma of the individual within a totalitarian state. With most of England still basking in the relief of Chamberlain's Munich agreement, Tippett felt that something must be done both to make clear the threat and voice compassion with the suffering peoples of a sort which which governments – capitalist governments – were plainly failing to express. Here was the 'objective correlative' for the feelings of outrage hitherto channelled into the Blake setting and the war-play: Tippett had the basis of his oratorio.

The work was composed rapidly in the first days of war, completed in 1941 and first performed in 1944.[33] By then the composer had spent three months in Wormwood Scrubs prison in London as a Conscientious Objector who refused to take part in any activity connected to the conduct of the war. That same intensity and integrity of feeling which underlies his rejection of war is the foundation of the oratorio: it is perhaps the most complete instance of a work whose deep, Romantic sensuality is quite inseparable from a political and aesthetic philosophy which, resting firmly on the contemporary political situation, is a passionate statement of the sanctity of the individual within the created world. For this reason it is of central importance in the phenomenon of forties Romanticism.

II

The main stream of Romantic social and aesthetic thought is present in almost every aspect of *A Child of Our Time*, dominating the overall structure, the selection of musical material and the libretto. The work embraces a series of stylistic and intellectual references to earlier forms of Romanticism, but this is not the most important way in which it is Romantic: it is the way in which all of these elements are drawn together and subsumed into a movement of great intensity and compassion, forming a human journey towards renewal described in terms of the natural world, and in which the listener is fully involved, that marks this off as a fully Romantic work in the philosophical and aesthetic sense and which reveals the bond between it and the finest painting and writing of the war years.

The overall structure of the work rests not on principles of Romantic music but on the far older forms of baroque oratorio. The three-part structure of the oratorio derives from Handel's appproach in *Messiah,* in which the first part deals with general statements and prophecies; the second with the movement from the coming of Christ to the day of judgement; and the third with spiritual and philosophical comments, largely drawn from St Paul. In *A Child of Our Time* this is developed so that the first part covers the general nature of twentieth-century oppression; the second, the story of the 'child'; and the third, the moral and emotional movement which underlies the individual story. Within this larger outline, the musical building blocks are once again familiar from earlier tradition: recitative is used to narrate events, arias and duets to make personal statements, and choruses draw larger and more general moral comments. Thus there is a sense in which, in using a form that is already familiar, Tippett is extending and developing a tradition rather than doing something radically new.

In itself this is an important concept. It shows the composer deliberately eschewing new or experimental structures and instead turning towards something that is familiar not only from Handel but also from the great many Victorian oratorios which use a rather similar form,[34] and this is a deliberate casting of the work within an established mould to make it accessible for both listeners and performers. Oratorios in England are very much public property: they belong to the large and not-so-large choral societies who perform them. Tippett's idiom is rigorously his own and is in no way compromised or simplified in this work; but nevertheless, by choosing the familiar oratorio genre Tippett is making the work accessible to a wide range of people in a way that is wholly appropriate to the social ideals of Romanticism and the socialist ideals of the composer.

This concern for accessibility is shown more strongly in the fundamental nature of the work's text. Within it is also contained the essential Romanticism of the work. In a BBC Radio talk which he gave in 1950, the composer said that the oratorio

> brings the events before us in recollection, not to judge, but that by terror and pity we may be moved to stop equating intellect with spirit, and to 'break open the heart'.[35]

This would seem to be a clear development of Wordsworth's idea of poetry as 'the spontaneous overflow of powerful feeling recollected in tranquillity':[36] the mood of the oratorio is contemplative, not active, so as to allow us to see it within a larger historical and moral context and undergo the spiritual regeneration this will produce. In a sense, this is a principle of drama which has been employed since Greek theatre, but the aesthetic espoused by Tippett here is truly Romantic because of the way that it stresses the relation between judgement, intellect and emotion. There are the healing aspects of 'terror and pity', which could conceivably have to do with Greek catharsis as much as the purifying effects of the Sublime; but the end result of these experiences is that we respond in a way which is purely spiritual. This comes very close to what is often referred to as 'the simple Wordsworth';[37] the poet's ideal that emotional and spiritual response occurs at a level above the intellect, revealed in those moments when 'we are laid asleep/ In body, and become a living soul'. . . and 'see into the life of things'.[38] This is, perhaps, something that is more possible when we listen to music than when we look at a painting or read a book; but, without getting too involved in matters of comparative aesthetic philosophy, it is I think quite clear that Tippett is conceiving his work in a context of moral sustenance and renewal in the face of one specific example of wholesale moral outrage, and considering at great depth the ways in which music and text may work together to induce a response of compassion and understanding in the listener by extending Romantic aesthetics to confront the issues of his age.

The most celebrated structural pillar of the work is the inclusion of five arrangements of what were in 1940 called 'negro spirituals' at key points of the work. On the one hand this is another development of tradition, Tippett extending the habit of composers of the Lutheran church of including chorales to be sung by the congregation as well as the choir in their cantatas and passions.[39] In another it is something radically new, not so much musically as politically and humanly. Composers had used such themes before: Delius had included specific songs in his *Appalachia*[40] and, while vigorously denying that he had used actual folk song, Dvořák had taken elements of such folk-tunes in his *Symphonie aus der Neuen Welt*.[41] What makes Tippett's use of them so new is their role in the emotional pattern and growth of the work. The spirituals have a universality of application, bringing together as they do British, American and African cultures in their language and the areas of experience they represent, but their breadth is far greater. In the oratorio they become the voice of enslaved peoples through the centuries, representing the suffering of all outcast and exploited races, whether Jews in ancient Egypt, blacks in imperial Africa and the slave plantations in the Southern States, or Jews and gypsies in Nazi Germany. Giving the moral voice of the text to a race still, in 1940, regarded as inferior – people in East Anglia will still tell you how appalled American servicemen were when blacks were served in the same bar as whites in pubs near air bases – shows the breadth of Tippett's vision and his desire to extend the Romantic notion of using the real language of men in a way that is politically forceful and wholly contemporary.

Yet it is not primarily a political dimension, but a personal one, which dominates, since the spirituals provide 'the folk element in the work' – folk music and folk poetry which represents 'a common, a folk-experience'.[42] The language of the spirituals is full of the large, open imagery of mythic poetry which has almost universal applicability; it expresses a moral journey through direct physical images of travelling, landscape, thunder, crossing the river and, at last, crossing over 'into camp-ground'.[43] It is language which has its roots in biblical expressions of journeys and is seen also in parables of life as a journey such as *The Pilgrim's Progress* – indeed, Tippett makes the point that the trumpet that 'sounds within-a my soul'[44] is the same trumpet that sounded for Mr Valiant-for Truth when he 'passed over to the other side'.[45] The landscape of journey is also strikingly a part of the Romantic equation of the spiritual with the external; one of the earliest uses of landscape as a reflection of inner state in the true Romantic sense comes in the poetry of eighteenth-century dissenters from high Anglican tradition – most particularly the hymns of Wesley[46] and, perhaps surprisingly, Joseph Addison[47] – which presents the process of life as a journey through a landscape changing with one's own spiritual state.

In all of these forms, folk-language has been absorbed into an artistic structure of no little complexity, and the same happens with the text of *A Child of Our Time*. This is true not only in the way that the spirituals simply slot into the remaining text of the libretto, but also because their folk idiom becomes a touchstone for the whole diction of the text – 'a kind of spirit-level folk poetry to which the rest of the text had to conform'.[48]

Tippett's intention to have the libretto written by T. S. Eliot is well-known, as too is Eliot's instruction that the text would be best written by the composer himself.[49] The desire to reflect the simple universality of folk-language is shown repeatedly in the diction. This is most pointed in passages such as the tenor solo in part one:

> I have no money for my bread
> I have no gift for my love[50]

but there is also a desire to reflect contemporary speech within this larger continuum of suffering. The Chorus of the Self- Righteous in Part Two includes these lines:

> They shall not work nor draw a dole
> Let them starve in No-Man's-Land[51]

These are sharply contemporary expressions raising sharply contemporary issues, the dole of the depressed thrities and the suffering of those caught in the exposed ground between the trenches of the First World War. Thus the libretto extends and modifies folk-language to become both contemporary and timeless. The composer's own feeling[52] is that the text is least effective when it uses psychological terminology which is not yet absorbed into common speech, as in the Tenor's cry

> I am caught between my desires and their frustration as between the hammer and the anvil.[53]

Fifty years on, the incongruity is less troublesome; what is happening instead is that contemporary language is being joined with references that are timeless; the psychological suffering is given utterance in parallel with a vivid, timeless image, and so folk and contemporary language come together. Like the use of spirituals, it is something which seemed new and strange at the time but which with distance is revealed in its rightness.

All of this is important primarily because it gives the work immediacy and depth of impact by making its human compassion both universal and incisively immediate; but it is also important because it shows an extension of the Romantic aesthetic, seen in Wordsworth and elsewhere, of absorbing folk elements into a complex aesthetic structure. However much we may see the *Lyrical*

Ballads as folk-poetry, what makes them succeed is the guiding aesthetic force of Wordworth himself and, in much the same way, the libretto of Tippett's oratorio is successful because it takes and develops folk elements and combines them with contemporary expressions and issues and a series of other Romantic concerns to make an aesthetic statement of spiritual and political needs. The presence of the refining intelligence is apparent in the music as much as the text:

> But the vital consideration must always be, whether this musical (or literary) vernacular can be purified, enhanced, de-sentimentalized enough to convey the charge of deeply serious artistic emotions.[54]

This applies to the 'purification' of the harmonies of the spirituals, which are changed from the cloying, conventional ones of the popular arrangements of the day to something of much greater originality. Tippett is above all a linear composer and the effect of the spirituals is almost that of a marriage between Elizabethan madrigal and southern swing; the slight astringency of the harmonies is usually the result of the interaction of the vocal lines, the whole being conceived horizontally rather than vertically. But there are moments of great effect which are wholly harmonic – for example, the shift to E major on the last chord of 'he calls me by the thunder' in the first spiritual,[55] which reveals the strength of the imagery and allows us to hear the melody more clearly by presenting it in a new harmonic context. What is happening is that, by presenting the spirituals in this new setting, Tippett is showing them with a new cleanness, stripped of their habitual and perhaps rather stale harmonic trappings; once more the traditional is seen afresh. Folk idiom is thus transformed and absorbed into personal artistic idiom, just as it is in the Romantic folk-song treatments of Beethoven[56] or the folk-song inspired compositions of Vaughan Williams.[57]

The spirituals are also united to the rest of the work by the way in which their frequent idioms become part of the melodic contours of its other movements. The minor third, flat seventh and open fifth which are characteristic of the spirituals' melodies are absorbed into other movements to give this further kind of unity. Most listeners are probably aware of this to an extent no greater than their awareness of the unifying intervallic progressions of a Brahms symphony, or of the tone row of a Webern song, but they add to the music's organic unity and thus provide a major sense of growth and development through it. Such organic unity is, of course, fundamental to Romantic music, reflecting as it does the idea of psychological change and growth, most obviously in Wagnerian *Leitmotive* but also in the thematic transformations of Liszt and all succeeding composers who have used the technique as a way of allowing the listener to share in an emotional or spiritual as well as an intellectual journey. Once again Tippett is using and developing a Romantic convention for his own purposes, namely to convey in terms wholly musical the emotional and spiritual journey made explicit by the libretto.

This continuity and change is also apparent in the textures of the music. The very opening, with its sombre brass chords followed by a limping string theme given forward impetus by a series of suspensions and retardations, reaching temporary resolution in B major seven bars after figure 1, is a re-working of several earlier conventions. The procession-like figure comes from the baroque overture; the suspension a device used by composers as far back as Monteverdi and Purcell to suggest extremes of emotion; the dark texture a typically Romantic figuration to suggest intensity of mood; the movement to resolution suggesting countless earlier equivalents implying some kind of temporary resting place on a journey. All these are modified by Tippett's own limpid linearity in a progression towards clarity and accessibility motivated by impulses of compassion and perhaps influenced by a hearing of Berlioz' *L'Enfance du Christ*,[58] an earlier Romantic work which attempts to tell a moral tale in a manner that is directly comprehensible to all.

Folk-style from the spirituals and stylistic elements from European Romanticism are joined by elements of contemporary popular music in the score's synthesis. This is clearest in the tenor solo from part one, 'I have no money for my bread',[59] which uses a tango rhythm to give ironic force to the movement: it is as if the material bankruptcy of the individual is shown to be the result of the spiritual bankruptcy of the society which has caused it. At the same time, of course, it makes the lament peculiarly contemporary; the idiom of the people is being used here, albeit popular by destination rather than popular by origin, and once more Tippett is continuing and extending the Romantic convention of using popular idioms.

Text and music thus come together in an expression of human compassion which is an extension of the Romantic in several dimensions in a deeply personal and deeply committed fashion. Yet it is in the nature and movement of the text that this may most fully be seen, and which we must now consider in greater detail.

III

As well as making use of a number of general Romantic conventions and approaches, *A Child of Our Time* also employs some very specific Romantic texts and attitudes. This it does not by quotation, but by referring to aspects of earlier works and developing them in its own fashion to confront the issues with which it is concerned.

The first reference of this kind is to a fundamental text of European Romanticism. The opening of the oratorio, the chorus 'The world turns on its dark side', has affinities with the opening of Part One of Goethe's *Faust*.[60] In this work's 'Prologue in Heaven', the world is seen spinning round

> Alternating Elysian brightness
> With deep and dreadful night[61]

While this is happening, Mephistopheles tells the Lord about the activities and ambitions of Faustus. What in the Renaissance was an allegory of the challenging of the old Boethian system of order and hierarchy becomes for the Romantic generation a symbol of man's yearning for the unattainable, which leads only to his destruction. Right at the start the narrative of the oratorio is, by implication, placed within the context of the discussion of what is proper for man to wish to attain. Is it, for example, proper for him to cast out a certain race, or to seek justice at his own hands for such an act of outrage? These questions are not explicitly raised in the libretto at this stage but they are certainly relevant to the movement of the text as a whole, and the reference to *Faust* introduces them subtly and perhaps almost unwittingly at the start of the work. The allusion is also impressive because it shows the degree of distance between the narrator and the events being described; the world is seen as a distant planet, with all human life remote, and this contributes a good deal to the force of the imagery of the seasons and the natural world which is central to the growth of the work and the emotional journey we undergo within it. All this, of course, is in addition to the primary impact of the image, in establishing the idea of winter as a season of the soul and of society in general at the start of the work. The progress from this winter towards a season of renewal and growth is one of the two main movements of the oratorio, and in this lies much of its significance as a piece of contemporary Romanticism. It is in the other progression that its major reference to a specific Romantic writer may be seen.

This second movement is implied in the work's epigram, 'The Darkness declares the glory of light'. This is a line from the last speech of the Chorus in T. S. Eliot's *Murder in the Cathedral*,[62] itself a subtle reworking of the opening verse of Psalm 19, 'The heavens declare the glory of God: and the firmament sheweth his handy-work'.[63] The point contained within Eliot's line is that even those who disparage goodness are evidence of its power since, as the Chorus continues,

> Those who deny thee could not deny, if Thou didst not exist; and their denial is never complete, for if it were so, they would not exist.[64]

This is related to a passage of the text which appears towards the end of Part III:

> I would know my shadow and my light,
> so shall I at last be whole.[65]

Here the theories of Jung come into play, Tippett having made a study of his notions of anima and animus, the contradictory impulses implicit within all human motivation, shortly before writing *A Child of Our Time*. But the contradictory impulses as they are revealed in many places through the work show much more clearly a development of the ideas of William Blake, that good is present within evil and evil within good, and that the one must subsume the other for any sense of completeness to be achieved. Only if compassion is extended towards the destroyer, and understanding gained of the self-destructive impulse within the good, may any lasting progress be made. This is something that Tippett makes explicit in his own writing about the work:

> in actual composition . . I got drawn by the work itself towards some deeper commitment which needed to embrace both sides: the self-righteous and the rejected. And yet with passion, and not an inert neutrality.[66]

At the start of the work, images of confusion abound. We are told that 'the living God consumes within and turns the flesh to cancer!',[67] a notion of the destructiveness of isolation and incompleteness which has elements of Blake's *Thel*[68] about it. The Chorus then asks explicitly 'Is evil then good?',[69] making the confusion perfectly apparent: in a world where oppression is endemic, the action of Herschel Grynsban in shooting vom Rath is an inexplicable coming together of good and evil. Rationally it is a crime; but in these circumstances reason would seem to have little relevance and we are left with the question of the Chorus, 'Is reason untrue?' The predicament is truly Blakeian, yet very insistently present in contemporary social ills. 'Reason is true to itself', the Alto soloist answers, 'But pity breaks open the heart'.[70] Blake's *Urizen*,[71] rationality unmodified by compassion, has no solution to the real world; and pity is ultimately self-defeating and degrading since, as he argues in the *Songs of Innocence and Experience*,

> Pity would be no more
> If we did not make somebody poor[72]

The progression of contraries continues as the 'child of our time' is seen as the 'scapegoat' in Part II and, unable to find his parents, falls victim to the evil within him:

> His other self rises in him, demonic and destructive[73]

In the third part, it is as if the boy has been not so much abandoned but wilfully destroyed by his God;

> God overpowered him – the child of our time[74]

So far from being a journey towards resolution, what seems to be happening here is that the boy, who began as the victim of the oppression of others, has now become the victim of his own evil and as a result has incurred the wrath of his God. The Blakeian unity of opposites seems to be leading only to destruction. Yet Blake again provides the key to the movement towards resolution.

Just after the beginning of Part III, the Alto solo sings

> The soul of man is impassioned like a woman.

> She is old as the earth, beyond good and evil, the
> sensual garments.
> Her face will be illumined like the sun.
> Then is the time of his deliverance.[75]

Tippett acknowledges[76] the source of this passage in one of Blake's plates in *The Book of Job*,[77] allying it most particularly to that part of the text where Job finds no difference between God and Satan, but where he is offered a vision of a new synthesis where good and evil are united and re-birth follows. This is most likely the eleventh of the series.[78] Job lies beneath the figure who is both God and Satan; he has a cloven hoof and is wound around by a giant worm, symbolising mortality. With his right hand he is pointing behind him to a stone tablet on which is carved the decalogue, familiar from the title-page of *Urizen*[79] as emblematic of the negative, destructive forces of reason unmixed with compassion. Yet the figure also has the hair in the form of rays of sunlight familiar from other images of the Old Testament God, and is reaching his left arm down protectively over the figure of Job. The next plate in the series contains the legend 'Lo all these things worketh God oftentimes with Man to bring back his Soul from the pit to be enlightened with the light of the living.'[80]

What is happening in Tippett's text is the dawning of the realisation that divine love sometimes works through instruments of evil to redeem its object, and that redemption is at hand even in the midst of persecution. Contained within these lines of texts are also the key Blakeian notions of the elision of male and female, and the idea that both are merely 'sensual garments' of the spirit. The 'boy' has indeed suffered greatly, but this is the inseparable corollary of his redemption. This is where the importance of the second of the two movements of the text becomes apparent; the renewal will take place not in the redemption of the boy as an individual, but in the regeneration of the natural world. And we now realise another reason for the distant viewpoint of the opening: if the world turning on its dark side is seen from a vast distance, the larger process of renewal will be visible more clearly and, most important, will be seen as part of a process involving the whole of the earth, a system of natural order of which humankind – the boy and his oppressors – is merely a part.

The natural imagery of the text is apparent from the very start in the opening reference to winter; yet even at the early stages there seems to be some suggestion of hope, albeit severely limited, when the Chorus claims 'we are as seed before the wind'.[81] Even though the Chorus is carried 'to a great slaughter',[82] they are still seed; they still have the potential for renewal and rebirth. Yet this is still a long way off; shortly later we hear

> When shall the usurers' city cease?
> And famine depart from the fruitful land?[83]

This combines a Blakeian image of the stifling effect of institutional greed with a similar idea of stagnation in the natural order; yet there is never the complete abandonment of the hope of movement, rather a statement of deathly stasis. Movement of a different kind is suggested in the spiritual at the end of Part One, 'Steal away to Jesus':[84] the only progression that is possible is that of a religious retreat – in the strict sense – in time of spiritual and natural desolation.

The second part of the oratorio, concerned as it is with the specific circumstance of 'the boy', contains fewer images of this sort, but towards its end continues the idea of stagnation in the assertion of 'The Mother' (Soprano) that 'The springs of hope are dried up.'[85] Yet a few lines later the Alto solo asserts 'The dark forces rise like a flood.'[86] The use of water imagery for both renewal and the evil which drowns out hope is important; it is a reflection of the idea of the similarity of good and evil which we have seen, developed from Blake, elsewhere in the oratorio, and this suggests again that only by the two forces coming together in some way will renewal be attainable.

It is in the last part that the imagery takes on its most important role in directing the progress of the oratorio towards a sense of release and renewal. We are told of the world's descent into 'the icy waters where lies the jewel of great price',[87] suggesting that the descent into evil is in itself some kind of redemptive process; and this indeed is continued in the bass soloist's assertion:

> Winter cold means inner warmth, the secret nursery of the seed.[88]

This is something of genuine renewal, and also of universal significance; it recalls such mythic archetypes as the Pluto and Proserpine myth and the legend of John Barleycorn, both ways of seeing the dearth of winter as an essential part of the natural cycle. Suggestions of hope continue: we are told that 'The garden lies beyond the desert'[89] and that 'Healing springs from the womb of time'.[90] Then, when we have been told of the boy being overpowered by God, the Tenor states the ideal of self-knowledge which it seems is one of the foundations of renewal: once the desire to know 'my shadow and my light' is acknowledged, regeneration is possible. 'Without contraries is no progression':[91] once this has been realised, there is at last a sense of movement:

> The moving waters renew the earth.
> It is spring.[92]

The four soloists sing together over a changed version of the limping theme with which the work has begun: as Tippett himself says, 'It is spring: but spring with an ache in it'.[93] The work concludes with the final spiritual 'Deep river'[94] – water again, but here suggesting progress, not stasis, as the children of Israel move across the Jordan to 'camp-ground' and the promised land. Rebirth – spiritual, human, natural – is achieved.

The progress of *A Child of Our Time* is essentially a dual one. The libretto develops the Blakeian idea of the benevolent unity of good and evil in contemporary, Jungian terms in parallel with a movement in the natural world from stasis to renewal in the ancient cycle of the seasons. The movement is both personal and global; we are drawn closely into the human conjunction and resolution of good and evil, yet also presented with the relation between humanity and the natural world by means of the changing seasons seen as from a vast, interplanetary distance. All of this is reflected in the passionate intensity of the music, and given wide relevance in the folk-idiom of both musical and verbal texts. Tippett has used the folk-styles, the Blakeian dialectic, and the seasonal, natural images – all fundamentally Romantic notions – in a manner that is totally appropriate to the oppression of his own day, creating a fusion which is among the finest of contemporary developments of Romantic traditions and outlooks.

Tippett has this to say of the spiritual movement of *A Child of Our Time*

> It's nothing less that the re-birth of the inner imaginative world, that is sought for. To plough the dark ground of our disorders that we may sow new seeds – to 'harrow hell'.[95]

It is characteristic of the composer's writing that this should draw together all the images of concrescence and renewal and give them final utterance in an image at once spiritual and earthy; harrowing hell. Romantic renewal is seen through the changing pattern of the seasons, both in themselves and as a metaphor of spiritual rebirth. It is this which makes *A Child of Our Time* both timeless and contemporary; and it is this which gives it its place within the main stream of Romantic painting and writing of the forties.

7

Midwinter Spring

I

"I shall be one with nature, herb, and stone",
Shelley would tell me. Shelley would be stunned:
The dullest Tommy hugs that fancy now.
"Pushing up daisies" is their creed, you know.
To grain, then, go my fat, to buds my sap,
For all the usefulness there is in soap.
D'you think the Boche will ever stew man-soup?
Some day, no doubt, if . . .

Friend, be very sure
I shall be better off with plants that share
More peaceably the meadow and the shower.
Soft rains will touch me, – as they could touch once,
And nothing but the sun shall make me ware.[1]

Wilfred Owen is here taking a concept from earlier Romanticism and extending it in the light of his immediate circumstances. The idea of unity with the earth is common in the literature and also the life of the First World War: at a time when the soldier spent a great deal of time sheltering below ground it is not surprising that physical proximity should spawn philosophical speculation, and the idea of being better off as an actual part of the earth must to many have seemed attractive. In this there is a bitter irony typical of much of the outlook from the trenches; Paul Fussell[2] has called irony the dominant mode of seeing of the whole war. Owen is bitter about Shelley's view of the place of the dead Keats within the natural world,[3] and suggests that the stance in *Adonais* owes little to an awareness of genuine suffering or the kind of unity with nature – 'rats', 'germs' and 'microbes' – which is the common experience of the soldier. Irony is also present in the expression 'pushing up daisies' which Owen quotes, an expression recorded by Eric Partridge[4] as a coinage of the trenches which develops the more passive 'under the daisies' of pre-war colloquialism.[5]

The serious element that is most apparent alongside the irony is a notion of release – after the passage quoted above the poem continues 'Your guns may crash around me. I'll not hear'. The poem overall makes clear that, when the soldier's body is at one with the earth, he will be 'better off' because he has escaped suffering. It is a view of unity with nature some way removed from Shelley's in *Adonais*.

It is also something far distant from a major line of writing and painting from the Second World War, which again takes a Romantic view of nature for its starting point, albeit less explicitly than Owen's 'À Terre'. We may see this view emerging in the late thirties, perhaps most particularly in a work which looks back to the trenches of the first war, David Jones' *In Parenthesis*.[6] In Part 7 of this work, Jones develops this idea of unity with the earth in a manner which seems to foreshadow a great deal of the finest writing and painting of the forties, yet is as explicitly rooted in the immediate experience of the trenches as any of Owen's poems. The sequence beginning 'Lift gently Dai, gentleness befits his gun-shot wound in the lower bowel' demonstrates this quality very well.

> Lower you lower you prize Maria Hunt, an' gammy fingered
> upland Gamalin – down cantcher – low – hands away me
> ducky – down on hands on hands down and flattened belly
> and face pressed and curroodle mother earth
> she's kind:
> Pray her hide you in her deeps
> she's only refuge against
> this ferocious pursuer
> terribly questing.
> Maiden of the digged places
> let our cry come unto thee.
> *Mam*, moder, mother of me
> Mother of Christ under the tree
> reduce our dimensional vulnerability to the minimum –
> cover the spines of us
> let us creep back dark-bellied where he can't see
> don't let it.

There, there, it can't, won't hurt – nothing
shall harm my beautiful.[7]

Despite its force and its deep roots in the actuality of experience, there is a tenderness to this passage which gives it a very different tone from Owen's poem and which is inseparable from the attitude it adopts towards the natural world. The passage begins with what seems to be a direct imitation of the language of soldiers, in the direction 'lower you prize Maria Hunt', but this is very different in significance from Owen's vernacular diction. 'Maria Hunt' is rhyming slang for cunt or vagina, an individual variation of the still current 'Berk' as abbreviation of 'Berkely Hunt'[8] but still familiar in the soldier's lexicon of abuse. This is a lot more than an obscenity: it is a reference to a generative part of the body which links with a large number of similar references to procreation and rebirth in the passage. Most apparent of these is the reference to 'mother earth' which is no mere conventional use of the expression. This is a maternal figure turned to for a protection which is both physical and spiritual. 'Mam, moder, mother of me/Mother of Christ under the tree' makes this clear and also shows the universality of the earth mother: the Welsh diminutive *Mam*, the Middle English *moder*, the earth that is the speaker's mother and the Mother of Christ are all drawn together in an image of generation that is timeless yet made immediate by the urgency – and the fatuous military jargon – of 'reduce our dimensional vulnerability to the minimum'. The earth is something the soldier burrows into, with a 'curroodling' or bodily caressing motion which suggests a sexual union: seen in this context, 'Maria Hunt' is still overtly a term of abuse to a cack-handed stretcher bearer but also a further enrichment of the idea of sexual replenishment and renewal in contact with the earth. And the diction of the succeeding line, 'hands away me ducky', seems to recall the instructions of a kindly prostitute – or perhaps an older mistress, echoing the 'mother' note – at the moment of penetration. Add these to the tenderness of the ideas of hiding 'in her deeps'; the sacramental presence of the 'Maiden of the digged places', completing the visions of earth as woman by adding the dimension of patron saint as well as mother and mistress; and the gentle concluding of 'nothing shall harm my beautiful' and we may see in the passage a vision of the earth as embodying procreative, nurturing and spiritually enriching qualities which merge human and natural processes in a continuum of care and renewal.

In the twenty years separating Owen's text from Jones's, the view of the natural world has changed. Both make use of a kind of Romanticism, Owen by ironically stressing the literal truth of a vision of unity with nature and Jones by showing the sacramental quality of the relationship between man and earth. The former is pessimistic and static, seeking to find in the natural world only a refuge from suffering by becoming insensate. The latter is imploring and dynamic, offering not only refuge but also tenderness, with the hope of renewal made strongly implicit by language of human sexuality and images of real and metaphoric motherhood.

It is this difference which is possibly the most striking shift between the view of nature in the first war and that of the second. Irony and refuge give way to a deep passion, an involvement and sense of renewal through the procreative processes of the natural world, often imaged in or linked with human sexuality. The timelessness of the Jones passage is also important: the ancient past is often seen as a time of harmony and inspiration, or regarded as synchronous with the present. It is the growing, nurturing earth which endures, and the varieties of this vision in word and image are the concern of this chapter.

II

Within the larger concern to redefine the relationship between humankind and the natural world are a whole series of styles and stances. The ideas of regeneration apparent in *In Parenthesis* are in a sense a forerunner of some of the most complete and self-sustaining of these; but there are other ways of seeing this relationship which vary in their character as well as in their effectiveness. Of these, three figures are of importance in suggesting a move, however tentative and erratic, towards the ideal of regeneration: Michael Ayrton, Cecil Collins and John Craxton. The range with which they address the issue is startling, showing once more that, with forties Romanticism as much as with its much earlier original, there is rarely any consensus of style.

Michael Ayrton is not an easy artist to discuss, wavering as he often seems to do between high Catholic iconography of the central European tradition and Grand Guignol Gothic which can dilute the power of his work in a disconcerting way. There are several of his images which show an awareness of the natural world, and a stance towards it, which can be seen as part of the movement towards renewal with which so many artists of the time are concerned; the difficulty lies in assessing the quality of his contribution to the theme.

The range of his sources and the nature of his style means that it is often hard to establish the significance of Ayrton's imagery. His *Orpheus*[9] is an early example. It shows a three-quarter length male nude clasping a lyre with four strings before an arid background of rocks and thin trees. Scraps of fabric are blowing from the topmost branches; otherwise, there is no sign of life or movement. Is this an allegory of the stagnation of the power of Orpheus, dry thoughts in a dry season reflecting the powerlessness of the artist in war? Or is it merely a piece of decorative art, almost in the tradition of Rex Whistler, whose wall-paintings[10] entertained his aristocratic patrons in the thirties?

The same doubt hovers over *Joan in the Fields*.[11] This may be read as an allegory of the female principle in the land, the artist's mistress Joan Walsh being shown against a richly autumnal scene of harvest fields, while two figures, a man and a woman, rest in the sun between a row of stooks and the corn yet to be harvested. The painting also has a clear debt to a much earlier work, Gainsborough's *Mr and Mrs Robert Andrews*.[12] The reference is clear in the whole composition, with the figure of Joan replacing the two patriarchal landowners in Gainsborough's canvas, and the cornfield stretching away behind in a similar manner. The reason for this reference, and the use made of it by Ayrton, are both less clear. The earlier painting is permeated by emblems of ownership – the landowner's gun and dog symbolising his power over all the animal life on his land, the ancient tree symbolising hereditary possession, the wife suggesting the extension of that ownership into future generations. Is Ayrton rejecting all this, saying instead that the country and the regenerative properties it embodies now belong to all? This is certainly an attractive idea, echoing the new accessibility of the countryside celebrated in Frank Newbould's posters and elsewhere. It is given further force by the presence of the kitten in Joan's lap, replacing the pheasant which Gainsborough may have intended to paint in the lap of Mrs Andrews as a further sign of ownership. The emblem of the game laws is thus ousted by a representative of amiable and domesticated nature – the sentimental fluffiness of which many onlookers will find hard to take.

Yet this reading does not convince. Joan *isn't* in the fields: she is sitting in a Windsor chair a little distance above them, as if on a terrace. Whether or not this is the naturalistic setting, the visual distance is still clear, and this floating separateness holds her apart from the fields and what is going on in them. In consequence, the idea of Joan as some kind of earth-mother is also denied. She is not bound to the fields in any literal sense, nor by colour or composition: the black hair, pink dress and flesh tones have no link with the tonality behind her. As Joan is separated from the fields, so are we, the onlookers: there is a feeling of inaccessibility here, cut off as we are by the high viewpoint – much more distant, ironically, than Gainsborough's – as much as by the discontinuity of space between Joan and the fields. The idea of the two figures in the fields as representing a modern Adam and Eve[13] is similarly unconvincing. Why so? They are labouring in the fields, certainly, but they are not presented as a couple and there is no eye contact between them; there is little to suggest that they are other than a pair of farm workers.

The painting's general lack of tension, too, prevents it from sustaining a reading of such depth; we are closer to fashionable portraiture or the original of a magazine illustration than to an allegorical statement of a latter-day Ceres-Pomona myth. Perhaps a greater closeness to the land is seen in *Mrs Chittendon*.[14] She at least is seen standing firmly within a field, clutching a cabbage which she has just harvested from it, and linked to it both by colour and texture and by the austere solidity of form which she shares with the landscape in which she stands. But again there is a lack of seriousness in the image: can we really impute this dignity to the painting? I think not. *The Earthbound*[15] offers another relationship with the land. A male nude lies supine in a partially-harvested cornfield, one hand outstretched at his side and the other folded across his stomach, legs wide apart and head back as if in sleep or death. A track divides the field into the growing corn on the left and the harvested sheaves on the right, stacked in an orderly line which recedes into the far distance. A few stray stalks remain near the figure, the heavy ears bending them down over his head. Is this an allegory of the regenerative cycle of the land, the nude symbolising the dead seed which will burgeon into the full-grown corn? Certainly there is a bond of texture and tonality between the body and the earth on which he lies. Yet again the painting's lack of weight argues against his being some kind of latter-day John Barleycorn; there is a simplicity of style here which again links it to a kind of popular illustration, the exaggeration and foreshortening of the hand and foot of the nude adding to this impression rather than giving a sense of immediacy and involvement for the onlooker. There is, of course, nothing to be said in principle against the use of such a lightness of style; but to be effective it would surely need to have a directness of impact and allegorical meaning to match?

There are several paintings of this time which are more completely concerned with landscape. *Winter Stream*[16] and *Entrance to a Wood*[17] both show contorted organic shapes of trees within naturalistic landscapes, approaching Sutherland's treatment of natural forms in the 'biomorphic' style considered later in this chapter, but lacking its incisive reorganisation of the growing matter it presents. *Gethsemane*[18] seems to be presenting the anguish of the central figure of Christ in the contorted shapes of the trees; yet once more there does not seem to be the concentration and intensity of the theme in the manner of execution. Ayrton's most celebrated work of this period is the angst-ridden *Temptation of St Anthony*,[19] which goes away from the natural cycles hinted at in the other paintings considered here. Perhaps it is an allegory of contemporary suffering, suggesting a kind of renewal in St Anthony's eventual triumph; but once again there is a lack of tautness and depth which places the painting's effects seriously at risk.

It may well be that his illustrations to Phoebe Pool's anthology *Poems of Death*[20] are his most successful work of the period: the greater narrative direction given them by the texts they illustrate removes the element of ambiguity and uncertainty so often apparent in the oils, and the smaller medium itself aids intensity, giving a concentration which, for me, the larger paintings lack. Ayrton is important in suggesting a link between human and natural worlds in broad terms and a clear, accessible style aided by his sweeping forms and intense colour; but this accessibility is inevitably accompanied by a lack of spiritual depth, and we need to look elsewehere for a fully satisfying statement of Romantic regeneration.

Cecil Collins approaches the relationship with natural forces in terms which are rather different. His concern is for a new bond between mankind and the land which is sacramental, very much in terms of the unification between the celestial and the everyday that is characteristic of much poetry of the seventeenth century – Donne[21] and Vaughan especially – along with the hieratic, almost ritualistic formalism of the finest Elizabethan art.[22] This is made clear in a painting which dates from just before the war: *Portrait of the*

Artist and His Wife.[23] The two figures sit at a table in the foreground of an interior dominated by natural textures – wooden floorboards, wooden table – on chairs upholstered in rich fabric, his gold, hers purple. The figures have a stiffness which seems to come from hieratic Tudor portraiture seen through a veil of European modernism. The woman's dress seems a simplified version of those worn by lesser dignitaries in Tudor portraits, and the man is wearing a dark-green suit, starkly contemporary in an arts-and-crafts manner. The faces of both have the mask-like quality of Elizabethan patterns and, taken with the rest of the painting, suggest that characterisation or any other kind of 'meaning' is to be found here by emblematic association rather than psychological revelation.

It is the relationship of the couple with the table and what lies on it which bears the main emblematic significance of the foreground, and which reveals the particular nature of the paradise which they inhabit. The two are eating fruit, the leaves of which lie scattered over the table's surface. Each clasps a tiny ankh, the Egyptian-Coptic symbol of life; at the rear of the table stands a chalice which can just be seen to contain red wine, and which has a delicately chased base. These details give the scene its sacramental qualities; the two are sharing the host, which has been united with both the pagan life-force – the ankh – and the emblem of the Christian Fall – the apple – in what seems to be a celebration of the full sensuality of the natural world of humankind's fallen state. Perhaps the serpentine chasing on the base of the chalice is further evidence of both the Fall and primitive natural forces. The apple-as-host implies that this is different from Milton's prelapsarian paradise, or even Palmer's. 'Blissed be the time/That apple take was!'[24] The fortunate Fall has always been near the centre of English theology, and Collins seems to extend the idea in this image.

The ideal state does not end there, though. It also seems to embrace elements of traditional English craftsmanship, in the elaborately-turned legs of the table, the heavy crockery and the cutlery. The forks have the three tines of earlier English designs,[25] suggesting a reversion to an earlier period of English history. The spoons are similarly archaic, having the small, teardrop bowls[26] of old English patterns and resembling the fork in their long, thin stems. The heavy woodwork and rough plates suggest aspects of the revival of native craftsmanship of the twenties and thirties, itself a continuation of the various craft revivals of the end of the previous century; the archaic design of the cutlery suggests a harking back to an ideal past which is visible in several aspects of British design of the earlier years of the century.[27] All of this is quite revealing: it suggests that for Collins the ideal is an arts and crafts paradise, perhaps related to his working at Dartington Hall in the thirties and during the war years. The perfect relationship between humankind and the natural world is here imaged in the craftsman's feeling for his natural materials in a self-conscious rejection of the mass-production of the mechanistic world; spirituality is a sensual closeness to nature aided by a revival of ancient craftsmanship.

Behind the schematic window of the composition's interior we can see out to a garden which is again suggestive of Collins' ideal. This is like one of those tightly-planned gardens which the Elizabethans saw, in their ordered layout, as representative of heavenly perfection. The fields of the middle ground are patterned with small plants which are a cross between the formalised English flowers on the dress of Queen Elizabeth which emblematise the native stock in formal portraits,[28] and the patterns developed from the same source in the wallpapers and fabrics of William Morris.[29] At the centre of the landscape is an incinerator which has been compared in shape with a chasuble,[30] but this likeness seems less convincing than to a censor, and one highly modified to suit the honest, outdoor tradition of the English mystical craftsman: it is, after all, spreading not catholic incense but good, honest, out-of-doors vigour in the form of English leaf-smoke. To the right stands a building recognisably Tudor in architecture, its exposed beams and raised structure revealing it as some kind of lodge or garden house. Behind it to the left, nude male and female figures sit in a boat, their long straight hair echoed in the straight rushes beside the pool: we are in the company here not so much of Adam and Eve but a latter-day English artist prophet, Eric Gill perhaps – certainly the straight hair is a motif in one of his less explicit sacramental-erotic drawings.[31] They are accompanied on the lake by seven swans – the kind of vague symbol, suggestive of royalty, grace and death as well as of unity with the natural world, which is frequent in the genre of half Christian, half pagan other-world saga popularised by Tolkien[32] and others. And the landscape recedes up a rolling hillside which suggests the Devonshire landscape of Collins' birthplace, covered in strong, native trees which will, one conjectures, either bring forth further apples for the table in the foreground or yield their timber to future generations of English craftsmen to make its replacement.

Collins' painting combines elements of Tudor emblematology

with ideas and actualities from the tail-end of the arts and crafts movement. It is a canvas which works through a series of separate analogies and allusions rather than any central drive or compulsion; certainly it lacks the risk-taking intensity of the painting of Sutherland or the involving immediacy of Rosoman. Collins is a painter who is often regarded as Romantic; yet this canvas seems only to reveal itself as a piece of self-conscious imitation of Tudor stylistics combined with some post-Morris moralising. The relationship with the land that is postulated here is sophisticated and, in its own way, redemptive; yet it lacks the instinctive sweep of the earlier Romantics and the intense spiritual immediacy of the finest work of the forties. Instead of, like them, taking what it needs from Romantic stances and developing this into a unified and genuine response to the exigencies of the time, it offers us an assemblage of references to a largely mythical earlier ideal. The spirituality is no doubt genuine; but, like Collins' other work of the period, the painting offers us a refuge and retreat from the threatening reality of 1939, not a direct confrontation with it. Collins is not a Romantic artist; he is a pictorial archivist. Looking at the work of both Collins and Ayrton, I find myself thinking of the words of Hopkins which Grigson quoted about Palmer, and finding in them a definition of what they lack:

> A kind of touchstone of the highest of most living art is seriousness; not gravity, but the being in earnest with your subject – reality.[33]

The position of John Craxton is rather different. As Chapter 2 has made clear, his early work shows the influence of Palmer and Calvert in its dark intensity and concentration on natural forms. As is the case with Graham Sutherland, however, this was only a passing stage, and his work of the later forties shows a related yet ultimately rather different stance towards the natural world and the idiom used to depict it. His work may be seen as a kind of progress between the twin poles of Romantic primitivism and contemporary biomorphism until it moves off in quite a new direction in the paintings from Greece of the later forties. The references to Palmer and Blake of *Poet in a Landscape* and *Dreamer in a Landscape* which have already been discussed as quite self-consciously a refuge from the problems of style which the artist then confronted are in a sense analogous to Collins' refugee style: yet they are stronger because they develop the earlier Romanticists' manner in a way which is far more deliberate and original, exploiting the duality of the landscape in a way that seems quite beyond the reach, and perhaps also the vision, of that artist. Two paintings which show one way forward from the derivativeness of the earlier vision are *Welsh Farm*[34] and *Harvester and Bird in a Cornfield*.[35]

The first of these is at first deceptively straightforward. The figure of a young man shouldering a pitch-fork is seen in profile in the foreground. The eye is then drawn upward to the gable-end wall of a limewashed stone farmhouse which stands just offset to the right of the centre of the image. To its left, the buildings bend stiffly round to form three sides of a quadrangle, their rectilinear shapes softened only by the arched top of a doorway which is amplified in the shape of a tree – or is it the moon? – at the joining of two outbuildings. The stark white is only little modified, given a silvery quality to suggest moonlight on two of the buildings, and replaced by a stark black and khaki-green on the third.

To the right of the central gable-end the landscape is quite different. Where before we are in a world of monochrome and geometrical regularity, here we are in a land of dynamic curves and rich organic colours. A mud-ochre track sweeps across from the right and then recedes beside the farmhouse, flanked by dark green and purple trees. Brighter ochres and green-blues suggest water or lighter vegetation at the edge of the canvas.

The composition might easily appear split into two unrelated sections remarkable for their stylistic difference. The buildings on the left are almost a parody of Ben Nicholson's playful *Painting 1937*,[36] with its circling motion controlled by the colour and size of a series of rectangles; the organic forms to the right, a version of Sutherland's *Entrance to a Lane*, with its dynamic curves and play of light and shade. Yet there is no such schism: the painting succeeds as a unity for several reasons. At the most literal, referential level it is held together by swathes of deep greens across the foreground, and the luminous yellows and browns of the courtyard paving. A pattern of colour is also used to hold the composition together. The blue-purple of the trees in the far distance at the right is taken up by the jersey worn by the man in the foreground, and the door of the building at the left margin, leading the eye backwards and forwards within the depth of the painting as well as across its width: and the red rectangle of the door in the centre both balances this and acts as a sharp division between the built, human environment of the farm and the organic one of the countryside at the right. There are also rhythmic forces: a series of variations on the rectangle is formed by the doors and doorways, the farmhouse walls and the hipped roofs, with further extensions in the semi-circular arches of the doorway and moon- tree figure. This rhythm is balanced by the free, dynamic sweeps of the right-hand side, and the whole is poised by the calming, static planes of the foreground and the still figure of the farmer.

All of this is very significant in the overall effect of the work as a whole: what is happening here is that the painting presents its landscape in terms more familiar from an abstract composition of shape and colour. In so doing, it is part of a technique which can be found in many of the finest works of English Romantic art. Cotman, for example in *Greta Bridge, Yorkshire*,[37] uses a system of arches, circles and rectangles to create a similarly abstract pattern within a representational context; Stubbs uses a mixture of dynamic rhythm and stage tableau to present his own highly idealised view of Arcady in *Haymakers*[38] and *The Reapers*.[39] And in so doing, all allow us to see the landscape in wholly new, non-referential terms, as a counterpoint to the experiential intensity which the reorganisation of landscape into such patterns itself represents. This is something we have already encountered as underlying the appeal of Romanticism for many forties painters, but here it is presented with an astringent purity that is original and vigorous, very different from the influence of Palmer's rhythmic forms on the earlier work of Craxton. In this painting, the quality allows us both to share the experience and to observe it as something radically distant from us. In using this approach, Craxton is both continuing the tradition of earlier Romantic painters, extending it by his freer use of abstraction to take account of the developments of the nineteen-thirties; and he is also allowing us to see the relationship between farmer, farmhouse and countryside as part of a new rhythm, something related to earlier visions but nonetheless strictly contemporary. There is no visionary intensity, no statement of biological renewal; but instead there is an awareness of place and involvement which develops earlier traditions and reveals the unity between man and land through the most basic of painterly techniques – colour and form. Even the most apparently abstract patterns, it seems to suggest, can be subsumed into this system of nature: Romantic unity is possible, through the land, even in a world of modernism and threat. This is no retreat into Romanticism; it is a genuine and strong extension of a tradition, full of vigour and hope.

Harvester and Bird in a Cornfield is different in style, lacking the precise line and careful balance of *Welsh Farm*. Yet it develops the earlier painting's quality of presenting figure and landscape as an abstract rhythm, further reducing the referential elements by using only two tonal planes, the yellow-ochre-brown of the figures and land and the deep blue of the sky. Instead of the recognisable figures of farmer and farmhouse, the painting uses exaggerated forms which recall the profiles of Picasso's *Guernica*.[40] This is important in itself: there is a strong element of European modernism which allows the painting to broaden and revitalise the British landscape tradition as well as to continue it. This newer freedom in the definition of forms also gives the painting its most significant effect: the profiled head of the harvester in the foreground appears as a parallel expression of the landforms to the left. Dark and threatening, these suggest sudden outcrops of rock in a desert, an impression heightened by the sand-yellow of the land before them. Between these two natural forms stretches the land itself – presumably the cornfield of the title – above which rises the figure of a bird, beak open and legs apart, apparently rising in panic having been disturbed by the harvester.

The quality of the landforms; the rapid action of the bird; and the sombre intensity of the scene, made sinister by the sensuously deep blue sky and shadowy moonlight, all suggest a relationship of disquiet between the separate elements. Yet there *is* a relationship between them; man and landform are drawn together by their profiles, and we are left feeling that the figure is in some way involved with the natural world. There is no simple or clear explanation for this; but figure and land exist as a unity, disturbing because of its newness of vision as much as its incomplete, unexplained quality. Once again Craxton has taken a Romantic stance and modified it; the response to contemporary uncertainties has created an uncertain bond between human and natural forms in a painting which has a direct engagement quite absent from the work of Ayrton and Collins. Unity and regeneration are in sight.

III

Craxton's exploration of the relationship between humankind and the natural world is not limited to the kind of suggestions made through spatial rhythms and tonal linkings in the two paintings just discussed. It goes further than this, to contribute to what may be seen as one of the more widespread stylistic approaches of the period, generally known as biomorphism. In different forms this can be seen not only in the work of Craxton but also in Graham Sutherland – who may be said to have first used and developed the stance – and, in a terrifyingly negative way, Francis Bacon. It is also possible to see in one or two of Paul Nash's paintings of the war years a personal development of biomorphism which embraces his own surrealist nature and his interest in Celtic myth. In literary forms it includes writing as diverse as the polemic of Cyril Connelly[41] and the early poems of Philip Larkin;[42] and, as the final section of this chapter makes clear, it is not unrelated to the most compassionate statements of renewal which may be seen in Henry Moore and T. S. Eliot.

This is far more than a stylistic mannerism: it is a suggestion, through the use of figures which combine animal and human features, of the commonality of the created, organic world which develops and extends the Romantic notion of the place of humankind within the living world. Only rarely is this a positive or comforting awareness; most often it suggests a disturbing, animal nature within apparently sentient beings, or a writhing towards human power without moral responsibility in animal life forms. Lacking explicit moral statement, it rests on the uncertainty of a time when the 'humane-ness' of humanity as both everyday reality and moral concept is seriously in doubt. Forms are ambiguous in both their literal and metaphysical states. If human, animal and vegetative life forms are combined by this view it is not within a divinely ordered pattern of hierarchy in the Boethian mould, nor is humanity placed in stewardship as in the Miltonic paradise. Instead, the whole is reduced to the uncertain, arbitrary processes of the chance multiplication of cells, in which before the onlooker's uncertain sight tree boughs shift into threatening jaws, rocks into malformed human torsos, shells into skulls. Visually liberating, the style is often physically and morally disturbing to the onlooker; yet there is at times within it a notion of growth and renewal in which the genetic processes of human change are seen as united with and symbolised in vegetative nature and, as in earlier periods of turmoil and dismay, the natural world is seen as the only way forward in a time of human self-immolation.

The stance is first discernible in Sutherland's work of the late thirties. The return to an 'object' signalled by Piper and Grigson[43] was in a sense irrelevant to Sutherland, or at most a public announcement of something that had been going on in his work ever since his flirtation with Palmeresque engravings had allowed him to create his own free vision of the natural world and its 'objects'. But these are objects seen both through the filter of personal experience inevitable and unavoidable in a post-Romantic world, and through an awareness of the abstract qualities of real shapes made more insistent by the Surrealist exhibition of 1936 and the painter's own sensitivity towards the rhythmic, spatial and abstract qualities of shapes in the natural world which as we have seen is never far away from a lot of older English Romantic painting.

Both the graphic work, such as *The Garden*, and the paintings, such as *Entrance to a Lane*, show the combination of referential form and purely abstract relationship which embodies the new 'object' suggested by Piper and Grigson, along with a tautness of texture and colour which has a purely aesthetic meaning: they are both self-defining and referential in the manner of the finest English Romantic paintings. This allows the onlooker to see the natural world being presented as familiar but distant, a world which we are a part of yet apart from: we are seeing the world almost as a wholly different set of species and genera. It is this quality which is developed in the latter into something we can more properly call biomorphic because the 'object' is referential in a deliberately confused, unclear manner. Sometimes the confusion is vague and threatening, as familiar natural objects become sinister, imprecisely symbolising an evil which is never made explicit; sometimes it is positive in an unexpected and moving way, showing a new natural relationship, a kind of twentieth-century visual *discordia concors* which offers us some hope of a way out of the immediate physical and moral impasse.

This first strand, the threatening ambivalence of natural forms, is first seen in work of the late thirties, in particular *Gorse on a Sea Wall*.[44] The central feature of the composition is a tendril of gorse which spirals out towards the onlooker, culminating in three spiky prongs; it stands against a minimal suggestion of a wall, while the background which we might otherwise assume to be sky is divided vertically into a sickly ochre and a deep muddy red. The impression is of a fragment of the natural world presented quite devoid of its habitual significance; in its lack of clear referential 'meaning' the image is far removed both from the rather decorative idea of the seashore as an assemblage of *objets trouvées* fashionable in some circles in the thirties and from a clinically observed botanical drawing. But most important is the fact that it is also a long way from the traditional experienced landscape of Romantic painting. There is no world view here which includes the artist and onlooker in a single vision of creation: instead there is one fragment, undefined in form and devoid of context, of which neither onlooker nor artist can offer a convincing single reading.

This quality is shown in the painting by the ambivalence of form. The gorse curls towards us in a spiral which is surely organic but cannot easily be categorised within the plant kingdom, which cannot be human yet has haunting human qualities. The three prongs at the end of the tendril are surely fingers, and elegant ones too; yet their elongation and their number argue logically against this reading. A doctor acquaintance of Sutherland's saw in the painting the form of the inner ear;[45] yet the formal arguments for this are belied by scale, colouration and texture. We are shown a form which is neither vegetative nor human, having the attributes and potential of both and the definition and context of neither: the result is deeply disturbing since, as with Elizabethan images of the fractured chain of being, the whole relationship between mankind and the natural world is called into question by this view which presents the human-vegetative as a wholly new, unexplained and morally undefined species.

Much the same response is evoked in other paintings of the same period. *Midsummer Landscape*[46] is at once an enlarged root-form given animal dynamism by the shoots running out at right angles from it, and a grotesquely enlarged ganglion; the vortex of the sky adds to the dynamic effect of the protruding shoots, yet there is no sense in which these shoots convey a sense of life or vigour in their movement. One is tempted to say that if there is energy here it is the energy of the *Totentanz*, but even that is too positive because too specific; the effect is again increased because it is general and imprecise, aided by the ambivalent scale of the painting. Are we standing before a large felled tree which recedes alongside a road, or kneeling to examine a fragment torn from ground supporting small plants and fungi? The same qualities dominate *Green Tree Form: Interior of Woods*.[47] Here the central figure is a bough which lunges across and towards us like a limb wrenched from its socket; the surrounding green gives no suggestion of size, and its lush, sensuous colour and texture deepens both the threat and the suffering of the torn limb by the contrast it presents. It is a grisly parody of Marvell's 'Green thought in a green shade', suggesting only violence and corporeal – and, by implication, spiritual – mutation and decay. The wash drawing *Blasted Oak*[48] is disturbing in a different way; whereas *Green Tree Form* owes much of its power to the discord between the threatening, suffering shape and the sensual background, the drawing makes its effect by presenting a figure which is both uprooted tree and a malformed beast with nothing but a gaping mouth and single claw. It is line which is the vehicle here; the image it presents is again imprecise in scale, devoid of context and symbolic of anguish both suffered and inflicted. In all these images there is no defined place for the onlooker: we strive for a context, a wider view, but are given only the immediate, unexplained forms. The Romantic unity of vision has been replaced by a reworking of another Romantic element; particularity and uncertainty, and the confusion of immediate experience.

Sutherland's biomorphism attracted its imitators. Craxton produced some work in this area, most notably the large oil *Welsh Estuary Foreshore.*[49] The crucial difference is that here we are offered a coherent view of a landscape, with recognisably receding forms, foreground and background, so that conceivably we may regard it as an extreme form of the experiential landscape. The lack of definition of the Sutherlands, their uncertain scale and incongruous juxtaposition of textures – all the key elements which give the images their peculiar quality – are absent here, and Craxton's painting becomes an English abstract landscape seen through the filter of *Guernica*. It is the same qualities which make Craxton's other significant biomorphic work of this period, his illustrations to Geoffrey Grigson's anthology *The Poet's Eye,*[50] similarly unsuccessful when compared with Sutherland's work. The cover vignette, showing a curled stone with a curved recess at one end and a circular eye at the other resting on a roughly ploughed landscape, seems to resemble more a parody of prevailing styles in English art, with references to Barbara Hepworth and Henry Moore's sculptural forms as well as to the post-Picasso school of portraitists. As with Ayrton, there is a problem of approach here; the work establishes neither a seriousness of tone nor a clear statement of parodic wit, hovering uncomfortably between the two. The same is true of the illustrations within the volume; too explicitly human for the menace of Sutherland's biomorphs, they offer a confusion and uncertainty of a far less intense kind than the works which are surely their point of origin.

To find something of the stature of Sutherland's biomorphic forms in the work of other artists we need to move to an unlikely source, Paul Nash. After his involvement with Surrealism in the thirties, Nash had returned at the beginning of the war to employment as war artist. Two aspects of his work from this period are relevant: the landscapes which use natural forms expanded and developed to vast proportions produced by the converging of the Surrealist and Celtic strands of his painting; and the larger canvases which he produced as a war artist. The former are discussed in the next section of this chapter; of the latter, three stand out as significant contributions to the art of the time. *The Battle of Britain*[51] uses the Romantic convention of experiential landscape to place us both within the battle and outside it; we see the events from an aerial viewpoint, yet from a considerable horizontal distance. The result of this is striking: instead of the uncertain, formalised stance of a detached viewpoint in Charles Cundall's *The Retreat from Dunkirk* we are presented with a view of the events as an abstract pattern, the vapour trails of the sky balancing the serpentine form of the river beneath and forming a strange frozen choreography which records the movements of the battle. *The Battle of Germany*[52] takes the process of abstraction still further, offering a pattern dominated by a central pall of smoke separating two areas of landscape, the whole united by motifs such as the pale circles familiar from Nash's surrealist works of the thirties[53] and ambiguous shapes suggesting vegetation in the foreground. Here the impression is not of threatening biomorphs or destructive military action, but rather of seeing events from a very great distance: the idea of an experienced landscape is taken to extreme lengths as we seem to see things *sub specie aeternitatis*, almost in the manner of Greek tragedy or a Hardy novel.[54] Both use Romantic convention in a new and striking way: they are among the most important compositions of the war for this reason, perhaps the only two which present mid-century battle in an idiom which is both totally contemporary and clinically detached – a lack of involvement which is strangely also apparent, in many different forms, in artists of far less originality through the war years in the form of a clinical, almost diagrammatic, style.[55] Perhaps it is another part of the tentative quality so often seen in the art of the time.

Nash's most forcefully original composition of the war years, which will perhaps ultimately be judged as one of the greatest images of any artist recording or commenting on the war, is his *Totes Meer*.[56] At the time of this painting Nash was fascinated by the fuselages of crashed German aircraft massed at a salvage dump at Cowley near Oxford and took many photographs[57] of the arbitrarily suggestive forms they adopted. In *Follow the Fuhrer. Above the Clouds*,[58] Nash had shown the relationship between a bomber aircraft and a predatory mammal by inserting the figure of a shark into a formation of German bombers; in *Totes Meer* he reverses the surreal association by placing the fuselages on the ground to form the waves of the dead sea of the title. The composition is sparse: to the right a beach extends into the far distance where, on the horizon, can be seen a thin line of hills with a few trees. Above them the moon, crescent yet discernibly a full sphere, stands pale and thin. The whole of the rest of the painting is taken up by wave-forms of broken fuselages and wings, which cross and merge in various stages of decomposition. In the right foreground the thinning of texture, with wings devoid of their surface cladding and now just a construction of ribs and spars, suggests waves breaking on a shore, an impression heightened by what seems to be a thin line of spray caused by the decomposing spars, and the yellow colour of the land. The painting's recessive movement is created by the interplay between the distant moon at the top left and an aircraft tail wheel near the bottom centre; the eye is drawn back and forth between these two, both to create depth and also to point the contrast between organic and metallic substance, created and built forms, enduring and decaying matter. At the far right, some way back along the shore, some seagulls circle, giving further depth and adding to the feeling of organic decay. The whole is unified by the dominant coloration, a thin, ghostly blue-silver, suggesting moonlight but also echoing the unreality of the scene.

At one level the painting is an elaborate visual pun, the metallic forms paralleling wave-forms in a manner that is clean, mechanical and totally in accord with surrealist ideas about form and meaning, and furthers that movement's preference for man-made rather than organic structures. Yet at another it is inevitably suggestive of the immensely destructive forces of warring humanity, wasteful of resources as well as of life, in comparison to the eternal cyclical processes of nature, represented by one of the oldest of all symbols in the moon and the tides. The title, too, is hardly neutral: *Totes Meer* suggests desolation of the spirit as well as of the forms presented. Is there a suggestion, though, that the decay of the aircraft is in itself something positive and progressive, with the crests of the wings and fuselages gradually merging with the crests and hollows of the landscape? Perhaps the presence of the seagulls suggests this, as scavengers suggestive of animal renewal; the recessive depth of the painting also implies a three-dimensional landscape, something frequently rejected or playfully distorted in the more overtly surreal paintings of the thirties – *Harbour and Room*,[59] say, or *Landscape from a Dream*[60] – but the presence of which may imply growth and renewal. The title argues for the former view; but even if we take it as a totally negative reading of human destruction, Nash's use of a natural landscape as the vehicle of the metaphor is powerfully innovative, a personal view of biomorphism which takes the Romantic tradition of experienced landscape and reverses it to make a statement that is both involved yet distanced, compassionate yet as intellectually witty and cynical in its own way as the painter's much earlier vision of war, *We are making a New World*.[61]

There is one further work to consider in this tentative canon of biomorphism as an ironic form of contemporary Romanticism. In 1945, Francis Bacon had made his own violent, disturbing parody of all the ideas of unity between humanity and nature in his forcefully literal *Figure in a Landscape*,[62] in which a figure dissolves into the rock-face behind it. This angry rejection of earlier nature-visions is also shown in the anguished *Three studies for figures at the base of a Crucifixion*.[63] Here the biomorphism of Sutherland's earlier form reaches an almost unbearable intensity. The three separate panels each depicts a half-human, half-animal form whose dominant feature is its mouth. Origins of the figures have been identified as Picasso's pre-war biomorphs, and the photographs of screaming mouths by J. A. Boiffard.[64] To this we should add Bacon's more personal concerns – with the textures of raw meat, with the theme of the dictator, and with the technical details of dentistry and orthodontics. But these are of secondary consideration – all is of secondary consideration before these screaming mutant forms, whose emotional intensity is raised by the untempered orange of their backgrounds. They have been seen as the pursuing furies of the *Oresteia*, as victims of Auschwitz, as mutants procreated at Hiroshima; they are all these, in a soundless, inarticulate scream of mid-century suffering, both victim and torturer, extending the 'superhuman inhumanities'[65] of which Wilfred Owen spoke in an earlier war to levels which can find no expression in habitual or familiar terms. Again the title is significant. These are too tentative to be complete figures, but instead are only studies; they are at the base of a crucifixion, not the crucifixion itself, hinting at even greater barbarism; and it is *a* crucifixion, not *the* crucifixion, so that any hope of Christian renewal and redemption is lacking. The triptych, the age-old form of devotional paintings and altar-pieces reflecting in its very structure the renewing and redemptive qualities of the trinity, is here bitterly ironic: there is no hope for the future, only the endless agony of the present in the scream of torturer and tortured. Bacon, like Sutherland and Nash, is using biomorphic forms to reject all of the familiar patterns of unity and renewal in the natural world developed by the Romantics; but the use of such devices to express pain is in itself a stance which can only be seen as a modification of the Romantic displacement to meet the desperate exigencies of the mid-century. Lacking the order of a narrative, they embody rather than chronicle. The spiritual anguish of the first Romantics has become terribly real: these contorted natural forms offer no hope in the natural world for a society which has outraged the natural order at Auschwitz and Dresden.

IV

The biomorphism of Sutherland and Bacon is only one version of the Romantic equation which lies heavy on the minds of artists and writers of the forties. Those images of disturbance and distress are balanced by stances which, though often tentative, are ultimately more hopeful. Not all biomorphic forms are negative and threatening; there are some which show a unity between humankind and the natural world which is both positive and regenerative. The work of Ceri Richards provides examples of biomorphism as a dynamic, almost turbulent force of renewal through the natural world; and there are other works which make far bolder statements about the hope of organic renewal through the land, for example John Minton's *Recollections of Wales* which was discussed in Chapter 2.

The sense of oneness between humanity and nature is shown with great vigour in Richards' *Cycle of Nature*.[66] The left of the canvas is dominated by animal figures – a horse or centaur which gallops to the left, its head turned back to face across the plane of the painting, and a curious bird figure, whose small head is almost that of a crowned human in some neo-classical emperor's portrait. In the centre, unidentifiable animal forms writhe, apparently trying to struggle out of the picture's plane. To the right, forms representative of generation proliferate: pistils, stamens, a bunch of grapes, shapes suggestive of vaginae and phalloi crowd in, and there is a hint of landscape in the green form at the right upper quarter. The whole seethes against a background of deep, pure blue sky and the colour and texture of stone below the horizon; Richards makes far more use of the textures of paint than does Sutherland, and the result is that the dynamism of the composition is given a further dimension, both literally and in terms of the greater sense of life this gives, a significant move away from the flat uses of colour which add to the still menace of the other artist's biomorphs. We are not far away here from the world of David Jones's 'prize Maria Hunt', the teeming procreative universe which continues despite all other intellectual and moral movements – or their absence – and which can be seen elsewhere in, say, the Pompey Bum scenes of *Measure for Measure*. In the context of forties Romanticism there is an exuberance here which is something new and startling; it may well lack a serious engagement with reality, as do the paintings of Michael Ayrton, but for wholly appropriate reasons, to create a harmony of idea and idiom these lack. It is embodying dynamic and exhilarating generation and growth rather than suggesting unclear notions of rebirth or chill moral stasis.

A different vision of the equation between humanity and nature is seen in Richards' *Welsh Landscape*.[67] The landscape is a line of chalk cliffs, texturally full and undulating in colour between rich, pink stone and darker greys in an extension of the lighting effects familiar in Welsh coastal areas. In the foreground lies a shape which is at first ambivalent, sharing as it does the coloration of the cliffs and being presented in an extremely foreshortened form. The figure soon reveals itself as the naked body of a woman, who lies with one hand at the back of her head and the other outstretched at her side, while the legs and feet extend thinly up shore. The blue-lilac of the sky is repeated in two patches in the foreground, perhaps cushions or towels, the square shape of that on the right stressing by contrast the flowing outlines of both body and landscape.

The symbolic significance of this painting is not precise, and we risk diminishing it by tethering it to something explicit. Yet the woman's body within a landscape suggests birth and renewal, the fish-like qualities implying a kind of rebirth from the sea. The shared tonality of woman and land extend this into a notion of renewal in all creation, and the circling form caused by the head, shoulders and outstretched arms is reminiscent of a natural spiral or vortex. It is too fanciful to relate it to an ammonite or the vortex used by Blake to suggest organic states,[68] but it does have some of the qualities of these. What is perhaps most striking is the placidity of the painting in comparison with *Cycle of Nature*. Frenzy has given place to calm, yet the unity between humankind and the organic world is in no way diminished; perhaps the calm adds an element of confidence to the relationship. Comparison with Sutherland's pre-war Welsh landscapes[69] is also revealing; for all their organic shapes and compassionate depiction of contours, these are still 'abstract' enough to omit any figures, with the exception of *Welsh Landscape with Roads*[70] – though even here the concern is more with rhythm and texture – and so do not postulate the kind of unity between humankind and the natural world that Richards suggests through structure, texture and tonality.

Richards' suggestion of this sort of unity is an extension of the Romantic idea of union which is perhaps particularly coloured by the artist's Celtic origins, and this is something which recurs in different forms in much of the more significant work of the time. David Jones's use of Welsh language and Welsh legend in the expression and structure of *In Parenthesis* is clear; so too is Richards' place within the mainstream of Welsh art and thought, perhaps most particularly so in his treatments of passages and themes from the poetry of another major Celtic artist, Dylan Thomas. Yet I do not think that Celticism *per se* is the most fundamental feature of the work of either of these; with them as with other artists whose work is discussed in the next few pages, Celticism or an awareness of ancient traditional links with the land is only one constituent of the idea of unity with the land as a regenerative force, one of a series of filaments which merge to give the fabric its final colour and shape.

This is perhaps best shown in the work of Paul Nash. Nash's output during the war years covers a bewildering range of style and medium. It includes landscapes in oil or watercolour which seem to continue his more traditional vein of the twenties; the synthesis of surreal and Romantic in *Totes Meer*; symbolic collages such as *The Rose of Death*;[71] and visions of landscape which combine ancient tumuli with a sense of the sacred places outside time in primeæval societies. These last are the most significant in terms of the relationship with nature they present, drawing together as they do elements of Druidic history, the ancient form of the landscape modified by tumuli and standing stones, the ideas gained from his reading of works of anthropology and the artist's own developing style linking surrealism with the indigenous landscape tradition to make a very precise and very personal statement within the larger context of Romantic regeneration of the war years.

Cumulus Head[72] illustrates well the change in Nash's approach to landscape which is visible in the last years of his life, in particular his synthesis of surrealist imagery with the more traditional, lyrical treatments of natural forms always present at one level or another in his work. Using the larger blocks of colour and freer textures of *Battle of Germany*, Nash here shows a form which is part cloud, part woman's head, above a thin line of sea and surrounded by further clouds which are more naturalistic. It has been compared with Odilon Redon's *Les Yeux Clos*,[73] and perhaps also owes something in its concept to René Magritte's use of cloud forms.[74] Certainly it reveals that European Surrealism has become absorbed completely into his work and linked with native idioms to a degree, and in a style, which is apparent in the work of no other English painter of his generation. But what is perhaps more striking is the way in which human and organic forms are combined. In the last years of his life Nash became progressively obsessed with the mystical and philosophical nature of flight, almost seeing it as the perfect human goal. Seen in this context, the painting becomes a kind of spiritual assumption painting, replacing the classical idea of apotheosis into heaven with Nash's personal ideas about flight. There is also a more specific symbolism: the human head becomes part of a natural cycle in the process of irrigation it joins, existing as a cloud as part of the regenerative cycle represented by the sea, the sky and the clouds. The ancient mythic significance of the sea as bringer of life and death, with the ideas of death by water and its associated practices in early societies, is something with which Nash would have been familiar from his reading of Frazer's *Golden Bough*.[75]

Over the next few years Nash's work undergoes a coming together which unites several strands which at first seem separate, but which in the last paintings are revealed as components of a larger fabric, and this fabric itself a development of the idea of unity between humanity and the natural world which is a very personal development of the outlook of English Romanticism. One of these strands concerns ancient places, in which Nash had been interested almost since the beginning of his career as a painter when Wittenham Clumps began to fascinate him. *Chesil Bank, Abbotsbury*[76] suggests one of these ancient places in a general way, also asserting cyclical continuity in the contrast between the aged tree at the foreground and the young sapling in the centre. *Maiden Castle*[77] gives a feeling of oneness with a much older landscape, reproducing the contours of the ancient mound and presenting it with the immediacy of a Romantic experiential landscape. Yet both of these lack intensity and completeness: Nash has not yet attained the final synthesis of his view of the natural world and its processes.

The same is true of the two *Sunflower and Sun*[78] paintings dating from 1942. Of these, the first and larger is the more striking. Executed in the style familiar from *Battle of Germany* and other paintings, with a much bolder use of colour and form than is found in many of Nash's oils, it presents a landscape simplified into large blocks of colour. On the horizon stand the Wittenham Clumps, but the composition is dominated by two linked figures, the sun in the top right and the figure of a sunflower, just unfolding its head from the seed, in the foreground of the painting. These are held together by a beam of sunlight which shafts diagonally down from the sun across the composition. The symbolic suggestion is clear: the sun regenerates life in the form of the sunflower, which is being drawn up out of the earth by the power of light and heat. The Clumps show that this is a timeless process; their presence reminds us that this is going on now just as it did thousands of years ago, adding a quality of stasis to the essentially dynamic process of natural growth. This paradox of stillness and renewal is something which Nash is not alone in using as an extension of the Romantic view of nature and its cycles.

It is not only the sun which has a part to play in Nash's cycle: the moon is also crucial. This is shown clearly in *November Moon*.[79] Once again the composition is dominated by related circles, here one aerial and two others terrestrial, in the moon and a pair of mushrooms which rest on a low terrace wall at the very front of the painting. To the left, the chill, chalky moonlight shines over an avenue of trees; to the right, warmer tones predominate. But in the chill light there is little suggestion of renewal, and the mushrooms, being fungi, suggest decrepitude rather than renewal. We may infer that they, too, are part of the cycle of nature, and that for Nash the cold of autumn and winter as much as fungal decay is a necessary stage in the growth towards spring; but there is little open statement of this in the canvas and the predominant feeling is one of a rather eerie stillness which almost suggests the dispassionate cool of his thirties landscapes.

The synthesis of these elements, and of Nash's view of the natural cycle, is arrived at in two final paintings, *Landscape of the Summer*

Solstice[80] and *Landscape of the Vernal Equinox*.[81] Both of these draw together the idea of a natural cycle with the notion of ancient places, by stressing the stage in the cycle at which the landscape is experienced as a key point in ancient views of nature. The first of these paintings again shows Wittenham Clumps, in semi-abstract blocks of colour on the horizon. Before this, at the very edge of the plane of the painting in the manner familiar from the preceding canvases, stand wild flowers, primarily St John's Wort. These are important as native wild flowers, and St John's Day is close to the date of the summer solstice; but there is a deeper significance. Nash was fascinated by the idea of Balder, the ancient earth spirit representing the life force equivalent to the sun, whose death each year was necessary for the subsequent coming of spring in one of many folk explanations of the necessity of winter. Frazer makes mention in *Balder the Beautiful*,[82] which Nash knew well, of the ceremony of the St John's Day fire in Baden, in which the height of the flames is supposed to predict the height of the crops of the following year. Thus in the painting the wild flowers suggest both the fires and the crops themselves, and so there is the suggestion of the coming together of succeeding stages of the cycle. The familiar rhythm of distant exchange between sun and flower emphasises the separateness as well as the unity of the two extremes: the cycle is both still and dynamic, synchronic and diachronic, in the frozen choreography of the painting.

There is one further element of importance in the choice of the solstice. Traditionally Midsummer's Day is the longest day of the year when the sun stands still in the sky, hence the word *solstice*: the painting thus represents both the unity of this season and the next, and an instant outside time. And as such it is the successor to Constable's *Landscape: Noon*: a moment of experience created as much as recorded by the artist, showing his unity with the created world and the cyclical quality of its processes, yet something which is outside time because of its frozen nature as paint on canvas. Nash is developing and extending the Romantic stance very clearly, combining it with his own concerns about natural resurgence and using an idiom which, in its free delight in the use of large blocks of colour and impasto techniques, is a twentieth-century extension of Constable's own free oil technique in the so-called 'sketches' for the six-foot canvases.

Cyclical process are clear, too, in the companion painting, *Landscape of the Vernal Equinox*. Here the process is reversed: the Clumps are shown here at the season when night equals day, the nadir which prefigures the coming of high summer and the full richness of the natural world. Once more the time is precisely fixed: we share a moment which is directly experienced yet also outside time. And in both of these paintings the present and the past coalesce, as we become part of the ancient landscape of Wittemham Clumps.

Eclipse of the Sunflower[83] and *Solstice of the Sunflower*[84] follow the same pattern in more compressed terms. In the first, the sun is eclipsed by the moon as the sunflower on the earth beneath falls to the ground in a tense concentration of the idea of the equinox; in the second, a vast sunflower cuts swathes through a field of corn to symbolize the sun's rays nurturing the crops through light and heat, while the sun seems, in Nash's own words, to be 'whipping the Sunflower like a top'.[85] This is the blessing and nurturing of midsummer fire; the two discs of sun and sunflower are united, and the cycle of growth and rebirth completed. Ancient myths of natural renewal are recreated in twentieth-century idiom, time present linked with time past and all united in the Romantic experiential landscape: Nash's vision is complete.

Both Richards and Nash modify Romantic ideas of continuity and renewal through landscape in their own very different idioms, which relate them each in their own way to contemporary, post- abstract styles. But although they both offer a way of coming to terms with the insistent issue of death and suffering, they might seem to a casual observer to retreat from the literal reality of that suffering since they do not present its most frequent site, the modern city.

A vision of natural regeneration which includes the city is much rarer, but it is not totally without the spectrum of forties Romanticism rebirth of the art of this time. It is this vision which lifts the blitz paintings of Graham Sutherland above those which seek merely to record or recreate the experience, uniting as they do the intensity of literal visions of the blitz and the imaginative tension of the earlier biomorphic studies, transforming the latter from frighteningly negative treatments of the organic world into statements of renewal which, both within their immediate contexts and when seen at a greater distance, remain some of the most insistently original Romantic imagery of the war years. That Sutherland should develop a vision of such a kind can be explained in various ways at a literal level. At the start of the war he entered the employ of the WAAC, shortly after having evolved the richly Romantic style of the Welsh landscapes familiar from *Entrance to a Lane* and the deeply disturbed view of nature in his biomorphic work. If we add to this the undoubted representational skills in depicting buildings within landscapes that are familiar from the etchings of the twenties, it becomes apparent that he is uniquely equipped to provide such a vision. At first he was given separate commissions to paint RAF bombers – 'I couldn't make much of them, I'm afraid'[86] – but was then employed as a war artist to record the effects of the bombing, first in Swansea and then in London. That he had immediate and comparatively unrestricted access to the sites of most complete devastation[87] is worth stressing, because it shows that his images of this time rest directly on personal experience which was then transformed by his imagination in the manner made clear in his 'Welsh Sketchbook' article.[88] These are no retreats from reality; they show once again how forties Romanticism is a direct and immediate comment on the experience of its age.

Sutherland's achievement in this area is most apparent in the series of paintings each bearing the title *Devastation* which he completed in London in 1941. As his biomorphic paintings show the uncertain, menacing qualities of unidentifiable natural forms, so these paintings show how the forms of wrecked buildings may adopt shapes which are apparently organic, and so unite built and growing environments, human and natural worlds, to offer some hope of organic renewal. Sutherland himself made clear the nature of this way of seeing:

> gradually it was borne on me amid all this destruction how one shape would impinge itself on another. A lift-shaft, for instance, the only thing left from what had obviously been a very tall building: in the way it had fallen it was like a wounded animal. It wasn't that these forms *looked* like animals, but their movements were animal movements. One shaft in particular, with a very strong lateral fall, suggested a wounded tiger in a painting by Delacroix.[89]

The parallel with Delacroix is significant: not only does it show Sutherland's interest in the relation between movement and line in organic and mechanical forms, but also points to larger similarities of composition. Many of the wartime works have the kind of turbulent, swirling lines one associates with Delacroix's most theatric compositions and the fact that they depict mechanic, not organic, structures, shows Sutherland's interest in uniting the two areas of experience.

The exact reference in this passage is a little confusing, as it seems more likely to refer to a lion than a tiger, most probably the animal in the foreground of *Lion Hunt*.[90] The painting which most completely resembles the twist of the neck in the lion is *Devastation, 1941, City: Fallen Lift Shaft*.[91] Here the shaft of metal girders is flung upward and falls towards the onlooker in a parabola exactly echoing that of the neck of Delacroix's lion. Its shape dominates the composition, the rest of the image consisting only of rubble and darkness. It is a metallic equivalent of the earlier biomorphs, though it is in no way mechanical. In those, Sutherland used flat colours as backgrounds to emphasise the uncertainty of the organic form: here, he uses sketchy, incomplete bodies of colour and free, bravura brush work to suggest the organic movement of what is otherwise an inorganic form – since, although the shaft's movement is curved, it is square in section and composed of metal girders. A balance and fusion is achieved between the constructed and the organic.

Much the same is true of *Devastation, 1941, City; Twisted Girders (1)*.[92] Here the girders burst from the centre of a ruined building, curving frond-like over the remains of its walls in a movement which suggests the trailing tendrils of a plant rather than the mechanical extrusion of metal forms, to give another version of organic growth within a built, urban setting in a sophisticated extension of the simpler idea of renewal seen in images of flowers blooming in bomb-sites. Yet the scene is still recognisably representational and in this painting we may perhaps understand Sutherland's own feeling about his work of this time. He felt that

> he could have purged them of the element of directness and immediacy and arrived at a more detached – not a more abstract – pictorial treatment.[93]

Perhaps the artist comes closer to this ideal in another of the series, *Devastation, City, Twisted Girders*.[94] The ruined building of the background is ambiguous in scale, appearing a single structure one moment and representing the whole blasted skyline of London the next. From the centre and the right-hand side leap thick girders, which then twist and curve right across and towards the painting's surface, the larger culminating in a jagged tear which is almost a metallic equivalent of the jaw in *Blasted Oak*. Beneath the span of these two larger girders, several smaller ones are twisted together. Their shapes and the pale yellow colouration suggest a natural object, perhaps the calyx of a flower, and once more the effect of the earlier biomorphs is reversed: instead of a natural object made threatening there is something metallic made organic. Romantic experiential landscape is here linked with an idea of renewal through nature in the city: it is a daring use of Sutherland's semi-abstract ideas of landscape to suggest that there is some possibility of organic growth even in the city.

Sutherland's most daring use of the idea of renewal comes in a painting which differs from the three so far discussed. From the office blocks of the city it turns to a typical street at the centre of London docks; perhaps the shift is significant, suggesting a Romantic concern for the everyday experience of the common man. This is important because, like Greene's *Ministry of Fear* and Bowen's 'Mysterious Kôr', it is concerned with human suffering, and not the destruction of the commercial areas of the other *Devastation* pictures; and while those are concerned with the suggested renewal of natural forms, this seems to go further and consider spiritual regeneration.

Devastation: East End Street[95] shows a street of terraced houses in Silvertown reduced to little more than two rows of façades mirroring each other across a rubble-strewn street. The colouration is richly sombre, each terrace being shown in a gold ochre against a night sky and road of muddy greys and browns. Were this the predominant effect, the scene would be merely a latter-day Picturesque close to the style of John Piper; but Sutherland's vision is far less direct. The viewpoint is immediately in front of the receding perspective, rather like the king's vantage point in a perspective set by Inigo Jones, so that the eye is led through the street towards the vanishing point at almost the exact centre of the composition. This placement is unusual; few artists would choose a composition so rigidly symmetrical, and the result is that the image has a mathematical balance about it which contradicts the desolation apparent in the houses themselves, suggesting an order in the midst of desolation. Yet this is not the main function of the perspective, which instead serves to funnel our view towards the end of the street. There, a row of houses which seem to be untouched by the bombing stands in clear white moonlight. Before them, a curved form, compounded of chrysalis and mummy, lies in the road. It has the ambiguity yet none of the menace of Sutherland's earlier biomorphic organisms, and its shape – curved, not rectilinear, created not built – is emphasised by the contrast it forms with the straight lines and rigid angles of the ruined houses. The tonality adds to the contrast, too, the cold white light of the central section, curiously suggestive of a gothic window in shape, marks it off as territory wholly different from the ruined houses. Is this perhaps some embodiment of the spirit liberated from the houses? Does it suggest that natural things live on despite the collapse of the city and the mechanism it represents? Can we perhaps see in this a Blakeian allegory of the release of the creative, organic force from the tyranny of mechanical reason? These questions, let alone any answers we might choose to put to them, are much too explicit: the painting has its effect in the balance of ordered structures and free growths emphasised by its composition and form.

We may choose to view the painting in various ways. It is in one sense a record; in another it is a composition which takes formal balance to the point almost of a wholly abstract painting; and in another it is a vision of some kind of liberation which the blitz brings. Perhaps it is best seen as an unspecified visual parallel to other kinds of release expressed in other ways at the time – release from ordered, constrained existence which the financial security of the war provided;[96] release from the anguish of mental suffering as external circumstances, too, became manic;[97] the release seen by Stephen Spender[98] of the spirit of the builders of the city, although heaven knows there is little enough of the spiritual about a street of terraced houses in Silvertown. Explication is diminution; this is an extraordinary painting in its vision and imagination, Romantic yet wholly contemporary.

Sutherland's use of twisted liftshafts, deformed factory chimneys and spiralling towers of girders show a re-working of the theme of natural rebirth, the turning towards the forms and textures of nature seen so often at a time of mechanistic holocaust. Yet they never seek to escape: in combining the strands of abstracted natural forms and broken mechanical structures they show the artist coming to terms with the destruction and hinting at a kind of regeneracy in which metal and concrete seem to be just as 'organic' as the roots of trees. Just as the many photographs of flowers blooming amid bomb sites show the power of nature to repossess the land, so Sutherland's images show an awareness of the organic beauty which these new forms have been given in their ordeal by fire. It is the fullness of natural processes seen through a twentieth-century sensibility, in which no open hope is given but some synthesis is achieved between created and invented worlds.

V

Perhaps the most explicit and certainly the most daring statement of the creed of renewal through the cycle of natural processes is provided in the poetry of Dylan Thomas. *Deaths and Entrances*[99] conveys the idea of rebirth even in the title, whose source – the sermon known as 'Death's Duel' by John Donne[100] – adds another layer of continuity in its reference to the Anglican tradition. Death is not an ending but a change of state; this assertion is apparent throughout the volume, which works not so much as a gathering of separate poems but as an organic growth of its own towards the state of childlike fulfilment attained at its close in 'Fern Hill'.[101] In the course of this process, the work contains three poems which are closely concerned with the blitz.

'Ceremony after a Fire Raid'[102] seeks to place the death of 'A child of a few hours' within a larger movement of sin, Fall, redemption and praise, referring in its central section to 'the legend/ Of Adam and Eve' which changes at the end into a ceremony which spreads out

> Over the sun's hovel and the slum of fire
> And the golden pavements laid in requiems,
> Into the bread in a wheatfield of flames,
> Into the wine burning like brandy[103]

Here the naturalistic surroundings of Sutherland's slum terrace are conjoined with images of natural renewal which in turn are emblematised in the bread and wine of the host; the renewal is within the organic cycle but it is also part of an established ritual. All is transformed and the 'ceremony' becomes not an occasion of mourning but a rite of passage in which the child is taken up into 'The sundering ultimate kingdom of genesis' thunder'. What begins as a poem of mourning ends as a literary, apocalyptic version of an Assumption painting; the rite of passage becomes an act of redemption in its ceremonial richness.

Assumpta est infans; ite missa est. In Thomas' poems, as in Greene's reference to the sense of dismissal the morning after a raid, there is a mood of taut emotion elevated and transformed into ritual. Not only is this a statement of continuity in the face of surrounding death and destruction; it shows a deep awareness of human needs in mourning, to recognise and express loss but to see these things within a larger process of renewal.

The idea of organic renewal in death is present also in 'Among those killed in the dawn Raid was a Man aged a Hundred'.[104] Its conclusion is a beautifully gentle image of release and renewal:

> The morning is flying on the wings of his age
> And a hundred storks perch on the sun's right hand.

But the process of renewal is by no means easy; we should not be led into thinking that there is no sense of anger within Thomas' attitude towards the dead. *Deaths and Entrances* also contains a poem of great anger at death, 'Do not go gentle into that good night'.[105] The anger is held in check and ritualised by the controlling structure of the villanelle in which the poem is cast, but it is still strongly there in the refrain:

> Do not go gentle into that good night
> Rage, rage against the dying of the light.[106]

This does not negate the sense of progression in the other deaths; it is simply another stage of the process of loss and renewal. First there is anger, then a ritualistic release through a religious ceremony, and finally an awareness of the continuity of the natural cycle.

The most powerful expression of this faith in renewal is given in 'A Refusal to Mourn the Death, by Fire, of a Child in London'.[107] It is a poem of breathtaking risk in its approach to the death of a child, refusing as it does to 'blaspheme down the stations of the breath' or to 'murder/the mankind of her going'. Only when the whole organic cycle has come to an end will the poet mourn: the moment of death is seen as another glorious assumption, in a contemporary parallel to the assumption of the nuns in Hopkins' *The Wreck of the Deutschland*.[108] The poem is a rich texture of images of natural renewal, culminating in the child's ceremonial unification with 'the grains beyond age, the dark veins of her mother'. Thomas is asserting that the child has not suffered death, but a fire-change into a new state within the organic continuity: 'After the first death, there is no other'. This a poem which compresses much of the thought of 'Ceremony after a Fire Raid' into a much tauter statement, linking the *hwyl* of the Welsh sermon – the elevated passion of the preacher – with a sense of great control in the single sustained crescendo of the poem which builds, in a sentence which spans the whole of the first two stanzas, to the climax in the first line of the third.

Taken together, these poems all show a remodelling of a Romantic notion of death and renewal which acknowledges the desolation of loss but turns it into a ritual which is not only psychologically sound but allows for a movement forward. The dead in these poems by Dylan Thomas are the twentieth-century equivalents of the object of the Lucy poems,

> Roll'd round in earth's diurnal course
> With rocks and stones and trees![109]

They are also more than that. Thomas confronts violent, agonising death and comes to terms with it in a way that is a direct confrontation of the immediate circumstances of mid twentieth-century destruction: Romanticism is extended in a literary and a human plane once more.

Thomas' compassion is personal and immediate, treading a narrow line between consolation and hysteria. An approach to the realities of the blitz and a statement of renewal which is no less intense but much more measured and inclusive in its statement of renewal is to be found in the last of T. S. Eliot's *Four Quartets*, 'Little Gidding'.[110] The poem takes its name from the village where, in the seventeenth century, Nicholas Ferrar chose to set up his religious community as a place of meditation and prayer. Simply in making this allusion Eliot is establishing the many-layered significance of the poem. It is concerned with the meditative life, yet one which is placed within the living countryside; it is something from the past, yet is still alive and real; the community and the chapel are both outside time and a part of it. All of these unities are expressed in the first two words of the poem's opening section: 'Midwinter spring'.[111] As the section develops it becomes clear that this is a time of stasis, which is outside the normal sequence of the seasons. Yet, as the very end of the section makes clear, it is both 'Never and always'.[112] The whole of the poem is concerned with this paradox, which is essential to one kind of Romantic perception: Constable's *Landscape: Noon* is a moment outside time, yet it is an intensely perceived moment of actual experience, Wordsworth, Coleridge, Keats and many others deal with states of experience that are visionary in their intensity yet have firm roots in the everyday.

As well as this fusion of stasis and movement, the moment

represents the state of death and loss which is necessary before any renewal may begin, the 'death of water and fire'. This is made explicitly real in contemporary terms in the poem's second section which refers to 'the uncertain hour before the morning'.[113] A spiritual uncertainty, yes, but also a literal one, as those who have endured a night raid are unsure whether at last it has ended. The poem's speaker encounters a wanderer, blown towards him

> like the metal leaves
> Before the urban dawn wind unresisting.[114]

The figure is urban and dispossessed, a remodelling perhaps of Stetson from *The Waste Land*,[115] representing a kind of loss of selfhood which is necessary as part of the movement towards renewal. Eliot combines imagery of organic cycles with that of urban destruction here – the figure is like a leaf, but it is metal, suggesting a fragment of shrapnel from the night's raid on the city. Perhaps there is also an echo of the leaf in the first of the 'Preludes' of 1917.[116] This and the hint of *The Waste Land* are more than incidental examples of Eliot's habitual intertextuality; they are an emblem of continuity of form which makes the ideas instantly familiar yet different, which in itself furthers the idea of self-recognition, development and growth which is important later in the poem. At the end of the section, we have some grasp of the nature of this redemptive change:

> From wrong to wrong the exasperated spirit
> Proceeds, unless restored by that refining fire
> Where you must move in measure, like a dancer[117]

Ceremony is once again important in the change, familiar from earlier Eliot as well as from Thomas; the 'refining fire' is similarly multivalent, suggesting both the purgative processes of Dante and the immediate agonies of the blitz.

In the third section it becomes apparent that the contradictions implicit within the poem from its start are the basis of the movement towards regeneration that it represents: 'Attachment to self and to things and to persons', detachment from all of these, and 'growing between, them, indifference'.[118] These are described in terms of the natural world, as flourishing 'in the same hedgerow'; and there is again a sense both of stillness and of progression, in that memory can allow love to expand beyond desire and so liberate us 'from the future as well as the past'. Here we are very close to the state of illuminatory experience which is fundamental to a great deal of Romanticism – a state which involves both a heightened awareness of ourselves and a loss of self-awareness in unity with the experienced world, and is both part of time because of the deeply felt reality of the experience and outside it because of its unique intensity. In this there is an element of the unity with sacred places of the past which we find in Nash – not surprisingly, since Nash like Eliot drew from Frazer – but Eliot takes things much further towards a cycle of renewal.

The introduction of a passage from Dame Julian's *Revelation of Love* is a part of this renewal, accepting as it does that 'Sin is Behovely' but that 'All shall be well'.[119] It is almost another version of the fortunate Fall. Section I addresses most directly the air raid itself, the 'flame of incandescent terror', but it is 'the dove descending' which produces this, the ancient symbol of the holy spirit, and we are then told that it is Love that 'devised the torment'.[120] All comes together in the final section, which presents the idea of a unity between death and life, then and now, stasis and progress, within a moment of perception in the chapel at Little Gidding expressed as part of a cycle of nature:

> We die with the dying:
> See, they depart, and we go with them.
> We are born with the dead:
> See, they return, and bring us with them.
> The moment of the rose and the yew-tree
> Are of equal duration. A people without history
> Is not redeemed from time, for history is a pattern
> Of timeless moments. So while the light fails
> On a winter's afternoon, in a secluded chapel
> History is now and England.[121]

The very end of the poem states this again, revealing the surrender of selfhood which is necessary before we may attain completeness, as part of a unity of opposites which includes both the destructiveness of the raid and the creation of the natural world; 'and all manner of thing shall be well'.[122] Eliot's vision of synchronicity through the land is one of great poise; it is perhaps the crowning achievement of literary Romanticism of the forties.

Writing in 1988, the critic Peter Fuller decribed Henry Moore's drawings of tube shelterers as 'among the finest ever produced in

Britain',[123] the result of a combination of acute observation and imaginative transformation of what he saw. In the context of forties Romanticism of the kind found in Eliot and Thomas, there seems little reason to disagree with this view. The ceremonial qualities of the poets are replaced by a freshness of vision which allows us to see the figures as almost a wholly different life form, but one which is approached with an immense tenderness and compassion so that, once again, the apocalyptic events are seen within a framework which presents humanity as both suffering and enduring.

It is easy to see why, on a purely visual level, the scenes which were commonplace in most underground railway stations in London from the autumn and winter of 1940 onwards should have appealed so strongly to Moore.[124] Here were great numbers of 'reclining figures', a seemingly endless series of variations on the form that so preoccupied him, their shapes swathed in blankets and consequently distorted and emphasised in all kinds of curious ways, their figures merging and interlocking, revealing all kinds of new forms defined as much as anything else by the apertures between them – another central concern of Moore's pre-war sculptures as a way of defining the three-dimensionality of a figure. But to see the drawings as no more than continuations of a series of formal concerns is to misunderstand their true value, which lies neither in this nor in the great human compassion they reveal but in the great and subtle balance they achieve between these two elements, form and response being perfectly united; once again, the inner-outer equation of forties Romanticism has been posed and perfectly solved.

Moore's work may be divided into two kinds of image: the series of rapid sketches made after forays into the shelters, which survive as two sketchbooks; and the series of finished watercolour and pen drawings which he completed slightly later but using the same basic material. Moore did not make sketches of the sleepers themselves: 'I never made any sketches in the underground. It just wasn't possible. It would have been like making sketches in the hold of a slave ship.'[125] Instead, he worked later on, entering into the sketchbooks ideas for subsequent development. The sketches are quick, full of risk and change, forms evolving through the use of his technique of 'sectional lines' which build up their mass in the way that contour lines build up the height of land on a map; the use of wax crayons to separate some areas of the drawings from the water-colour washes allows forms to be defined precisely with no loss of energy or immediacy. Whether or not Moore was responsible for inventing this technique is immaterial; what matters is that he was using a modification of the technique of Romantic wash-drawing which allowed him to convey the external reality and his response to it in his own reworking of the figures, amplified by the intimate knowledge of the human figure from his earlier work in two and three dimensions.

It is impossible here to do justice to the depth and range of these figure drawings, nor do they need fulsome elucidation. Some are almost realistic in their depiction of groups of figures against recognisable backgrounds; that on page 36 of the British Museum[126] sketchbook shows a family group seated in front of a wall, presumably in the 'Tilbury', a large shelter made in the basement of a warehouse. The number of the bay and a 'no smoking' directive are visible on the wall, as is a sheet of paper headed 'Notice'; to the right a square doorway reveals a corridor receding through similar openings. Before this gaunt, rectilinear drop sit and lie a group of people, probably a family, their bodies highlighted – through the use of the wax technique – to show harsh stripes of white and yellow light. The bodies themselves have small heads and exaggeratedly large bodies, massive shoulders and thin forearms; there is a rhythmic quality to the balance of each body against the next which takes Stubbs' frieze-like movement and adds to it a tenderness formed by the contact between the people. A woman is holding a young child standing on her lap; another holds a baby in her arms while another figure, perhaps a woman, sleeps with her head on her shoulder. In the foreground a larger figure lies, with knees drawn up almost into the foetal position, his head resting on the thigh of a woman sitting beside him. Despite the degree of intimacy, the contact between the figures is never sentimentalized: although we are moved by these figures, we are also distanced from them by the expressionless faces, the lack of detail, the suggestions of bodies simply as large, vague masses; yet there is a tenderness here which is quite characteristic of all the shelter drawings.

Others show individuals or groups of figures, either against a similar naturalistic background or in isolation; some have scribbled notes about future compositions, most of which were never completed. Depicting as they do men, women and children in air raid shelters, mainly those underground and so cut off from the events from which they are taking refuge, they are studies of the vulnerability of humanity at a time of threat and in circumstances of dislocation. These qualities are revealed in the sombre colourings, the lack of facial features, the postures of exhaustion. Yet the drawings also show great strength: the figures' shoulders are often massive, leading down to arms which encircle children to suggest a nurture which is deeply compassionate.

The relation between the figures and the outside world is shown in some of the drawings. That on page 6 of the British Museum collection has four separate compositions, held together by tonality and rhythms. At the top a long, thin group of people is shown, the mother and baby at the left familiar from other sketches, as a kind of apocalyptic, enduring madonna and child. Before her, two figures sleep outstretched, the first with his or her head on the thigh of the second, who sleeps, foetus-like, with hands drawn up under her cheek. There is compassion and tenderness here both in the human contact and in its depiction; but there is something more. These figures have the rhythmic undulations of a natural landscape, a line of hills folding over and towards us; as we look at the image, it resolves first into people, then into a landscape, until each becomes a metaphor for the other. The idea of continuity and regeneration seen in the mother and child flows out into something larger, the enduring qualities of the land. This is extended in the remaining images of the page, four separate images which suggest – no more than that – landscapes which are close to Sutherland's biomorphs in their imprecise outlines and, like them, suggest the possibility of both desolation and renewal.

This link with the outside world is shown more completely in the sketches on page 62 (see front cover). At the left, in an image headed 'blanketed figure in bombed street', a figure stands facing straight out towards us before a bomb-damaged Victorian terrace. The figure is familiar from the other sketches, and stands monumental in the wrecked street. Is there a suggestion here of the enduring power of created, human things amid the collapse of cities? The composition bears a striking but probably quite coincidental resemblance to Sutherland's Silvertown painting but, instead of the sombre splendour of its colouration, has muted pinks and greys; the whole is much more intimate, suggesting that Moore's response is more personal and approaches its subject more nearly than do Sutherland or Thomas and Eliot. The second image, at the right, shows two loosely-sketched figures in the remains of a bombed house while, in the background, the ruined skyline of the city is suggested. The scribbled title reads 'seated woman and child'. It is almost a latter-day treatment of the rest on the flight into Egypt;

woman and child, ageless symbols of regeneration, sit firm and solid within the rubble, suggesting again that cities shall pass but human compassion and regeneration will live on.

The most complete image of this is presented in the third of the sketches on the page. In the background a city street, damaged but still standing, is shown in grey, washed over with pink to suggest fire, and overall suggesting a combination of built, urban stasis and destructive, organic energy. Before this, in the foreground, lies a woman, a characteristic Moore reclining figure with the elements of massiveness and vulnerability familiar in all the shelter drawings. The fluent undulations of the body contrast richly with the angularity of the row of buildings; here is an organic form, of both humanity and landscape, which suggests endurance and renewal in the face of desolation.

Moore's drawings have not always been popular. Many Londoners felt insulted by them when they were first displayed, and they have been accused of sentimentality.[127] Perhaps; yet they tread a line of great risk, responding as they do with immediacy and human concern to conditions of great suffering. Their confrontation of these issues is direct; and it is also Romantic, in stating human compassion, in re-creating events and scenes through the refining inner consciousness, and most completely in showing the triumph of humanity as part of an organic, created world, something which merges visually and philosophically with landscape, in the face of the desolation all around.

The work of the sketchbooks is complemented by the larger drawings – complemented, not completed, because both have different things to say, the sketchbooks urgent, immediate and experiential, the drawings more distanced and contemplative. One must stand as representative here: *Sleeping Shelterers: Two Women and a Child*.[128] We see the figures as if standing at their feet as they lie swathed in blankets; at the left, one of the women sleeps with arms drawn up around her head in the circling, enfolding gestures frequent in Moore's madonna and child sculptures. Again, the shoulders are massive, defined by the sectional lines; yet there is a vulnerability in the instinctive, open posture adopted by the woman in sleep. At the right, the other woman is shown only as a head, mouth agape, and a single hand curled around the blanket. Between them only the child's head is visible; it has a quality of serene stillness about it, suggesting that the child is lying on its back and apparently sleeping quite untroubled. What unites these figures is the sweep of the blanket over them, suggesting as it does the undulation of landscape. The depiction is far more accurate and detailed than many of Moore's drawings, certainly than the sketches; we can see the facial features clearly. Yet the distortion of the shoulders is still clear, to show the strength of these figures even when they are at their most vulnerable. The two women seem to create a landscape of nurture within which the child sleeps; there is a guarded hope of renewal here, through the human individual and through the land, essential features of forties Romanticism.

Moore, Thomas and Eliot all see the immediate circumstances of the blitz as a kind of renewal, a literal and terrible ordeal and transformation by fire. Their response, like those of all the artists considered in this chapter, is to see renewal as a force of great power through both the individual and the land. These, to me, are the finest achievements of forties Romanticism, compassionate yet formal, innovative yet within a long tradition. Ultimate judgements are still perhaps not possible; we are too close to the time and perhaps to the experience. In 1943 Keith Vaughan reviewed an exhibition of war art with his usual intelligence and fluency; it is fitting that his words about Moore should close this chapter:

> I think these drawings are very moving because Moore has not withheld himself from the full impact of this strange and tragic situation, but going beyond the apparent, has tried to discover and express those human and enduring qualities which would ultimately triumph and vindicate it . . . . these motionless swathed figures belong to no accidental setting of time and place. Rather they are memorials to the enduringness of things, of stone and human patience and courage.[129]

8

Roots that Clutch

I

Throughout the foregoing chapters I have stressed the fact that Romanticism in the arts of the Second World War is in many ways a confrontation with the reality that surrounded it rather than an idealist retreat from it. The philosophy of Romanticism, as it evolved in the late eighteenth and early nineteenth centuries, has a great deal to do with political and social theory: Rousseau,[1] after all, evolved the theory of interchange with nature into a paradigm of education and social life which was to sweep across Europe, and we should not forget that Wordsworth and Coleridge, as well as Blake, came into conflict with the authorities over actions which were taken to be subversive.

Chapter 1 advanced the proposition that the 'social realism' of the thirties was in many ways a direct development of Romanticism, and that it certainly shared many of its features in terms of aesthetic style and stance. The chapters which followed have revealed other ways in which Romanticism during the war years confronted the reality which surrounded it. The posters of Frank Newbould present the country as a place of spiritual re-creation to all, not simply the landowning classes; images of the city see in it a new aesthetic beauty which places it almost in the context of emotional mentor seen in Wordsworth's view of the countryside; and the two come together in the hoped-for union between town and country seen in *Land at War*.

Paintings of the Sublime instinctively adopt a stance which allows fear and distress to be turned towards something which offers a psychological tautening, a balance of inner and outer turmoil which, as a means of living through apocalypse, seems almost to be an expression of the mind's power to come to terms with suffering, as suggested in the study of mental illness during the blitz. The paintings of Richards, Craxton and so many others all use the approaches of earlier Romantics to reconcile the inner and outer planes of experience skewed by war by seeing the cyclical process of nature as a healing force. These are, in a sense, two very similar ways of approaching contemporary issues through contemporary reworkings of Romantic outlooks; in a way they are brought together in Michael Tippett's oratorio which, in both music and text, suggests a movement of organic growth and renewal to overcome human evil by recognising and subsuming it into a pattern of forgiveness and reconciliation imaged in the ancient rhythm of the seasons. An idea of renewal through these processes and of synchronicity with earlier ages is offered as another way through by poetry of the forties; and the work of Henry Moore offers human compassion at a level that is both tentative and monumental, uniting his view of the figure with a sense of the rhythms of landscape and above all revealing the primacy and dignity of the individual, anonymous yet precious, within the tube shelter's unique combination of dehumanising threat and mutual nurture.

All of these are direct, Romantic confrontations of circumambient reality and threat. It seems to me that they are all held together by two principles. First, there is the acceptance of the individual, regardless of origin, condition or status, as something of unparalleled importance, seen in the constant stress on the uniqueness and equality of individual experience, whatever the kind. Secondly, there is the stress on the curative, revivifying and sustaining qualities of the natural world, either in literal terms or as a powerful metaphor of spiritual renewal and very often in some combination of these two.

These ideas lead to a question: is there a way in which these outlooks can be seen to go beyond the aesthetic to underlie political and social movements of the time? It would be naïve to expect there to be an easy answer, and arrogant to try to produce one in the confines of this concluding chapter. Nevertheless, it is valid to speculate for a little while on some of the evidence, and to consider, however inconclusively, the degree to which the two central principles advanced at the start of this paragraph come together in some of the more important social and political developments of the war and its immediate aftermath.

II

In Chapter 3, I quoted some passages from an article by B. L. Coombes to show the way in which Wordsworthian experiential writing was being used not only to record events but also to reveal a passionately-held political conviction which they have largely induced in the writer. This kind of Romantic realism is something which is extended into a more overt political vision in two other articles in the series 'The Way We Live Now'. One is the essay by Louis MacNeice[2] which has already been discussed, in which he recounts his feelings on his return to London from New York. Quite regardless of what MacNeice says or the way in which he says it, the factual implications of this voyage must be seen in the light of the not inconsiderable importance they would have had at the time. At the start of the war, MacNeice was one of a group of prominent writers and intellectuals who sought refuge in the United States, others including Spender, Britten and of course W. H. Auden. The act of returning is thus an act of public commitment to the European cause, a declaration of personal involvement, which is intensely Romantic because it places a cause first, and feeling above reason and self-preservation. What MacNeice says at the close of the piece is a forthright Romantic statement about the supreme importance of the individual.

> The typical Englishman contains, paradoxically, an anarchist; this can be seen from English poetry. Any social revolution which is to suit this country must take account of that anarchist. The notorious defects of the English are not least the defects of a people who respect the individual human being. A world view? All right, we need a world view (we can't be empiricists for ever) but the world is made up of human beings. Any ideology which ignores the individual human being is ripe for the scrap-heap. For the sake of man we must have an economic programme – but only for the sake of Man and that means men and that means not Citizens 7601, 7602, etc., but Tom, Dick and Harry. When we come out of the tunnel we must still have faces – not masks.[3]

This is not a piece of representative thirties fellow-travelling; MacNeice was certainly never a member of the Communist Party and his allegiance to Socialism was tenuous, delayed and grudging;

what we have here is a piece of good honest liberal humanism of which E. M. Forster himself might not have been ashamed. It is important because it uses English poetry as evidence of the anarchy that is fundamentally present within the English, and because it stresses the need for human consideration within any economic system: an extension of the Romantic stress on heroic individualism and the primacy of individual experience is being linked with an awareness of the systems of the modern state within the international community. Is it reasonable to call this a political philosophy based on a reconsideration of Romantic individualism in the light of contemporary circumstances? It seems to me that it is.

Something rather different happens in the second of the *Penguin New Writing* articles, which appeared in the issue after MacNeice's contribution, and whose author called himself 'Captain X. Y. Z.'.[4] It begins with a conventional account of a group of privileged and rather bored officers as they drift into the mess after dinner, and then turns to the reader to ask 'And what about you? Will you come with us and watch the old, old farce?'.[5] This is both a literal and a metaphorical performance, a play the officers are considering going to see and the performance they are themselves making as they return from having eaten too well. The writer's anger then becomes clear:

> You ox. This is your condemnation, not ours. It is you who have allowed this. Make no mistake. Our minds are your responsibility, not ours.[6]

Read in one way, 'this' is the war, and the passage an angry condemnation of public complacency along the lines of Day Lewis's 'Newsreel'. But it soon becomes clear that there is another, more corrosive 'this':

> What Idea, then, will you give us? You do not know? We know *our* answer, but we have given up our right to make it. Shall we hint, with vague phrases, at a vision of plenty? Plenty for you, me, him, the batman, the brigadier, the writer, the miner, the bellhop? Plenty for *all*? . . . Watch us again, as we consciously idle from the dining room to the ante-room. We have eaten too well and now the batmen are serving coffee. Take in every detail. Is this how it will be, for ever and ever and ever, world without end?[7]

Once again there is the concern for the individual – batman, brigadier, miner – within a new system; the old order, it is implied, has failed and therefore lost the right to continue to make decisions: it is the reader, a kind of self-defining common-man, on whom the responsibility now rests. This is a challenging statement of the idea of individual primacy because it takes the Romantic convention of address to the reader and changes and extends it; instead of the indirectness of *The Prelude,* where the reader is almost involved in a kind of eavesdropping in an exchange between friends, the address is immediate and terse. Romantic concern for the individual does not only give importance to all; it gives responsibility to all, too.

It is intriguing to take the process further and ask how far this particular strand of Romanticism may be seen to underlie the larger social movements and changes of the forties – the movement which culminated in the establishment of the welfare state by Attlee's Labour government of the immediate post-war years. Examining the ideological origins of all this is too long a path to travel here, but we may instead glance at some of the key documents involved. First, Attlee's broadcast to the nation[8] on the eve of what was known as 'the Appointed Day', when the new unified social insurance system came into operation. Attlee stresses the fact that as far as possible everyone will be treated equally to avoid the 'sense of injustice' caused hitherto by the range of schemes in operation. The principle of equality is also stated: 'The aim is to ensure that the provision of proper care and treatment shall not depend on financial resources, and that when you are sick you will be free from the money worries which so often accompany illness.'[9] Here is the state recognising the importance of the individual, of whatever nature: it is very close to the society advocated by Captain X. Y. Z. It also moves towards the awareness of individual human beings for which MacNeice pleads:

> One word on administration. National Insurance is a service dealing with human beings who need sympathy and personal consideration. The aim of the new service is to give this through a network of local offices, staffed by men and women who will give friendly guidance and help and information to everyone.[10]

It is too easy to dismiss this in hindsight with a series of hollow laughs founded on hard experience; but the idealism and commitment behind Attlee's words are real enough, and there is a clear link between them and MacNeice's pleas. Is this evidence of Social Romanticism in action? The evidence is incomplete, the question too large, the other factors involved too many; but the resemblance is nonetheless there.

A second document allows us to bring together a consideration of the Romantic view of the individual and the concern for ideas of nurture and regeneration through the processes of the natural world. *Social Insurance and Allied Services*,[11] the Beveridge Report, was the document upon which the eventual form of the welfare state rested. Designed for popular reading and discussion, it became the most unlikely bestseller of the decade, selling 635,000 copies when it appeared just before Christmas 1942. At its heart was this statement:

> Now, when the war is abolishing landmarks of every kind, is the opportunity for using experience in a clear field . . . Social insurance fully developed may provide income security; it is an attack upon Want. But Want is one only of five giants on the road of reconstruction and in some ways the easiest to attack. The others are Disease, Ignorance, Squalor and Idleness.[12]

Here is one of the fundamental pronouncements about the new social state; it is expressed in terms of landscape and a journey, the journey as a metaphor of moral progress which is familiar from early Romantic hymns and countless Romantic poems which show exterior forms as an image of inner state. Is it conceivable that literature of this sort, and the political and philosophical notions of equality which underlie it, resting as they do on the idea of the primacy of the individual's experience and their expression through natural forms, lies somewhere at the foundation of Beveridge's concept? Perhaps this is stretching credibility too far; but the resemblance of language is there, and the preceding chapters should, if nothing else, have made clear the prevalence of such imagery and stance in writing and painting of the time.

The strands of individualism and organic nurture are also woven together in powerfully visual ways which have to do with key social and political issues and developments of the time. A very particular visual formulation of the new world that is to come after the war is provided by the posters designed by Abram Games for the Army Bureau of Current Affairs in 1943. These are part of the 'Your Britain – Fight for it Now' campaign which we have already encountered in the posters by Frank Newbould, but Games approaches the concept in a markedly different way. Whereas Newbould presents a gentle vision of a rural paradise now available to all, Games shows real social ills and suggests ways in which they are to be cured. The three deal with health, housing, and education.

Of the three the most striking is that which deals with health.[13] It is a composition which is a remarkable blend of the representative and the symbolic. A representation of what looks like an architect's model of a building in international modern style, identified as Finsbury Health Centre, is shown on a plane which runs at a slight diagonal across the poster. Examination of the edges of this plane reveals it to be a brick wall – the façade placed in front of a scene which shows crumbling stone walls surrounding a squalid interior in which a child with the thin, brittle limbs of rickets stands awkwardly; the words 'disease' and 'neglect' are scrawled on the walls, and a gaunt, broken tree stands in a far corner. The brief text makes clear the message; that modern medicine, founded on periodic health checks, will eradicate the disease of the past. It is a clear and direct statement that, in the better world after the war, the individual – symbolised by the child – will be the subject of the state's care, symbolised in the Finsbury Health Centre which in itself stands as representative for one of the more enlightedned London boroughs in terms of attitudes to health and slum clearance in the thirties. In no way could this be called an escape from pressing contemporary problems: so distressingly real was the figure of the child with rickets that the poster was withdrawn and stocks destroyed on the personal instructions of Winston Churchill.[14]

Finsbury Health Centre, designed by the Tecton group led by Berthold Lubetkin, was one of the most celebrated new buildings of the thirties, praised for its functionalism and regarded by one critic as 'the type of the modern city building'.[15] Its use gives a firm rooting in actuality to a poster which otherwise is idealistic. There is no place here for a Romantic view of the countryside, but instead we have a vision of the city which embraces the idea of the nurture of the individual as completely as any other image of the war years. In its idealism, and in the figure of the child as an object of nurture, it is a poster which is firmly in the Romantic tradition which stresses the primacy of the individual regardless of origin.

The poster concerned with housing[16] shows a line of Victorian slum houses receding at the left, looking not unlike the bombed terraces in Sutherland's *Devastation* painting discussed in Chapter 7.

Here, though, their decay suggests the squalor and neglect endemic in pre-war slums rather than the work of the Luftwaffe, and the reason is clear: to provide a contrast with the block of model flats which is shown in idealised form at the right of the composition. The text informs us of the importance of 'clean, airy and well planned dwellings' and goes on to identify the building as 'a block of workers' flats built in London in 1936'. Again, the idealism is concerned with the idea of the nurture of the individual by those in a position of authority: both here and in the other image there is an assumption that authority involves responsibility, something which develops the fundamental Romantic notion of the primacy and equality of the individual but adds to it ideas of responsible government in the contemporary social state.

What is striking about this image, however, is that it is not wholly urban in nature; the block of flats is presented behind a lawn, with a young tree growing to the left. This is far more than mere visual decoration: it is an emblem of the fact that the flats stand in an area of land that has been carefully 'landscaped' to resemble a version of the countryside within the boundaries of the city, and it is thus representative of the major way in which the Romantic notions of nurture and nature come together in English social and political life of the forties.

In 1941, Nikolaus Pevsner began a series of lectures for Birkbeck College, London University on the nature of English art. In 1955 these became the Reith Lectures, and were published as *The Englishness of English Art*[17] in the following year. The view of Englishness they present, with its emphasis on the relationship between national character and art, on the English view of nature, and the importance of linearity in much English painting and architecture, has since become well known and it is not my aim to support or refute its general assertions. Its relevance here is in its discussion of the nature of English architecture and town-planning, and the claims it makes which are borne out very strongly by a range of government reports and items of legislation. There is a common ground between what these reports have to say about the building of urban settlements and Pevsner's historically-conscious approach which suggests that the influence of certain very specific aspects of Romanticism is strong on them both; and, in turn, this implies that a Romantic outlook was common in areas far more diverse than what, for want of a better word, we may call the 'pure' or 'fine' arts of the time.

Pevsner argues[18] that the unique contribution of the British to the growth of the town has been in extending the tradition of the landscape garden, first through eighteenth-century squares and crescents, then through the creation of individual buildings such as Buckingham Palace which are more country houses transplanted than urban palaces, and finally through the tradition of the garden city, begun by Ebenezer Howard at Letchworth and espoused by imitators elsewhere in the early years of this century. Extending this to contemporary practice, he argues that what is needed is a return to the principle of the Picturesque, made clear by Uvedale Price, that the *genius loci* or spirit of place must predominate. Thus not only is a distinguished architectural historian saying that the English townscape owes much to the Picturesque – the advance party of the Romantic view of the countryside – but he is also advocating a return to it in the face of the present housing difficulty. This evidences the prevalence of the Romantic continuity discussed in Chapter 2, as well as showing its revival in architectural debate; but when we examine what was happening in town planning in England during the early forties – when Pevsner was writing the first drafts of his lectures – we are made aware that the continuing presence of the Romantic outlook on the countryside is strong in a far more practical way.

The first consideration is the siting of New Towns. For this, according to the New Towns Report,[19] 'a reasonable degree of undulation is to be welcomed, since it may add greatly to the beauty and interest of the town.'[20] Once the site is chosen, development should follow according to its character:

> The beauty of a town depends not only on its buildings but also on its relation to the surrounding landscape and on the disposition and treatment of the natural features, existing or introduced, within the boundaries. To fit happily in the regional scene it must either have harmony or considered contrast therewith. The contours and vegetation of the surrounding land form its permanent setting, and the flow of the land with its distant views may often suggest the direction of roads and placing of buildings within the town. The layout should therefore take full account of the topography, and beauty should be a constant consideration as well as convenience of building plots and easy road gradients. As examples, planting on higher ground can accentuate contours; and ribs of high ground and woods, or alternatively parkways in

> valleys, may be used to define boundaries between neighbourhoods or to separate industrial from residential zones.[21]

Reading this passage is rather like reading something from Uvedale Price or Humphrey Repton;[22] the idea of using and improving the landscape is fundamental to it, underlying which is the notion of beauty in landscape as something deliberately to be sought and exploited. That this beauty of landscape is intrinsically 'better' as a site than something unattractive yet well-located is an assumption implied at an even deeper level; it is as if the state of living in or surrounded by country is automatically assumed to be morally better than that of living in a town. This is, of course, the underlying assumption of the whole 'New Town' philosophy; a self-contained community which exists from the fruits of its own labours, it is perhaps the last expression of the ideal of the self-sustaining country estate.

There is, of course, a difference. A country estate belongs to a landowner; the New Towns, at least in theory, belong to their inhabitants. Egalitarianism of access to the country has been extended into egalitarianism of ownership. That this was a prime aim is shown again in the New Towns Report: there is a regret that 'a tendency towards segregation by income group'[23] is present in existing towns, and the following advice:

> If a socially homogeneous community is to be created, a conscious and sustained policy to that end will be needed on the part of the agency itself, and of the leaders of local industry and commerce and social activity.[24]

The homogeneous community, without segregation into income groups, can only be achieved by adhering to the fundamental Romantic principle of the primacy and equality of each individual; that this is aimed for, within a new town which is sited in beautiful countryside, shows the coming together of the two basic strands of Romantic philosophy, modified to suit the conditions of the time, and absorbed into official policy.

Visions of the future are not always so tangibly based on the aesthetic theory of the past; but before leaving this line of thought it is pertinent to consider for a moment the outlook suggested by Arthur Bryant,[25] a writer who was probably the most popular historian of his day, and who used his readings of the past to offer a view of the future. Bryant argues that there *are* lessons of the past, which can be learnt and applied to the future with a Socialist zeal and passion for the primacy of the individual over the economic system that cries out with the voice of Shelley and Blake against the institutional greed he sees around him. There is much here that is very strictly contemporary, written in a style to rouse the spirit of a nation at war by stressing the English values of freedom and justice: but there is also a great deal which suggests a return to the system implicit within the Romantic world view, in which individuals take precedence over systems. Bryant laments the betrayal of the hopes of those who had fought in the First World War who had been offered 'a land fit for heroes':

> But when the soldiers came home they found a world designed for stockbrokers and *rentiers* and civil servants. It was built not in the image of their apocalyptic dream but in that of the utilitarian labyrinth of the money-changers from which they had gone forth in 1914.[26]

And, a little later;

> Man should be master of his tools, not his tools of man. It used to be the glory of England that its craftsmen took pride in their work. Under the modern system the artisan is denied the joy of giving quality to his task and is usually employed on a temporary basis. He is at the mercy of forces over which he has no control. He is not truly that which his English instinct prompts him to be – a free man.[27]

All of this is a rather simplistic rejection of a modern economic system which places share-dealings and commodity markets above the actual production of wealth, and it argues for a return to a system which is more immediate in its response to the individual. In this it is basic to that strand of Romantic philosophy which is deplored by Goldsmith, breeding wealth at the expense of men, by Blake, in his glorious anger at the 'charter'd' city, by Constable, in his cyclical images of worked landscapes. The irony, of course, is that it is a view which most people today would have no difficulty in seeing as 'romantic', but so in the popular sense of escapist and unrealistic. What the answer is, Bryant does not say: he implies that it lies in the English passion for justice and for freedom and we must remember that he was writing at a time when the welfare state was still a matter for heated debate and speculation. Perhaps that – the welfare state itself – is the balance between the heroic individualism of Romanticism and the modern system of international economics.

In one of his Reith lectures, Pevsner quotes Emerson: 'Only the English can be trusted with freedom';[28] both freedom of line in the garden, the descendant of the flaming line of English Gothic and Blake's spiritual linearity, and the freedom of speech and idea of Shelley and Cobbett.[29] Today, in the brittle glamour of Thatcherite *enrichissez-vous* economics, the ideas of the forties seem bravely idealistic, and about as far away from us in time and as unattainable in practice as the ideals of worked landscape that we see in Constable. But in the forties, things were different; the past is not quite another country, but it is certainly another countryside.

For a little while, in the visions of the past and the future put forward by historians and politicians, art historians and architects, something approaching a philosophy of Romanticism takes on a new life. At times, as in the New Towns movement, there is a coming together of the primacy of the individual and the nurturing force of the countryside, within a modern social state. It is the product of many other forces, and its debt to Romanticism is hard explicitly to define; it is transient and offers the hope of things which are perhaps unattainable. Yet it seems to me that, just for a moment, historical study, political and social actuality, and the reality of applied aesthetics come together: Romanticism is a living social force once more.

III

I do not know how much of this is valid, much less true; so much depends on one's own viewpoint, and whether it be a place of immediate involvement or one of calm distance. The Romantic ethic in larger concepts of social organisation is one of a great number of factors and influences, merging and cross-pollinating within the process of social change. Perhaps the Romantic, experiential outlook is so fundamental in its nature and effect that, once established in a nation's culture, it becomes irreversible. Perhaps the rekindling of Romantic ways of seeing, along with the movements for social reform of the thirties and forties, coalesce into the larger stream of welfare planning. Quantification is impossible, if not ludicrous; but it does seem that the relationship is one which needs to be considered even if, on reflection, it is rejected.

What of the value of the remainder of the work considered in these pages? In my earlier *Art and Survival in First World War Britain* I tried to show the ways in which popular and fine art aided the psychological endurance of those who lived through the war, by informing, consoling, placing events within a context of heroic myth, and sometimes by offering a view of events which offered hope and a way through based, often unknowingly, sometimes not, on almost total distortion of reality. This book has different aims, but the question is still a valid one: what was the achievement of British Romantic art in the Second World War?

For those who were there, much of it offered some of the things listed above. Simply informing is rare; since a common thread is that the artist creates as much as records what he or she experiences, documentary impartiality is not frequent. The recording of experience in this way is cathartic for the artist and allows a genuine human sharing with the reader or onlooker, establishing trust and human contact at a time when these were often in danger. Even those works which seem to do nothing but present external reality, but which on deeper study are shown to be full of interpretation, had much to offer in this way. Charles Cundall's depiction of Dunkirk, apparently so straightforward, is on reflection a profoundly political statement. But for those who lived through the time, it perhaps gave comfort by providing a sense of order and courage in the death of a soldier for families eager to share his last moments, hungry for consolation and purpose. A later and more distanced generation may ask whether this is valid, or whether it is a greater distortion because it offers an order which is untrue and a purpose which is doubtful; but those who had such needs saw it differently. Those works – the writings, in particular – which present fragments of experience as yet without order must have appealed to a sense of sharing, reinforcing the sense of bewilderment that many must have felt during the strange new times, and in this offering a kind of common-ground which, even in its uncertainty, was human and therefore reassuring. Cundall and Bone apart, there is little ordering, little myth-making in most of the work we have considered; it could be found elsewhere, in the more popular work, but in so much of the work discussed in these pages it is the quality of shared tentativeness which is more often predominant.

What of the body of work – poetry, painting, music – which presents a view of the natural world? We should be aware that here we are dealing with 'high art' which would be accessible to the few as well as with images of nature which are popular by destination. *Land at War* doubtless gave pleasure, information and a sense of renewal to many, and helped in a rediscovery of the countryside during the war years. The idea of the country as shared spiritual resource in Frank Newbould and others presumably had much to offer in very practical terms, both in hope for the future and in recalling memories of the past in a Wordsworthian way. In comparison with these images, the ideas of renewal which we may now find the most powerful – those of Sutherland, Moore, Eliot, Dylan Thomas – were far less accessible then. Moore's shelter drawings drew little public acclaim and some open ridicule and rejection; the cyclical processes of Thomas and Eliot perhaps offered consolation to those bereaved in war, but it is impossible at this distance to say categorically if this is so or to quantify instances.

We are left with the function of offering ideals which is present in a large number of works of different kinds; ideals of freedom, peace and justice which seem inseparable from a view of the English countryside in so many films and pieces of popular writing, and ideals of the precious integrity of the individual, underlined by all the writing based on personal experience, however fragmentary – the very things suggested as the basis, if not of the new society of *après la guerre fini*, at least of its new towns.

Looking at it in a larger context, we may see the return to the land as something that recurs throughout English culture in periods of stress or change: it happened in the great flowering of European mysticism of the late fourteenth century which accompanied the black death and the social turmoil of the peasants' revolt; it happened in the social and political convulsion of Romanticism; it happened again when the land was threatened by invasion in the forties. Perhaps some of the forties generalisations about the importance of the land for the English, and about English art being innately a Romantic art, have a kind of validity.

What does the art of the forties have to say to us as people, not art historians? Just as the writers of the thirties and forties reinvented Romanticism in their own image, so we inevitably reconstruct the work of the forties through our own tunnel vision: we cannot help but see it through green-tinted spectacles. In the course of writing this book, on frequent and increasingly frenzied trips to the University Library in Cambridge, I passed through fields of East Anglian wheat ripening in just the same way, and through just the same agencies, as those described in *Land at War*, a powerful emblem of the continuing organic cycle. But, of course, they are not the same; the land is now largely poisoned by phosphates and nitrates, and the 'Widow Makers' from the nearby airforce bases that fly low over the corn make their contribution to global warming which will perhaps lead to the fields being flooded in my son's lifetime. Even at the height of the blitz, Dylan Thomas could write 'After the first death, there is no other': now it is no longer true.

Auden said, 'All I have is a voice/To undo the folded lie'.[30] All natural cycles come down to individual actions: to people, not systems. Philip Larkin, who in many ways inherits the priorities and the tentative mood of the Romantics of the forties, writes in 'The Mower' of an event which is apparently trifling – running over a hedgehog with a lawnmower. It becomes a statement of loss and a plea for nurture which continues and extends the greatest compassion, for the precious individual, for the created world, of the forties. It is a suitable end; and a suitable beginning:

> The first day after a death, the new absence
> Is always the same; we should be careful
>
> Of each other, we should be kind
> While there is still time.[31]

Notes

Sizes of paintings are given in inches, with height preceding width.

CHAPTER 1 SOME VERSIONS OF ROMANTICISM

1. Graham Sutherland, 1939; oil on canvas, 23 5/8 x 19 5/8, Tate Gallery, London.
2. T. S. Eliot, 'East Coker', *Four Quartets*, 1944, p. 23.
3. 'No book is genuinely free from political bias. The opinion that art should have nothing to do with politics is itself a political attitude.' 'Why I write', *Collected Essays*, 1961, p. 422. Although this statement dates from 1947, it is quite clearly a distillation of opinions which are apparent throughout his writing of the thirties.
4. See, for example, Charles Harrison, *English Art and Modernism 1900–1939*, 1981; P. Ray, *The Surrealist Movement in England*, Ithaca, 1971; Arts Council of Great Britain, *Thirties: British Art and Design before the war*, exhibition catalogue, 1979; Marlborough Fine Arts Ltd, *Art in Britain 1930–40 Centred around Axis, Circle, Unit One*, exhibition catalogue, 1965.
5. Bernard Bergonzi, *Reading the Thirties: Texts and Contexts*, 1978, p. 55.
6. 1936; conveniently available in *The English Auden: Poems, Essays and Dramatic Writings 1927–1939*, ed. Edward Mendelson, 1977, pp. 169–99.
7. 1819–24; conveniently available in *Byron: Poetical Works*, ed. Frederick Page, rev. John Jump, 1970, pp. 635–858.
8. 1927–8; *ed. cit.*, pp. 1–17.
9. 1817; *ed. cit.*, pp. 390–406.
10. 1939.
11. William Wordsworth, 1805 rev 1850; *The Prelude: 1799, 1805, 1850*, ed. Jonathan Wordsworth, M. H. Abrams and Stephen Gill, 1979.
12. 1939; *Collected Poems 1928–1953*, 1955, pp. 80–1; passage quoted from p. 81.
13. 1819; conveniently available in *Shelley: Poetical Works*, ed. Thomas Hutchinson and corrected by G. M. Matthews, 1970.
14. c. 1938; *Collected Poems 1954*, 1954, pp. 171–2; passage quoted from p. 172.
15. In *Keep the Aspidistra Flying*, 1936.
16. 1793; *Blake: Complete Writings*, ed. Geoffrey Keynes, 1966, pp. 189–195.
17. 1789–94; *ed. cit.*, pp. 111–26, 210–21.
18. 1798; ed. R. L. Brett and A. R. Jones, 1963.

19. Article in *Sight and Sound*, Winter 1933–4; quoted in Forsyth Hardy, *Grierson on Documentary*, 1946, rev. 1966, p. 16.
20. 1936; John Grierson, for the GPO Film Unit.
21. 1935; Alberto Cavalcanti, GPO Film Unit.
22. 1934.
23. 1935; Edgar Anstey and Arthur Elton, British Commercial Gas Association.
24. Harold Lowenstein, 1936.
25. *Sight and Sound*, Vol. 5, No. 18, Summer 1936, p. 30.
26. The sequence in occurs in *Listen to Britain*, Humphrey Jennings, 1942; Ian Dalrymple for the Crown Film Unit.
27. A selection from their work is provided in *Speak for Yourself: A Mass-Observation Anthology 1937–1949*, ed. Angus Calder and Dorothy Sheridan, 1985, which also contains a full bibliography of M-O publications and an outline of other material still held in its archives. Dorothy Sheridan, 'Mass Observing the British', *History Today*, Vol. 34, July 1984, pp. 42–6 provides an introductory account of the organisation's work.
28. *May 12th Mass-Observation Day Surveys*, ed. Humphrey Jennings and Charles Madge, 1937.
29. These were all topics discussed in Charles Madge and Tom Harrisson, *Britain*, a Penguin Special published in 1939.
30. Launched in August 1937.
31. Launched in October 1938.
32. 1937; *The Collected Poems of Louis MacNeice*, ed. E. R. Dodds, 1967, pp. 84–5.
33. 1937; *ed. cit.*, p. 207.
34. 1939; *ed. cit.*, pp. 245–7.
35. 1830; oil on canvas, 102 3/8 x 128, Musée du Louvre, Paris.
36. 1945; oil on cardboard, 30 x 40, Estate of Leslie Hurry.
37. ed. Keidrich Rhys, 1941.
38. *Poems of the Second World War: The Oasis Selection*, ed. Victor Selwyn *et al.*, 1985.
39. 1984.
40. The series, called *New Excursions in English Poetry*, made known a good deal of poetry from earlier periods, Romantic and otherwise. Important among its volumes were *The Poet's Eye*, ed. Geoffrey Grigson, ill. John Craxton, 1944 and *Poems of Death*, ed. Phoebe Pool, ill. Michael Ayrton, 1945.
41. See Chapter 5, note 35.
42. Launched in 1940; issued at increasingly wide intervals from January 1940 as paper became more difficult to obtain.
43. Launched in January 1940.
44. 1977.
45. 1988.
46. In *British Cinema History*, ed. James Curran and Vincent Porter, 1983, pp. 144–63.
47. Oxford, 1980.
48. 1986.

49. *Ministry of Morale: Home Front morale and the Ministry of Information in World War II*, 1979.
50. *Official History of the Second World War*, 1950.
51. 1982.
52. *A Paradise Lost: The Neo-Romantic Imagination in Britain 1935–55*, 1987.
53. Graham Sutherland, 'Welsh Sketchbook', *Horizon*, Vol. 5, No. 28, April 1942, pp. 224–36; passage quoted from p. 234.

CHAPTER 2 THE ROMANTIC CONTINUITY

1. Geoffrey Grigson, 'Samuel Palmer: The Politics of an Artist', *Horizon*, Vol. IV, No. 2, November 1941, pp. 314–29; passage quoted from p. 314.
2. *The Picturesque: Studies in a Point of View*, Putnam, 1927.
3. *Ibid.*, p. 17.
4. *Ibid.*, p. 2.
5. *Ibid.*, p. 275.
6. See below, with reference to the paintings by Charles Cundall and Muirhead Bone in Chapter 3.
7. *The Picturesque*, p. 57.
8. *Ibid.*, p. 57.
9. *Ibid.*, p. 80.
10. *The Gothic Revival*, 1928.
11. Horace Walpole, 1784.
12. Of *The Battle of Germany*; quoted by M. and S. Harries, *The War Artists*, 1983, p. 179. Clark did to some extent redress the balance in his autobiography *The Other Half*, 1977, p. 23, where he mentions Nash's 'two or three beautiful and moving pictures', but then refers to *The Dead Sea of German Aeroplanes* – presumably *Totes Meer* – and *Battle of Britain* as 'the splendid tonic'. The error over the title of the first and the nationalistic reading of the second do seem, however, to suggest a continued lack of sympathy with the paintings.
13. *The English Romantic Revival in Art and Poetry: A Reconsideration*, Fifth Rickman Godlee Lecture, Thursday, 24 October 1935.
14. *Ibid.*, p. 5.
15. Sense A.1 in the *OED*; this meaning is also explored by Logan Pearsall Smith in 'Romantic Words', *Words and Ideas*, 1925 and Hans Eichner, ed., *'Romantic' and its Cognates: The European History of a Word*, 1972.
16. Binyon *op. cit.*, p. 7.
17. *Ibid.*, p. 23.
18. *Ibid.*, p. 24.
19. *English Watercolours, from the work of Turner, Girtin, Cotman, Constable and Bonnington*, 1939. The paintings were reproduced 'in 8-colour process on the IRIS Press in Switzerland' by Dr Hans Zbinden of Berne.

20. 1805; watercolour, 9 x 13, British Museum, London.
21. *English Watercolours*, p. 8.
22. Geoffrey Grigson and John Piper, 'England's Climate', *Axis*, Autumn 1936, pp. 4–9.
23. *Ibid.*, p. 5.
24. *Ibid.*, p. 9.
25. *Ibid.*, p. 9.
26. *Ibid.*, p. 9.
27. Myfanwy Evans, ed., *The Painter's Object*, 1937.
28. Edmund Burke, *A Philosophical Enquiry into the Origin of our Ideas of the Sublime and the Beautiful*, 1756
29. 'Lost: A Valuable Object', in Evans, *op. cit.*, p. 70.
30. Evans, *op. cit.*, p. 6.
31. *Ibid.*, p. 8.
32. Graham Sutherland, 'An English Stone Landmark'.
33. John Piper, 'England's Early Sculpture'.
34. Paul Nash, 'Swanage, or Seaside Surrealism'.
35. John Piper, *British Romantic Artists*, 1942.
36. *Ibid.*, pp. 15–16.
37. Most probably *Woody Mountain Landscape with Peasant and Cattle on Bridge*, c. 1783; oil on canvas, 15 3/4 x 19, National Gallery, London. Of the three paintings listed by Ellis Waterhouse, *Gainsborough*, 1958, closest to the title given in the article, this is the most likely as it was displayed in the National Gallery during the thirties.
38. *British Romantic Artists*, pp. 11–12.
39. 1800; watercolour, 11 8/10 x 20 1/4, Tate Gallery, London.
40. *British Romantic Artists*, p. 14.
41. *Ibid.*, p. 26.
42. *Ibid.*, p. 14.
43. *The Romantics: An Anthology Chosen by Geoffrey Grigson*, 1942.
44. *Ibid.*, p. 335 n. 44.
45. 'A View of English Painting', *Penguin New Writing*, No. 31, 1946, pp. 131–45; passage quoted from pp. 138–9.
46. 'England's Climate', p. 6.
47. *Ibid.*, p. 6.
48. *Ibid.*, p. 5.
49. *Ibid.*, p. 6.
50. *Ibid.*, p. 6.
51. *Ibid.*, p. 6.
52. *Ibid.*, p. 6.
53. Myfanwy Evans satirises this profusion in her introduction to *The Painter's Object*, 1937.
54. 1935; oil on canvas, 6 x 12, S. John Rivers.
55. 1937; oil on canvas, 48 x 60, John Piper.
56. *Oxon (Shell Guides)*, 1938; later reissued as *Oxfordshire, not including the City of Oxford*, Shell Guides, 1953.
57. 1939; oil on canvas, 20 x 16, J. R. Haines.
58. 1939–40; oil on linen, 25 x 30, Manchester City Art Gallery.
59. The theory and practice of the landscape at Stourhead is discussed

in Kenneth Woodbridge, *Landscape and Antinquity: Aspects of English Culture at Stourhead 1718 to 1838*, 1970.

60. Charles Harrison, *English Art and Modernism 1900–1939*, 1981, p. 321.
61. 1942–3; ink, watercolour and gouache, 17 x 19, Reresby Sitwell.
62. 1942; watercolour, 15 1/2 x 20 1/4, British Council.
63. 1941; watercolour, 28 x 21, H. P. Juda.
64. S. John Woods, *John Piper: Paintings, Drawings and Theatre Designs 1932–1954*, 1955, p. 13.
65. 1940; oil on canvas, 20 x 24, City Art Gallery, Coventry.
66. 'What to Look for in a Picture: part of a discussion by Clive Bell, Herbert Read and V. S. Pritchett', *The Listener*, Vol. XXVI, No. 666, 16 October 1941, pp. 529–30; passage quoted from p. 529.
67. 'Art and Life: part of a discussion between V. S. Pritchett, Graham Sutherland, Sir Kenneth Clark and Henry Moore', *The Listener*, Vol. XXVI, No. 670, 13 November 1941, pp. 657–59; passage quoted from p. 657.
68. *The Passage to the Control Room at S.W. Regional Headquarters, Bristol*, 1940; oil on panel, 30 x 20, Imperial War Museum, London.
69. *John Constable the Painter*, 1924.
70. *John Constable RA*, 1926.
71. *Constable*, by André Fontainas, trans. W. Jackson, *Masters of Modern Art* series, 1927.
72. *Letters to C. R. Leslie*, introduced by C. Holmes, 1931.
73. C. R. Leslie, *Memoirs of the Life of John Constable*, edited and enlarged by A. Shirley, 1937.
74. 1829; oil on canvas, 48 1/4 x 66, National Gallery, London.
75. 'Died April 1st, 1837: John Constable', *The Architectural Review*, Vol. LXXXI, No. 485, April 1937, pp. 149–51; quotation from p. 150.
76. 'From a Painter's Note-Book-V', *Penguin New Writing* No. 28, July 1946, pp. 141–47; quotation from p. 141.
77. 'A View of English Painting'. *Penguin New Writing* No. 31, 1947, pp. 131–45.
78. *Ibid.*, p. 137. The reference to Cézanne is intriguing: in 1927, Hussey had rejected the idea of a likeness of vision between that painter and the earlier English Romantics; a few years later both Piper and Vaughan recognise the link in perceptual stance underlying the difference of style.
79. *J. W. W. Turner: Watercolour Drawings in the National Gallery*, 1904.
80. A. W. Finberg, *The Life of J. M. W. Turner*, 1939.
81. Graham Sutherland, 'A Trend in English Draughtsmanship', *Signature*, July 1936, pp. 7–13; quotation from p. 13.
82. 1785; oil on canvas, 93 x 70 1/2, National Gallery, London. In 1936 it belonged to Victor Rothschild, who lent it to Philip Sassoon for the Gainsborough exhibition at his house in Park Lane, London.
83. 'Henry Fuseli RA 1741–1825', *Signature*, 10, 1938, pp. 11–13
84. *Complete Writings of William Blake*, ed. Geoffrey Keynes, 1925.
85. *The Engraved Drawings of William Blake*, 1926.
86. See, for example, Frances Spalding, *British Art Since 1900*, 1986,

pp. 130–132, and Charles Harrison, *English Art and Modernism 1900–1939*, 1981, pp. 322–23.

87. *The Followers of William Blake: Edward Calvert, Samuel Palmer, George Richmond and Their Circle*, 1925.
88. In 'Samuel Palmer: the Politics of an Artist', *Horizon*, Vol. IV, No. 2, November 1941, p. 328. Grigson here wrongly dates the volume as 1926.
89. 1822; watercolour, 2 3/4 x 4 1/8, British Museum, London.
90. The first is John Linnell's *Sheep Resting under a Tree*, 1818; etching, 5 9/16 x 9 1/16, collection of Robert N. Essick, an important contribution to the tradition of small engravings of pastoral scenes.
91. The images are reproduced in David Bindman, *The Complete Graphic Works of William Blake*, 1978, as plates 602–18. The quality of reproduction in Binyon's text is better than that of Bindman's, largely because Binyon's book is printed on unglazed paper.
92. Bewick's *A General History of Quadrupeds* had appeared in 1790, and the *History of British Birds* in 1797 (Vol. I) and 1804 (Vol. II).
93. Binyon, *op. cit.*, p. 3.
94. *Georgian Poetry 1920–22*, 1922.
95. *Samuel Palmer, being a Lecture delivered to the Print Collectors' Club on Wednesday November 16th, 1927*, publication No. 7, Print Collectors' Club, 1928, p. 9.
96. *Ibid.*, p. 9.
97. c. 1829; watercolour and gouache, 11 x 8 3/4, Victoria and Albert Museum, London.
98. Hardie, *op. cit.*, pp. 10–11.
99. See Chapter 1.
100. 'Samuel Palmer at Shoreham', *Signature*, November 1937, pp. 1–17.
101. 1947.
102. 'Samuel Palmer at Shoreham', p. 15.
103. *Ibid.*, p. 15.
104. *Ibid.*, p. 16.
105. R. G. Alexander, *A Catalogue of the Etchings of Samuel Palmer*, Print Collectors' Club Publication No. 16, 1937.
106. James Laver, 'The Place of Samuel Palmer in the History of British Etching', *Artwork*, III, 1927.
107. Frank Jewett Mather Jr, 'Samuel Palmer's Virgil Etchings', *Print Collector's Quarterly*, Vol. 24, No. 3, 1937, pp. 253–64.
108. Raymond Lister's *Edward Calvert*, 1962 has few reproductions of the later work and none in colour, as does Binyon.
109. A. J. Finberg, 'Edward Calvert's Engravings', *Print Collector's Quarterly*, Vol. 17, No. 4, 1930, pp. 138–53.
110. 1827; wood-engraving, 3 1/4 x 5 1/8 (including inscription), British Museum.
111. Quoted in Roger Berthoud, *Graham Sutherland: A Biography*, 1982, p. 51.
112. *Ibid.*
113. 1923; etching, 7 1/2 x 8 3/8.
114. 1924; etching, 5 1/8 x 6 1/8.

115. 1925; etching, 4 3/4 x 4 7/8.
116. 1833; oil and tempera on panel, 13 x 18, Tate Gallery, London.
117. 1928; etching, 3 3/8 x 2 7/8.
118. 1830; tempera on canvas, 11 7/8 x 7 1/8, Tate Gallery, London.
119. 1926; etching, 4 7/8 x 7 1/4.
120. 1926; etching, 4 3/8 x 6 3/8.
121. 1925; etching, 5 3/8 x 7 3/8.
122. 1925; etching, 6 7/8 x 8 7/8.
123. 1929/30; etching, 4 3/4 x 6 3/8.
124. 1930; etching, 5 1/8 x 7 5/8.
125. 1931; etching, 8 1/2 x 6 1/8.
126. 1825; pen and ink, 7 x 9, Ashmolean Museum, Oxford.
127. 1825; watercolour mixed with gum, 7 1/8 x 10 7/8, Ashmolean Museum, Oxford.
128. 1941; pen and wash, 21 x 29 1/2, Christopher Hull Gallery, London.
129. 1942; black ink and white chalk on paper on board, 21 6/10 x 30, Tate Gallery, London.
130. Present whereabouts unknown.
131. Present whereabouts unknown.
132. c. 1944; conté crayon on blue paper, 17 x 24 1/8, Christopher Hull Gallery, London.
133. Whitechapel Art Gallery, *John Craxton: Paintings and Drawings 1941–1966*, 1967, p. 6.
134. Geoffrey Grigson, *John Craxton: Paintings and Drawings*, 1948, unpaginated.
135. *Ibid.*
136. Vol. V, No. 27, March 1942, facing pp. 188 and 189 respectively.
137. c. 1945–7; pen, ink and wash on paper, 21 x 29 1/2, Tib Lane Gallery, Manchester.
138. Early 1940s; pen, ink and body colour; size and present whereabouts unknown.
139. 1944; ink and body colour on paper, 19 1/2 x 24 3/4, British Council.

CHAPTER 3 ROMANTIC REALISM

1. 'Spots of time and *The Haywain*' in *Romantic Landscape Vision*, Wisconsin, 1975, pp. 3–28.
2. 1821; oil on canvas, 51 x 73, National Gallery, London.
3. Jonathan Wordsworth, M. H. Abrams and Stephen Gill, eds, *William Wordsworth, The Prelude 1799, 1805, 1850*, New York and London 1979: Book 11, lines 257–72, pp. 428 and 430.
4. I, 290; *ed. cit.*, p. 8.
5. *Ibid.*, p. 428 n. 2.
6. See the forewords to Muirhead Bone, *The Western Front; Drawings by Muirhead Bone*, 2 vols, each of 5 parts, 1917.
7. *War Pictures by British Artists*, 1942; passage quoted from inside front dust-jacket.

8. *War Pictures by British Artists*, Second Series, *1; Women 2; Soldiers, 3; Production, 4; Air Raids*, 1943.
9. *Ibid.*; inside front dust-jacket.
10. 1940; oil on canvas, 40 x 60, Imperial War Museum, London.
11. Frances Spalding, *British Art Since 1900*, 1986, p. 141.
12. Meirion and Susie Harries, *The War Artists*, 1983, p. 174.
13. These figures are those quoted from Admiralty records in Winston Churchill, *The Second World War, Vol. II: Their Finest Hour*, 1949, p. 102.
14. That no less a figure than Churchill himself was aware of this tendency and its danger can be seen in his opening words to Parliament on 4 June: 'We must be very careful not to assign to this deliverance the attributes of a victory. Wars are not won by evacuations'. Quoted in *Their Finest Hour*, p. 102.
15. Stephen Spender, *War Pictures by British Artists, Second Series, 4: Air Raids*, 1943, p. 6.
16. 1940; chalk, wash and pen, 22 1/8 x 30 7/8, 1940, Imperial War Museum, London: reproduced in *War Pictures by British Artists*, IV, *Army*, plate 17.
17. Alex Henshaw, *Sigh for a Merlin: Testing the Spitfire*, 1979, p. 37.
18. 1940; wash, 13 3/4 x 18 5/8, Imperial War Museum, London.
19. *War Pictures by British Artists*, II, *Blitz*, 1943, pp. 5–6.
20. A glance at the published selections of these files will confirm this. See Tom Harrisson, *Living Through the Blitz*, 1976, repr. 1978, chapter 5.
21. *Blitz*, p. 5.
22. 1940; water-colour, 8 1/4 x 9 1/8, Imperial War Museum, London; reproduced in *Blitz*, plate 11.
23. 1940; water-colour, 8 x 12 1/8, Imperial War Museum, London; reproduced in *Blitz*, plate 12.
24. Water-colour, 10 1/8 x 14 1/2, IWM; reproduced in *Blitz*, plate 13.
25. The conditions here and in other public shelters was exposed and bitterly criticised in *Picture Post*, Vol. 9, No. 6, 9 November 1940, pp. 14–15.
26. *Blitz*, p. 61.
27. It should in fairness be pointed out that not all of Ardizzone's images lack compassion: his later *A Battle in an Orchard of Almond Trees in Sicily* (1943; water-colour, 14 3/4 x 21 1/4, Imperial War Museum, London) makes sensitive use of the desolation of nature to show the suffering of the battle in which, as the artist laconically records himself, 'Casualties were heavy' (Imperial War Museum, *A Concise catalogue of Paintings, Drawings and Sculpture of the Second World War 1939–1945*, 2nd edn, 1964, p. 10).
28. 1941; chalk, 10 1/2 x 15 1/4, South London Art Gallery, Camberwell.
29. No. 13, April–June 1942, between pp. 64 and 65.
30. Ink and wash; 8 3/8 x 10 1/2, private collection.
31. *The Colours of War*, 1983, p. 120.
32. Present whereabouts unknown.

33. Present whereabouts unknown.
34. Present whereabouts unknown.
35. 'Instead of a Carol', *Poems from the Forces*, edited by Keidrich Rhys, Routledge and Kegan Paul, 1941, p. 65.
36. For example, *Battle of Britain, August–October 1940: An Air Ministry Account of the Great Days from 8th August–31st October 1940*, issued by the Ministry of Information on behalf of the Air Ministry, HMSO 1941. A 32-page pamphlet, this sold 300,000 copies on the day of publication.
37. *We Speak from the Air: Broadcasts by the R.A.F.*, issued for the Air Ministry by the Ministry of Information, HMSO, 1942.
38. *Over to You: New Broadcasts by the R.A.F.*, prepared for the Air Ministry by the Ministry of Information, HMSO, 1943.
39. *Somme Battle Stories* recorded by Capt. A. J. Dawson, illustrated by Bruce Bairnsfather, published for *The Bystander* by Hodder and Stoughton, 1916.
40. Jennings' own stance is perhaps most apparent in *Words for Battle*, produced by Ian Dalrymple for the Crown Film Unit, 1941, which matches film of wartime Britain with poetry by Blake, Milton, Browning and other poets, ending with the Gettysburg address read over shots of tanks going past the Houses of Parliament and a 'coda' showing people in the streets of London accompanied by Handel's 'Water Music'.
41. Tom Harrisson, 'Crisis By-election', Vol. 1, No. 6, 5 November 1938, pp. 44–9.
42. B. L. Coombes, 'Unemployed', Vol. 2, No. 3, 21 January 1939, pp. 11–19.
43. *Penguin New Writing* No. 2, January 1941, p. 7. Lehmann's reference to 'each month' was optimistic; the paper allowance the magazine was given after the success of the first issue was withdrawn next year so that, from June 1942, it appeared quarterly.
44. *Penguin New Writing* No. 2, January 1941, p. 9.
45. *Ibid.*, pp. 9–15.
46. *Ibid.*, p. 14.
47. *Ibid.*, p. 15.
48. *Ibid.*, p. 15.
49. Preface to *Lyrical Ballads*, 1800, edited by R. L. Brett and A. R Jones, 1963, p. 245.
50. *Penguin New Writing* No. 3, February 1941, pp. 9–15; passage quoted from p. 10.
51. *Ibid.*, p. 10.
52. *Ibid.*, p. 11.
53. *Penguin New Writing* No. 8, July 1941, pp. 9–15.
54. *Penguin New Writing* No. 11, November 1941, pp. 9–16.
55. *Penguin New Writing* No. 9, September 1941, pp. 9–17.
56. *Ibid.*, p. 9.
57. *Ibid.*, p. 12.
58. *Ibid.*, p. 17.
59. *Penguin New Writing* No. 5, April 1941, pp. 9–14.

60. *Ibid.*, pp. 13–14.
61. *Penguin New Writing* No. 13, April–June 1942. The first 'Report on Today' section in that issue contained William Chappell's 'The Sky Makes me Hate it', Richard Nugent's 'From a Pilot's Diary' and Dan Davin's 'Under the Bridge'.
62. *Penguin New Writing* No. 12, April 1942, pp. 9–12.
63. *Ibid.*, p. 10.
64. *Ibid.* p. 12.

CHAPTER 4 BLITZ SUBLIME

1. Edmund Burke, *A Philosophical Enquiry into the Origin of our Ideas of the Sublime and the Beautiful* (1756), ed. J. T. Boulton, 1958, p. 136.
2. *Ibid.*, p. 137.
3. *Ibid.*, p. 136.
4. For example James Ward, *Gordale Scar*, 1812?–14; oil on canvas, 131 x 166, Tate Gallery, London.
5. For example Henry Fuseli, *Thor Battering the Midgard Serpent*, 1790; oil on canvas, 51 8/10 x 35 8/10, Royal Academy of Arts, London.
6. 1802. Conveniently available in *Samuel Taylor Coleridge (The Oxford Authors)*, ed. H. J. Jackson, 1985, pp. 117–18.
7. *The Prelude*, 1805, I, 372–426, *ed. cit*, pp. 48 and 50.
8. *The Way of All Flesh*, ed. R. Hoggart, Harmondsworth, Middlesex, 1947, rev. 1966, p. 45.
9. 1941; oil on canvas, 30 x 36, Imperial War Museum, London.
10. 1835; oil on canvas, 36 x 48, Museum of Art, Philadelphia.
11. See, for example, 'Fire-Fighters!', *Picture Post*, Vol. 10, No. 5, February 1 1941, pp. 9–15.
12. 1944; oil on canvas, 14 1/2 x 21 1/2, Imperial War Museum, London.
13. For a comment on his painting *The Ballooon Apron* see my *Art and Survival in First World War Britain*, 1989, p. 143 and plate 20.
14. 1940; watercolour, 22 x 29 1/2, City of Bristol Museum and Art Gallery.
15. Quoted in the Rev E. S. Shipley (ed.), *Bristol Siren Nights*, 1943, p. 24.
16. Directed by Arthur Cameron Menzies with music by Arthur Bliss and screenplay by H. G. Wells, produced by London Films, 1936. It is based on Wells' *The Shape of Things to Come*, 1933.
17. 1941; oil on canvas, 36 x 30, Imperial War Museum, London.
18. Both men are shown briefly in Humphrey Jennings' *Fires Were Started*, Ian Dalrymple, Crown Film Unit, 1943; the film gives an understated view of the life of a fireman which offers some valuable comparisons to Rosoman's painting.
19. See, for example, the photographs in *Front Line 1940–1941*, Issued for the Ministry of Home Security by the Ministry of Information, HMSO, 1942, especially those on pp. 28–31. This volume also

contains (p. 23) a photograph of St Clement Danes on fire, which makes a telling comparison with Carr's painting of the same scene.

20. *An Avalanche, or ice-fall, in the Alps, near the Scheideck, in the valley of Lauterbrunnen*, 1803; Oil on Canvas, 43 1/4 x 63, Tate Gallery, London.
21. See, for example, *Conference de peinture et sculpture*, Paris, 1698. The first English version, *The Conference of Mr Lebrun upon Expression*, appeared in 1701; English versions of this and other works appeared in the 1750s, 1780s and 1790s, and James Barry is among the artists known to háve used his theories as a source for their paintings.
22. Interview with Meirion and Susie Harries, quoted in their book *The War Artists*, 1983, p. 181.
23. For example, *A Radar Predictor, H.M.S. Formidable*, 1945, gouache, 15 1/2 x 20 1/2, Imperial War Museum, London.
24. *War Pictures by British Artists, Second Series, 4: Air Raids*, 1943, p. 59.
25. For an introductory survey of these and similar works of the war years see Robert Hewison, *Under Seige: Literary Life in London 1939–45*, 1977, Chapter 2.
26. Probably the best-known example of this kind of work is H. E. Bates, *Fair Stood the Wind for France*, 1944. Popular fiction of the war is surveyed in Holgar Klein, ed., *The Second World War in Fiction*, 1984.
27. Herbert Wilcox, Associated British Picture Corporation, 1945.
28. Robert Greenwood, 1943.
29. Humphrey Jennings and Harry Watt, GPO Film Unit for the Ministry of Information, 1940.
30. 1943; page references are to the Collected Edition, 1973.
31. Greene discusses in detail the circumstances of the book's writing in the introduction to the Collected Edition and in *Ways of Escape*, 1980, pp. 73–8. This also contains (pp. 79–88) the journal of blitz experiences which Greene kept at the time.
32. *The Ministry of Fear*, p. 3.
33. *Ibid.*, p. 5.
34. *Ibid.*, p. 258.
35. *Ibid.*, p. 259.
36. *Ibid.*, p. 260.
37. *Ibid.*, p. 260.
38. Emily Brontë, 1847.
39. Ann Radcliffe, née Ward, 1794.
40. *The Ministry of Fear*, p. 25.
41. Burke, *op. cit.*, p. 136.
42. *The Ministry of Fear*, p. 73.
43. *Ibid.*, p. 193.
44. *Ibid.*, p. 205.
45. *Ibid.*, introduction, p. xiii.
46. 1948.
47. *The Ministry of Fear*, p. 136.
48. 'Dion', V, ll. 96–9, *The Poetical Works of William Wordsworth*, ed. E. de Selincourt and Helen Darbishire, Oxford, Vol. 2, 1952, p. 277.

49. *The White Doe of Rylstone, or, The Fate of the Nortons*, 1815 ll. 1053–6; *ed. cit.*, Vol. 2, 1952, p. 277.
50. *The Borderers*, 1795–6, II. 618–20; *ed. cit.*, Vol. 3, 1940, p. 152.
51. For a further discussion of this see Tom Harrisson, *Living Through the Blitz*, 1976, p. 41.
52. R. M. Titmuss, *Problems of Social Policy (Official History of the Second World War)*, 1950, p. 23.
53. *Ibid.*, p. 345.
54. Accounts are given, for example, in Harrisson, *op. cit.*, pp. 132–4, 148 etc.
55. Figures are those given in the Official History, A. S. MacNalty (ed.), *The Civilian Health and Medical Services*, Vol. 1, 1953, p. 185.
56. P. E. Vernon, 'Psychological effects of Air Raids', *Journal of Abnormal Psychology*, Vol. 36, 1941, pp. 457–76.
57. Irving Janis, *Air War and Emotional Stress*, 1951, p. 75.
58. *Op. cit.*, p. 347.
59. Quoted in Harrisson, *op. cit.*, p. 78.
60. *Ibid.*, chapters 4 and 5 *passim*.
61. 1949.

CHAPTER 5 THE NURTURING EARTH

1. Oliver Goldsmith, *The Deserted Village*, 1769; *The Collected Works of Oliver Goldsmith*, ed. Arthur Friedman, IV, 1966, pp. 273–304; line 51, p. 289.
2. 'Elegy in a Country Churchyard', 1751; *The Complete Poems of Thomas Grey*, ed. H. W. Starr and J. R. Hendrickson, 1966, pp. 37–42.
3. The key figure here is Paul Sandby, whose early work such as *Distant View of Lieth*, 1747, watercolour and pencil, 6 3/8 x 17 13/16, Ashmolean Museum, Oxford is important in establishing a tradition.
4. Views on the continental grand tour are important here, but fashionable scenes in England are more significant in the growth of indigenous landscape. In these views of the Lake District and parts of Wales are most frequent, watercolours such as John Warwick Smith's *Hafod House*, 1793, 13 5/8 x 22 1/8, Private Collection, being representative.
5. Richard Payne Knight's *The Landscape: A Didactic Poem in Three Books* appeared in 1794 with an engraving after Thomas Hearne showing the shaggy and irregular textures fundamental to the Picturesque, as defined in Uvedale Price's *Essay on the Picturesque* which had appeared earlier in the same year.
6. Unlike the Picturesque and the Sublime, there is no tradition of visual embodiment of the Beautiful: perhaps the topographical watercolours of Paul Sandby come close to this in one manner whereas those of the English Claudians, such as Richard Wilson, do so in another.

7. 1781; oil on canvas, 26 1/2 x 41 3/8, Tate Gallery, London.
8. 'Lines Written a few miles above Tintern Abbey, on revisiting the banks of the Wye during a tour, July 13, 1798', *Lyrical Ballads, ed. cit.*, pp. 113–18; line quoted from p. 114.
9. The so-called *Sketch for Hadleigh Castle*, 1829, oil on canvas 48 1/4 x 66, National Gallery, London is the most outstanding example, but all the mature works show the quality to some degree.
10. It is almost absurd to limit this to a single example, but *Norham Castle, Sunrise*, 1845–50, oil on canvas, 35 3/4 x 48, Clore Gallery, London demonstrates the quality exquisitely.
11. Evident, for example, in the work of many painters of the Norwich School, such as John Crome, *Grove Scene*, 1810/20?, 25 6/10 x 18 3/4, oil on canvas, Castle Museum, Norwich.
12. Letter to the George Keatses, 21 April 1819, *The Letters of John Keats*, ed. Hyder Edward Rollins, Cambridge, Mass., 1958, Vol. 2, p. 102.
13. This is apparent in many places, for example the frontispiece to *Songs of Innocence*, 1789; facsimile, ed. Geoffrey Keynes, Oxford and Paris, 1967.
14. *Tales*, 1812; *George Crabbe: The Complete Poetical Works*, ed. Norma Dalrymple-Champneys and Arthur Pollard, II, 1988, pp. 132–42.
15. c. 1833; oil on paper on panel, 8 1/5 x 10 17/20, Yale Center for British Art, New Haven, Connecticut (Paul Mellon Collection).
16. 1828; line-engraving, 3 1/32 x 5 3/32 including inscription, British Museum, London.
17. *A Revelation of Love*, late fourteenth-century, ed. Marion Glasscoe, Exeter, Devon, 1976.
18. The figure of Christ crucified on a cross formed of lilies is in the east window of the Clopton Chantry Chapel, Holy Trinity, Long Melford, Suffolk: it dates from about 1350.
19. c. 1100; ed. Michael Swanton, Exeter, Devon, 1987.
20. *Piers Plowman: The Three Versions*, ed. George Kane and E. Talbot Donaldson, 1988.
21. In particular, *Silex Scintillans: or Sacred Poems and Private Ejaculations*, 1650, in L. C. Martin, *The Works of Henry Vaughan*, 2nd edn, Oxford, 1957.
22. *Poems, Centuries and Thanksgivings*, ed. Anne Ridler, Oxford, 1966.
23. The outstanding examples are the series of books of this sort produced by A.&C. Black and those of Batsford in the thirties, but there are many others, for example Arnold Fellows, *The Wayfarer's Companion*, 1937 and Edric Holmes, *London's Countryside*, n.d. (1927).
24. For example, the former's *The Moat, Grange Farm, Kimble*, 1922, oil on canvas, 30 x 20, Tate Gallery, London and the latter's *Landscape at Iden*, 1929, oil on canvas, 27 1/2 x 35 3/4, Tate Gallery, London.
25. See, for example, Sutherland's posters for Shell-Mex and the London Passenger Transport Board.
26. *Cornwall Illustrated in a Series of Views, Shell Guide*, 1934; *Devon, Shell Guide*, 1936. Betjeman was general editor of the series, which was published first by the Architectural Press, 1934–7, then by Batsford, 1937–9, and subsequently by Faber.

27. This is shown by the inclusion in Harry Batsford's series of books on the countryside of *The English Countryside: A Survey of its Chief Features*, 1939, which included essays on the evolution of different kinds of landscape.
28. This is discussed by Geoffrey Grigson in 'Samuel Palmer: The Politics of an Artist', *Horizon*, Vol. IV, No. 23, November 1941, pp. 314–29.
29. My own *Art and Survival in First World War Britain*, 1989 discusses the political significance of this in Chapter 8, 'England, Whose England?', pp. 132–53.
30. See, for example, David Mellor (ed.), *A Paradise Lost*, 1987; Raymond Durgnat, *A Mirror for England*, 1970 and other works mentioned in Chapter 1.
31. The Archers, 1944.
32. Directed by Michael Powell and produced by Alexander Korda, with a story by Ian Dalrymple, 1939.
33. 1938; released under the title *Do It Now* in 1939.
34. *For Ever England: an Anthology*, 1943.
35. Collins' series *Britain in Pictures* and *The British People in Pictures*, which included John Piper's *British Romantic Artists*, 1942, John Betjeman's *English Cities and Small Towns*, 1943 and Harry Roberts' *British Rebels and Reformers*, 1942 are representative and important; so, too, are the Batsford *Home Front Handbooks* series which included Harry Batsford's *How to see the Country*, 1940; Edmund Vale's *How to look at old Buildings*, 1940 and Doreen Wallace's *How to Grow Food*, 1940.
36. 1942; photo-lithograph; 19 7/8 x 29 3/4, Imperial War Museum, London.
37. On the effects of some of its efforts to stimulate discussion by the production of posters about post-war welfare, see Chapter 8.
38. The evolution of these is delightfully chronicled in Brian Cook Batsford, *The Britain of Brian Cook*, 1987.
39. See Chapter 8.
40. Photo-lithograph, 29 1/2 x 19 3/4, Imperial War Museum, London. The genesis of this poster is discussed in Ian McLaine, *Ministry of Morale*, 1979, p. 31.
41. 23 September 1939.
42. Photo-lithograph; 19 7/8 x 29 3/4, Imperial War Museum, London.
43. 1916; auto-lithograph, 39 7/8 x 25, Imperial War Museum, London. For a more detailed discussion of this poster see my *Art and Survival*, p. 133.
44. Photo-lithograph; 19 7/8 x 29 3/4, Imperial War Museum, London.
45. Photo-lithograph; 19 7/8 x 29 3/4, Imperial War Museum, London.
46. Published annually in the thirties; the 1938 edition, for example, contains a full-page illustration in sepia photogravure of Salisbury Cathedral seen through the trees.
47. *Lyrical Ballads, ed. cit.*, pp. 113–18; lines quoted from p. 114.
48. *Land at War*, HMSO, 1945, p. 7.
49. *Ibid.*, p. 15.
50. *Ibid.*, p. 12.

51. *Ibid.*, pp 12–13.
52. *Ibid.*, p. 7.
53. 1924; etching, 6 7/8 x 9 3/4, Twenty-one Gallery, London.
54. 1924; etching, 5 1/8 x 6 1/8, Twenty-one Gallery, London.
55. John Piper was perhaps catering to similar tastes in his articles such as 'Decrepit Glory; A Tour of Hafod', *The Architectural Review*, Vol. LXXXVII, No. 523, June 1940, pp. 207–10. The article is also of interest as a latter-day re-creation of a visit to one of the most popular destinations of the earlier Picturesque tour of Britain.
56. *Land at War*, p. 10.
57. In, for example, *The Milkmaid's Garland, or The Humours of May Day*, installed in a supper-box at Vauxhall Gardens, c. 1741–2, Victoria and Albert Museum, London.
58. In paintings such as *Autolycus*, 1836; oil on canvas, 21 x 29, Victoria and Albert Museum, London.
59. *Ed. cit.*, p. 245.
60. *Land at War*, p. 87.
61. *Ibid.*, p. 20.
62. *Ibid.*, p. 25.
63. *Tess of the D'Urbervilles*, 1892; New Wessex Edition, ed. P. N. Furbank, 1974, pp 348–9.
64. 1815: oil on canvas, 20 1/4 x 24 1/2, Victoria and Albert Museum, London.
65. *Land at War*, p. 94.
66. 'September Journal', *Horizon*, Vol. 1, No. 9, pp. 221–2.
67. 'Upon Westminster Bridge', 1807, *ed. cit.*, Vol. 3, p. 38.
68. 'Songs of Innocence and Experience', *Blake: Complete Writings* ed. Geoffrey Keynes, 1966, p. 216.
69. *War Pictures by British Artists, Second Series, IV: Air Raids*, 1943, Introduction, p. 7.
70. 1940; Humphrey Jennings and Harry Watt, with commentary by Quentin Reynolds; GPO Film Unit for the Ministry of Information.
71. In particular a series of photographs of St Paul's Cathedral seen from the sites of ruined buildings, conveniently available in *Lilliput goes to War*, edited by Kaye Webb, 1985, pp. 101–5.
72. In, for example, *The Incredible City* by Mrs Robert Henrey, 1944 and the same writer's retrospective study, *The Virgin of Aldermanbury: Rebirth of the City of London*, 1958.
73. Stephen Spender, 'September Journal', *Horizon*, Vol. 1, No. 9, p. 224.
74. *Penguin New Writing* No. 20, 1944. Page references here are to the reprinting in *The Collected Stories of Elizabeth Bowen*, 1980, pp. 728–40.
75. 'Mysterious Kôr', p. 728.
76. Most obviously *Two Men Contemplating the Moon*, 1819; oil on canvas, 13 3/4 x 17 3/10, Staatliche Kunstsammlungen, Gemäldgalerie, Dresden.
77. See P. B. Ellis, *Rider Haggard: A Voice from the Infinite*, 1978, p. 117.

78. *He: by the authors of 'It', 'King Solomon's Wives', 'Bess', 'Much Darker Days', 'Mr. Morton's Subtler', and Other Romances*, 1887.
79. Letter to H. Rider Haggard, 12 July 1887, quoted in Ellis, *op. cit.*, p. 109.
80. *The Examiner*, January 1818; *Poetical Works*, ed. Thomas Hutchinson, 1905 repr. 1970, p. 551.
81. In the story, Elizabeth Bowen misquotes l. 3 as 'Mysterious Kôr, thy *walls* forsaken stand' (my italics).
82. *The Complete Works of Thomas Chatterton: A Bicentenary edition*, ed. by D. S. Taylor in association with B. B. Hoover, 2 Vols, Oxford, 1971.
83. For example *The Shepherd's Dream*, 1793; oil on canvas, 60 6/10 x 84 6/10, Tate Gallery, London.
84. 'Mysterious Kôr', p. 730.
85. *Ibid.*, p. 738.
86. *Ibid.*, p. 739.
87. *Ibid.*, p. 740.
88. *Ways of Escape*, 1980, repr. 1982, p. 79.
89. Humphrey Jennings, Letter to Cicely Jennings, 28 July 1942, quoted in Mary-Lou Jennings (ed.), *Humphrey Jennings: Film-maker, Painter, Poet*, 1982, p. 29.
90. Discussed, for example, in Ritchie Calder, *The People's War*, 1969 repr. 1971, pp. 210 and 192 respectively.
91. 1944; lithograph, 39 3/4 x 24 7/8, Imperial War Museum, London.
92. 1945; tempera on panel, 11 1/2 x 14 1/2, Imperial War Museum, London.
93. 'Wild flowers bestow beauty on London's "blitzed" sites', Vol. 201, No. 5396, 19 Sept. 1942, p. 334; 'Nature makes her own garden in a blitzed site: wild flowers now blooming in New Bond St.', Vol. 206, No. 5540, 23 June 1945, pp. 678–9.
94. Ealing Studios: screenplay by John Dighton, Angus MacPhaill and Diana Morgan from the short story 'The Lieutenant Died Last', *Collier's Magazine*, 29 June, 1940. In the USA it is known as *Forty-Eight Hours*.
95. See Chapter 8.

CHAPTER 6 A CHILD OF OUR TIME

1. *King Arthur*, 1691.
2. *Dido and Aeneas*, 1689
3. *Acis and Galathea*, c. 1720, for example, has a text by John Gay.
4. *Messiah*, 1741.
5. *The Dream of Gerontius*, 1900.
6. *A Mass of Life*, 1898–1905.
7. *A Sea Symphony*, 1903–9.
8. For example, *God puts a mark on Cain after he killed Abel*, 1781; black chalk heightened with white, ink and black wash, 24 8/10 x 20 9/10, Kunsthaus, Zurich.

9. For example, *Titania and Bottom*, 1780–90; oil on canvas, 85 x 107 9/10, Tate Gallery, London.
10. For example, *Satan with Adam and Eve*, watercolour, 1807/8, 19 1/20 x 15 3/10, Museum of Fine Arts, Boston and the larger version of the same composition with image reversed in Henry E. Huntington Library, San Marino, California.
11. For example, *The Inscription over Hell gate*, 1824–7; watercolour, pen and ink, 20 5/8 x 14 1/2, Tate Gallery, London.
12. The first collecting was done by the Rev. John Broadwood, whose *Sixteen Sussex Folk-songs* appeared in 1843. Baring-Gould began collecting in 1888, and published his first collection, *Songs of the West*, in 1889. *A Garland of Song* followed in 1895.
13. Sharp's *Folk Songs of Somerset* appeared in 1904, and his influential *English Folk Songs for Schools*, written in collaboration with Baring-Gould, was published in 1906.
14. Vaughan Williams absorbs the melodic structures and harmonic implications of folk-song in almost all his mature work, as well as using actual folk-songs as the foundations of particular works. *In the Fen Country*, 1904, rev 1935, is an example of the former kind; *Norfolk Rhapsody No 1*, 1906, rev 1914, of the latter.
15. In, for example, *A Somerset Rhapsody*, 1906–7, dedicated to Cecil Sharp.
16. Grainger's most characteristic use of folk-song is probably to be found in *A Lincolnshire Posy*, 1937–8.
17. 1927–30.
18. 1936.
19. Vaughan Williams drew his text from *The Complete Poems of John Skelton* edited by Philip Henderson, 1931, which modernised the texts presented in the standard edition, *The Poetical Works of John Skelton*, ed. by the Rev. Alexander Dyce, 2 vols, 1843.
20. 1938/9.
21. Set by Britten as *Rejoice in the Lamb*, Op. 30, 1943.
22. Op. 31, 1943.
23. Letter xxii, 1810; *ed. cit.*, Vol. 1, pp. 564–74.
24. Op. 33a, 1945.
25. *A Child of Our Time*. Oratorio for soli, chorus and orchestra. 1944.
26. 1934.
27. This dates from the mid-thirties; Tippett himself does not refer to it in his *Moving into Aquarius*, 1958, nor does it receive extensive mention elsewhere.
28. Tippett's political attitudes at this time are discussed in Meirion Bowen, *Michael Tippett*, 1982, pp. 19–24.
29. 1789–90; *Blake, Complete Writings*, ed. Geoffrey Keynes, 1966, pp. 148–60; passage quoted from p. 159.
30. These are conveniently collected in Meirion Bowen (ed.), *Music of the Angels: Essays and Sketchbooks of Michael Tippett*, 1980.
31. Grynsban's photograph was published in an article on the pogrom following the death of vom Rath, 'Back to the Middle Ages', *Picture Post*, Vol. 1, No. 9, 26 November 1938, p. 13.

32. 1938.
33. For a discussion of the writing and first performance see Bowen, *Michael Tippett*, pp. 43–6.
34. The diversity of subject – if not of musical nature – is remarkable: Mendelssohn's *Elijah*, 1846, and Samuel Coleridge-Taylor's *Hiawatha's Wedding Feast*, 1900, use the same basis of recitative, aria and chorus.
35. Michael Tippett, 'The Nameless Hero: reflections on *A Child of Our Time*, BBC Radio, 22 April 1950, reprinted in *Music of the Angels*, pp. 188–92; passage quoted from p. 190.
36. Preface to *Lyrical Ballads, ed. cit.*, p. 266.
37. After the title and main thesis of John Danby's book *The Simple Wordsworth*, 1960.
38. *Lyrical Ballads, ed. cit.*, p. 114.
39. Bach's use of traditional melodies and popular songs as the basis of his chorales in the cantatas is an early parallel to Tippett's use of the folk idiom of spirituals.
40. *Appalachia: Variations on an old Slave Song*, 1896.
41. Symphony No. 9 in E minor, Op. 95, 1896.
42. 'The Nameless Hero', p. 188.
43. *A Child of Our Time*, full score, p. 151.
44. *Ibid.*, pp. 45–6.
45. John Bunyan, *The Pilgrim's Progress from this World to That which is to Come*, 1678, ed. J. B. Wharey, 2nd edn, rev. by R. Sharrock, Oxford 1960, p. 309.
46. For example, 'Love's redeeming work is done', *Hymns Ancient and Modern Revised*, No. 141.
47. For example, 'The Lord my pasture shall prepare', *Hymns Ancient and Modern Revised*, No. 179.
48. Michael Tippett, programme note for York Festival, 1963, reprinted in *Music of the Angels*, pp. 192–5; passage quoted from p. 194.
49. The story is told by Tippett himself in 'T. S. Eliot and *A Child of Our Time*', *Music of the Angels*, pp. 117–26; pp. 117–19 are expressly relevant.
50. *A Child of Our Time*, pp. 34–5.
51. *Ibid.*, pp. 62–4.
52. 'The Nameless Hero', p. 188.
53. *A Child of Our Time*, pp. 35–6.
54. York Festival Programme note, p. 194.
55. *A Child of Our Time*, p. 45, bar 5.
56. *A Select Collection of Original Scottish Airs for the Voice with Introductory and Concluding Symphonies and Accompaniments for the Piano Forte, Violin and Violoncello*, 1804.
57. The works already cited in note 14 exemplify this, but perhaps the most complete examples are to be found in the *Symphony in D Minor*, 1925?–1943, and the opera *The Pilgrim's Progress* on which Vaughan Williams worked intermittently from 1906 but which was not finally performed until 1951.
58. 1854; text by the composer.

59. *A Child of Our Time*, pp. 33–8.
60. 1801; *Faust. Der Tragödie Erster Theil*, Werke Goethes, herausgegeben von der Deutschen akademie der wissenschaften zu Berlin unter leitung von Ernst Grumach, Berlin 1958.
61. The translation is by Shelley, published in part in *The Liberal*, No. 1 and in full in the *Posthumous Poems* of 1824. The text is available in *Shelley: Poetical Works*, ed. Thomas Hutchinson, corrected by G. M. Matthews, Oxford, 1970, pp. 748–62; passage quoted from p. 749.
62. 1935.
63. The text quoted is taken from *The Book of Common Prayer*, 1662.
64. *Murder in the Cathedral*, p. 90.
65. *A Child of Our Time*, pp. 136–7.
66. Note by the composer dated June 1968, *Music of the Angels*, pp. 195–7; passage quoted from p. 196.
67. *A Child of Our Time*, pp. 11–12.
68. *The Book of Thel*, 1789; Keynes, *ed. cit.*, pp. 127–30.
69. *A Child of Our Time*, p. 14.
70. *Ibid.*, pp. 14–15.
71. *The First Book of Urizen*, 1794; Keynes, *ed. cit.*, pp. 222–36.
72. 'The Human Abstract', Keynes, *ed. cit.*, p. 217.
73. *A Child of Our Time*, p. 75.
74. *Ibid.*, pp. 133–4.
75. *Ibid.*, pp. 114–21.
76. See Bowen, *Michael Tippett*, p. 48.
77. *Illustrations to the Book of Job*; title-page and 21 line engravings, 1825.
78. Reproduced in plate 636 in David Bindman, assisted by Deirdre Toomey, *The Complete Graphic Works of William Blake*, 1978.
79. Bindman, *ed. cit.*, plate 186 reproduces the copy in the Pierpont Morgan Library, New York; a colour facsimile of the title-page of the copy in the Lessing J. Rosenwald Collection of the Library of Congress, Alverthorpe Gallery, Jenkintown, Pennsylvania is conveniently available in *The Book of Urizen*, ed. Kay Parkhurst Easson and Roger R. Easson, Memphis, Tennessee, 1978, p. 11.
80. Bindman, *ed. cit.*, plate 637.
81. *A Child of Our Time*, pp. 18–19.
82. *Ibid.*, p. 20.
83. *Ibid.*, pp. 25–32.
84. *Ibid.*, pp. 44–8.
85. *Ibid.*, p. 89.
86. *Ibid.*, p. 101.
87. *Ibid.*, pp. 109–10.
88. *Ibid.*, pp. 123–4.
89. *Ibid.*, p. 127.
90. *Ibid.*, p. 131.
91. William Blake, *The Marriage of Heaven and Hell*, 1790–3, Keynes *ed cit*, pp. 148–60; line quoted from p. 149.
92. *A Child of Our Time*, pp. 139–40.
93. York festival programme note, p. 194.
94. *A Child of Our Time*, pp. 150–7.
95. 'The Nameless Hero', p. 190.

CHAPTER 7 MIDWINTER SPRING

1. 'À Terre', *The Collected Poems of Wilfred Owen*, ed. C. Day Lewis, 1963, p. 65.
2. In *The Great War and Modern Memory*, 1975. Fussell discusses the point throughout the book, most concentratedly on pp. 7–18; on p. 8, for example, he remarks 'the Great War was more ironic than any before or since'.
3. 'I shall be one with nature, herb, and stone' is a half-remembered quotation from *Adonais* (1821), stanza XLII:

   He is made one With Nature:
   . . . a presence to be felt and known
   In darkness and in light, from herb and stone

   See *Shelley, Poetical Works*, ed. Thomas Hutchinson, 1905, p. 441.
4. Eric Partridge, *A Dictionary of Slang and Unconventional English*, 1937, pp. 205 and 671.
5. *Ibid*., p. 205. Further exploration of the language of the trenches is provided in *Songs and Slang of the British Soldier 1914–18*, edited by John Brophy and Eric Partridge, 1931.
6. 1937.
7. *In Parenthesis*, pp. 176–7.
8. See Eric Partridge, *op. cit*., p. 48.
9. 1941; 29 1/2 x 19 3/4, Mrs Fay Pomerance, Sheffield.
10. For example, those at 19 Hill Street, London, 1930–31 and Plas Newydd, Anglesey, 1936–8.
11. 1943; oil on board, 18 1/2 x 23, private collection.
12. 1748?; oil on canvas, 27 1/2 x 47, National Gallery, London.
13. Suggested by Michael Yorke in *The Spirit of Place*, 1988, p. 202.
14. 1943; oil on canvas, 20 6/10 x 24 6/10, private collection.
15. 1944; oil on canvas, 19 1/4 x 29 3/4, Sotheby's, London.
16. 1945; oil on board, 22 1/2 x 32 3/4, Aberdeen Art Gallery.
17. 1945; oil on canvas, 28 1/2 x 36, Arts Council of Great Britain.
18. 1944; oil on canvas; present whereabouts unknown.
19. There are several versions of this theme from the forties; that referred to here is the most familiar version, 1942–3; oil on panel, 22 9/10 x 19, Tate Gallery, London.
20. Frederick Muller, 1945.
21. In particular the *Holy Sonnets*. See John Donne, *Poems*, ed. H.J.C. Grierson, 1933.
22. This is most apparent in the emblematic portraits of Queen Elizabeth, such as the so-called 'Ditchley' portrait attributed to Marcus Gheeraerts, c. 1592; oil on canvas, 93 x 59, National Portrait Gallery, London.
23. 1939, oil on canvas, 47 1/10 x 36, 1939, private collection.
24. The anonymous fifteenth century lyric from which these lines come is probably the most immediate embodiment of this particular doctrine.

It is conveniently available in R. T. Davies, *Medieval English Lyrics: A Critical Anthology*, 1963, pp. 160–1.

25. Four-pronged forks do not appear in England until the late seventeenth century: see Gerald Taylor, *Silver*, 1956, p. 112.
26. Such forms were current in the fifteenth and sixteenth centuries: see Taylor, *op cit*, p. 44.
27. This is clearest in some designs by C. F. A. Voysey. A fork designed in 1902, made in electroplate by Charles William Fletcher of Sheffield, has three tines; a teaspoon designed in 1908, made in sterling silver by Edward Barnard and Sons Ltd., has the teardrop bowl and both have the long, thin shaft. See John Brandon-Jones, *C. F. A. Voysey: Architect and Designer 1857–1941*, 1978, pp. 135–7.
28. In, for example, the 'Rainbow' portrait, attributed to Marcus Gheeraerts, c 1600–1603; oil on canvas, 50 x 39, Hatfield House, Hertfordshire.
29. Seen, for example, in the 'Daisy' pattern, 1861.
30. David Mellor, *A Paradise Lost: the Neo-Romantic Imagination in Britain 1935–55*, 1987, p. 20.
31. *The Nuptials of God*, published in the magazine *The Game*, 1923; wood-engraving, 2 6/10 x 2.
32. See *The Hobbit, or There and back Again*, 1937 and *The Lord of the Rings*, 1954–5.
33. Quoted by Grigson in 'Samuel Palmer at Shoreham', *Signature*, November 1939, pp. 1–17; passage quoted from p. 16.
34. 1944; oil on board, 18 x 24, Christopher Hull Gallery, London.
35. 1945; ink and gouache, 7 x 10 1/4, private collection.
36. 1937; oil on canvas, 62 3/4 x 79 1/4, Tate Gallery, London.
37. 1805; watercolour, 9 x 13, British Museum, London.
38. 1785; oil on panel, 35 1/4 x 53 1/4, Tate Gallery, London.
39. 1784; oil on panel, 35 1/2 x 53 7/8, Tate Gallery, London.
40. 1937; oil on canvas, 137 1/2 x 305 3/4 Prado, Madrid.
41. See 'The Ant-Lion', *Horizon* Vol. 1, No. 1, January 1940, pp. 25– 30.
42. The approach is clear in several of the 'Early Poems, 1938–1945' published in *Philip Larkin: Collected Poems* ed. by Anthony Thwaite, 1988, for example 'The hills in their recumbent postures', p. 234; 'Time and space were only their disguises' p. 260 and 'All catches alight', pp. 272–3.
43. 'England's Climate', *Axis*, Autumn 1936, pp. 4–9; Myfanwy Evans (ed.), *The Painter's Object*, 1937.
44. 1939; oil on canvas, 24 1/2 x 19, Ulster Museum, Belfast.
45. See John Hayes, *The Art of Graham Sutherland*, 1980, p. 72.
46. 1940; gouache, 26 3/4 x 18 1/2, City Museums and Art Gallery, Birmingham.
47. 1940; oil on canvas, 31 x 42 1/2, Tate Gallery, London.
48. 1941; pen and wash, 15 x 12, Colin Anderson, Jersey.
49. 1943; oil on burlap, 44 1/4 x 71, Scottish National Gallery of Modern Art, Edinburgh.
50. 1944.
51. 1941; oil on canvas, 40 x 60, Tate Gallery, London.

52. 1944; oil on canvas, 48 x 72, Imperial War Museum, London.
53. See, for example, *Pillar and Moon*, 1932–42; oil on canvas, 20 x 30, Tate Gallery, London, in which the stone ball at the top of the pillar in the foreground and the white moon at the rear of the composition parody each other and define the inner recession of the painting.
54. The comparison is made closer by Nash's own interest in stone circles and other prehistoric ritual elements at Stonehenge, recalling Hardy's use of these features to give universal significance to *Tess of the D'Urbervilles* (1891).
55. See, for example, the wash drawings of Edward Ardizzone and Eric Ravilious, both of which, though differing greatly in style, present a detachment which perhaps reflects a refusal to judge or interpret which is a marked feature of much art of the time.
56. 1941; oil on canvas, 40 x 60, Tate Gallery, London.
57. These are now in the Tate Gallery Archive, London.
58. 1942; chalk, watercolour and newspaper photograph on buff paper, 15 2/10 x 22 1/4, private collection.
59. 1932–6; oil on canvas, 36 x 28, Tate Gallery, London.
60. 1936–8; oil on canvas, 26 3/4 x 40, Tate Gallery, London.
61. 1918; oil on canvas, 28 x 36, Imperial War Museum, London.
62. 1945; oil on canvas, 57 x 50 1/2, Tate Gallery, London.
63. 1944; oil on board; triptych, each panel 37 x 29, Tate Gallery, London.
64. See Dawn Ades, 'Web of Images', in *Francis Bacon*, catalogue to Tate Gallery exhibition, 1985.
65. 'Spring Offensive'; *Collected Poems of Wilfred Owen*, ed. C. Day Lewis, 1963, p. 53.
66. 1944; oil on canvas, 40 x 60, National Museum of Wales, Cardiff.
67. 1945; oil on canvas, 10 x 12, Peter Nahum, London.
68. In, for example, *Newton*, 1795/c. 1805, colour print finished in pen and watercolour, 18 1/8 x 25 5/8, Tate Gallery, London. Here Blake uses the image with his habitual ambivalence to depict the end of the rolled-up scroll on which Newton is making geometric drawings, so that it represents both the free creative impulse and the mechanistic restraints of the reason.
69. For example, *Pembrokeshire Landscape*, 1936; pen and ink and gouache, 14 x 21 1/2, National Museum of Wales, Cardiff and *Sun Setting Between Hills*, 1937; watercolour, 9 7/8 x 14, Lord Clark of Saltwood.
70. 1936; oil on canvas, 24 x 36, Tate Gallery, London.
71. 1939; collage of colour reproduction of Bartolommeo Vivarini's *Adoration* and mother-of-pearl sequins, size unknown: destroyed by the artist.
72. 1944; oil on canvas, 16 x 24, Fine Art Society.
73. 1890; oil on canvas, 15 1/2 x 13 3/4, Musée du Louvre, Paris.
74. Most celebratedly in *Le temps menaçent*, 1928, oil on canvas, 21 1/4 x 28 3/4, Penrose Collection, London.
75. James Frazer, *The Golden Bough*, 12 vols, 1890–1915. Of these the final volumes, *Balder the Beautiful*, were the most important in this phase of Nash's work.

76. 1943; pencil, chalk and watercolour with colour notes, 11 3/4 x 15 1/2, Patricia Raeburn.
77. 1943; chalk and watercolour with colour notes, 11 1/4 x 15 1/2, Michael Culme-Seymour.
78. 1942; oil on canvas, 20 x 30, National Gallery of New South Wales: 1942, pencil, chalk and watercolour, 15 1/2 x 22 1/2, Mrs James Fell.
79. 1942; oil on canvas, 30 x 20, Fitzwilliam Museum, Cambridge.
80. 1943; oil on canvas, 28 x 38, National Gallery of Victoria, Melbourne.
81. 1943; oil on canvas, 28 x 56, Queen Elizabeth the Queen Mother.
82. *Balder the Beautiful: The Fire Festivals of Europe and the Doctrine of the External Soul*, 2 vols; see vol. 1, pp. 117–18, 145 and 167 ff.
83. 1945; oil on canvas, 28 x 36, British Council.
84. 1945; oil on canvas, 28 x 36, National Gallery of Canada.
85. From 'Picture History', unpublished writings by Nash about his last paintings, quoted in Andrew Causey, *Paul Nash*, 1980, p. 334.
86. Article by Sutherland in Roberto Tassi, *Sutherland: the Wartime Drawings*, 1980, p. 20.
87. *Ibid.*, pp. 19–20.
88. *Horizon*, Vol. V, No. 28, April 1942, pp. 224–36; quoted in Chapter 2.
89. Tassi, *op. cit.*, p. 19.
90. 1861; oil on canvas, 30 1/16 x 38 11/16, Potter Palmer Collection, Art Institute of Chicago.
91. 1941; gouache, 25 1/2 x 44, Imperial War Museum, London.
92. 1941; gouache, 26 x 44, Ferens Art Gallery, Kingston-upon-Hull.
93. Douglas Cooper, *The Work of Graham Sutherland*, 1961, p. 28.
94. 1941; pen and ink, charcoal and gouache, 25 7/8 x 44 1/8, Ferens Art Gallery, Kingston-upon-Hull.
95. 1941; pen and ink and gouache, 25 3/8 x 44 7/8, Tate Gallery, London.
96. See the reference to R. M. Titmuss, *Problems of Social Policy*, p. 347, in Chapter 4.
97. As I suggest above in Chapter 4.
98. See the passage from Spender's introduction to *War Pictures by British Artists, Second Series, IV: Air Raids*, 1943, p. 7, quoted in Chapter 4.
99. *Deaths and Entrances*, 1946. For ease of availability, subsequent references are to the poems in *Dylan Thomas: the Poems*, ed. Daniel Jones, 1971.
100. 'Deaths Duell, preached at Whitehall before the King's Majesty in the beginning of Lent, 1630, on Psalms 68.20', in Evelyn M. Simpson and George R. Potter (ed.), *The Sermons of John Donne*, Berkely and Los Angeles, California, 1962, X, pp. 229–48. The specific passage to which Thomas is alluding occurs on pages 231–2: 'Our very *birth* and entrance into this life, is *exitus à morte*, an *issue from death*'.
101. *Ed. cit.*, pp. 195–6.
102. *Ibid.*, pp. 173–5.
103. *Ibid.*, p. 175.

104. *Ibid.*, pp. 172–3.
105. *Ibid.*, pp. 207–8.
106. *Ibid.*, p. 208.
107. *Ibid.*, pp. 191–2.
108. 1875; *Poems now first published*, ed. Robert Bridges, 1918; text available in *Poems of Gerard Manley Hopkins*, 4th edn, ed. W. H. Gardner and N. H. Mackenzie, 1967.
109. Wordsworth, *ed. cit.*, Vol. 2, p. 216.
110. *Four Quartets*, 1944, pp. 49–59.
111. *Ibid.*, p. 49.
112. *Ibid.*, p. 51.
113. *Ibid.*, p. 52.
114. *Ibid.*, p. 52.
115. 1922.
116. *Prufrock and other Observations*, 1917.
117. *ed. cit.*, pp. 54–5.
118. *Ibid.*, p. 55.
119. *Revelation of Love, ed. cit.*, p. 28.
120. *ed. cit.*, p. 57.
121. *Ibid.*, p. 58.
122. *Revelation of Love, ed. cit.*, pp. 28–9.
123. 'Henry Moore: An English Romantic', Susan Compton, *Henry Moore*, exhibition catalogue, Royal Academy of Arts, 1988, pp. 37–44; passage quoted from p. 41.
124. Moore's own writings about his feelings about the subject are usefully collected in *Henry Moore on Sculpture*, ed. Philip James, 1966.
125. Introduction by Moore himself in *Henry Moore: A Shelter Sketchbook, with a commentary by Frances Carey*, 1988, pp. 9–10.
126. *Henry Moore: A Shelter Sketchbook, with a commentary by Frances Carey*, 1988. This is a facsimile of the first of the two sketchbooks used by Moore; some pages from the second have been reproduced in *Shelter Sketch Book*, London and Berlin, 1967, and a selection of pages from both was published under the same title by Editions Poetry in 1945.
127. For this and other contemporary responses to the drawings see Roger Berthoud, *The Life of Henry Moore*, 1987, pp. 175–6.
128. 1941; pen and ink, wax crayon and watercolour, 13 1/8 x 20 5/8, Robert and Lisa Sainsbury Collection, University of East Anglia, Norwich.
129. 'Art Critic' (pseud. Keith Vaughan), 'War Artists and the War', *Penguin New Writing* No. 16, January 1943, pp. 108–17; passage quoted from pp. 114 and 113.

CHAPTER 8 ROOTS THAT CLUTCH

1. Most particularly in *Du Contrat Social*, 1762, but also in *Discours sur l'origine et les fondements de l'inégalité, 1755* and *Émile ou de l'Education*,

1762.

2. 'The Way We Live Now – IV', *Penguin New Writing* No. 5, April 1941, pp. 9–14.
3. *Ibid.*, p. 14.
4. 'The Way We Live Now – V', *Penguin New Writing* No. 6, May 1941, pp. 9–13.
5. *Ibid.*, p. 10.
6. *Ibid.*, p. 13.
7. *Ibid.*, p. 13.
8. 'The New Social Services and the Citizen', broadcast on 4 July 1948 and printed in *The Listener*, Vol. XL, No. 1015, pp. 39–40.
9. *Ibid.*, p. 40.
10. *Ibid.*, p. 40.
11. *Social Insurance and Allied Services – The Beveridge Report in Brief*, 1942, presented the main findings and was the version sold in largest numbers, at 3d a copy or 10s for fifty copies.
12. *Ibid.*, p. 4.
13. *Your Britain. Fight for it Now*, 'Modern medicine . . . '. 1942; photogravure, 19 7/8 x 29 5/16.
14. See Joseph Darracott and Belinda Loftus, *Second World War Posters*, 1972, p. 33.
15. J. M. Richards, *An Introduction to Modern Architecture*, 1940, pp. 115 and 117. Richards was assistant editor of *The Architectural Review* under Betjeman.
16. *Your Britain. Fight for it Now*, 'Clean, airy and well planned dwellings . . . ', 1942, photo-gravure, 19 7/8 x 29 5/16.
17. The 1956 edition was published by *The Architectural Review*, but the lectures are best known in the revised edition by Penguin Books Ltd of 1964 and subsequent reprintings.
18. In chapter 7, 'Picturesque England', pp. 172–92 of the 1964 edition.
19. Ministry of Town and Country Planning and Department of Health for Scotland, *Final Report of the New Towns Committee*, Cmd. 6876, 1946. The committee was chaired by John Reith.
20. *Ibid.*, p. 11.
21. *Ibid.*, p. 19.
22. In *Sketches and Hints on Landscape Gardening*, 1795, and *Fragments on the Theory and Practice of Landscape Gardening*, 1816 respectively.
23. *Op. cit.*, p. 10.
24. *Ibid.*, p. 24.
25. Bryant's most celebrated work of this period is contained in his three books *English Saga 1840–1940*, 1940; *The Years of Endurance 1793–1802*, 1942; and *The Years of Victory 1802–12*, 1944.
26. *English Saga*, p. 316.
27. *Ibid.*, p. 330.
28. Pevsner, *op. cit.*, p. 178; he is quoting from Emerson's *English Traits*, chapter xviii. Emerson actually writes 'only the English race can be trusted with freedom' (*English Traits*, 1856; ed. H. M. James, Cambridge, Mass, 1966, p. 97). Pevsner's own circumstances as a refugee from Nazi persecution no doubt explain the deletion.

29. Cobbett himself provides an interesting unity of concern for individual freedom and nurture through the land: his *Cottage Economy* appeared as a series of pamphlets in 1821–2 after his radical journalism. His advice on the rearing of fowls is especially to be recommended.
30. 'September 1, 1939', 1939; *ed. cit.*, pp. 245–7; passage quoted from p. 246.
31. 'The Mower'; 12 June 1979. First published in *Humberside*, the Hull Literary Club magazine, Autumn 1979; reprinted in *Philip Larkin: Collected Poems* edited by Anthony Thwaite, 1988, p 214.

Select Bibliography

Aldgate, Anthony, *Britain Can Take It*, 1986.

Alexander, R. G., *A Catalogue of the Etchings of Samuel Palmer*, Print Collectors' Club Publication No. 16, 1937.

The Architectural Review.

Arts Council of Great Britain, *Thirties: British Art and Design before the War*, 1979.

Auden, W. H., ed. Mendelson, Edward, *The English Auden: Poems, Essays and Dramatic Writings 1927–1939*, 1977.

Axis.

Bergonzi, Bernard, *Reading the Thirties: Texts and Contexts*, 1978.

Berthoud, Roger, *The Life of Henry Moore*, 1987.

Binyon, Laurence, *The Followers of William Blake: Edward Calvert, Samuel Palmer, George Richmond and their Circle*, 1925.

Binyon, Laurence, *The English Romantic Revival in Art and Poetry: A Reconsideration*, Fifth Rickham Godlee Lecture, Thursday 24 October 1935.

Binyon, Laurence, *English Watercolours, from the work of Turner, Girtin, Cotman, Constable and Bonnington*, 1939.

Blake, William, ed. Keynes, Geoffrey, *Blake: Complete Writings*, 1966.

Blake, William, ed. Bindman, David, assisted by Toomey, Deirdre, *The Complete Graphic Works of William Blake*, 1978.

Bowen, Elizabeth, 'Mysterious Kôr', 1944; *The Collected Stories of Elizabeth Bowen*, 1980.

Bowen, Meirion, *Michael Tippett*, 1982.

Bryant, Arthur, *English Saga, 1840–1940*, 1940.

Burke, Edmund, ed. Boulton, J. T., *A Philosophical Enquiry into the Origin of our Ideas of the Sublime and the Beautiful*, 1958.

Calder, Angus and Sheridan, Dorothy (eds), *Speak for Yourself: A Mass-Observation Anthology*, 1985.

Causey, Andrew, *Paul Nash*, 1980.

Clark, Kenneth, *The Gothic Revival*, 1928.

Compton, Susan, *Henry Moore*, 1988.

Cooper, Joseph, *The Work of Graham Sutherland*, 1961.

Darracott, Joseph and Loftus, Belinda, *Second World War Posters*, 1972.

Durgnat, Raymond, *A Mirror for England*, 1970.

Eliot, T. S., *Four Quartets*, 1944.

Ellis, P. B., *Rider Haggard: A Voice from the Infinite*, 1978.

Evans, Myfanwy, *The Painter's Object*, 1937.

Finberg, A. J., 'Edward Calvert's Engravings', *Print Collector's Quarterly*, Vol. 17, No. 4, 1930.

Greene, Graham, *The Ministry of Fear*, 1943; Collected Edition 1973.

Greene, Graham, *Ways of Escape*, 1980.

Grigson, Geoffrey, 'Samuel Palmer at Shoreham', *Signature*, November 1939.

Grigson, Geoffrey, 'Samuel Palmer; The Politics of an Artist', *Horizon,* Vol. IV, No. 2, November 1941.
Grigson, Geoffrey, ed., *The Romantics: An Anthology chosen by Geoffrey Grigson*, 1942.
Grigson, Geoffrey, ed., *The Poet's Eye*, 1944.
Grigson, Geoffrey, *John Craxton: Paintings and Drawings*, 1948.
Grigson, Geoffrey and Piper, John, 'England's Climate', *Axis,* Autumn 1936.
Haggard, H. Rider, *She*, 1887.
Hardie, Martin, *Samuel Palmer, being a Lecture delivered to the Print Collectors' Club on Wednesday, November 16th, 1927*, publication No. 7 of the Print Collectors' Club, 1928.
Harries, Meirion and Susie, *The War Artists*, 1983.
Harrison, Charles, *English Art and Modernism, 1900–1939*, 1981.
Harrisson, Tom, *Living Through the Blitz*, 1976.
Hayes, John, *The Art of Graham Sutherland*, 1980.
Hewison, Robert, *Under Seige: Literary Life in London 1939–45*, 1977.
His Majesty's Stationery Office, *Social Insurance and Allied Services – the Beveridge Report in Brief*, 1942.
His Majesty's Stationery Office, *Land at War*, 1945.
Horizon.
Hussey, Christopher, *The Picturesque: Studies in a Point of View*, 1927.
Illustrated London News.
Imperial War Museum, *A Concise Catalogue of Paintings, Drawings and Sculpture of the Second World War 1939–1945*, 2nd edn, 1964.
Imperial War Museum, *The Neo-Romantics: Drawings and Watercolours*, 1982.
Janis, Irving, *Air War and Emotional Stress*, 1951.
Jennings, Humphrey and Madge, Charles, *May 12th Mass-Observation Day Surveys*, 1937.
Jennings, Mary-Lou, *Humphrey Jennings: Film-maker, Painter, Poet*, 1982.
Jones, David, *In Parenthesis*, 1937.
Klein, Holger, ed., *The Second World War in Fiction*, 1984.
Kroeber, Karl, *Romantic Landscape Vision*, 1975.
Larkin, Philip, ed. Thwaite, Anthony, *Philip Larkin: Collected Poems*, 1988.
Lilliput.
The Listener.
MacNalty, A. S., ed., *The Civilian Health and Medical Services (Official History of the Second World War)*, Vol. I, 1953.
Madge, Charles and Harrisson, Tom, *Britain*, 1939.
Marlborough Fine Arts Ltd., *Art in Britain 1930–40 centred around Axis, Circle, Unit One*, 1965.
Mather, Frank Jewett, Jr, 'Samuel Palmer's Virgil Etchings', *Print Collector's Quarterly*, Vol. 24, No. 3, 1937.
McLaine, Ian, *Ministry of Morale: Home Front morale and the Ministry of Information in World War II*, 1979.
Mellor, David, *A Paradise Lost: The Neo-Romantic Imagination in Britain 1935–55*, 1987.
Ministry of Information, *Front Line 1940–41*, 1942.

Ministry of Town and Country Planning and Department of Health for Scotland, *Final Report of the New Towns Committee*, Cmd 6876, 1946.

Moore, Henry, *Shelter Sketch Book*, 1945.

Moore, Henry, *Shelter Sketch Book*, 1967.

Moore, Henry, *Henry Moore: A Shelter Sketchbook, with a Commentary by Frances Carey*, 1988.

Moore, Henry, ed. James, Philip, *Henry Moore on Sculpture*, 1966.

Orwell, George, 'Why I Write', *Collected Essays*, 1961.

Owen, Wilfred, ed. Day Lewis, C., *The Collected Poems of Wilfred Owen*, 1963.

Partridge, Eric, *A Dictionary of Slang and Unconventional English*, 1937.

Partridge, Eric, and Brophy, John, *Songs and Slang of the British Soldier 1914–18*, 1931.

Penguin New Writing.

Pevsner, Nikolaus, *The Englishness of English Art*, 1956, rev. 1964.

Picture Post.

Piper, John, 'Died April 1st, 1837: John Constable', The Architectural Review, Vol. LXXXI, No. 485, April 1937.

Piper, John, 'Decrepit Glory: A Tour of Hafod', *The Architectural Review*, Vol. LXXXVII, No. 523, June 1940.

Piper, John, *British Romantic Artists*, 1942.

Print Collector's Quarterly.

Ray, P., *The Surrealist Movement in England*, 1971.

Reilly, Catherine W., ed., *Chaos of the Night*, 1984.

Rhys, Kedrich, ed., *Poems from the Forces*, 1941.

Ross, Alun, *The Colours of War*, 1983.

Sight and Sound.

Selwyn, Victor *et al.*, *Poems of the Second World War: The Oasis Selection*, 1985.

Sheridan, Dorothy, 'Mass-Observing the British', *History Today*, Vol. 34, July 1984, pp. 42–6.

Sillars, Stuart, *Art and Survival in First World War Britain*, 1988.

Sutherland, Graham, 'A Trend in English Draughtsmanship', *Signature*, July 1936.

Sutherland, Graham, 'Welsh Sketchbook', *Horizon*, Vol. 5, No. 28, April 1942.

Tassi, Roberto, *Sutherland: The Wartime Drawings*, 1980.

Thomas, Dylan, ed. Jones, Daniel, *Dylan Thomas: the Poems*, 1971.

Thorpe, Frances and Pronay, Nicholas, *British Official Films of the Second World War: A Descriptive Catalogue*, 1980.

Tippett, Michael, *A Child of Our Time*, 1944.

Tippett, Michael, ed. Bowen, Meirion, *Music of the Angels: Essays and Sketchbooks of Michael Tippett*, 1980.

Titmuss, R. M., *Problems of Social Policy (Official History of the Second World War)*, 1950.

Vaughan, Keith, 'A View of English Painting', *Penguin New Writing*, No. 31, 1946.

Vernon, P. E., 'Psychological Effects of Air Raids', *Journal of Abnormal Psychology*, Vol. 36, 1941.

War Pictures by British Artists, First series, 4 vols, 1942; Second series, 4 vols, 1943.

Whitechapel Art Gallery, *John Craxton: Paintings and Drawings 1941–1966*, 1967.

Woodbridge, Kenneth, *Landscape and Antiquity: Aspects of English Culture at Stourhead 1718 to 1838*, 1970.

Woods, S. John, *John Piper: Paintings, Drawings and Theatre Designs 1932–1954*, 1955.

Wordsworth, W., ed. Wordsworth, Jonathan, Abrams, M. H., and Gill, Stephen, *The Prelude*, 1979.

Wordsworth, W., ed. de Selincourt, E. and Darbishire, Helen, *The Poetical Works of William Wordsworth*, 1940 and 1952.

Wordsworth, W., and Coleridge, S. T., ed. Brett, R. L., and Jones, A. R., *Lyrical Ballads*, 1963.

Yorke, Malcolm, *The Spirit of Place: Nine Neo-Romantic Artists and their Times*, 1988.

Index

A King's Journey

A novel by
Tony Boucher

Published in Great Britain in 2025
by AGB Publishing

ISBN 978-1-0683726-0-5

For

The Hidden People

Also by Tony Boucher:

The Unfortunate Basil Albright

driver boy

The Tukul with the Blue Door

The Drowning Mary

(sequel to The Tukul with the Blue Door)

Anna and the Knight

Alone

Close

(sequel to Alone)

Alone and **Close** are also published as one novel

An Incorrect Opening

Contents

Kings were destined to be my enemies, as I would be to them.

And the other hundred and twenty? Well, fifteen were there to protect me, sacrifice themselves for the better good if necessary.

The rest? They had their own rulers, their own monarchs, they only existed to try and conquer me, although I would always survive to fight another battle, even after defeat. That's why I was created all that time ago, for no other reason.

So here I am now, in this great establishment, in this great city, my Queen still by my side. I've been here for one hundred and thirty-seven years, and that's only a fraction of my existence so far. I'll probably be here for a lot longer, longer than you could imagine, longer than you will ever know; and the longer I exist the more important I will become. I will gain more strength, more respect. Where you humans learn to die, I have to learn to live, only because you have to be alive to die, as I once was; and yet I still live on.

Nor do I fight battles now, I haven't for hundreds of years. I suppose you could say I am at peace, shoulder to shoulder with my adversaries. In many ways I feel lucky, so much could have gone wrong, my survival has hung in the balance so many times, a lot more than you could imagine, as you will soon discover. It may still do, although it now feels as if I am immortal.

And the other seven Kings? Well, they still exist, one is with me now. Most were taken elsewhere to another great establishment. Sixty-one other pieces reside there now, along with the discs and a buckle. Six were then taken from there to be close to the place where we were discovered during my last liberation.

Most of us have survived. All our Queens. All our clergy, although I must say one had a lucky escape. Our Horsemen bar one. Thirteen Warriors are still here, one having emerged only a few years ago, the one rescued from our first incarceration, then only to be separated from us again. I heard he was taken

to a faraway place, away from his monarch, away from his fellow compatriots, destined to live a solitary life.

Maybe we will all be reunited one day.

I doubt that too.

It was our front line that took the greatest loss, thirteen lost from our first incarceration. Eight perished in the inlet at Mealasta, spread over the ocean-bed, never to be seen again. Twenty-four had been found in Ireland, only to be lost again.

My story begins before I was crowned...

My Host

1283

It all started seven hundred and forty-two years ago. I was living on top of the world at the time, where the land is pristine white and the sea is a clear crystal blue. A place where only the few can live. My Host managed it though, until you humans decided he had something you desired.

He was only seven months old at the time, just a calf suckling his mother's milk, although nearly three hundred pounds in weight he was merely a pup. It was at this time I started to erupt through his skin. That was my first encounter with the outside world, not that I was visible, just a tooth hidden under his muzzle.

And as My Host grew, so did I.

It was nearly two years later when I became visible to the world, or I should say, when I became aware of the world and it became aware of me. It was only then I realised I had a twin, just a few centimetres separating us, growing at the same rate as me, like a mirror image of myself. I can tell you now, his destiny was never to be as regal as mine.

My Host's mother kept him close to her at all times, on

shore or on an ice floe, also in the water. Never at any time would she abandon him, even under the greatest danger, sometimes keeping him protected between her flippers and in touching distance of the sea, ready to make their escape at any sign of danger. Some mothers would leave their young with another while they went foraging: not My Host's mother, she trusted no one. Everywhere she went he went, even having to fight another mother to get the best feeding places or a superior spot on a floe.

My Host would watch with unwavering attentiveness as she dived underwater. He would always follow to see her floating upright, as if standing on her head, her snout just above the seabed. Flapping her flippers or squirting jets of water into the sand to expose any food, using her whiskers to feel for signs of movement, her own tusks to hunt out exposed sea creatures. She taught My Host how to suck the flesh from a clam, feeding on thousands in one session, the seabed becoming a blanket of crushed and discarded shells. On a rare occasion she would grab a young seal and crush it to death, devouring every part of it, nothing wasted. She taught My Host how to prod myself and my twin into the ice edge, so to haul his great body onto a floe, then using us and his flippers he would drag himself along the surface.

Polar bears were their greatest fear on land, prowling around the fringes of the herd, drawn to the mothers with the youngest calves, sniffing out any sign of weakness, hoping to separate them so she would leave her calf alone and vulnerable. At one time My Host's mother protected him with such voracity that she hurled herself onto the starving hunter's back as it made an attempt to pull My Host away and me along with him. Dropping her substantial head she sunk her tusks into its flesh. The bear fled, its thick white fur stained with red.

Even the sea wasn't safe. Killer whales would hunt out helpless and slow moving calves. But My Host's mother knew how to keep him safe at all times. Sensing danger from afar she

ignored by my host, the smaller ones preferring to keep their distance, not being able to compete with his size and impressive display. Maybe they were just there to learn. Then one larger bull tried his luck. He attacked my host with such voracity I thought it could only end in his and our death. I thought our time had finally come. Many times myself and my twin were locked in with our rival's tusks. Pulling, pushing and twisting, attempting to show who had the greatest strength. Then as soon as we became untangled we began stabbing at each others neck, deep cuts being left in his and My Host's flesh. The water around us began to turn red. It seemed to go on for ages until slowly but surely My Host was becoming the victor. Wounded and bloodied, his rival accepted defeat and swam away into the distance. This was my first experience of a real battle.

Looking back, it was as if to show me what was to follow.

It was soon after this victory, one of the females slipped off the ice sheet and into the sea. She begun nuzzling up to him. Copulation was soon achieved.

This same ritual was played out for several weeks. My Host swimming out to sea, searching out his harem, occasionally fighting another hopeful male, using me and my twin as weapons, always winning the battle: I think it was because he had the most to lose. Then one day it just stopped and he returned to the old routine of eating and basking, the occasional battle. The following year the same mating routine would start all over again.

Then there was another day, *the* day, the day of the 'great slaughter.' All the signs of what was about to happen were there, as I said, I had seen it before.

It was early in the evening...

Over a hundred of the dragon boats appeared on the horizon, more than I'd ever seen before, and with them the hunters and their weapons. The first we heard were dogs barking on the decks, their ferocious noise sending confusion and terror throughout the herd. The larger bulls around us started jostling

each other in panic as they tried to fight their way into the sea. Many did, the water looking as if it had become a boiling mass of huge grey bodies.

The hunters landed close to shore, but away from the herd, as they always did. They then headed towards us, stopping on the water edge, blocking any escape route. Many bulls had failed to make it into the water, as My Host had. More panic continued to break out, each bull trying to make a path for themselves. When they couldn't, they changed direction. It seemed not one knew which way to turn. Confusion grew. Mayhem continued.

Huge males, some bigger than My Host, tried to make their escape towards the sea, only to find themselves blocked by the wall of carcasses. One by one each of these magnificent beasts received a blow to the back of the head, rendering them lifeless. The hunter with two hands clasped around the hilt of a sword would thrust the blade downward into their heads, piercing their brain and hopefully killing them instantly. Slowly the wall of carcasses began to build up, until they too became impenetrable. Panic-stricken, some bulls would attempt to breach this vast wall of bodies. That's when the hunters would spear their bodies with long lances, many rebounded off the tough skin, some managed to puncture it. They only stopped when three or four had penetrated into the thick layer of fat and flesh. Some blades would break as the hunter tried to retrieve them, leaving the metal spearhead inside the animal; and yet the huge bulls wouldn't die, for these it would be a slow painful death.

One magnificent bull managed to break through a gap. A hunter not seeing the great beast had been crushed under its great weight. The bull never made it to the water.

My Host, knowing his fate if he went towards the sea began to head inland and towards safety. Along with his flippers he used me and my twin to quicken his escape, working together to haul his great body over the rocks. That's when a huge chunk of my twin broke off, losing several centimetres from the tip.

From that moment his fate was sealed.

It wasn't long before My Host soon found himself alone and vulnerable. That's when some of the hunters began to venture inland, picking off any isolated bulls, the ones with the most impressive tusks sought after first.

As I was.

It was then I sensed the club fall towards us.

My Host's head dropped to the ground after a thunderous cry of pain. An eye popped out of a socket and hung beside me. He then fell into silence, all movement ceased, the hot breath I had felt for the past twenty-seven years began to slowly fail. His great body felt as though it was gradually melting into the ground. Then the blade came down, as if it had fallen from the sky. My Host's breathing finally stopped.

Being too heavy to be moved, My Host was skinned and butchered where he fell, the blubber and skin pulled back for the skull to be detached from the body with both me and my twin still rooted to it. The hide would be taken away to make rope and rigging for the dragons. The assassin responsible for his demise rewarded with the liver and tongue, to be taken and cooked as delicacies.

But it was me and my twin they truly wanted.

We were known as 'Arctic gold.'

I parted company with My Host soon after.

I would never see him again.

My Creator

1311

The first time I came into contact with My Creator was a year after the 'great slaughter'. I was laid out near the water's edge with many more of my own kind. It felt like there were hundreds of us, maybe thousands, all placed in neat regimental rows on the stony ground, leaving just enough space for our captors to walk between. Myself and my twin had already been hacked away from the skull of My Host. There we lay side by side, my twin now a shadow of its former self. I couldn't tell you exactly how long we had been there, time has never had any effect on me. I think it may have been many days and nights. That's all I can say.

I was aware of four people approaching. The first to notice me was a timid middle-aged man of slight build, he was wearing a knee length blue tunic knotted at the waist with a thick black cord. Wrapped around his lower leg were leather shoe bindings, virtually hiding any existence of his lower breeches.

I can tell you now, it was he who was to become My Creator; the equivalent of your own God I suppose you could say. Whoever that may be: you have so many.

compatriots at the beginning. Mostly there to heat up the porridge or prepare the lefse and skyr, topping up the mugs with fresh water when called for. Every now and then Olav would call his son over to show him the best way to use a bow saw or fill the cracks with a mixture of stone paste and fish glue. To know the depth of the smooth creamy outer layer. All the preparation needed before carving.

Olav took each day as it came, he had little choice. Disease and illness were never far away, taking many family and friends from them, some far too young. Olav's eighteen year old daughter Astrid was the latest, a year before my creation, adding to the two sons and one daughter he had already lost, two before they had even taken their first breath. Astrid, like so many, had died from the coughing disease; and like all the others suffering from it, she had drowned in her own fluid.

Kjeld the Elder knew what was to come for him. He had watched as every gurgling intake of air she took had become more and more painful, as if she was trying to breath underwater, the sweat from her body making it seem as if she was. Then one day she stopped eating and drinking altogether, like she had accepted her fate and wanted to get it over with quickly. A few days later the weakening rise and fall of her chest finally stopped.

It was Grete who chose the grave in the burial ground. In some ways she was fortunate that Astrid had died in early summer: many of the graves had already been dug in spring because the ground was far too hard in winter, the gravediggers knowing they would never be short of people to fill them. It wasn't uncommon to have no graves left by the end of Autumn. Olav paid the gravediggers in kind, several combs, two textile beaters and a wristful of bracelets were passed over.

The loss of his beloved granddaughter broke Kjeld the Elder's spirit and body even more. With his unceasing cough and laboured breathing, he knew it would be only a matter of time before he was to join her.

Olav chose to throw himself even more into his work, keeping his surviving two sons close by his side.

The workshop was a large timber building with a stone base and topped with a sod and bark roof. It had been built on church owned land and stood close to the recently built Nidaros Cathedral, the stave church being the most magnificent in all of the North lands. Their neighbours were tanners and cobblers, blacksmiths and carpenters, along with many more trades. All having to pay extortionate rent to the church, either in kind or money.

The workshop was once the building where Jakob Bengtsson worked, some say the greatest wood carver of all time. They also say his spirit still resides within the walls and with Olav's skill being so great it was rumoured he had been possessed by Jakob. Olav wanted to say his talent was his and his alone. He didn't though, as long as people paid him handsomely because of it, then he was happy to encourage the stories.

An open hearth stood in the centre, permanently glowing to ward off the extreme cold. The smoke, along with the work-dust giving the interior a permanent haze. In the winter months much of the work would be conducted close to the fire. On some days it got so cold and their fingers so numb they had hardly any feeling at all, the conditions rendering it impossible to carry out any intricate carving. Then they would take on a chore that occupied a great deal of their time, more than the workshop did on some weeks: the neverending task of chopping wood, the difference between having hot or cold food, being chilled or frozen, working or not working.

Wooden boxes of different shapes and sizes sat on the worktop with all manner of tools: axes and chisels, adzes and scorpers, all filling their own spaces. There were raps and gouges, awls and punches, many kept in circular compartments with the ends pointing up to the wooden beamed frame of the roof. Bow saws and bone drills hung from wooden spikes, ready

to be snatched away at the blink of an eye. Next to them lay antlers and bones, whale's teeth and walrus tusks, some in differing sizes and states of honing and carving. You could say the place had an organised chaos about it, a scene of order and routine.

Within all this there was one worktop that was left untouched, this was in the corner tucked away by the entrance. It was where they displayed the toils of their trade: hair pins and combs, belt buckles and clasps, textile beaters and bracelets, all simply carved, knowing these were affordable objects they could sell for produce at the local market. Separate from them were the more elaborate pieces, reliquaries and pendants, all manner of ornaments, most replicating religious art or warriors from sagas long gone, also gaming pieces for tafl sets. All intricately carved, many taking weeks to complete. Only the aristocracy and clergy could afford such creations as these.

Day by day the sun circled the earth and the moon passed through sickle to full; the four in the workshop continued to go about their duties. Until one day, a day that was to be different to any other.

For me, it was the first time my creation was to be discussed...

Bjarne of Bjarkoy

1313

A large man had entered the workshop, a man with a bull-neck and a thick beard the colour of rust, his disproportionately large forehead mostly hidden by a leather Skjoldehamm hood, the sides of which covered his wide shoulders. He looked more like a creature of the forest by the amount of facial hair and fur draped over his body. A short sword hung from a waist band, one hand encrusted with dirt resting on it, ready to be drawn in the blink of an eye. It was his eyes though, there was a cold alertness about them, a man that had seen more than his fair share of suffering in life; and probably the cause of much of it. As the man entered, he immediately studied every part of the workshop. One by one he held his blackened glare on the people inside. He eventually looked behind him, gave a slight nod and stood to the side.

Another man stepped up and walked passed the first. He was wearing a long hooded cloak that hung loosely to the ground, more like a monk's habit, although Kjeld the Elder knew there was nothing sacred about this man, trying to make himself appear like a peasant, but was far from it. Under one

that, the revenue from those farms would remain in his family. Names are just words anyhow.

Then wanting to compound his King's strength even more, and with it, his own, Bjarne of Bjarkoy lead the anti-ecclesiastical movement. The all powerful clergy were also overstepping their own privileges, mostly by creating more laws favourable to themselves.

The power should come from the king himself, and only you, Bjarne of Bjarkoy told him. It is you that is appointed by God himself he had to remind his sovereign.

In doing so Bjarne of Bjarkoy found he had been excommunicated by the powerful Archbishop Jon Raude. Bjarne of Bjarkoy was a man that had never lost a battle, as many had discovered to their detriment. Rumours had spread within the church that Archbishop Jon Raude's life was in danger. This caused him to flee to Sweden with many others. From then on the king could appoint all the high ranking clergy himself, with Bjarne of Bjarkoy's guidance of course.

Then one day, Baron Erlingsson of Bjarkoy's life changed dramatically, one his own immense power had no control over. His son and sole heir to the Giste Bjarkoy estate had died. Thinking it was God's revenge for his past sins against the church he tried to make amends by paying for much of the Nidaros Cathedral's construction. He also started wearing simple sack like clothing, having to suffer the cold and the chafing in doing so. His penance to God.

So thereafter, Baron Erlingsson simply became Bjarne of Bjarkoy.

What has this to do with my story?

His power also extended to the massacre of hundreds of walruses for their Arctic gold. This included My Host. So you see; it was Bjarne of Bjarkoy who sealed my fate.

"So you know who I am?" Bjarne of Bjarkoy asked.

Olav had to think carefully, was it a question or statement?

He knew one ill-considered word could go badly wrong for him. "How could I not squire," he replied. "It is an honour to have your presence in my humble workshop."

"And you are also wondering why I am here?"

Olav didn't know how to answer, thought it best to remain silent. So he did.

"I have seen your work Olav Leifsson." Bjarne of Bjarkoy paused for a moment, waiting for a reaction. None came. "The hnefatafl pieces."

Olav remembered them from last year. He also recalled it had been someone else who had commissioned them, another dignitary, not of the rank of Bjarne of Bjarkoy. He returned a slight nod.

"The best I have seen anywhere in this land."

Olav breathed a sigh of relief. "Thank you squire."

"You know I have travelled far and wide Olav Leifsson."

Olav continued to listen, having no choice but to display compliance.

"I have been to distant lands where I have seen great artistry." Bjarne of Bjarkoy paused for a moment. "As is yours."

"You are too kind squire."

"I have also met many powerful rulers on my travels. They have bestowed upon me many worldly gifts," Bjarne of Bjarkoy took the wooden box from under his arm and set it down on the worktop.

Olav gazed down at the small chest and saw the exquisite workmanship, the varying woods, light and dark shades, all complimenting each other. There were ones Olav had never seen before. Having learnt some of his trade in carving wood he thought he had got to know them all. He then spotted mother of pearl and other shells, again, some new to him, all inlaid into intricate patterns. He also thought he saw what looked like a precious gemstone, a sapphire of the deepest blue, like a full moon reflecting on the ocean surface.

Olav glanced back up.

"Look inside," Bjarne of Bjarkoy told him.

Olav lifted the lid and lowered his gaze. Inside were strange looking objects, stones that weren't stones. Some were green, others brown, the shapes of which he had never seen before. But they were nothing special, nothing that got anywhere close to matching the fine workmanship of the box.

Olav looked up once again. "Hnefatafl?" he said, making it sound more like a question.

"You are right in one aspect, they are gaming pieces, but not hnefatafl," Bjarne of Bjarkoy replied, as though he had guessed what Olav was thinking.

Olav looked down again, raised a hand slightly, as if asking permission. Bjarne of Bjarkoy returned a single nod. Olav picked one up, a smaller piece, turned it around in his fingers. They weren't ivory or bone, he knew that, he wasn't sure what they were made from, he also knew they weren't from his own land. He then wondered if Bjarne of Bjarkoy wanted him to replicate these. An easy task he thought. In some ways he felt it was an insult to his skill.

"I don't understand," Olav remarked.

"These are pieces from a game played in a distant land, a game they call shatranj." Bjarne of Bjarkoy gazed long and hard at Olav, as though his silence could say more than words. "A powerful vizier taught me how to play. He also told me if I could beat him I could have a set. This set." He looked as if he was about to break into a smile, but didn't. "This man also told me how the game was created from a land even further away from his. Probably from a father showing his son how a great battle was won."

Olav wondered when he would get to the reason why he was standing before him.

Bjarne of Bjarkoy continued. "In this game there is a King next to his advisor, there are chariots and elephants and horsemen on the back line, the front line are where the foot-soldiers stand. They play on a board of sixty-four squares.

He took a piece out, near the top of it was a single projection poking out from the front. "This horseman can move one or two squares to the side, front or back, in any order, it can also jump over another piece, capturing the enemy on the square it lands on. He took out another, like it had sunk in the middle. "This chariot can move horizontally or vertically, as many squares as it wants, strong, but weak at the same time," he said. He then took out another. This piece had two projections, like short tusks. "This is the elephant, it moves two squares from corner to corner of the square, and can jump over a piece if necessary." Bjarne of Bjarkoy searched in the chest. And this is the advisor, the weakest piece because it can only move one square from corner to corner. He placed it back in the chest and pointed to the piece Olav was holding, a cone shaped pebble with eight sides and a flat base. "This is the smallest piece, but working together they are strong. It can move one square forward, or diagonally if it wants to capture one of the enemy. This is the piece from the front line. And lastly, the shah, the king. It can move one square in any direction, usually when it's on the run. The game is won when the king has nowhere else to go. The battle is lost."

A long silence followed.

"I know what you are thinking Olav Leifsson. The pieces before you look nothing like kings or men on horses or even chariots. This is because their religion is different to ours, they believe that anything living can only be created by God himself." He paused for a short moment. "But we are not of that religion are we Olav Leifsson? We are only servants to our one God."

Olav was confused. "Yes squire."

Bjarne of Bjarkoy picked up a reliquary laid beside the box, a hollowed walrus tusk with intertwining ornate carvings and a hinged silver lid, a chain fixed at both ends for carrying. A beautiful piece of workmanship only the most skillful of craftsman could have produced. "You will make four shatranj

Bjarne of Bjarkoy replied curtly, the fragility in his voice gone.

Olav saw his father-in-law's unease. "We only have enough morse for..."

Bjarne of Bjarkoy interrupted. "I have sent men to the north, to the white land of the frozen water. They have collected morse tusks. There will be many for you to choose from. Take what you need, take more if you wish, keep those for yourself. As long as I have my four sets that is all that concerns me. Nor will anyone see the morse before you. You will be the first Olav Leifsson."

Kjeld the Elder spoke again. "But squire, how do simple peasants like us know what a King or Queen, or even a..." He stopped when a cough stole his words, just managed to continue. "Or what even a warrior should look like. We are simple people of peace."

Bjarne of Bjarkoy glared long and hard at him, a sympathetic expression now masking his true feelings. He knew the old man had the coughing disease, that his time in this world was not for much longer. He was glad Olav wasn't suffering from the same fate. "You will work with the finest artist, the best in the North lands. One that has drawn our own King and Queen, our bravest warriors. She will draw the finer details for you, from her you will know what is required. I will also send attendants, they will model for you. There is nothing you will want Olav Leifsson."

Kjeld the Elder knew exactly what he meant by attendants: spies to report back on their progress.

"May I ask who the beneficiary of these sets will be?" Olav asked.

"One will be for a Vizier to the Sultan Oljeitu. The very same person who gave me this shatranj set. A very important man with great wealth and influence. Many trade routes pass through their kingdoms, all carrying wonderful treasures. This box the shatranj pieces came in, the precious stone, they could all be yours Olav Leifsson. Not only gemstones like this, but

the finest cloths, spices and fruits, dyes you have never seen the colour of before." He stopped to glare at Olav. "Ivory from animals the size of houses."

"Animals the size of houses," Olav said, then wondered what beasts like these would look like.

"But you asked for four sets my squire?

"I did. Another is for our own great King Haakon Magnusson, the third is for the church. And the fourth, well the fourth is for me Olav Leifsson."

"And the boards squire, what of the boards?"

"You will deal with the pieces alone, the boards I have commissioned Fredrik Bengtsson to make."

Fredrik Bengtsson, the son of Jakob, and like his father his reputation as a great carpenter had become widely known throughout the North lands.

Bjarne of Bjarkoy continued. "Each square...," he looked around and picked up a lead stone, drew a shape on the worktop, as if from memory. "This will be the size of the square each piece will sit on. The King will be the largest, the horsemen the deepest, so you must allow for this when you create them."

Olav gazed down at the roughly drawn shape.

He dealt in accuracy, not guesswork.

"You will do as I ask," Bjarne of Bjarkoy said.

Olav paused, wondered if it was a command or question. Either way, he knew there could only be one reply. "Yes squire, I will do as you ask."

"Good."

"But the oils in the morse will need time to dry."

"How long."

"Six months at the least, maybe longer."

"You have some here that have already dried."

"Yes, but..."

"Good enough for what I require."

"Yes."

"Then use them, you can replace what you use with double

that, more."

"What you ask will take time...," Olav began to say, wondering if he had overstepped the mark.

"One year, that will be the next time you will see me. That is when I will collect them."

Bjarne of Bjarkoy turned and stepped towards the door, he stopped and drew his attention towards Kjeld the Elder. "The king will hear of Kjeld Ragnarsson. He will remember your name as I have done." He then turned back to Olav. "Also yours Olav Leifsson, and your sons." He stopped, as if waiting for something.

Olav glanced at the older of his two boys. "Leif Olavsson," he said, then looked over to the boy. "Kjeld Olavsson, my youngest."

Bjarne of Bjarkoy gave a single drop of the head. "Do me proud Olav Leifsson and your rewards will be great and many." Without another word he turned and left the workshop, taking the box and the shatranj set with him. The large man followed close behind.

Olav went to step away, realised he still had the shatranj piece in his hand, one from the front line. It was as if Bjarne of Bjarkoy had left it with him on purpose, as if he was wanting to tell him something. Olav then realised he had never described the pieces from the front line. He gazed down at the piece in his hand and knew it was a test.

A King is Crowned

1313

It was Kjeld the Younger who carried me from the cart into the workshop, unwrapped me from my cloth and set me down with all the other chosen ones. It was there we were scrutinised once again, this time in a lot more detail. Measurements were taken, lines were drawn. It seemed to take ages before My Creator made the final decision of who would make the grade and who wouldn't. Those who didn't were carefully discarded to the back, destined to become a lesser piece, maybe one from the front line or not for the shatranj sets at all: a hair pin or a fabric breaker, a gaming disc.

It was Kjeld the Elder who finally picked me up, appearing to have the most say in my destiny, studying me in great detail as he had done by the waterfront. My Creator had joined him in his scrutinisation, giving a look of approval. It felt as if both knew what the other was thinking without a word being spoken. In the end My Creator circled two lines around my girth using a lead ingot, one line close to the tip and another about ten centimetres below. Kjeld the Elder then placed me to the side.

There I remained. For how long? I couldn't tell you.

She ignored him.

Along with them came a box full of tunics and capes, some of the finest cloth they had ever seen. Also crowns and mitres, swords and spears, some more ornate than others. There were false beards and wigs made of human hair, croziers and wooden blocks in the shape of books. There were shields and helmets, all of differing styles and sizes. The last to be brought in was a seat, like a throne, plain in appearance, as if the wood had been hammered together in a matter of minutes, but sturdy enough. The last and by far the largest object was a wide bark stripped tree trunk sat on four legs, at one end was the stump of a branch angled forward then down to suggest a horses head.

Birgit the Gifted worked closely with Leif for the first few weeks, ensuring the shapes were correct for the next stage. My Creator had soon realised that she had been given the same explanation from Bjarne of Bjarkoy as to what was required of her. One hundred and twenty-eight pieces, with the unique appearance that separated the individual pieces. More importantly, the nature of the carving.

By the way Birgit spoke it was obvious she had been close to Bjarne of Bjarkoy at one point in her life. My Creator wondered in what form this relationship took. Regardless, he knew his authority could now be questioned, that this was going to be a combined effort between him and her. Not to do so could be very much to his detriment.

Kjeld the Elder was still convinced the attendants were Bjarne of Bjarkoy's spies. His abruptness and discourtesy to them had caused many a rift with the male attendant, who himself was no pushover (working on a farm has a tendency to build up a man's strength). Leif, who was also a strapping lad, had to play the go-between on a few occasions, trying not to take sides. Birgit always stood back, not wanting to get involved, although she was impressed with Leif's diplomacy. The old man kept his suspicions to himself so no one knew why he was acting with such animosity. Everyone thought it was

Kjeld the Elder being his usual self, that it was the lung disease getting on top of him, or maybe it was because they were nothing like him in looks, as My Creator thought; Sihtric with his dark hair and Tovild with her black skin. All he knew was the task had to be completed, whatever their differences. As long as that continued, then like Birgit, he also kept well away from petty disputes.

The actual work of creating the pieces started when Birgit the Gifted instructed the male attendant to pull on a full length leather gambeson. She then placed a tall kite-shaped shield in his left hand, My Creator having to press it tight against his body so there was no space between him and it. A sword was then put in his right hand, the blade pointing upward. Again My Creator pressed it against his cheek, marking where the sharp end touching the coned helmet, only so he knew exactly where it should be placed at all times. The attendant had soon been transformed into a warrior, a brave fighter guarding his monarch. The same piece that would occupy the four corners of the board.

My Creator studied the tusks Kjeld the Younger had sawn from the one marked with the sign of a shield. After replacing the first two, he kept the third in his hand.

He told the attendant to stand beside the hearth, under the light from the hole above him. Oiled pottery lamps were also lit. My Creator knew the attendant would have to keep that same statue pose for hours, that the fire would help to keep him warm.

He scrutinised the attendant for some time before scratching lines on the surface of the carving. He then began working with a scorper along with his narrowest chisel, marking the ivory and scooping out a small amount at a time. That's how he continued, the deepest areas were hollowed out first: under the beard, behind the shield, the blade of the sword, not too much to begin with, only stopping when he thought he had gone deep enough, sticking to his own mantra 'least is best.' He would then go to another area, returning later to the same places

when the cuts needed to be made deeper. Sometimes he would hold it at arms length, keeping the attendant in his line of sight, turning it in his fingers, as if he could picture the final piece in his head. The edges of the blade came next, leaving a small rounded area for the hand and pommel. He knew the piece would be chunky in shape, kept solid, no weak areas. This was morse, not wood.

The fingers would come later, just three scratched lines gripping the handle. He returned to under the chin and behind the shield, deeper and deeper the morse was honed out until he came to a stop again. He knew where not to have too much detail at the beginning. Any finer details would follow later.

Sometimes his eyes would glaze over, as if he had entered a trance, transported to another world, when everyone knew not to interrupt him.

The tapered body was next. With each scoop, with each cut, with each hollow, the piece began to take shape. Minute by minute, hour by hour he continued without rest. On occasions he would stand back and think, sometimes staring at the attendant as if he wasn't a real person, just an inanimate object, another tool to work with. Sometimes forgetting the attendant needed a rest. Then My Creator would glance back down at the small figure, as if it was slowly coming to life. He was annoyed with himself, realised he hadn't left enough for a full beard, decided he would have to be hairless around the chin. A simple cleft in the chin would suffice for this piece.

The head was next, no eyes or mouth, leaving a slight protrusion for the nose. He then worked on the coned helmet, the point at its tip, a line around its base, gouging a row of small holes below that, no nasal guard on this warrior, the line of the leather helmet would stand proud across its brow. Next came the folds of the coat, firstly drawn on the morse by Birgit the Gifted. She had gripped the leather tunic worn by the man, nearly causing the attendant to lose his balance, making them laugh. Not Kjeld the Elder though. Birgit explained that the coat

should look the same at the back as it does in the front. My Creator finished with the facial features, as he always did. A line for a mouth, turned down at the corners, a slight hollow below it to give the hint of a lip, this was where too much detail could spiral out of control. My Creator wondered if it was too mournful, not terrifying enough. He decided that would have to come with the later pieces. He knew there would have to be sixteen of them in total, this one would be diluted into the rest. Hopefully Bjarne of Bjarkoy wouldn't see it; and if he did: then My Creator would say he had done it on purpose, that each piece has its own character. The eyes were last, as if bringing the piece to life. Cutting the shape of a protruding oval. Two tiny holes were gouged out for the pupils, the first was slightly off centre, a mistake, the other eye he made the same. This warrior was looking away towards the enemy. That's what he would say anyway.

The attendant was finally stood down.

My Creator's goal was to complete this piece before the end of the third day, if he could do it in that time then hopefully he could do others in two days, maybe one. The sun was high in the sky, days were long, natural light would be on his side. Three more followed in five days, all similar to the first, though this time he left enough room for the beard, the eyes he managed to carve so they were looking directly ahead. On another piece the height changed slightly, he had to make it smaller, only because of a crack running down the morse: he pressed boiled fish glue into it, gave the piece a tap to get the thick liquid deep in the crack, stopping it from widening. On the whole he kept them to what he thought was acceptable, to what Bjarne of Bjarkoy had specified; and there was no way he could keep them all the exact same size. He had enough samples to show Leif and Kjeld the Elder. He knew another eleven warriors would have to be made. He also knew he would have to delegate many of them to his eldest son. Regrettably his father-in-law would expect to be involved

her at first, telling Birgit he wanted the male attendant. "Warriors are white-skinned," he had told her. "Also men."

"The shield-maiden was a woman and also a feared warrior." she replied curtly.

Kjeld the Elder couldn't disagree.

"And just as strong as any man," she added.

This time My Creator had to intervene, jabbing himself in the chest as he did. "If we fail it will be me who is fed to Ymir," he told his father-in-law curtly. "And try to make them look like warriors, they are not monks." He then glared at Birgit the Gifted. "Or nuns."

He felt he had regained his authority.

It was when he was halfway through the first warrior, Kjeld the Elder decided to position the shield so it was held in front, he soon realised he had carved it far too close to the face, that the top of it would be slicing into the warrior's chin. He had to think of a way out before his son-in-law discovered his mistake. That's when it came to him: stories of fearsome fighters throwing themselves into wild frenzies before entering the battle. How they would howl and slash their swords through the air, sometimes drawing their own blood before releasing their terror on the enemy. More importantly he had heard about them biting their shields. This he would do, telling his son-in-law that it was done on purpose. It also gave him great enjoyment when he told the woman attendant to bite onto the shield, which she reluctantly did. His shaking hands made accidental scratches on the surface of the coat: chain mail he decided.

My Creator appeared happy when he saw the finished result. "Make four," he told him. "Just so they can be part of the same set."

Ten weeks had passed and another payment had arrived. Three chickens, a live hog, a goat, a leg of venison, more nuts, more wheat, more barley, more cereals. Along with them came a large pot of honey, a rare luxury for My Creator and his family; and like the dates, it was the first time they had ever

seen a fig. Also spices they had never encountered before: saffron, nutmeg and cinnamon, which pleased and confused My Creator's wife at the same time.

Her name was Grete, taught by her mother, from a young age she knew how to make the most of the little they had; and she never asked for much, but always made sure the family had enough to survive. She had learnt how to manage the food through the coldest of the winter months, and if it continued beyond what was normal, Greta knew how to ration what was left. Some weeks they would have nothing to eat but gruel. If they were lucky she could mix in some dried cod or herring, sometimes salted meat if the workshop had a good day at the local market. In times of plenty they had beef stew with mushrooms and onions cooked in a soapstone pot. Using flatbread heated on a hot slate tablet they would soak up the little that was left. Other days she would make lefse, spreading it with buttermilk or skyr.

But not this year, this year she had everything in abundance: bags of oats to make enough porridge for an entire army. There was barley and grain for baking bread, also dried fruit and salted meat. The milk from the cows would keep them in butter, cheese and yoghurt. They even had roasted chicken, a rare luxury, even with the seven she had been given by Bjarne of Bjarkoy, more than she's ever had in her lifetime. Usually chickens were kept for eggs, only eaten when they failed to lay. Even so, she still felt guilty when neighbours around them were struggling.

The entire family, including Grete's sister Dina and two young nieces shared a turf roofed longhouse, built at the bottom of a hillock to protect them from the bitter winds. Dina's husband had died several years ago in a fishing accident. The more people in the house the more heat that could be generated. They also helped at the market stall when the men were busy in the workshop. The walls were made of stone and wattle, dried mud filling any gaps, the corners rounded so as not to detain

the biting wind. Square wooden pillars spaced equally apart held up the spider web of timber frame beams which held up the roof. Each of the pillars was ornately carved, used by Leif and Kjeld the Younger to practice their carving skills, which they often did. Several pairs of skis also hung from the sides, waxed and ready for a heavy snowfall. Everyone in the family was an expert skier, sometimes learning before they could walk. A fire was lit permanently in a hearth at the centre of the house, also used for heating up the food, a hole in the roof allowing some of the smoke to escape. Long benches ran the length of the sides, used for both sitting and sleeping, the seats covered with woollen blankets, sheep fleeces and elk hides.

Their livestock, when not in the pasture, were kept in the two outhouses in the summer months, only bringing them into the byre at one end of the home during the bitter winters. This was on a lower level than the rest of the room, divided with a wattle and mud wall, a space at the top to allow the heat through.

Several more weeks had passed and the work on the pieces continued. Everyone had fallen into their own routines, only the noise of the tapping of a hammer and the gouging of tools broke the silence.

A few days later a cart full of logs turned up. The time they were spending at the workshop meant their own stack was becoming low, both in the workshop and at the house. It was as if Bjarne of Bjarkoy knew, or as Kjeld the Elder suspected, had been informed. Pulled by two weary oxen, the cart was full of seasoned birch. It was My Creator's preferred wood, not only did it last longer, it also carried a sweet scent when burnt. He then wondered where it had come from. What family had not paid their rent? Who was going to be low on their winter fuel this year? Who would freeze to death? He felt guilty and wanted to refuse it. He didn't. He couldn't.

A Bishop was to be carved next. Birgit the Gifted spent a great amount of time searching out the correct attire, dressing

the male attendant in an under-smock first, the chasuble had to fall over the arms in neat flowing folds. She then placed the mitre with the points to the front and back, the two lappets hanging from the back. A crosier in the right hand, the curve of the crook resting on the cheek. Bjarne of Bjarkoy was adamant that none would hold crucifixes. 'I want Bishops, not Archbishops,' he had told her, as he had done with My Creator. She knew about the episode with Jon Raude. 'Also no stoles, they are at war, not preaching sermons.' The following Bishops wore copes tied at the top and open at the front. Some had a prayer book in the left hand, one had it open, threatening the enemy with God's words as Kjeld the Elder put it. As with the other pieces, the deepest cuts came first. My Creator worked by intuition, as he often did, having confidence in his own skill. Two days it took to complete the first clergyman.

Five more soon followed.

The male attendant complained of his arms becoming tired before the sixth. Birgit knew it must have become very uncomfortable for him, and if he had protested about something at the farm it would have probably resulted in his dismissal; and the loss of everything that accompanies employment: food, clothes, a roof over his head. There were plenty more labourers from where he had come from. She allowed him to swap the crosier and bible, just to rest one arm. She then permitted him to abandon the book altogether so two hands could hold the centre of the crosier. It was when My Creator was about to start the ninth, the attendant complained that he couldn't stand any longer, that his legs would collapse from under him if he did. With Birgit the Gifted's suggestion and under Kjeld the Elder's protests, My Creator allowed the attendant to sit on the makeshift throne, knowing he had to make four the same. In the end, eight were made this way. During the last two, Birgit the Gifted suggested the attendant should hold two fingers up in blessing. "More for yourself," she had told him, bringing much needed laughter into the workshop.

attendants arm, who grudgingly placed a flat hand on the cheek of the mask, holding it in place. Birgit stopped for a moment, stared at the attendant. She then turned towards My Creator, a grin came to her face. "There you have your answer Olav Leifsson."

"I can't keep it like this," the attendant protested.

"Rest your other hand on your leg, hold your arm up with that one," Birgit told her.

The attendant did exactly that.

My Creator said no more and began carving, first using a scorper and an awl, then various chisels to create the folds in the smock. A row of dots was punched between two lines on the crown, then the same at the hem of the veil. With a bow drill he made random small holes before gouging out the hollow for the crown. He then realised he had gone too deep in one area, it was too late to do anything about it, decided he'd fill it with stone paste and fish glue later on.

My Creator trusted Leif to start working on the other pieces, satisfied he had come a long way since carving the last of the horsemen, "Keep a close eye on him," he told Birgit the Gifted.

Kjeld the Younger started on the pieces for the front line, proud at last to have become part of the carving process. My Creator told him to use the shatranj piece as a guide, resulting in the first few taking on that same octagonal shape. Birgit the Artist then decided to change the design, irritating My Creator, who felt he was losing his authority to her again.

"Now they look as if they are from our land," she said as she began drawing symmetrical shapes for Kjeld the Younger to scratch onto the fronts and backs.

"They look more like headstones," My Creator remarked coldly.

"That is the idea." Birgit replied. "It is a battle, we have to bury the dead somewhere." More than once she had made the comment that the game of shatranj was very Norse, that there

would probably be more blood spilt away from the board than on it. "You folk from the North don't like losing,' she told him.

Twenty weeks had passed.

A pony and cart had been delivered to the workshop, that was it, nothing else, no food this time. The farmhand transporting it told My Creator it was for Kjeld the Elder, that he was given specific instructions to say it was for the old man's use, and his only. That his squire had heard he had been struggling with the journey from the house to the workshop, and that his cough and breathing were getting worse.

My Creator wondered how Bjarne of Bjarkoy knew. He turned to look at Birgit. He knew his father-in-law was finding the journey hard going, sometimes suggesting to him that he should stay at the house. He just thought if Birgit the Gifted was conveying what was happening then some good had come out of it.

My Creator had started carving the back of the throne on the Queen. This was when he could display his true craftsmanship. Everything he had learnt from carving wood in the stave churches: the great door at Urnes, the pillars inside the church at Borgund, how his predecessors were influenced by carvings from distant lands to the south, ones the North people had held themselves. He would try to do the same: stick to what you know, it's only a fraction of the size he had told himself.

After a while, the female attendant complained the throne was far too uncomfortable, that the wood was too hard to be sat on for any length of time. She asked for some kind of padding to be placed over the seat, this Birgit did, lifting the attendant higher. She also draped a blanket over the back, leaving a part of it on show. My Creator carved that into the piece, knowing it would give it some uniqueness.

Six more Queens followed, some varying in size and shape. One had become more hunched than the others. One looked stretched, distorted, another appeared squat. My Creator made sure each had a hand held to their cheek, that was important,

only needing Tovild to keep the mask in place while he carved the face, allowing her to lower it when working on another area. Because of it, no matter on size or pose, they all had that same pensive expression. Each piece was richly carved with interlaced scrolls. Sometimes Birgit the Gifted would draw the patterns beforehand. Some took on what looked like impossible shapes: a chain that couldn't link together, but somehow did, as if she had put it there to fool the eye.

My Creator thought she was certainly living up to her name.

Tovild had complained of being thirsty on two occasions. Birgit had given her a drinking horn filled with cool water: the vessel was also carved into those pieces, although it irritated him when she removed the mask each time she took a sip. It was the Queens expressions though, each one said so much: grief, sadness, concern, mindfulness, reflection, it was all there in that one simple line for the mouth.

"She has a smile," Birgit had remarked about one.

My Creator couldn't see it.

Leif could.

Twenty-five weeks had passed.

Three more chickens, a slaughtered boar which Kjeld the Elder had to share the cart with on the return journey, complaining that he had become no more than a pig, and a dead one at that. More boxes of vegetables, more oats and barley, a roll of material. Grete had never felt such soft cloth before.

It then came the turn of the Kings. My Creator had left them until last. He knew these would be the most important pieces. Two he had completed within a week. He felt annoyed with himself, they were far from his best work. It was the face he wasn't happy with. The first had its eyes too far apart. The next had a snub nose. Then a failed beard. The backs of the thrones were becoming inferior, the twisted vines and dragon tails were far from the intricate carving he had produced with the Queens. He also had to seek advice from Birgit about its

size, something he rarely did. He decided one was far too small, maybe he was looking for reassurance. She picked out a Queen, shorter than the others, said it would make a perfect companion. The second was slightly larger, again, still not big enough, another Queen was found.

As the days passed My Creator continued with the Kings. He was becoming more tired with each monarch, sometimes exhausted, working longer than he should, missing meals. He knew time was looming ever closer, he needed them finished. "I should have started with the Kings at the beginning, when I was fresh of mind," he told his father-in-law.

Nine months had passed in total and two more payments were made, one had more spices and fruits never seen before. The second had more of the finest cloth.

Forty-seven Pawns, fourteen Warriors, thirteen Bishops, fifteen Knights, seven Queens and five Kings had been made. Ten pieces had been discarded so far. No part of the tusk was wasted, the morse between the pieces was made into gaming discs.

Then it came to my creation, my coronation, my birth, however you want to put it.

Leif had sawn me into my first simple shape, using guides drawn on by My Creator, a right-angle cut, that's all it was. Birgit the Gifted had dressed the male attendant in the finest material and placed a crown on his head, four braided twists of hair hung down from the back. She then sat him on the makeshift throne and stepped away.

My Creator began. Firstly he chiselled out the area behind the sword held across my knees, my fingers wrapped around the hilt, my other hand around the scabbard, as if I was sitting in judgement. Six cuts to make the shape of the throne, leaving a raised area on the front of the armrest. My Creator thought it was another touch, different to the others. I slowly started to take shape. My round powerful shoulders became evident, behind them was enough morse for the hair. A cloak was draped

same. “No one will know the difference.” He hoped.

I and seven other Kings were finally completed, all of us on thrones with swords held across our knees, all sitting in judgement.

The eight Queens had been finished three weeks before, also seated, all with a right hand held to their cheek. The sixteen on horseback had spears. Sixteen Bishops with mitres and croziers. Sixteen warriors standing proud, holding swords and shields, four biting their shields. Sixty-four pawns, sixteen like tombstones, forty-eight octagonally shaped.

Bjarne of Bjarkoy had been very specific about the colour, he had specified a vivid red, Olav remembered him saying that cinnabar stones should be used and he didn’t have them at the time of the visit, how they were very rare and he would have to supply them at a later date. Birgit had explained how they should be crushed into powder and mixed with oil from a cod’s liver, then rubbed into one side of each set, giving them several coats.

A year had passed and none had arrived.

Sihtric had returned to working on the farm and Tovild to the kitchen. Kjeld the Elder never stopped thinking they were spies, although in the last months he had softened towards them, thinking they probably had no choice.

Neither were seen again.

Four weeks had passed and still no cinnabar stones.

Olav continued to wait.

Birgit the Artist continued to visit the workshop, telling Olav it would be best if she showed him how to make the dye. In waiting she spent most of her time with Leif, helping him with motives for carving combs and textile breakers, going for walks with him, sometimes visiting his home, helping Grete prepare the food for the evening meal, then joining them for the feast, after all, she had earned the food as much as anyone else.

On several occasions Grete had commented to her husband that she could feel Baldr blowing a warm wind in their

direction; and with it a great celebration was to follow.

My Creator knew Grete was deeply immersed in her village's customs, ones that were passed down through the generations from her mother and her mother before her. Sacrificing a calf and spilling the blood into the sea would bring them an abundance of cod in early spring and halibut in autumn. Worshipping Odin while cleansing yourself would bring wisdom. Thinking of Frifgg while making love would bring fertility. Baldr would bestow love itself. There were many more, even Grete would admit she never knew them all. All she got from the Christian church was greed and misery.

Six weeks had passed and still no sign of Bjarne of Bjarkoy. Another payment missed. Four shatranj sets, one hundred and twenty-eight pieces sat unwanted at the back of the workshop.

Life soon returned to how it was before, producing simple combs and bracelet rings, hairpins and needles, clasps and brooches, pieces that would easily sell at the local market. The commissions from rich patrons and the church began to return, some from far afield, a religious ornament, a reliquary inlaid with wood. These were pieces Olav had had no choice but to refuse over the last year, one mention of Bjarne of Bjarkoy dispelled any discord at the time.

Grete was correct about the wedding, Baldr had indeed blown a warm wind in their direction, and with it joy and love.

Leif and Birgit the Gifted were betrothed to each other.

Olav knew an amalgamation of the two families would be beneficial for all concerned. Thinking back he could never remember her ever speaking about her family. Whenever he or Kjeld the Elder tried to broach the subject an awkward silence would descend, she would ignore them, sometimes walking away, silently continue with her drawings.

"She will tell us in her own time," Grete had told her husband. "When the green light dances above the white forest." she had said. "Then we will know the time is right."

Olav knew the coupling between Leif and Birgit would be

made from love, unlike his marriage to Grete, when they had met only the once before the ceremony, just for the betrothal. She was fourteen and he seventeen. They were told love would come, it could take time though. 'Cleanse yourself and ask Baldr for love,' Grete's mother had told her. She did and love followed.

For many it didn't.

It was a moonless evening when Grete saw the light above the white forest, the huge curtains of green dancing above the horizon, more than she had ever seen before.

"Now Birgit the Gifted, it is time. Will you tell us about your family?" Grete had asked her.

After a moment's thought. "I have no family," she replied.

"I'm sorry to hear that," Grete immediately said, placing a hand on Birgit's wrist. She knew death came early for many, as it had done for some of her own family. It wasn't uncommon to hear of disease taking an entire family, sometimes leaving a single member on their own.

"No, they are still alive," Birgit told them.

Olav turned his attention towards Leif, wanting to study his reaction. It was obvious he already knew.

"I was once betrothed to someone else, I was very young, it was not long after my becoming a woman. He was a person very much above the status of my own family," Birgit stopped, her expression dropped. "Also a lot older than me. And I mean a lot older," she repeated softly. "He had a reputation of being a bully, an abuser. Nor would I be his first wife."

"So you disobeyed your..." Kjeld the Elder started to say.

Grete interrupted. "So what happened?"

Her father shot her an angry glare.

"I refused to marry him. I told my parents I wanted to learn about art. I wanted to be an artist. I loved to draw, even at a young age." She paused to catch her breath. "My father beat me every night, and every night I refused to capitulate. I would rather die than marry that man." Birgit the Gifted gazed down

to the floor. "In the end I ran away. That was the last I saw my family."

"Where did you go?" Grete asked.

"I miss my mother and sister," Birgit said, as if she had never heard Grete's words. "I also worry about my sister."

An uncomfortable silence followed.

"Where did you go?" Grete asked.

"I found a farmer's hut on the edge of the forest."

"In the forest!" Grete cried out, knowing how dangerous it was. Not only the wolves and bears but also the tales she had heard about the trolls that lived there, how they would snatch people and keep them as slaves.

"I tried to light a fire but the kindling was too damp. I nearly froze to death that night, another and I would have. I was very frightened, I heard the wolves howling. Strangely, I didn't mind, I knew dying was better than being found by this man. He would have probably killed me anyhow. It was what he would have done before that frightened me." She stopped for a moment and gazed at Grete, her eyes dark with sadness.

"And after?" Olav asked.

"A farmhand found me next day, I was unconscious and on the verge of death. He carried me to his home where I warmed up, his wife gave me food from the little they had. They saved my life." Birgit paused for a second. "Margreta Nikolasdatter was the owner of the farm. She was told about me and gave me a job working in one of her houses."

"A servant!?" Kjeld the Elder asked.

"Aren't we all." Grete replied, irritating her father even more.

Birgit spoke again. "I had somewhere warm to sleep, food in my belly."

"That's all we need," Olav told her.

"And love," Grete added.

"And I was also free of that awful man. Most of all I could start drawing again. That is all I wanted. I don't ask for much."

herself in a bath of warm water and blaveis petals before plaiting her hair and looping it around her head, the ends held together with colourful beads. They then dressed her in the bridal gown and veil, her future mother-in-law and two cousins singing songs dedicated to Odin and Baldr as they did.

Leif bore the family sword, the hilt strapped to a belt fastened by an ivory buckle, one Olav had meticulously carved himself with intricate patterns and metal fastenings.

During the ceremony, Kjeld the Elder handed them both a birch branch to hold as they stood before Father Moen. "Think of Frifgg and you will have many children," he told them as they took it.

Rune rings were exchanged, each with an inscription of their love for each other. This was their contract of marriage. Leif also gave Birgit a gift of an ivory ringlet, one he had carved himself with symbols similar to the ones she herself had drawn for the carvings on my own throne.

Birgit presented him with a painting on wood of a bride giving her lover a blaveis flower. "This flower will be permanently in bloom," she told him. "Every time you look at it, it will bond our relationship deeper."

The festivities followed the marriage ceremony, lasting for two whole days and one night. Lengthy speeches were delivered, some with humour, some not so much. Vast quantities of mead were consumed, which fuelled their enthusiasm for more music, more dancing, more food and even more speeches. Olav allowed one of his cows to be slaughtered. Two pigs were also roasted on a spit. Many candles and logs burnt. He silently thanked Bjarne of Bjarkoy for his payments and wished him a speedy return.

And when it was time for the actual coupling: the guests, accompanied by drummers and pipers followed the nervous couple to their new home. Six entered the house with them and watched as the bride and groom climbed under the wedding blanket. The witnessing had been completed. The guests

departed. The coupling was sealed.

After that, the festivities gradually abated and people returned to their daily routines.

Kjeld the Elder coughed himself to death a week later, it was like he had stubbornly waited for the wedding until he could finally depart this world.

As were his last wishes; he was dressed in his finest attire and cremated on a pyre with one treasured belonging: the rune ring he was given to him by his long departed wife at their own wedding.

While the flames took Kjeld the Elder, prayers were chanted with more food and mead consumed in great quantities. Once again Olav thanked Bjarne of Bjarkoy. He was only glad there wasn't to be another ceremony.

During the funeral Father Moen gently coaxed Olav away from the gathering. "I've been speaking to Archbishop Kortin Arnosson," he said when they were away from earshot.

Olav had the feeling that the Father looked uneasy about something.

"It is about Baron Erlingsson."

"Bjarne of Bjarkoy."

Father Moen cleared his throat. "Yes, of course, Bjarne of Bjarkoy."

Olav felt as if the Father was trying to delay what he was wanting to say.

"Not that it matters now," the Father said.

Olav's expression dropped, he felt as if all the air had been sucked out of him. He knew that could only mean one thing.

"Your daughter-in-law, Birgit the Gifted."

"What about Birgit?"

"I believe she thought of Bjarne of Bjarkoy as a father to her."

"She did...does."

"I believe she couldn't find him to invite him to the wedding?"

"No, but we tried. We sent word far and wide, no one knew of his whereabouts."

Olav watched the priest take a deep breath.

"I have news of Bjarne of Bjarkoy." Father Moen paused for a moment, as if he was wanting to pick up the courage. "I thought it best that you tell Birgit the Gifted yourself." Another pause, another deep breath. "Bjarne of Bjarkoy travelled to Bergen at Queen Isabel's request. From there she instructed him to travel to Scotland to speak to her brother Robert Bruce. He was at war with the English, trying to regain the land that had been stolen from them. But it was at great sacrifice to his own warriors. With our help the conquest would be over sooner, saving many lives, also making our lands rich. That is why she sent Bjarne of Bjarkoy to Scotland. To offer Norway's help." He stopped to study Olav's reaction. "Queen Isabel had other reasons, ones personal to her. She wanted her revenge on the English for the entrapment and humiliation of the women in her family." Father Moen's face dropped. "Especially her beloved niece Marjorie. She had heard what they had done to her."

"But I thought she no longer has the authority."

"Our own King was aware. And yes Olav, he approved. He took it as an opportunity for Bjarne of Bjarkoy to strike a deal with the Scots at the same time. Like I said, with peace can come great wealth."

"So what is it you want me to tell my son's wife?"

"There was a storm on their return journey. A great wind had whipped up the seas."

Olav closed his eyes in realisation. His only thought at that time was the outstanding payments owing to him. The wedding and his father-in-law's burial had taken so much, hardly anything remained. He had never given up hope that it would be replenished.

Father Moen saw Olav's sympathy, thought his compassion was only for Birgit. He placed his hand on his shoulder. "Some boats did manage to make it to land, although I'm afraid many

didn't."

"And Bjarne of Bjarkoy was on one of the boats that didn't?"

Father Moen stared long and hard at Olav, saw a man in grief. Realised his task of telling Birgit was going to be a heavy one. "It seems the fleet had become separated and Bjarne of Bjarkoy's boat was caught in the worst of the storm."

"So Bjarne of Bjarkoy is dead?" Olav said, the words sounding neither a question or statement.

"No one witnessed the sinking."

Olav's face opened up. "So he might be alive?"

Again, Father Moen thought his optimism was for Birgit. "It is not only him we lost. No one knew the outcome of the talks with the Scots. Archbishop Kortin tells me Queen Isabel is beside herself."

"And the King?"

"Money can also be made from misery."

"Or money can be lost from misery," Olav added more to himself.

"I think it best that it is you who informs Birgit the Gifted of this sad news," Father Moen said before stepping away.

Olav remained where they had been talking. He had to think: not only to consider his losses, but what to do with the pieces. It wasn't a foregone conclusion that Bjarne of Bjarkoy had perished. He could turn up at any moment and ask for the four sets. Olav couldn't risk it. Even in death this man could still wield great power. What if he had given instructions for someone else to collect the pieces if something should happen to him, like his boat sinking in a storm. He might send the guard that had accompanied Bjarne of Bjarkoy. Olav had to do something he thought. Then again, maybe doing nothing would be better.

So for safe keeping he put the figures in a ceramic pot and stowed it away in a small stone kist at the back of the workshop, along with other items, including the discs made from the morse

England had arrived in Bergen. Only it wasn't just wool and timber they were trading, rats had also stowed away, bringing something far smaller with them: the fleas that fed on them. Not satisfied with rats, the fleas then began to feed on the humans, leaving something even smaller and nastier in their bodies.

Like a murderous tidal wave, a deadly disease began to quickly spread far and wide, showing no mercy. Nor was there any discrimination, anyone could come under its curse, and they were, quicker than they could be buried. Many had to be taken out to sea to prevent the disease spreading. The Church blamed it on the people themselves: that it was their sins that brought the wrath of God they told them. Out of the three hundred priests in the North lands before the epidemic, only forty had survived.

'The Black Death,' it was called; and no other name could have been more appropriate.

Leif and his wife Birgit the Gifted had become two of its victims, being in their late sixties they didn't stand a chance. On the first day it was a fever and a chill. On the second, black spots started to appear. One spot amalgamated with another; and then another. They had seen frost bite many times before, but nothing like this, this wasn't only fingers and toes, this was entire arms and legs, until the whole body was covered. Birgit took three days to die. Leif watched every wretched moment of it. He knew he would soon follow the same excruciating demise. He did, four days it took. More than half the people from the North lands suffered the same fate.

The two people who knew of my whereabouts had now gone.

Mainly through self-imposed isolation, Kjeld the Younger managed to survive. For most of his life he had known nothing but grief. When one period of mourning finished, another would begin, with each loss his wound became deeper. The only period of happiness he could remember was back in the workshop when we were created. It seems My Creator could bring

happiness to his life when all other Gods failed.

With the huge loss of the North land's people he had little choice but to be recruited to work on a neighbouring farm, paid with just enough vegetables to ward off starvation.

Kjeld the Younger was fifty-two.

He had also left the family house, the one he had lived in his entire life, setting up home at the workshop, even though it had become dilapidated and barely fit for human habitation. It meant he had only one place to keep warm and keep working at the same time, although the need for morse carving was not in the forefront of people's minds at that time.

Many of the survivors had to fend for themselves by using timber from unoccupied buildings, of which there were many. Kjeld the Younger started with his parents and brother's house before anyone else got to them, even if he knew the wood was unsuitable for burning, causing the workshop to fill with thick pungent smoke. He had no choice, once the shivering stopped, then so would he.

In Leif and Birgits house he found the belt buckle, the one his brother had worn at his wedding. Kjeld the Younger had kept it to remember them both, the only thing he did keep. He kept it at the back of the workshop beside a clay pot.

It was on one of these days when he was sat by the hearth, the meagre glow giving him just enough heat to stave off the cold. He raised his heavy head and looked around at the tusks and tools laid around the worktops, a thick layer of wood dust covering them. As he had done many times before, he recalled all those years ago after that visit from Bjarne of Bjarkoy. The exquisite workmanship, the intricate carving, the best his father had done, also his grandfather and brother. Kjeld the Younger also included himself in this, even though his father only allowed him to tackle the pieces from the front line, ending up like tiny monoliths: he was still part of it though. He also remembered his sister-in-law Birgit the Gifted, the two attendants, how they all worked as a team. He felt their spirits

were still with him.

Kjeld the Younger did not pity himself. He had made a decision. From the few remaining tusks in the workshop he would make one last shatranj set, just to prove something to himself. It would be for the spirits of his father, for his brother and Birgit, for his grandfather, even for the two attendants. He knew he had the skill, he also knew he could put his own mark on them, for them to stand out as his. It would be a tribute for everyone he had known.

He recalled how his father had become exhausted before carving the Kings. How the first two were not up to his usual standard. So Kjeld the Younger decided to work on this first, going through the initial stages of the basic shaping: the head, the torso, the throne. As it slowly took form he realised it had that same hunched appearance, as though the monarch was looking down on his subjects.

Kjeld the Younger was pleased, it meant he had become an equal. He then remembered the sword resting across the knees, the diagonal cuts on the sheath, the fingers gripping it at both ends. He did the same. Also the folds on the cloak and tunic, like waves washing across his legs. The four twisted braids of hair flowing down his back. Next was the carving on the back of the throne. This he tackled with great care and detail when drawing it on the morse. He remembered how meticulous Birgit the Gifted had been whenever she had done the same. Kjeld the Younger searched into the deepest depths of his imagination: saw strange bird like creatures biting the tails of another, the frame of the throne in the jaws of mysterious beasts, entwined serpents with grabbing claws filling the spaces between. The crown was next, maybe he had become too confident. Two of the points were of different height to the others, the base wasn't level. He was angry with himself, maybe he was becoming exhausted, just like his father had done. The face was next: eyes bulging. He remembered the way Leif had drawn circles around the hole for the pupil, Kjeld the Younger did the same. The

mouth was just a short single cut, no emotion, but seemed to say so much. The nose was perfect. He carved the beard last, braided, a natural crack running down the side of the face, this he used to indicate the edge of the hair.

Kjeld the Younger finished the piece two weeks later.

The Queen would be next.

He remembered when the first Queen was created, how she too was sat on a throne, the veil flowing over her head and shoulders, cascading down her back in neat folds.

Kjeld the Younger tried to recall all those years ago, he remembered the two beasts biting the top frame, their tails hooked around each other. He pictured the gouging of the tiny holes running down the hem of the mantle, this he tried to emulate. He started to carve the crown, recalled the trouble he had experienced with the King. It was then he remembered seeing an image Birgit had drawn for Leif. She had said it was from her travels further south, where the crown had fur edging to make it more comfortable to wear, that it had a cloth interior which sat on top of the head like a cap, only so it would fit the boy prince of that country at the time. Kjeld the Younger would make it the same, thought of it as a tribute to her. He remembered the Queen's pose, how she was sat with her hand to her cheek, that it was held up by the other hand (he wasn't present when they had the discussion about the female attendant having to hold the mask to her face). He didn't think anymore about it, just thought it was what Bjarne of Bjarkoy had told his father when describing the pieces. It was when he finished the Queen a week later that he realised the pieces created all those years ago had their right hand to cheek. His Queen's was on the left. Kjeld the Younger was left handed. It would do he told himself.

A Warrior was to be next. Kjeld the Younger remembered how they were made with the sword pointing upward, the blade resting against the side of the face; like the Queen's hand had been held to her cheek, he remembered his grandfather telling

In his hurry the farmhand had knocked her off the worktop at the back of the workshop and left it where it fell.

The Warrior? Another merchant bought him, his boat was shipwrecked just off the island of Oland in Sweden. Many of the sailors managed to swim to land. Just over a hundred years ago a farmer was digging the foundations for a new barn when he saw these two bulging eyes staring up at him. That Warrior now resides at another establishment in the capital of that nation.

The Horseman Kjeld the Younger became so fond of? The merchant who bought this piece from the farm labourer was Danish, he then sold it to a Frenchman who then sold it to an Italian. It eventually found the respect it deserves and now resides in the city of Florence.

There we remained, in a pot under the workbench.

The Hidden People
1537

I remembered feeling a slight movement, then a tremor, as if the pot was being shaken. I could then feel us being shifted backward, as though we had been caught on the crest of a wave and washed to the rear. We were being tipped-up, that much I could tell. A narrow ray of light entered the pot. The opening was then filled by two eyes peering in on us. The gap slowly widened and the head drew back, we were completely swathed in sunlight. Soon after a boy's hand reached in and started removing us one by one.

As I was lifted out I realised the workshop no longer existed, most of it reclaimed by nature itself. The only indication that a structure had been here was the amount of stones scattered around, the walls having long collapsed from the shifting ice and melting snows. The chamber we were in had also crumbled. One stone from higher up had glanced the side of the pot several years ago, causing a fragment to break away. Several discs and pieces fell through it, thirteen from the front line, most disappearing in the gaps between stones. We also lost two Warriors just before a Horseman fell side-on

against the hole, blocking any more of us from falling through.

The boy's eyes widened. He was young, fresh faced, not long from casting away his boyhood, but old enough to have a downy beard.

More pieces followed, each one placed on the ground beside me.

It was then I realised the changing of the seasons had started to take its toll, the ice crystals beginning to create scar channels all over our bodies.

A Bishop was next, which he studied in great detail, scrutinising it in minute detail. I could tell he couldn't believe what he was seeing, as if we were real people shrunken in size. A Warrior was next, the only one wearing a pot hat, where Kjeld the Elder had encountered the blunted shape of the morse he had carved it from. He lifted another piece out, another Warrior, one biting the top of his shield. The young man's eyebrows furrowed even deeper, he held the Warrior closer before swiftly pulling it away, as if the piece would suddenly come alive and impale him with its sword. As each piece was liberated from its confinement the young man's expression became more confused, his frown deeper. He picked me up and studied my throne in great detail: the two beasts biting the top frame, the entwined vines.

He eventually placed me back down with the others.

Everything was different, all the tools had gone, all the morse and antlers, they had all vanished. The hearth was just the remnants of a cold metal frame half submerged in the earth. The only real evidence that there was once a workshop here were the stones that once raised the walls off the ground. Beyond that, all the other workshops had also perished, just a rectangle of stones remained, a hint of what was once a thriving industrious area. Everything else had virtually vanished, reclaimed by the land or taken to be used in other homes. The stones from the workshop would eventually surrender to the same fate.

The young man cupped his hands together and threw as many as he could back into the pot, breaking a sword from one of the other Kings, a chip fell away from a Queen's crown. He had also scooped up one of the fallen Warriors: the many hard winters it laid outside had caused it great harm, like a war-weary fighter who had lost the battle before it had even started. The young man searched around the stones, turning several over to see what was underneath, some were boulders, so he had to use all his strength to roll them out of the way. He found one of the Queens Kjeld the Younger had created, the one that had fallen off the worktop, also the buckle from Leif's and Birgit the Gifted's wedding. The boy replaced the lid and held the pot with the hole against his chest.

A fear began to surge through him. He remembered the tales his Pappa had told him when he was a child, stories about evil creatures. Were we from one of those the boy thought? What misery would we unleash on the land? Another plague? But they were just tales he had to tell himself. We were not real. He could feel a pounding in his head. He had only one choice. Without thinking any more he began running towards the Church. Father Brynjar was the wisest man he knew. If anyone would know what to do then he would.

With heavy breaths he stopped outside the huge wooden doors of the cathedral. Keeping the pot tight against his chest he stepped through the wicket door and into the gloomy interior of the nave.

Looking down the aisle he saw three people kneeling in front of the altar, their hands held tightly together in prayer. The young man breathed a sigh of relief when he recognised the one in the middle as Father Brynjar. The other two he guessed were parishioners, the one on the left was a man, the other a woman. He waited just inside the door as the prayers continued. It sounded intense, the words vibrating down the aisle, as if they were asking for forgiveness. The lad wondered what transgression the man and woman had done to want to pray in

Erik remembered being told that these little people lived in their own tiny villages in the forests and meadows, that humans never knew where they were. How they were ruled by their own kings and queens and there were probably bishops and horsemen in these tiny villages, also warriors to protect them. That the tombstones he saw were for the Hidden People who had died: they had to be buried somewhere. But what was worse, if a human were ever to see them they would bring great harm onto that person.

His father used to joke that Erik himself was a changeling and his mother has been beating him every day with a stick, and yet he still wouldn't change back. Erik wanted to tell him that he only knew the half of it.

"Well, what do *you* think they are Erik?" Father Brynjar asked.

For several seconds Erik tried to think, wondered if he should tell him. "My father would say they are the Hidden People."

"The Hidden People?"

"Yes, he told me it was the Hidden People that caused the plague."

Erik stared wide-eyed at the Father, trying to absorb what he was thinking. It felt as if the priest was annoyed about something. It made him wonder what evil he had unleashed into the world.

"And you think these are the Hidden People."

Erik didn't know how to answer. He was starting to regret coming to the church. "Yes Father."

"And they are going to cause misery amongst our people, maybe another plague?"

Erik didn't know what to say.

A heavy silence followed.

"No Erik, I'm afraid your father is wrong." Father Brynjar knew of Erik's father's opinions on the Catholic Church, that he was part of a growing group asking for reformation and their

actions were becoming more extreme. "It was the sins of the people that caused the plague, not creatures from our imagination. It was God who needed to punish these sinners, as he will still do if some do not change their ways."

Erik wondered if he had sinned in saying what he had just said about the Hidden People. It was what the Father said next that took him by surprise.

"They are not the Hidden People. They are no more than morse carvings, and made by a very skillful craftsman by the look of it. They will do no more harm than that clay pot you are clutching like a baby, unless you were going to hit someone over the head with it."

Erik clutched the pot tighter to his chest.

"So what do you want to do with them?"

"I don't know."

"Why not take them home, after all, they are yours. It was you who found them."

"No!" Erik realised how abrupt that sounded. "Sorry Father, my parents wouldn't like that."

"Because they will think they are the Hidden People."

Erik gazed down in shame. "Yes Father, they will."

Erik didn't tell Father Brynjar the entire truth. That his mother often resorted to beating him for no reason. 'Maybe I was a changeling,' Erik began to think. She would certainly scold him for bringing us home, thinking we would bring bad luck to their house, even if he did tell her we were no more than gaming pieces. Then again, how could he say it was Father Brynjar who told him? Nor could he tell them that he had seen the Father, if anything, that would bring on a worse thrashing.

"Things are better left where they are, she would tell me," Erik said, not wanting to divulge the true reason.

The Father didn't pursue it. He knew.

"Come with me?" Without another word Father Brynjar had taken a rag-torch from a metal ring and strode away, stopping a couple of arm's length away. Erik was surprised

when he saw him open a small door, like a panel made from the same wood as its surroundings, rendering it virtually invisible. The Father turned to look at Erik, holding his gaze on him, as if to say he should follow. He stepped through and vanished from sight.

Erik followed with the pot still held tight to his chest, stepping into a bare stone room. That was until he could just make out shapes and colours on the walls. Through the dim light the rag-torch allowed he could just make out a painting. It appeared to be of a battle scene, of a warrior wearing a crown and wielding a long sword. Father Brynjar only paused for a second, just enough time to allow Erik time to take in the image. He then strode across the room and went through another arch. Eric followed, soon halting, aghast at what was in front of him.

Just proud of the floor and at the centre was laid a slab of stone, rectangular in shape, the size of a large coffin. What surprised Erik were the squares of a bright metal glistening in the flame of the torch. Something else caught the light, small objects encrusted in the metal: like sparks were igniting on it. Father Brynjar walked around to the other side and crossed himself. He held up the flaming torch and turned to look at Erik at the same time. On the wall was an altar, semi-circular in shape, bordered by square cut stones framing colourful images. In the middle was a picture of a saint in a blue shawl, wearing a crown encircled by a halo. Below was a picture of a battle, similar to the one on the walls in the previous room. In this image was a man sitting on a grey horse, he looked proud. Erik knew immediately who it was: St Olav, the Patron Saint of the lands leading to the North. Erik couldn't help but feel in awe of the bones that lay only a short distance from him.

"He is not here," the Father said.

Erik was surprised. "Oh, where is he?"

"The archbishop moved his remains to Steinvikholm Castle. There is a large garrison there. He will be better protected."

Before Erik could say anymore, Father Brynjar turned and walked under yet another arch, along a short brick stone corridor and into another room, also empty. In the corner of this room, and hardly visible, were spiralling stone steps, steep and narrow, like they were snaking around a huge, round pillar made of blocks of stone perfectly cut to shape. Father Brynjar began to descend deep into the depths of the Cathedral. Erik had to hurry to keep up, it was obvious the Father had done this journey a thousand times before, like he was floating downward. Erik struggled to follow the flickering orange light, knew he would be plunged into darkness if he didn't keep up, there would be a good chance he would miss his footing and tumble downward, probably taking the Father with him.

They entered a smaller room which appeared as if it had been carved out of the rock itself. Erik noticed the face of the walls had small alcoves cut into them, archlike recesses randomly spaced, some were near the ceiling, others lower down at the floor. There seemed to be no rhyme or reason for their position. Some were empty, others had pots all of different sizes and decoration, from the ornate to the very plain, from a poor state to looking nearly new. Strangely, the pot he was holding would not look out of place in one of these recesses.

Erik gazed around, saw a strange space in the corner. Another entrance? A way out? It was deceptive from the flickering shadow the flame was creating. The facing wall wasn't connected to the one adjoining it. He wished he could see more.

His attention was drawn back towards the pots in the recesses.

"They are the ashes of the Fathers no longer with us," Father Brynjar said. He carefully took the pot from Erik and placed it in one of the empty recesses.

"No one will know but us," Father Brynjar whispered to Erik as if the spirits of the departed Fathers were in the room with them. He pointed to the pot. "Don't worry, that place is

put the pot inside that recess thought Erik, because the priest knew that no one would be there to put him there.

Erik looked up at his mother. Where was his father? He so much wanted him to walk through the door.

"Gunna Aanenson said you had some of the Hidden People in the pot."

Erik knew if he said anymore, that would mean provoking her even more, triggering more punishment. He remained silent.

"You know what the Hidden People have done to this land. You know they will do the devil's work again."

Erik felt he had no choice but to defend himself, even if he knew the consequences. "Father Brynjar said they were ivory carvings. He said they are harmless." His voice had lost all fear, replaced with loud determination.

"Father Brynjar will say whatever suits him. And he won't be a priest for much longer now you have summoned all the evils onto this land. You know they will want their revenge on us." She raised her hand again, a lot higher this time. "Now your father has had to go and sort out the mess you've made."

Erik wondered what she meant by that. "I don't understand Mamma."

"Your father and other men from the village have gone to destroy them."

Eric thought, that's all the excuse they needed. Now he realised why Father Brynjar had moved St Olav's remains. He also knew they would never find us in that room, it was like a labyrinth just to get down there. Then again, they could torture Father Brynjar to find out where. He also knew the Father wouldn't tell. Then they will kill him! He had to go and warn the Father. Erik stood.

"Where do you think you are going?" his mother screamed, taking a step towards him.

Before she could get any closer Erik gave her a hard shove, causing her to trip on the corner of the hot hearth and fall backward onto the hard ground.

He was as much in shock as she was. "Sorry Mamma, but I have..." He stopped when he saw the rage in her face. She rubbed her head and saw blood smeared over her fingers.

Erik swiftly ran through the door, not stopping until he was out of sight of the house.

As he got to the brow of the hill he could see the smoke on the horizon, a black cloud billowing up to the sky. He ran as fast as his legs could carry him. As he got closer the plume became thicker and darker, the smoke rolling upward in huge balls, the flames flicking higher up into the sky. The nave was on fire, flames were breaking through the roof and reaching high up to the sky. All he could think about was Father Brynjar.

Erik arrived by the side of the church. He peered around the corner and saw a crowd of angry men holding flaming torches.

He heard a voice. "Erik!?" It was one he immediately recognised: his father.

Most would run from a fire, but not Erik, he had to warn Father Brynjar and made a swift dart towards the wicket door. Without stopping he entered into the nave. He saw thick black smoke filling the far end, the altar burning with bright red flames. A beam in the stave cracked, the timbers thudded to the ground causing embers to fly through the air, searching out fresh wood to set alight. Erik knew the roof would soon follow.

"Erik!" The voice turning to panic. "Erik!"

His father was by the door, soon he would enter the church. Erik didn't want that.

Erik grabbed a rag-torch and quickly disappeared through the small door, the same one he had when he followed Father Brynjar only a short while ago. He slammed it shut before the putrid smoke could follow. No one would know where he had gone, especially his father.

Once inside he took the same route Father Brynjar had travelled the first time. Passing the empty tomb and down the narrow coiling steps into the room where all the other pots had

been placed. His pot was still there, in the exact same place the Father had left it. He grabbed it. As he did a piece fell out, it was a Queen, the same one Kjeld the Younger had carved. It dropped onto the stone floor and smashed into fragments. Erik looked down when he heard the crack, saw just a head staring up at him, part of a hand held to the cheek, the arm broken away. There were two smaller pieces to the side of them. He left them where they fell.

Erik knew he had to warn Father Brynjar. He wondered if the priest had already made his escape. He began to make his way back up the steps, along the corridor and through the rooms, discovering the smoke had already infiltrated them. When he got to the last room he saw a putrid thick smog had penetrated into it. Erik held his breath and made a dash towards the door, grabbed the handle but snatched it away as the heat scolded his hand. He wrapped the corner of his tunic around the metal and managed to keep hold of it long enough to open the door.

There in front of him was a wall of flaming red, the heat smacking him harder than his mother ever could. He heard the sound of more falling timbers, knew to enter into the nave would be suicide. He could see the wicket door was open. Erik just hoped his father had made his escape.

He retraced his steps, knowing there was only one choice, that mysterious space in the corner, if that failed then his ashes would be joining the others already there.

He entered the small room again and took one of the pots from its recess, turned it upside down and began spilling the contents into it. "Sorry Father," he said to the pile of grey dust on the ground. "If I wasn't going to hell before, then I will be now."

"I forgive you Erik, although I'm not sure if our Lord will."

Erik jolted his head up. Standing in the corner was Father Brynjar. Gone was his cassock. Instead he was wearing the clothes of a peasant: a thick, brown woollen tunic, the elbows

patched with leather. Replacing his velvet fur-lined slippers were scuffed leather boots tied tight around his calfs. A sack was thrown over his shoulder.

"That was Bishop Henrikson," Father Brynjar told him.

Erik looked down at the small mound of ash. "Sorry Bishop Henrikson."

"He says he forgives you. Now come Erik, there is no time. We must hurry."

Erik looked up again, as if asking permission.

"Yes, if you must, but hurry."

Erik tipped up the broken pot and transferred us into our new home, sharing the space with what was left of Bishop Henrikson.

"Come quick." Father Brynjar vanished into the space.

Erik had no choice but to put his trust in him once again and soon found himself inside the narrow tunnel. The chiselled marks from the tools were still evident on the soft stone. Erik could only guess that it must have been dug out by the monks long gone. He quietly thanked them.

He continued to follow Father Brynjar, having to hurry to keep the orange glow of the torch in sight. It wasn't long before the tunnel had returned to natural rock. After a few more steps it had tapered down to a narrow space. Erik had to exhale all the air from his body to squeeze through the tiny gap, having to keep the pot high above his head. They were then confronted by a steep drop the height of a man. Erik negotiated the crude steps carved out of the rock, careful not to slip on them. He heard trickling ahead and soon had to wade through the freezing, ankle deep water, it felt as if he had lost all feeling in his feet. The drips from the ceiling began to soak into his clothes, the cold penetrating his bones. Erik could only think it would be impassable during the Great Melt, a shiver went through him as he realised it would have been a choice of drowning or burning to death if it had.

On they went, neither saying anything. It seemed to take

Silence.

For a second he thought Father Brynjar was about to change his mind. He didn't. "Where will we go?" Erik asked.

"I have a friend who will take us to Bergen. At first light tomorrow we will make contact with him. The day after that we will set sail. I will warn you Erik, it will be a long and hard journey. The boat is old so there is a good chance we may end up on the seabed."

"We survived burning Father, so we can also survive drowning."

"Good lad." Father Brynjar looked down at the pot, then back up at Erik. "You will have to leave that behind."

"No! No I won't. I can't." Erik said with resolute determination. "I will not," he added softly. "I promise, I will not let it get in our way." A smile came to his lips. "Anyhow, Bishop Henrikson will be protecting us."

"Then Bishop Henrikson is your responsibility." The Father then puffed out a laugh. "Although the only thing he would want protecting is his money."

Father Brynjar was true to his word. They made contact with his friend the following day. It was the sound of chopping Erik heard first, the slow thud thud of an axe echoing through the trees, followed by the rip of splitting of wood.

Then Erik noticed the space between the trees was becoming wider, until through them he could sea the glint of the sea. They then came to two huge stacks of chopped logs. It was the barking of dogs they heard next.

A man appeared around one of the stacks holding an axe in a threatening manner. Four elkhounds were by his side. On seeing Father Brynjar the man threw his hood back and yelled at the dogs, they immediately stopped barking. He embedded the blade into a tree trunk and approached with his arms held wide. With a hug and several pats on the back they warmly greeted each other. Both gripped their shoulders as they parted, their eyes locked onto each other. Silence followed, as though

so much was being said without a single word being spoken.

The man then looked at Erik.

"This is Erik," Father Brynjar told him. He then held a hand in front of his friend. "And this is Bunde Storstrand," he said, like it was nothing.

Erik froze when he heard the name Bunde Storstrand. He always thought the man was a myth, just a name in a tale. There were rumours that Bunde Storstrand could talk to the creatures of the forest, that he was brought up by the wolves and the bears, that his friends were trolls and the Hidden People, that he was once married to a mermaid. It was said he could give messages to the ravens to take directly to Odin. Also a fearsome fighter and brave warrior who killed a hundred men in a single battle. It was rumoured that Tyr himself had given him these powers.

The man looked long and hard at Erik, not making any sound or movement. Only these weren't the eyes of a fearsome fighter who was brought up by wolves, whose friends were trolls and the Hidden People. These were the eyes of a compassionate man, someone that was merciful and kind; not that Erik could see much of Bunde Storstrand. His face was virtually hidden by a mass of fair hair, just those eyes and strong cheekbones on display. He was also large, a giant of a man, his age indeterminable, he could have been anywhere between thirty and sixty. Erik held his gaze on this Bunde Storstrand, wanting to prove his own worth.

"Erik is with me." Was all the Father offered as an explanation.

Bunde returned a sharp drop of his head, as if that was good enough for him. With a baffled expression he looked down at the pot Erik was holding.

Erik realised this was a man of few words.

Father Brynjar released a hearty laugh. "Open it."

Erik raised the lid and cautiously held the pot out for Bunde to peer in. He wondered what this man of the land and sea

would make of the strange figures.

The eyes had a childlike naivety as they looked down at us. I then felt hard calloused fingers as he raised me into the light. His expression changed from bewilderment to admiration. He placed me back in and drew out another piece, one from the front-line, he replaced that. Then another, a Horseman. Then a Bishop, one standing, holding two fingers up in blessing, the crook of a crosier pressed against his cheek.

He looked towards Father Brynjar and crossed his chest.

Father Brynjar offered him a thin smile, although he remained silent.

Erik didn't know if he should say it, but if anyone should know then this man should. Erik looked up at the huge man. "My mother says they are the Hidden People. She says they will bring misery into the world."

Bunde looked down at Erik with a glint in his eyes. "Then who am I to contradict your mother. Nor is she wrong about the suffering. But I wouldn't blame these little fellows." He then looked at Father Brynjar. "Hnefatafl?" Bunde asked, although his frown said otherwise.

The Father shrugged. "Maybe, then again, maybe a game like hnefatafl, but not hnefatafl," he replied. "Morse?" he added, like it was a question.

Bunde turned it around. "Morse, yes, without a doubt Father," he replied. "Several of the poor beasts would have had to be sacrificed for this many."

He wasn't wrong.

Without anymore being said, Bunde placed the Bishop back into the pot. He then turned and led them towards the house. With a snap of his fingers the four elkhounds obediently followed, keeping close to their master at all times.

They rounded a tall wooden frame with rows of drying cod hanging down, the bitter wind stopping them from going mouldy. When they arrived at the house, Erik was surprised to see a solid building with thick walls made of stone and mud

mortar, he was expecting something less substantial. They stepped in. The first he saw was a simple altar on the far wall, just two candles with freshly picked flowers either side of a crudely carved crucifix. Erik realised this was a man with unwavering devotion, a man who obviously lived his life as a religious hermit, probably not seeing another human for months on end. A hearth was at the centre of the room, a pile of logs next to it. A byre at one end, but no animals. Erik could only guess that they were outside in their pens. He placed the pot on the floor and sat next to the hearth to warm up. He was cold, wet and exhausted. It had been a long night with no sleep.

A meal of elk meat and turnips with flatbread was served up, the dogs getting thrown large chunks of the meat as though they were included in the feast. When one was missing out, Bunde would feed her by hand.

"Without these it would just be turnips," he told Erik.

Bunde and Father Brynjar talked when the meal was finished, the Father telling him that the nave of the Cathedral had been completely destroyed, if not the entire church, reassuring Bunde that St. Olav's shrine had been relocated.

Erik listened, feeling ashamed, knowing his father was one of the people responsible. He said nothing.

When they had exhausted all conversation the Father told Bunde that he would understand if he didn't want to make the journey.

"I am a simple fisherman Father helping two weary travellers. What harm can that do?" he replied with a grin. " If they want to take umbrage over that then so be it," he said looking at a sword fixed to the wall. And that was that, no more was discussed on the matter.

"What about the dogs?" the Father asked.

"Mikkjel has agreed to take them for the time I am away. They are good elk hunters, he will be pleased to have them." Bunde patted the largest on the shoulder, one that Erik thought looked more like a wolf than a dog. "Balder here will be happy

was also a devout Catholic, a friend of Archbishop Olav Engelbrektsson who Osbern had helped escape to the Netherlands in one of his boats.

Erik's job was to load the goods, mainly fish, mostly herring, or white gold as Osbern the Merchant liked to call them, their profit so great. That's where Erik and the Father lived, staying at his large house on the edge of the port along with his wife and four daughters.

Erik knew Father Brynjar's advancing age was beginning to take its toll, that he had never got over the long and hard journey from Nidaros. Sometimes having to give his blessings from his bed.

Then one day a man with an upturned moustache and a cheerful disposition came to visit Osbern the Merchant. A Spanish hildago who entered the house with two black servants. He introduced himself as Gunisalvo Moctezuma de a Cueva Valenzuela, so everyone called him: 'the Spaniard.' He was here to initiate trade deals, as he had done in many other countries. He brought samples of his items to display to Osbern, mostly wines and sugar, along with some other items, including the two servants. All he wanted in exchange were furs, pelts and yes, Arctic gold, which apparently Osbern said he could get by the boat load.

It reminded me of something!

Whenever Erik opened the lid to the pot and displayed us to visiting folk, we would see the same enquiring eyes and baffled expressions, occasionally a look of horror, especially when a Bishop was first seen. So strange were we that some even took the same path as Erik's mother, saying we were the Hidden People ready to bring another catastrophe into the world. It was only when Father Brynjar stepped in with his explanation that they reluctantly accepted we were simply morse carvings.

That was until The Spaniard set eyes on us.

His reaction was totally different, it was as if he knew

exactly what we were.

He picked out a King first (not me), then a Queen, then a Horseman. Each one he studied with great admiration, followed by gushing praise which no one understood, but they could see his appreciation from his animated excitement, only to be quietened when he saw the exquisite workmanship. He then picked up a handful from the front line, fingered through them as though they were precious gemstones. Next was a Warrior, which caused him to frown in confusion.

As always, it was the Bishop that created the strongest reaction, but not the same as for other people. At first he slowly nodded, then glanced back to Erik. He held the Bishop up for all to see and spoke in Spanish. No one understood, although Erik could tell it was spoken in a positive tone.

"We think they may be part of a game called hnefatafl," Father Brynjar remarked. "Our ancestors used to play it. Many still do."

The Spaniard shook his head. "No," he said, like he had blown a hole into the air. "Hnefatafl no, chess yes." Another moment's silence. "Yes, chess," he repeated softly.

On his second visit the Spaniard requested to see us again. Foregoing his broken North lands language he started making strange and animated shapes with his hands, firstly drawing a square in the air, pinching his white tunic as if to say a plain cloth would suffice. After a lot of confusion, Arna, Osbern's youngest daughter eventually opened a chest and pulled out a large sheet of linen. The Spaniard nodded, then indicated what size he needed it to be, also something to draw with. He acted like he was a person who shouldn't be refused, someone who was used to having his commands obeyed; and quickly. Osbern nodded towards Arna. She skillfully cut the linen to size. The Spaniard cleared a space on the bench and began to draw an eight by eight chequered image, shading in each alternate square.

Everyone there looked on with fascination.

He then started picking up the pieces and placing them each on a square. When the Spaniard had finished there were two armies facing each other; four lines of eight with the four rows between them laying vacant, a space for the battle to be held. The Bishops he put in each corner of the board, one Warrior he placed next to the two Kings (I was one), another beside each Queen. He looked confused, as though something wasn't correct. He swapped the Bishops and Warriors, gazed down and smiled. The Spaniard then started making strange hand gestures, indicating to his dark boots, then to one of the armies. It was Arna who eventually clocked on, saying that one side should be a different colour to the other.

The Spaniard nodded. "Yes." He pointed to the other side. "White?"

Father Brynjar who had pointed to the other side. "Black," he said.

"Yes black," the Spaniard confirmed, then held his hands up, as if to say he didn't understand why they weren't. He called Erik over and told him to sit. He pointed to his eyes, then the board, as if telling Erik to watch.

Firstly he picked up a Warrior, began sweeping the piece over the chequered battleground. The Bishop was next, sliding it down the entire length of the diagonal. He indicated that it could capture a piece if from the opposing side, that it would then remain on that square. He gestured how a piece from the front line could move two squares on its first move, how it captured, pointing to the dark boot again when he wanted to show it was the opposing side. When it was a piece from the lighter side he would pinch his white tunic. Next was the Queen, moving the same as the Warrior and Bishop together. Last was myself, the most important.

So that's how it continued, without a word being spoken. The Spaniard occasionally glanced up at Erik to make sure he understood.

I noticed the moves were different to the way Bjarne of

Bjarkoy had described them to My Creator.

Then next day The Spaniard paid Osbern the Merchant another visit, carrying a length of black ribbon. He then went about cutting it into shorter strips and tied them around each piece on one side, including me.

At the beginning it was more of a lesson, the Spaniard making the moves for Erik, as if he was playing against himself. With each game his influence on Erik's side became less and less, until the second day when Erik needed no help whatsoever. On the third day Erik beat the Spaniard. His tutor appeared more than pleased; he had taught him well. There was no more to do.

The Spaniard left Bergen soon after.

Osbern the Merchant told Erik that the Spaniard had sailed away contented. He had got what he came for, securing the trade for furs and pelts, and of course: Arctic gold. Not only that, he had passed on the game of chess to the North lands: and wanted Erik to pass his skill of the game on. He also said the next time the Spaniard came to visit Bergen he would bring a consignment of Spanish chess sets with him, which he thought were the best in the world.

"Until he saw yours," Osbern told Erik. "He also said that when he returns to his own country he will ask for a set to be made with Bishops, as yours is."

Soon after the Spaniard left, Erik taught Arna the game of chess. Only it wasn't their eyes that met over that chequered battleground: instead of war, love was exchanged.

Erik married Osbern the Merchant's daughter not long after. It was Father Brynjar who conducted the marriage ceremony.

The priest died three months later.

Arna and Erik had six children. Three girls and three boys. All learnt how to play chess.

Osbern the Merchant died twelve years after Father Brynjar.

Erik immediately took over the business. Entertaining

lines of dogs.

It was at the end of the story when the captain noticed us in the gloom. He stepped over and immediately indicated for his associate to join him. As always, their expressions went through that same scale, from bemusement to confusion to admiration.

Captain Conor O'Clery picked me up and studied me in great detail. He then turned to Dagr and held me up.

"Oh those, they belonged to my father," Dagr said as though we were nothing.

The associate translated.

"What are they?" Captain O'Clery asked.

"They are used in a game called chess."

"What is chess?" Captain Conor O'Clery asked.

"It's like a game of war. My father taught me, but I never really bothered with it that much. It's not much fun getting slaughtered all the time."

"Who made them?"

"We don't know."

"Where have they come from?"

"My father found them amongst some ruins when he was a young man."

"Here in Bergen?"

"No, a place called Nidaros. My father escaped with them during the Reformation. He had to flee with a priest. The story of their journey is..." Dagr stopped for a moment. "Shall we say...interesting."

The captain's associate continued to translate.

"Was your father a priest?" Captain O'Clery asked.

"My father?" Dagr just managing to stop himself from laughing. "No, he was not a priest."

"Then why did *he* escape?"

"He never told me, even when I pressed him about it."

Captain Conor O'Clery picked me up and blew the dust away. His scrutiny became even more thorough, the

appreciation of the carving more intense. He rubbed his thumb over my intricate carving: it reminded me of the time when My Creator used a similar touch.

"There's more," Dagr told him.

"More what?"

"Pieces."

"More pieces you say."

"Yes."

"Where?"

"In a pot somewhere."

"A pot, where?"

"I'm not sure but my father said they would make four sets in total."

Captain O'Clery thought some more. "Four sets?"

"Yes, although there are some pieces missing."

A thoughtful silence followed.

"But there are enough left to make a complete set," Captain O'Clery asked.

"Yes."

"Are they for sale?" he asked.

Dagr thought. He would be glad to get rid of them, especially for money. He also remembered his father telling him never to divulge what you are thinking. "At the right price," he said.

Captain Conor O'Clery spoke to his associate in his native tongue. He then turned towards Dagr. "What price?" he asked.

"They are very unique, very sought after. Like you, many people have asked about them."

The Irishman was no ones fool. By the amount of dust on us he knew this man from the North lands was not telling the entire truth. Nor did he know where the pot with the others were. "What do you want for them?" he asked.

Dagr never had his father's or grandfather's astuteness in trade deals.

Two sacks of potatoes were eventually decided upon.

The pot was found and we were all placed back into the darkness of its interior again. Captain O'Clery then looked inside, taking several pieces out, as if he had made some sort of decision. When he pulled out the Queen Kjeld the Younger had made, thinking it looked different from the rest, he passed it over to his associate with several pieces from the front line.

Captain Conor O'Clery departed Dagr's house with the pot tucked under his arm.

My journey was about to take another path.

The Pirate and the Clansman

1607

Captain Conor O'Clery had loaded enough cargo on his fifty foot sloop for it just to stay afloat. It was a boat he'd not long brought back from a trip to Bermuda, a much larger and sturdier ship than the one he had travelled there in; only because it could carry twice the amount in the hold.

The island of Bermuda had so much to offer: tobacco, salt and so much more, especially the different exotic foods, ones he never thought could exist. Not in his wildest imagination could he have thought a fruit could look like a pineapple, or taste like it. The profit he made from that one expedition alone virtually paid for the boat. He even renamed it 'Seamrog,' just for luck.

He and his crew departed Bergen and set sail for Ireland.

On this particular journey from the North lands the cargo hold was packed to the seams with different items, rare timbers, various hides and furs, exotic feathers, whale bone, antler and of course, what every self-respecting merchant would want to

seas though, where the perpetrators could quickly vanish into its huge vastness. Never where they were; and he had sailed these waters many times, although he had heard these rogues had started using faster and more agile boats, becoming more fearless, their intention more hostile. Rumours of deaths and kidnapping were rife. Their tactics had also changed, combats had become closer to land, hiding away in a cove so they could ambush their victims. All Captain O'Clery and his crew had in defence were six small canons fixed onto the gunwale, three either side. None had been fired, not even in practice, he didn't think it was necessary. As much as he could, the captain made sure he kept land close by, he could look over the port side and see the Hebrides coming into view: just a thin and dark misty line on the horizon.

Captain Conor O'Clery had to make a decision. Firstly, he could wait it out and see who they were. With a bit of luck they would simply change direction.

Secondly, he could head for the safety of land, but then again, not knowing the lay of the land the Seamrog could be smashed against the rocks. Also stories of clansmen being hostile were rife, they would certainly take his cargo. He was Irish though, not English, maybe they would look on him with some camaraderie.

Thirdly, he could continue on course to their homeland. Try and make haste.

The captain chose the third. He didn't want to take any chances.

"Hoist the main and foresail," he shouted. "And be quick about it. We're heading home lads" Then added softly. "So we are."

Seamrog soon picked up speed, this was what it was built for. Jasperd Staffurd chose to tack starboard so as to get the most out of the wind. Captain Conor O'Clery knew there was no better man who could get the most out of his boat than Jasperd.

With every passing minute the distant sails were growing

ever larger. It was then the captain realised he couldn't outrun them.

He could now just make out the size of the boat sitting high in the water, one that would be able to ride the waves far easier than his sloop. He knew it would only be a matter of time before they caught up with them.

The Seamrog battled on through the waves.

For a second the captain thought they had vanished. He was about to breathe a sigh of relief, that was until he looked over the stern.

It was as if the ship had suddenly appeared out of nowhere. Behind them and fast approaching was a brigantine, two masted, double the length of his own boat, not large but fast and easy to manoeuvre.

Captain O'Clery looked starboard, a feeling of relief when he saw the ensign of a white saltire on a blue background. This soon turned to dejection when he saw the ensign lowered and replaced by one with a black background, the saltire had become crossed bones. It was his worst fear, these were pirates! All his cargo would be taken, probably their lives along with it.

Captain O'Clery could see a hive of activity onboard the brigantine. Several hands were scurrying around, all disciplined in their tasks. He thought about fighting, loading his canons, maybe try and pierce a hole low into the hull, hope it would sink the ship. He looked along the row of gunports on the brigantine, all probably manned: the captain knew he and his crew would perish trying.

Sails had been reefed. The brigantine's speed had dropped, slowly coming broadside to the Seamrog. That's when the captain could see the name Priam high up on the side of the hull.

The ship was closing in on them. Captain O'Clery was concerned, even a slight meeting of the two boats could mean Seamrog being capsized. Everyone on it would quickly perish in the freezing sea.

He heard the barking of commands. These were men well

drilled in their tasks, probably having executed this same manoeuvre many times before.

The Priam remained at the same distance, the height of three to four men between them. He wondered what their next tactic would be. This was cold, undulating water, a man's body would go numb immediately, turning his blood to ice, no one could survive swimming that short distance. That's when he saw him, peering over the gunwale. The man had a sharp face with a devil's beard, even from that distance Captain O'Clery could see his two blue eyes piercing into him. The man raised his tricorn, as if in an arrogant salute, revealing hair like a lion's mane. This was the so-called captain of the Priam, of that Captain O'Clery was in no doubt.

Another man appeared, standing not far from the Priam's captain. "Reef your sails captain," he yelled down. "Your boat is now under the command of Captain Peter Love."

Captain Conor O'Clery looked towards Jasperd, saw he was still battling to keep the Seamrog a safe distance from the Priam, as though his boat was being sucked towards the larger vessel.

Captain Conor O'Clery needed time to think; he had none.

"We are seizing your boat," the man shouted, looking agitated. "Captain Peter Love orders you to reef your sails now."

The next Captain O'Clery saw were two muskets, each either side of the Priam's captain, aimed at him and only him. He then looked at his own crew, saw their eyes were also on him, waiting. He tried to read what they were thinking: concede or try and evade capture? All he saw was cold fear. It would be his decision to make and his alone.

"Reef the sails lads," Conor said in defeat, then added, more to himself. "We await our fate so we will." He looked up, Peter Love had gone. The muskets remained.

The only noise was the strain of creaking wood as both boats rose and descended the waves; and yet the narrow gully between them remained the same.

A scraping noise revealed a long, thick beam of wood slid out through a gap in the gunwale. A rope threaded through a hole at the end and back onboard. A sailor suddenly swung out, the beam was given more length, the men pushing it attempting to gauge the distance to the Seamrog. The man held on tightly as he waited for the rope to stop swaying. A rope tied to it was pulled in. The sailor eventually swung above the Seamrog, not by far, just a couple of feet. When the time was right he slid down and dropped onto the deck. Another sailor quickly followed in the same fashion, then another, until there were four of them.

All this time the muskets remained on the captain.

The Seamrog's crew were expecting lice-ridden scoundrels who had no concern for their appearance, but these rogues wore clean clothes, two had a bandanna covering their hair. They were also well fed, muscular. One even joked to Jasperd about him trying to outrun the Priam. That's about as far as their amiability got when the crew of the Seamrog saw the cutthroats. One had an axe, another with two pistols tucked into his sash, the butts pointing outward: one for each hand.

Captain Conor O'Clery knew to try and take them as hostages would be suicide, that the captain of the Priam would have no concern about his own crewmen and would probably fire their muskets randomly into the Seamrog. Captain O'Clery thought if there was ever a misnamed person, then Peter Love was it.

One of the Priam's crew vanished into the cargo hold.

I recall feeling a presence, and not a good one. He was moving along the narrow gap at the centre. At one time he felt close, as if he was studying the pot we were in. I was half expecting to see the lid being removed, it remained in place.

The man appeared on deck again, took a bright yellow handkerchief from his belt and waved it vigorously towards the Priam. Shortly after, one of the sailors dismissed Jasperd Staffurd with threats from his cutthroat. It was far from an idle

Jasperd took a step back.

Captain Conor O'Clery's body stiffened, his hands flat on the deck, his knees bent that little bit more, ready to jump this man called Johnne Cokis. He also knew the consequences would be tragic. With Aengus next to him they could get at least two he thought, him and that man called Dauld. Maybe Fergus and Cael would get the other two.

But then what?

The Englishman pointed the pistol over the bow, slightly to the port side. "See them pointy stacks, like mules ears they are."

Jasperd stared ahead and nodded.

"That's where we're heading."

Captain O'Clery relaxed, he knew why they needed Jasperd. No one knows a boat in treacherous waters better then it's own helmsman.

Johnne Cokis spoke. "Dauld will direct you. Do as he says or we'll all be fed to the little fishes."

Cael and Aengus raised the sails and Seamrog changed direction, began it's journey towards land.

Captain Conor O'Clery looked up to the sky, where the clouds were brightest. They were heading southeast, towards the Hebrides.

It wasn't long before they could see the green top of an island. Soon after a grey rock face appeared, stretching above the gunwale. Slowly it began to loom ever higher.

The sails were taken down and the Seamrog dropped its anchor. The rocking of the boat lessened, they were in calmer water. Captain O'Clery tried to see where the Priam was, but it was nowhere to be seen.

The crew of the Seamrog waited their fate.

They heard the rhythmic swash of oars, then the grinding of wood against wood and a gentle knock against the hull, followed by several more knocks. He guessed there were four boats in total, all small. Then came the sound of voices, most

in the Scottish dialect. Several men climbed onto the Seamrog's higher deck, all wearing great-kilts. One was the leader, that was obvious, even the four from the Priam appeared to offer him respect. With hardly a glance towards the Seamrog's crew he disappeared down into the hold.

I felt movement. The lid to the pot we were in was opened. Two deep-set eyes with thick red brows peered in at us. A face jolted back. Next a calloused hand came towards us, one finger extended, poking us one by one, as though we would come alive.

Captain O'Clery realised his fate, also the fate of his crew. His boat was in the hands of a merciless clansman and a pirate called Peter Love. There could only be one outcome. His mind drifted to his home, to his family, knowing he would never see them again.

He heard another rowing boat, thought there must be around five by now, it was as if they were completely surrounded. Three men climbed on board, two carrying muskets. Captain O'Clery immediately recognised the third: the same man who had peered over the gunwale at him, the captain of the Priam.

Peter Love stared down at the captives. He then glared at the Seamrog's captain. "Name?" His voice was clear and refined, English, from the south.

"Captain Conor O'Clery. I am in command of this boat."

Peter Love ignored his comment, appeared to think for a moment. "Irish?"

"Yes."

The Priam's captain studied each one of the Seamrog's crew in turn, his gaze stopping at the youngest. "You the dish scrubber?"

Captain O'Clery began to answer for him. "He helps load..."

"Shark got your tongue lad?"

The boy shook his head, more like a tremble. "Like the Captain said, I help load." His voice changed to a willful tone.

"And I also scrub the deck if told."

The Priam's captain spat out a laugh. "A grubber!" He then glared long and hard at him. "Don't just sit there lad." He flicked a finger towards the stern. "Go and wait there."

The boy looked at his own captain, as if asking permission.

Captain Conor O'Clery returned a single nod. He knew it wasn't worth arguing, especially after the episode with Fergus. He guessed Peter Love wouldn't be so charitable.

Peter Love then glared at Jasperd Staffurd. "You the helmsman?"

"I am."

The captain of the Priam grunted.

A few seconds later the Scotsmen came up from the hold, the pot in his hands. "Captain," he said, greeting Peter Love.

"Ah, Mr MacLeod, good to see you are still with us."

"Aye captain, take more than a bunch of gommy southrons to capture Neil MacLeod."

Neil MacLeod? You could look at Neil MacLeod in two ways: freedom fighter or bloodthirsty feudal lord.

Freedom fighter? For years the MacLeods had laid claim to the tenure of Lewis. After all, that was the land his family had fought over for many centuries.

King James VI saw it differently. He thought the ownership of the land should be handed over to the Crown, namely himself, meaning all the profits from the rents and fishing would go to him. So to initiate this takeover, the King appointed a group of mainland noblemen to colonise the island, 'the Gentleman Adventurers of Fife,' they were called. Only there was nothing gentlemanly about these men, or noble. Some landed with an army of over six hundred fighters and immediately made themselves known to the local residents of Lewis; and if any of them were in dispute with this new arrangement? Well, many vanished, never to be seen again.

Bloodthirsty feudal lord? Over those few years Neil

MacLeod witnessed the Gentleman Adventurers of Fife's attempt to colonise his island with their own tenants. All came from the mainland, not that they had much choice.

Neil MacLeod managed to summon more than two hundred men from his own clan and began raiding the new settlers, slaughtering twenty of these impoverished folk on one excursion, seizing everything they owned. On a second raid he had killed sixty. His reputation as a bloodthirsty feudal lord had become renowned.

This led to another clan chief with just as lethal a reputation. Only this one was different, he had laid his oath to the King himself. Kenneth Mackenzie was his name and he had been given a commission of fire and sword, which basically meant he was to hunt down Neil Macleod and his followers, bring them back dead or alive, preferably alive. For this, Kenneth Mackenzie would be awarded the title Lord Mackenzie of Kintail and everything that went with the title, including the Isle of Lewis.

Peter Love hacked out a laugh. "Of that I have no doubt Mr MacLeod. Now, what have we down in the hold?"

"Usual captain, pelts and hides, tusks and timber." He opened the lid to the pot and stretched out his arms. "Aye, and these."

"And what have we here Mr MacLeod?"

"Little devils up to no good if you ask me captain."

Peter Love picked one out: a Queen.

Men were scurrying back and forth, loading the cargo from the hold onto the rowing boats.

Peter Love then looked down to the captain of the Seamrog. "What have we here captain?"

Captain Conor O'Clery shrugged. "They're nothing. Gaming pieces so they are."

Peter Love waited, as if he was wanting more.

"They're worthless, two sacks of potatoes. Take them."

Grub drew his knees up and pulled the sack closer to his chest, knew he had little choice. He nodded.

At least Jasperd and Grub will live thought Captain O'Clery as he watched his helmsman and cabin boy head towards the Priam.

Neil MacLeod and his men had also boarded their boats and embarked in the opposite direction, towards one of the smaller islands. That left two rowing boats. Captain Peter Love remained on the Seamrog's deck, along with Johnne Cokis, Dauld Howart and two seamen called Abraham Mathie and Nicolas Phillopes, the ones who held the muskets.

"Get your men to hoist the sails and raise the anchor," Peter Love told Captain O'Clery. He then pointed to Fergus. "You, old man, you will take the helm."

They were to be scuttled in deep water with them still on board the Seamrog, Captain O'Clery thought. In the distance he could see the Priam ahead at half-rig. The Seamrog had been following them, towing the two rowing boats in their wake. That's how it was for several hours until the land vanished and they saw the sails on the Priam lowered. The Seamrog continued towards it until they were only a stone throw away.

Pistols and muskets were cocked, fingers poised on triggers.

Captain O'Clery waited for that bright flash of gunpowder. There was nothing. Maybe they were taunting him, making him wait for his punishment. For the second time he closed his eyes and thought about his wife and children back home in Sligo. It was then he heard the words.

"Climb onboard."

Captain O'Clery opened his eyes and saw Peter Love's finger pointing towards a rowing boat on the starboard side. He and all the other members of the Seamrog crew climbed onto it.

Peter Love glared down at Captain O'Clery, his eyes piercing into him. "Remember captain, I will..." He then

stopped to eye the rest of Seamrog's crew. What he was about to say was for all of them. "I will never be taken alive." He held his glare on them. "Nor will your helmsman and grubber. Now be away with you." He gave the rowing boat one hard shove.

As Cael and Aengus rowed, Captain O'Clery took one last look up at the Priam, saw Grub and Jasperd gazing over the side at them, desperation written over both their faces, the sack held tightly in Grub's arms. The next they saw was Peter Love's rowing boat heading back to the Priam. Cael and Aengus stopped rowing, all their gazes were drawn towards the Seamrog as it sunk lower into the water. For a moment it appeared to resist it's watery fate, as if fighting for another breath. That was until they saw it roll to one side, the mast reaching out to them in one last desperate attempt to be saved. Captain O'Clery and his remaining crew watched as Seamrog was swiftly swallowed by Mother Sea.

They were alone and drifting.

Captain O'Clery's main concern at that moment was Tan, who was still shivering from his drenched clothing. The captain cupped a hand over his eyes and looked up to the sky, saw nothing but dark clouds. He needed to head away from Neil MacLeod's land and searched out a glimpse of brightness; they would head south east. No one knew the seas better than Captain O'Clery; while he still had a breath in his body there was always a chance. He knew one high wave could easily roll the small boat, or worse, take them further out to sea if the current was stronger than they could row. Peter Love had left them no provisions. In a few days they would be delirious with thirst, not long after that their bodies would be craving food. They may even have the urge to drink seawater. He knew once the madness sets in, they may even start looking towards each other as food. Captain O'Clery had heard the stories. There weren't any weapons to defend themselves, although he knew if it got to that stage then death would be preferential. He looked over at the vast expanse of ocean, towards the west, where the

sun would dip behind the horizon. After that he would have to rely on the moon and stars, if they were visible.

"Let's get your clothes dry," he told Tan.

Grub remained on the Priam, the sack hidden behind some barrels at the stern in the hold, under his only blanket. This was the place where he slept, although damp and cold it was his sanctuary, his escape from this hell.

Peter Love and the crew of the Priam continued with their piracy. Their reputation had become unrivalled around the Scottish islands. With their confidence feeding their greed it caused them to venture further afield, sometimes closer to Ireland. In his second year their notoriety was crowned with the capture of a ship owned by the rich and powerful Scottish royalist Thomas Fleming. Captain Love kept him as a prisoner before handing him over to Neil MacLeod: a hostage to be used for negotiating: if Thomas Fleming was lucky.

At the end of that year Peter Love had his most successful plunder. A large Dutch merchant ship, earning him his largest hoard so far: muskets and pistols, ginger and cinnamon, also discovering a pouch of precious stones and a small chest of silver coins in the captain's quarters. The battle was intense, with the crew of the Priam killing several Dutch sailors. Peter Love also lost two of his own. Grub witnessed the captain free the Dutch survivors as he had done with Captain O'Clery and the others, leaving them to drift in the vast open seas. This time he didn't give them much hope.

As he had done with Grub and Jasperd he kept five of the Dutch crew as slaves, as reassurance, also as punishment for his own losses. They weren't as compliant as Grub and Jasperd. Every day the five dutchmen were made to regret it.

Grub had become no more than a slave. Not only to the captain, but also to the rest of Priam's crew. Commands came from every direction; and they did, as if they were enjoying their torment: carrying food to the mess deck, having to keep watch through the night, sometimes for what seemed an eternity. Then

he would have to force himself to stay awake, knowing the consequences if he didn't. Running messages from the captain to his navigator, then to the helm and back to the captain. The worst times were when he had to climb the rigging to trim the top sails, scaling heights very few of the hardened sailors would venture. One slip would mean certain death, not that anyone would care. Grub sometimes thought it would be an easy way out.

On occasions he had to carry a message to Jasperd Staffurd. Grub noticed the helmsman was becoming like the rest of the crew, even joining in with goading and tormenting him. Once he watched Jasperd become involved with the fighting when they seized another boat. He knew the helmsman had been given the same ultimatum as the other crew: obey or perish. Jasperd had little choice, he had seen how Peter Love treated the Dutchmen.

And wherever Grub went, we went with him, like he had become our guardian angel; and as his body matured and he got stronger he had started to keep the sack with him. One cord slung over his shoulder and one tied around his waist. The sack itself hung down his back, hidden under his tunic, like it had become an extension of his own body. He was sure people thought of him as being deformed: a hunchbacked dwarf. To Grub, it was his connection to the past, to Captain O'Clery, the Seamrog's crew, his own family back home, everything he had lost. The only time he took the sack off was when he slept behind barrels. It was then he would take a few of us out, me included, when he would talk to us, tell us about his mother and father, his two sisters back in Ireland, about his dog Clover. All he had at that time was us. We were his family.

Just off Lewis is the small island of Bearasaigh. This was also the place where Neil MacLeod and some of his fellow clansmen made a home for themselves, on a low part of the flat top, where they couldn't be seen. A safe base he could return to after his many raids.

raised, ready to take any down if they countered resistance. One of the Priam's crew had managed to grab the wrist of a clansman as he tried to raise his pistol, causing it to fire into the clansman's foot with a haunting scream of pain. The seaman was immediately skewered through the belly with a cutlass and fell to the ground, alive but not for much longer as his throat felt the cold metal of another blade.

The Priam's crew soon discovered they were greatly unprepared and outnumbered. One of the Priam's men was shot in the chest, died immediately. As did another. Several more were injured, one being Johnne Cokis, another was Nicolas Phillopes. Jasperd Staffurd stood watching, neither fighting or running. Captured or be killed, it made no odds to him.

Torquil Blair and his men had taken the Priam without any resistance. In the absence of their captain there was no order to fight, so they didn't. It even appeared that some were relieved, just like Grub, the crew had been given their freedom. None were more relieved than the five Dutchmen held as slaves. When Torquil Blair opened the door to their cell he thought he saw five corpses lying there, until he saw one move. They were fed, given a rowing boat and released. It was only the money and other items Torquil was interested in.

Ishbel who was sitting on Peter Love's lap at the time swiftly removed herself. As she did the pirate saw Neil MacLeod stood in front of him with his pistol cocked, his finger on the trigger, the dark opening of the barrel held only inches away from his face. "Surrender or die," MacLeod said, hoping the captain would choose the latter, even if Kenneth Mackenzie had explicitly said he wanted the pirate alive.

The outcome would be the same for Peter Love whatever he did. He swiftly lunged forward and waited for the musket ball. Instead, his legs were immediately whipped away from him. William and Rauri MacNeil were soon on top of him with Malcolm Blair keeping guard, just in case one of his crew tried a rescue attempt. None did. When clear he tightly bound the

pirate's ankles and wrists with rope.

In the commotion Grub had slunk away behind one of the drystone walls. When he was sure no one had followed he made a run to where the rowing boats had been moored. He clambered down the rock and untied the ropes to all bar one. He pushed them away as far as he could, hoped they would be taken out to sea or dashed against the rocks, unable to be reached anyhow, only so no one would be able to follow. He climbed into the remaining boat and untied the moorings. Before shoving himself away he glanced up at the rock, hoped to see Jasperd climbing down to join him: there was no sign of the Seamrog's helmsman.

Grub rowed away as hard as his meagre strength would allow him.

As promised, Neil MacLeod had handed Peter Love over to Mackenzie, who after a time gave him to the authorities in Edinburgh, along with the nine surviving members of his crew. This included Johnne Cokis and Dauld Howart, Abraham Mathie and Nicolas Phillopes, also Jasperd Staffurd. Just to accommodate the huge crowd they all danced the hangman's jib on the sands of Leith. Watching this spectacle were Captain Conor O'Clery and three other Irish seamen. Unfortunately Tan died on the small boat, it was as if his body had shut down. As much as Captain O'Clery tried to speak up for Jasperd, no one would listen.

All his enquiries as to the whereabouts of his grubber came to nothing.

Lord Kenneth Mackenzie of Kintail was true to his word and gave Neil MacLeod and his clansmen their freedom, but not the Isle of Lewis, that would still belong to the Mackenzie clan. Neil MacLeod had no choice but to agree.

Unfortunately for Neil MacLeod, Mackenzie died a year later. The agreement died with him.

King James was not so honourable. This time a plan was

hatched against the feudal clan leader. Under the impression he was going to get the written agreement for the ownership of Lewis, he unwittingly travelled to Glasgow. Neil MacLeod was tried for high treason and every other offence they could throw at him, many of which he didn't commit.

Three years after Peter Love hung, Neil MacLeod alone danced the hangman's jig at the city's Market Cross. He was decapitated and his head impaled on a spike for all to see.

From then on the Isle of Lewis remained in the hands of the Mackenzies.

The Red Ghillie

1610

Iain Blaikie was employed as a ghillie. That meant whenever his master, the uncompromising tacksman George Mor Mackenzie of Baile-na-Cille needed someone to help him haul in a fish or bind together the legs of a deer or even herd the cattle to another pasture, then his ghillie was that person.

Iain was the surviving child of Janet and Robert Blaikie who lived in Perth when Iain entered this world. They also had two other children seven years later: twins, a boy and a girl, Ayleen and Donald. Unfortunately Iain had only known them for a couple of hours before God wanted them more than he wanted Iain. That's what he was told anyhow.

Shortly after this, Janet and Robert Blaikie were persuaded by their landlord Patrick Leslie that a better life for them would be on the Island of Lewis, there they could forget their loss, start a new life. He would even supply them with a house and land. What Patrick Leslie failed to tell Janet and Robert was that they would be murdered by Neil MacLeod and his followers within five months of settling there. Unfortunately this left the boy to fend for himself. That was until George Mor Mackenzie heard

than him by four or five years.

The boat eventually reached shallow water, the boy rowed as close as he could get to the beach. He then drew in the oars and laid them in the boat. The boy jumped out, the freezing water coming just above his knees. The Red Ghillie watched as he strained to pull the boat onto the beach. The bow rested on the sand with the boat refusing to go any further.

Then he watched as the boy reached in and lifted out a sack. More importantly to the Red Ghillie, it was bulging with something.

The boy then pushed the boat back into the water and scrambled onto the shore. Exhausted, he fell to his knees onto the sand, his chest heaving. He took his jacket off, slung the cord of the sack over his shoulder and tied the rest around his waist, as he had done a hundred times before. He then pulled his jacket back over his body, the sack now hidden. No one would know it was there. The Red Ghillie did though, which made him wonder even more what was inside it. Probably money and riches, even better: food. He was hungry, all he had eaten was porridge at first light, then stale bread and cheese for midday, which he had eaten long before then.

After escaping the Island of Bearasaigh, Grub had rowed for several hours, his arms and legs were so weak he could hardly pull on the oars anymore, a few more dips of the blades was about all he could muster. The little remaining strength he had left had been virtually used up.

Grub had unstrapped the sack and placed it on the floor of the boat to make it easier for rowing. There it lay in the ever deepening pool of freezing seawater.

He rested for a while and searched over the vast expanse of water. No one had followed him, that was his only blessing. He was thirsty and hungry, wished he had taken food from the feast when he had the chance, not as if filling his belly or quenching his thirst was in the forefront of his mind at that time.

On top of all this, the light was starting to fade, in a few hours it would be pitch black, any moonlight would be shrouded by the thick, grey cloud above him. The wind was also whipping up. He knew if left to the anger of Mother Sea then she would most definitely claim him as hers.

Grub had no choice but to change direction and head towards land, if only to find a place to hide out of the biting wind and rain. He wished he had headed towards the large sandy bay he had seen a little while back. At the time he thought it would leave him too much in the open, especially when he saw the grey stone houses and the smoke rising above them. They could be members of the MacLeod clan, they would know what had happened, they would think he was a member of Priam's crew. He was.

Grub couldn't take the chance. He had managed to get this far. There had been nothing but sea stacks and walls of sheer dark rock until then. No safe place to make land. That's when he saw it in the distance, behind some small islets. What looked like a white patch of sand. This was his chance, he may never have another, either this or certain death. He tugged on one oar to swing the boat around, began heading towards it. It was as if he had found a new hidden strength.

'I am going home,' Grub said to himself.

He entered the inlet. The quiet of the sea had swiftly been replaced by the intermittent roar of the waves. He took a quick glance behind him and saw the sand getting closer. As he turned back a wave had hit the boat at an angle, turning it sideways and nearly capsizing it.

Grub had to grip onto the sides, releasing the oars, one had jumped out from between the wooden pins, he just managed to rescue it before it dropped into the water and was swept out of reach. The sack was flung to the side, smacking hard against the wooden hull, nearly propelled overboard, only to slide back down into the salty pool of water again. The wash of the water had also loosened the opening of the sack.

Five from the front line and a Horseman were washed out.

Grub managed to turn the boat before it was nearly upended by another wave, only this one took him closer to the shore, like a sea-god had lifted it out of the water and carried it towards land. A loud clunk as the bow hit a rock just below the surface, sending Grub flying off the seat. A much louder thud as another submerged rock hit the side of the hull. Water began spurting in through a crack.

Another wave took the boat even closer. Grub quickly lay the oars across the two seats and placed the sack over them, ready to be snatched away, not noticing the six pieces swirling around underneath it. With the little strength he had remaining he swung his leg over and slipped into the water, hoping it was shallow enough: it was. He then began tugging on the bowhook of the boat, his feet sinking into the soft seabed as he did. He took the sack out and dragged himself onto the sand, removed his jacket, strapped the bag over his shoulder and covered it back up. He then looked at the boat, waited for a retreating wave and shoved it back into the water, hoping it would get smashed on the rocks.

The Red Ghillie waited to see what the boy's next move would be. He knew he didn't have much time himself. He had to get back to Baile-na-Cille before George Mackenzie began to wonder where he was. He had herded the sheep as told. They were secure in the pen.

The Red Ghillie watched as the boy made his way up the beach to where a line of stones and kelp separated the pasture from the white sands. The boy stumbled and slipped across them until his feet were on soft grass. There he stopped and glanced to the north, then to the south. It was then something held his gaze. The Red Ghillie looked to where the boy was staring, there was nothing but a heap of large boulders on a headland. He watched as the boy then looked inland, this time it was the sheep pen that held his attention, saw his lips move,

wondered what he was saying. The boy then turned towards the stone wall where the Red Ghillie was hiding, he ducked further down, made himself into a tight ball.

Grub was cold, wet, exhausted, hungry and thirsty, on the verge of collapse, felt he couldn't get any closer to death. More than that, he was scared, this was a land alien to him, probably the same place where Neil MacLeod ruled. Then again, that could be a good thing, that is if the clansman remembered how Grub had helped him during the feast.

With the little strength he had remaining, he stood, his legs just about keeping him upright. He then headed towards the green of the land, his feet sinking into the soft sand made the effort twice as demanding. Grub then clumsily hobbled over some small rocks until he felt the grass underfoot. He stood and looked to the north, saw nothing but a hillock and a few rocks strewn around. He then turned to the south, to a headland nearby, just a narrow piece of land jutting out into the sea. It was what was on that though: a collection of large boulders piled on top of each other. At least they might shelter him from the wind he thought. He may be able to get some rest, recoup his strength. Grub was also starving. He looked inland, saw several sheep held in a pen. He thought about the mutton stew he had served up at the feast. He would have to slaughter and butcher the beast, light a fire to cook it. He had no knife and everything around was wet and damp. He looked back at the sheep. 'You get to live another day so you do,' he mumbled to himself. He then saw a rectangle of crumbling rocks in the distance, the ruins of a house he thought, unfortunately not enough to give him shelter. Grub then thought he saw something move between the stones, something red. He was exhausted, it must have been an illusion. His mind was playing tricks with him. Not surprising.

Grub looked back up at the headland. He had no choice but to make his way towards the boulders. He needed to get some

replied.

"Then friend give friend sack."

"No, friend let friend keep sack."

"You not friend," the person made another grab for the sack and tried to snatch it from him.

Grub had survived everything that had been thrown at him while on the Priam. He had been tormented by men much larger, much rougher and much tougher than this person standing before him. All he knew was he had to get away.

Grub bent down to pick up his coat. A sudden movement directly in front of him, it didn't register what it was. He then felt a searing pain on the back of the head.

Then nothing.

The Red Ghillie saw the boy move out from underneath the overhang. He waited, not moving.

The boy stood.

The Red Ghillie waited some more.

The boy made a strange noise, words that weren't words.

"What's in the bag?" The Red Ghillie asked.

The boy said something, again, it sounded as if a strange noise was coming out of his mouth.

The Red Ghillie was still feeling hungry. "Food?" was the only word he said.

More strange noise.

The Red Ghillie held his hand out. "Give me the bag." He had to have it, whatever it took. He would try another tactic, one he thought the boy couldn't refuse. "I'll let you be my friend if you give me the bag."

More noise. By the boy's reaction, the Red Ghillie guessed he was refusing to give it to him.

"You want to be my friend?" the Red Ghillie asked.

He did understand the first word spoken back to him, 'yes.' The sack was his. "Then friend give friend sack."

Another word, another one he understood. 'No.' Not the

one the Red Ghillie wanted to hear. He made a quick grab for the bag, pinched the material and tugged it towards him. The boy snatched it back, then bent over to pick up his coat.

The Red Ghillie glanced down, saw a rock by his feet, he quickly picked it up and swung it towards the boy's head with a loud thud. The boy's head split open, spilling blood and grey matter over the stones. The boy dropped to the ground, his eyes open but not seeing.

The Red Ghillie unstrapped the sack, pulled it open and looked in.

Of all the eyes I've seen staring in at us, I've never seen any as wild as these. They were round and fierce, like the devil was inside of them.

A hand reached in and pulled one of us out: a Horseman. He studied it before throwing it back in. He then began to take out another, a Bishop. He dropped it back in, like he had grabbed something evil. For several seconds those eyes filled the opening, like his face was breaking through the surface of water.

The cord was pulled tight and we were plunged into darkness once again.

The Red Ghillie looked down at the limp body, he knew he couldn't leave it where it was, not with the contents of his head splattered over the rocks. People would know the boy had died in suspicious circumstances, even the Red Ghillie knew that much. His master would soon hear about it. He would know his ghillie had been there at Mealasta herding his sheep.

The Red Ghillie tried to think. It suddenly came to him. He remembered how a calf had wandered off and got stuck in a peat-bog not far from where he was. How it was sucked down into the soft earth, unable to free itself until it eventually drowned, only to be found weeks later, like a large fish floating just below the surface. He couldn't have the boy floating up like the calf. How to weigh it down? Rocks! How to carry them? He looked down at the sack, it was obvious. He would have to hide

the contents first. The Red Ghillie knew of a hidden souterrain not far from the House of the Black Women, a place set deep in the earth near the beach, just short of a man's height in length. The dry stone entrance had collapsed and been covered with earth and rocks, like it had been returned to the land. The Red Ghillie knew where it was though. He ran to the entrance with the sack in hand and began scooping out the sand and earth, eventually coming to the layer of rocks. He removed them one by one until there in front of him was a dark empty space.

Maybe he could dump the body there he thought, decided there would be more chance of it being found. He couldn't risk it. He would stick with the peatbog.

He poured in the small figures. As he did a Bishop had rolled further into the dark space. Not only that: a loose thread at the bottom of the sack had got caught around a Warrior's shield.

The Red Ghillie replaced the rocks and earth, topping it with tufts of grass. He ran back to the boulders, firstly stopping at the line of stones separating the beach from land. After filling the sack with rocks he returned to the boy's body, threw him over his shoulder with the legs dangling in front and arms swaying behind: he began the short journey. The Red Ghillie was surprised how light the boy felt, the same as when he had carried a fawn back to his master after finding it caught in a trap. The sack he threw over the other shoulder.

It was starting to get dark, he was glad no one would see him, he also knew his red tunic would lose all colour at that time. Then again, a peatbog could also be a dangerous place, even in daylight. One wrong step could have him pulled down into the upper layer of peat. Or worse, get stuck, slowly sink further and eventually drown, just as that calf had done. Unable to get his legs out he would starve to death; and how would he be able shout for help with a dead body thrown over his shoulder?

The Red Ghillie had no choice.

Trekking over the rough land it seemed to take ages before he began to feel the squelching underfoot, his feet sinking into the soft earth. He knew he had to get into deeper water if the body was to be completely submerged. Searching out the domes of harder ground he made his way further into the bog. With the fading light the Red Ghillie was beginning to struggle. Feeling he couldn't go any further he eventually stood on a small area of dry earth and gazed down. Below him he could see the glint of ripples stroking the water's surface.

The Red Ghillie placed the body on the ground and hurriedly began stuffing rocks in places where they would be held tight. With half of them still left in the sack he strapped the cord tightly around the body, wrapped it around his neck and under the armpits, he pulled it as tight as possible. He then rolled the body into the water. His heart rose to his throat, the body had remained at the surface, the head facing upward, the eyes appearing to look at him, it was like the boy was asking why he was doing this. The Red Ghillie leant forward and gave the body a hard shove down. With relief it slowly sunk. The eyes still staring up at him as they faded into the murky blackness of the water.

I was glad the Warrior tangled in the sack had accompanied Grub as he entered his watery grave. For all that time on the Priam he had kept us safe, hidden behind the barrels or under his coat. He deserved to have this fearless fighter to protect him.

The Red Ghillie made his way out of the bog and soon realised he was a long way from home, at least a two hour journey, closer to three in the dark, and it wouldn't be easy over the rocky surface and boggy ground. He thought about going back to the souterrain. How would he explain the strange looking objects to his master? Nor did he have anything to carry us in. For the time being he would leave us where we were, hopefully collect us at a later date.

It was when he wasn't far from the farmhouse at

At first the man displayed a mixture of fear and confusion, wondered how this large man knew about the others. He angled his head to the side and spoke in a foreign tongue. Four men slowly appeared from behind the stony ruins of the dun, each with their palms held outward, as if to convey the absence of weapons. Each one looked on the verge of death. Even in the gloom, the Lewis men could see the gaunt features, their eyes dark, their cheeks sunken.

"We friends," the first man said.

George Mackenzie drew his attention towards the Red Ghillie. "How many did you see?"

The Red Ghillie gave an excited nod, as if to say that was all of them.

"Where have you come from?" the tenant farmer asked.

"We from Netherlands. we taken..." the Dutchman began.

"No, now!" George Mackenzie spat, still highly suspicious. "Where have you come from *now*?"

"We slaves, we go."

"Go from where?"

"From boat."

"Which boat?"

"Boat called Priam. Captain name is Peter Love. He very bad man, make us slaves after capture boat."

The four Mackenzies shared suspicious glances. All four had heard the name Peter Love. All knew of his barbarity, his deviousness. Also that he was involved with Neil MacLeod. This could be a trick.

"What was your boat?"

"The Breda."

"Who was the captain of Breda?"

"Captain Jan Feicken."

"First mate?"

The questions were coming fast, not a second between them. It was obvious George Mackenzie was trying to trip him up.

"Sorry I do not..."

The Red Ghillie saw the hesitation. "They are dangerous master," he said, wondering why all these questions were being asked.

"Helmsman, who was the helm?"

"Jacobus Vitell."

The Red Ghillie spoke again. "You must slaughter them master."

The five Dutchmen noticed the ghillie's scorn. Their bodies tightened, the fear in their eyes obvious.

George Mor Mackenzie looked towards the sea, he could just make out the dark outline of a small boat on the sands. "You say slaves?" he asked, dropping his tone.

"Yes, but we are not slaves we are...how do you say, we are sailors on a mer...merch." The Dutchman stuttered. "I do not..."

"Merchant." One of the farm workers finished the sentence for him.

"Captain Love wanted us to join him. We say no. He make us slaves."

"So how did you escape?"

"Other man capture Priam. I not know name. He older but strong. He came with many others, carry food for crew. They take crew, none fight." The Dutchman turned to point at the small boat on the sands. "It was other man who told us to take boat and go."

"Who was this other man?"

The Dutchman shrugged. "Captain Love went to island, meet man called Neil MacLeod."

For a second George Mackenzie froze. He himself had had run-ins with the MacLeods, although his own reputation as a fearsome fighter and his many years of tenure meant he and his own farms were mostly left alone. Neil MacLeod and his men were mainly after the new settlers; as the Red Ghillie would know more than anyone. George Mor Mackenzie also knew of Kenneth Mackenzie's bounty on Neil MacLeod.

"One man say name, Torquil."

It was then George Mackenzie knew it was Torquil Blair. He must be telling the truth, how else would the Dutchmen know this.

He took the five Dutchmen back to Baile-na-Cille. Allowed them to stay in one of the old black houses, although he and his farmhands kept a close eye on them that night.

For the five Dutchmen it was freedom.

To discover the truth, George Mackenzie went to visit Kenneth Mackenzie the next morning.

Once there he was taken to an outhouse. There he saw clamped in irons and heavily guarded were Peter Love and his nine crew.

"You kidnapped five Dutchmen, kept them as slaves," George Mor Mackenzie asked.

A smirk came to Peter Love's face. "What of it?"

"So you admit it."

"Maybe I do. Maybe I don't."

"Tell the truth." Kenneth Mackenzie told him. "You're going to hang anyway."

The captain tried to kick out. The manacle dug deeper into his already torn flesh. He squirmed in pain. "You can go to hell Mackenzie."

A muted chuckle came from one of the chained men with him. It was Jasperd Staffurd.

Kenneth Mackenzie crouched down and spoke quietly in Peter Love's ear. "I wonder what your head will look like sat on the end of a pole. Do you know what the people will do to it captain?"

Peter Love tried to turn away.

Kenneth Mackenzie grabbed him by the back of the hair and yanked it to the side so Peter Love could face him. "They spit and throw rotting food at it," he hissed. "After that the birds will fly down and peck your eyes out." Kenneth Mackenzie then gave a hard tug on the shackle.

Peter Love released a loud yelp.

Jasperd Staffurd looked on some more, he was enjoying seeing the captain in pain.

"We're wasting our time," Kenneth Mackenzie said.

George Mackenzie towered over Peter Love. "Maybe I should bring the Dutchmen here, let them have a few hours with you." He turned to slide his eyes over the other nine. "Also your crew."

"You have the five Dutchmen?" Johnne Cokis asked nervously.

"Or maybe we could tighten your shackles ourselves," Kenneth Mackenzie said. "Then again, maybe we will loosen them if you tell this gentleman what he needs to know," he added.

Johnne Cokis spoke again, his voice shaking, he in particular had given the Dutchmen a rough time. "Tell them captain, what have we got to lose," he said through a grimace, blood trickling over his frozen feet.

"You kidnapped these five Dutchmen and held them as slaves, or were they part of your crew?"

"No, not crew," Peter Love finally said as though he had accepted his fate. He then wondered how this man knew about them. "I left them locked up on the Priam."

"So they were your prisoners?"

Peter Love glared long and hard at the huge Scotsman towering over him. He then lowered his gaze to the dagger stuffed into his belt. "Yes," he said. "They were. And if you would be so good as to cut my throat now. You will be doing me a great favour."

George Mor Mackenzie and Kenneth Mackenzie stepped out of the byre, leaving the shackles as they were.

On that same day, while his master was away, the Red Ghillie decided to collect the strange figures. He needed to have them closer to him, just until he could decide what to do. They may even have hidden powers, he could cast spells on his

Knowing his tendency for fantasy, and thinking it was the last rantings of a condemned madman, the authorities chose to ignore him. Not helping his cause: the Dutchmen had already returned to their homeland and therefore were not able to confirm the existence of either.

The Red Ghillie danced the hangman's jig soon after.

The Tenant Farmer
1831

Just for simply being a tenant farmer, just for trying to scrape a meagre living from the little they had, Malcolm MacLeod and his wife Agatha, along with their four children had lived in fear for the entire time they had inhabited their home in the tiny village of Penny Donald on the Island of Lewis.

That dread was for a very good reason.

For eighteen years Malcolm had witnessed the forced evictions of many of his fellow islanders, from the place they had lived and worked their entire lives, where their parents and their families before them had also lived.

Malcolm MacLeod knew his own time would come. When that would be he didn't know, but as sure as night followed day and day became night, he knew it would. It was like the earth that had provided his family with food and warmth for all those years was about to be whipped away from underneath their feet.

For Malcolm MacLeod it started over thirty years ago. He was aged ten when he began to realise the injustice in what was happening, along with the cruelty and exploitation that accompanied it.

Their landlord, the Seaforth Mackenzies wanted to create larger sheep farms, bringing in their own flocks from the Lowlands, knowing the return from them would be far greater than the rent the small tenant farmers like Malcolm MacLeod paid.

Malcolm's first recollection of the suffering was when he overheard a conversation between his parents, when his father had uttered that one sentence he would never forget. 'All we can expect is to live as beggars and die as slaves,' he had said.

When Malcolm became fourteen, he heard about the first village being cleared, the entire population of Ciet a'hog was evicted. The landlord used the excuse that several of its occupants were caught poaching on Mackenzie land, the same place their families had hunted and fished for generations. Within months the residents of Knlochroag and Scaliscro were also driven out. Malcolm had heard it wasn't only the farmers that were removed: weavers and stonemasons, carpenters and millers followed the same fate. The landlord knowing the loss of these trades would also have a detrimental effect on the farmers.

It was when Malcolm had reached the age of thirty-nine. This is when the villages in Uig had started to become the victims of the same 'back door' tactics by the factor's henchmen. To reduce their land so they wouldn't have enough to survive; and in doing so they also took away their rights to peat cutting, their only means to keep warm. That gave them no choice but to relocate somewhere else where they would probably suffer the same fate.

In that time, Malcolm MacLeod's head of cattle had been reduced from twenty-three to just seven. The few that were milking were barely enough to sustain his own family, any surplus was hardly worth selling.

It was a Saturday in March, a strong wind was howling in from the sea. Malcolm had gone outside to gather his herd, four were waiting by the cowshed as if pleading to be let in. He soon

found the fifth, then the sixth, quickly returned them to the byre. He went out again to find the seventh, not finding it immediately he headed towards the beach at Ardroil, a place where they had strayed many times. The sand whipped around him as he approached the dunes. Even with the scarf wrapped around his face he could still feel the crunch of grains in his mouth. He rounded a dune and there she was munching on a tuft of grass, appearing oblivious to the conditions. As he was about to lead her back, the wind suddenly shifted direction. That's when he noticed the remnants of a small stone chamber exposed in one of the dunes. There he saw a piece of ragged material poking out from the inside. Inquisitive to see what it was, Malcolm reached in and pulled on the cloth. It was a bag of some kind, made from sack cloth. He opened it up and looked in.

Malcolm froze in wonder.

For that short time he had become oblivious to the wailing of the wind, to the sand lashing around his face. He narrowed his eyes in confusion.

I recalled seeing this strange face, not human. At first I thought it was some kind of sea monster. I wondered if that was going to be our fate, in the belly of some ocean dwelling beast. Whatever it was had the smallest misshaped eyes, like scars, but the strangest thing of all, it had no mouth. Everything about it was tan coloured, as if it had risen up from the depths of the dunes. Then I saw a hand coming towards us, a man's hand, he lifted six of us out out: along with myself was a Bishop and a Warrior, also three from the front line. Out of shock he dropped us onto the sand. It didn't take long for the wind to cover us with sand, two completely. I thought he was going to leave us there. That was until he picked myself and the Bishop up, placed us back into the bag. A second after that we were in the dark again.

Malcolm covered the bag with stones and returned the cow to the byre. He would leave us in the dune until the weather improved. At the same time he would make sense of what he had just seen.

"Reverend MacLeod would then say the only way to get forgiveness was to seek it from his church, just so he can force people to join his congregation. Or we should all leave the island, only because that's what his paymasters want. I'd rather ask the devil himself."

"Then you will be taken those things home to their..."

Daniel interrupted his mother. "Why don't we go and see Captain Ryrie?"

A thoughtful silence followed.

"He's right," Malcolm finally said. "We will go and see Phineas. He'll know what to do." (Malcolm had became a friend of Reverend Hugh Munro's son John; Hugh Munro was Reverend MacLeod's predecessor. Another who became a frequent visitor to the manse was Captain Phineas Ryrie, someone that had been in the same regiment as John. After an injury he sustained during the Egyptian campaign he spent many days convalescing at the manse. During that time Malcolm and Phineas had become good friends, even continuing after John perished at the battle of Batavia).

Agatha remained silent.

"That's agreed then." He looked at his wife and smiled. "Just for you we'll keep them in the byre until I visit the captain."

For several weeks the creel was kept in the corner of the cowshed, hidden behind a peat-spade and under the cover of an old cloth.

Malcolm knew word of them would soon get around, that gossip travels as fast as the wind on the island: and so it did.

Visitors came from far and wide to set eyes on the small figures. He was always careful not to say where he found them, nor where they were hidden, telling whoever it was to wait by the sheep fank. Then he would skirt round to the back of the byre. Only when he was out of sight would he enter and collect the pieces, always the same ones, never the Bishops. A Horseman, the battered Warrior, a heavily scarred King (not me)

and Queen, two from the front line.

Only one day was different to the others. A young family from Mealasta came to see him. Donald and Annie Graham were their names. As he was showing them the small figures he saw them throwing glances at each other, as if there was no surprise in what they were seeing. It was after a minute when Donald drew something out of his pocket and held it up for Malcolm to see. It was a Bishop, the same as the others kept in the creel, only this was one Malcolm hadn't seen before.

"Where did you get it?" Malcolm asked.

It was Donald who answered. "By the ruins at the House of the Black Women. There is an old souterrain there. It hasn't been used for a long time, not since I can remember. I was thinking of opening it up again, that's when I spotted this inside, near the back."

"And that was the only one?" Malcom asked.

"Aye, as far as I can tell there was no other."

Malcolm stretched his arm out to give it back. "Then it is yours to keep Donald."

"No! Please, we do not want it," Annie said abruptly.

"But it was you who..."

"Look at it," she said. "At first we thought it was a gift from God, that it was sent to bring us some good, and not before time. We are simple folk Mr MacLeod. We do not ask for much." She puffed out a weary breath "We hoped it might save us from, well, you know." Her eyes dropped. "All it has done is bring us more misery."

Donald glared long and hard at Malcolm. "As yours will do to you."

"It may be dressed as God's messenger but it is the devil's work it bears," Annie added.

Malcolm used the same argument with them as he did with Agatha. "It is not this that has brought you misfortune, it is the tyrants from the south that have blighted our lives." He stretched out his hand. "Here, take it, it is yours."

"No!" Donald said, taking a step back. "We do not want it. We have heard about these others you have. Now we have seen them."

"You must take it and destroy them all before they destroy us," Annie said and without a further word, she and Donald strode away, not looking back.

Malcolm remained by the fank with the Bishop in his hand, decided he would keep it separate from the others.

Another day dawned, one that Malcolm knew would eventually come, a day he was dreading. While he was stacking blocks of peat with Daniel, a roaring voice came from afar, as if a wild animal was fast approaching. "Where are they?"

"It seems we have company," he whispered to Daniel, keeping his head down.

Both continued piling up the peat.

"Let me see them MacLeod."

Malcolm looked up. "And a fair day to you Reverend."

"Let me see them," the clergyman demanded.

Malcolm stood up, straightened his back and pulled his shoulders back. "And what may *them* be Reverend?"

Daniel took a step back. Unlike his father he was petrified of the Reverend.

"Those blasphemous messengers of our Lord," the Reverend bellowed.

"Blasphemous messengers?" Malcolm asked, knowing the Reverend's fondness for doom and gloom.

Reverend Alexander MacLeod softened his voice. "You should give them up for the sake of your soul Malcolm. Only a man of God would know how to purge these sins from this land."

Malcolm knew exactly why the Reverend wanted the figures: so he could hold a Bishop up in his sermons to exert fear and guilt into his parishioners.

Reverend MacLeod continued. "It is common knowledge amongst my flock what you have hidden away." The

clergyman's eyes became the size of saucers. "That they are Devils in God's attire."

"Do you mean they are dressed in the finest material embroidered with gold thread, that the fabric costs more than a man could earn in his lifetime Reverend?"

Malcolm waited, he knew Reverend Alexander MacLeod was a man of opposites, obliging one second, hostile the next. No one ever knew which it would be. He also had spies keeping tags on the people who hadn't attended his services, summoning them to his manse so he could play on their guilt, tell them it was a sin in the eyes of God not to be present on a Sunday morning. That way he could draw in crowds from great distances, sometimes in the many hundreds, more than the church could accommodate on some days.

But not Malcolm, he knew the preacher was a Seaforth man, that it was the Lady Hood MacKenzie herself who had appointed him to Uig, allowing the clergyman's stipend to be four times the amount of the teacher in his parish. More than that: Malcolm had a very good reason not to like the Reverend MacLeod. The clergyman had become very critical of his friend the Reverend Hugh Munro, who he regarded as unspiritual, choosing to criticise him at every opportune moment.

Malcolm continued. "They are no more blasphemous messengers than a...' A smile came to him as he said the next words, knowing how the Reverend disliked local tales and traditions, that he saw them as ungodly. "Than a Kelpie."

"A Kelpie is just a myth MacCleod."

"As there are many others in our lives Reverend."

Malcolm was sure the Reverend's skin turned purple.

"Let me see them MacLeod."

Malcolm knew the preacher wouldn't be satisfied until he had set his eyes on the figures, how he would drag his name through the mud if he didn't, how upset Agatha would be if that were to happen. He felt he had no choice.

"Wait there, I'll bring them to you." Malcolm stepped

Captain Phineas Ryrie? He had moved to the Isle of Lewis after receiving a leg injury during the Egyptian campaign. Because of that he was invalided out of the Ross-shire Buffs. His great friend Lieutenant John Munro also served in the same regiment. This led to John's father, the Reverend Hugh Munro and his wife Mary helping Phineas recuperate at the manse. He spent two years there, much of it walking on the sands at Uig, taking in the clean air, at the same time becoming acquainted with a tenant farmer in the area called Malcolm MacLeod.

Captain Phineas Ryrie decided to remain on the island, falling in love and marrying a Stornoway girl called Catherine Morison. Together they had two sons William and Robert, adding to his first son Roderick from a short-lived previous marriage when living in Edinburgh.

A young man opened the door: he was around the age of twenty. He remained framed in the opening, staring at the farmer stood before him. Nothing was said.

Malcolm thought he had a mousy timidness about him, that his silence was probably more out of shyness than rudeness. Maybe something had happened to Phineas he thought, that this stranger now lives in the house, considering he hadn't seen his friend for nearly a year it was entirely possible. He was just about to open his mouth when another man appeared out of a side door.

Malcolm immediately recognised that same straight backed posture, those thrown back shoulders, that air of pride, but most of all, it was his limp, as though he was dragging his foot behind him. Even with Reverend Munro's wife's persistence, he refused to use a walking stick, as if being peppered in the leg with shrapnel wasn't enough.

His step quickened towards the door, his right foot following. "Malcolm." The word spoken with a mixture of delight and surprise. "What have we the pleasure of..." Stopping

as he spotted the creel and the tartan material covering whatever was in it. "I see you are bearing goods. Maybe a wedge of that wonderful cheese your good wife makes. I remember it so well." He took in a long a sniff and laughed. "Thank God not herring, I can't stand the..."

Malcolm interrupted. "Nay, it's neither. I've come to seek your wisdom Phineas."

Phineas's laugh deepened. "Are you sure you have come to the correct house Malcolm?" He swept his arm behind him. "For God's sake man, come out of the bitter wind." He turned his head. "Catherine," he shouted. "We have a visitor."

A woman appeared, looking flustered, Malcolm couldn't help notice her skin had lost its glow, strands of untamed hair curled over her forehead. On one side of her and gripping tightly onto her apron was a young boy. On the other was another, several years older. "Malcolm, what a lovely surprise," she said and coaxed the older boy forward. "Do you remember William?"

"Aye Catherine, I do." Malcolm gazed towards the boy. "You have grown since the last time." He looked to her younger son, no more than three years of age. "And this is the strapping wee lad I remember from last time?"

The boy tightened his hold on his mother.

"And how is your family Malcolm?" Catherine asked. "Two are twins are they not?"

"Archie and Annie are at school in Carnish. Edward is still getting around on the chair and Daniel helps out around the farm now." He paused for a moment. "We are still there."

That's all Malcolm said about the Clearances. He knew better then to broach the subject in Phineas's presence. His friend felt the island needed to move with the times. In many ways so did Malcolm, but not in the manner it was being executed. "They're all grand, thank you for asking."

"Good." Phineas said, also knowing Malcolm's opinion. He then turned to the young man who had answered the door.

This is Roderick, he's my..." He stopped, his eyes shot to the floor and back again. "My son," he finished saying as if the words had got snagged under his feet.

Roderick stretched out an arm. "Nice to meet you."

Malcolm felt the soft skin of the young man's hand tighten, as though he was trying to prove something.

"I live with my mother in Edinburgh," Roderick said. "I'm just visiting for a short while," he added as if he should explain his presence.

Malcolm knew Phineas had been married before, a son had never been mentioned though.

"Good, good, that's introductions over with,'" Phineas said, needing to change the subject. "Let us go into the drawing room. I'm intrigued to find out what this piece of wisdom is you are wanting."

Malcolm and Roderick stepped into the small room, the amount of dark furniture making it appear even more diminutive than it was. The captain followed, immediately sitting, blowing out a heavy sigh as though it was a relief to get off his feet.

"Well?" Phineas asked.

Malcolm placed the creel on the floor in front of Phineas and opened it up. He knew this man had seen many things in his life, that it would take more than a few tiny figures to shock him.

After a moment of silent scrutinisation, Phineas looked up at Malcolm. "Where did you get them?"

"A cow strayed into the dunes in Ardroil. When I went to retrieve him I saw the wind had blown the sand away exposing some stones. And there they were."

Phineas looked in again. "If this has something to do with my so called wisdom, I'm not sure I can..."

"I need to get them away from the island, and fast, I've got the Reverend MacLeod on my back."

Phineas muttered something about the preacher.

"I don't know what to do with them Phineas. I was hoping

you might advise me."

It was Roderick who placed a hand into the creel, stopping before he got to the pieces. "May I?" As if asking for permission.

"Aye, be my guest," Malcolm replied.

"What do you want to do with them?" Phineas asked.

"Sell them." Malcolm took a glance towards his friend. "I don't ask for much, and you never know when I might need the money," he said as if there were more behind his words.

"And pray tell me Malcolm, where are we to sell such things as these?"

Malcolm had heard that tone before, when Phineas would revert to his army officer days, as if he was speaking to one of his lower ranks.

"That's why I'm here Phineas, I hoped you may know..."

Roderick interrupted. "I will take them."

A stunned silence fell into the room.

"I'm going home the day after tomorrow, I can take them with me. Edinburgh is antiquated in more ways than you think Mr MacLeod." Roderick took a deep breath, completely filling his lungs with air, as though just talking had caused him to be out of breath. "I'm sure I'll find someone that wants to buy them."

"That's very kind of you Roderick." Malcolm searched inside the creel and took out the Bishop, the one Donald and Annie Graham had left with him. "Not this one. This one doesn't belong to me."

"What do you mean it doesn't belong to you?"

"Someone else found it."

"Someone else?"

"Aye, their names are Donald and Annie Graham, they have a small holding in Mealasta. They found this one near the ruins called the House of the Black Women. Donald found it in a souterrain near there."

"Let me get this right Malcolm," Phineas pointed to the

cabinet full of leather bound books. Through all its modesty the room had an air of academia, as if many a scholarly debate had been thrashed out within these four walls as learned professors meticulously studied weird and wonderful artifacts from a time long past.

Maybe they would do the same with the small figures Roderick had brought with him, no one else seemed to know what they were. All he hoped for was a favourable outcome for his father's friend, to sell the pieces for enough money so Malcolm MacLeod and his family could start a new life elsewhere. Roderick knew exactly what the crofter had been trying to say without actually saying it. At the same time he would prove to his father his worth in society. Kill two birds with one stone so to speak.

Opposite the table and in front of a window were three leather chairs with metal studs running down the armrests. In each was a man adorning townsmen's attire of velvet coats, bulging cravats and austere expressions. Either side of them were two other men, one younger, as if his face had been carved from stone. He was leant back on the window sill, his legs outstretched in front of him, as if he wanted to melt into his surroundings. He reminded Roderick of his father, although that could have been the smoke from thornapple leaves taken before entering the establishment. The one to his left was older, noticeable by his silver hair and pale skin.

The gentleman who had shown Roderick up to the first floor had introduced himself as David Laing. His ring of unruly brown hair wrapped around a domed head made him appear around fifty, although guessing by the exuberant and youthful tone he was probably younger. He informed Roderick that he was an antiquarian specialising in literature and owned a bookshop on South Bridge, saying he mainly advised the Society of Antiquaries of Scotland on literary donations or purchases, but quick to add that his interests also lay further afield, as if he was wanting to put his guest's mind at rest.

Roderick thought of him as friendly and polite, although whenever he spoke about various items he appeared to be on the verge of animated euphoria. David Laing talked the entire time they entered the building, constantly thanking him for the letters they had exchanged, considering Roderick had only written the two. The first described the tiny figures, the second agreeing to the meeting on this Monday.

David Laing then noticed Roderick's forced breaths, as if the air was catching in his throat. "Would you like to sit my dear sir, if you don't mind me saying it looks as if you need to."

"That's very kind of you," Roderick replied, he felt he had to justify his breathing, as though it was becoming an embarrassment to him. "I have a slight chest infection," he said as he pulled out one of the chairs beside the table, relieved to take the weight off his feet.

David Laing turned to the five men. "And this gentlemen is our esteemed visitor Roderick Ryrie," he spoke like it was an announcement.

Roderick had never thought of himself as being esteemed, far from it, although he was pleased to see there were only six people in the room: he envisaged thoughts of standing in the pit of an amphitheater with rows of learned men staring down at him.

The first man was introduced, as if he was the most important person there. Roderick noticed he was immaculately dressed. His fingers hung over both armrests like talons, tapping the leather armrests as though it was some kind of musical instrument. Roderick felt he was impatient, as if it was a chore just to be there. He also thought of him as being between sixty and seventy, his skin tanned, heavily weather-beaten, as if the two went hand-in-hand. Roderick decided this was a man who was well travelled.

"May I introduce Lord Elgin," David Laing said. "And if I may say your Lordship, we are honoured to have your esteemed company today."

That word again thought Roderick, as though being esteemed was a necessary requirement to be allowed in this room.

"I hope your trip from Broomhall House was a pleasant one my Lord?"

"Only to be expected Laing," he replied with a frosty tone, like it had been an inconvenience.

"I just hope we can make it worthwhile for you."

"We shall see Laing." The fingers stopped drumming and the man leant forward, reluctantly reached out an arm, but not by far, as if it was Roderick who had to make the effort to approach him.

Thomas Bruce (Lord Elgin)? A man respected by some and held in deep contempt by many others.

Thirty years before this meeting, Thomas Bruce had dispatched a group of artists and sculptors to Athens to produce drawings and casts of the ancient monuments and artifacts. Strangely, to achieve this aim he erected a lot of costly scaffolding around many of the various buildings, including the Parthenon. Not long after, a royal mandate from the Ottoman government had strangely fallen into Thomas Bruce's prossession, stating that he had permission to remove the marble frieze and many other sculptures from the temple.

This vast collection eventually embarked for Britain, encountering many difficulties on the journey, including his ship the 'Mentor' becoming wrecked off the coast of Kythira, taking three years to recover the precious cargo from the seabed and at great cost. Twelve years after leaving Greece, the shipment finally arrived in England. The marbles were then purchased by the government for a princely sum and transferred to the British Museum.

Even a word was created to describe the taking of the sculptures: 'elginism,' meaning an act of cultural vandalism.

His most notably critic was Lord Byron, who penned this

poem about the marble's removal.

Cold is the heart, fair Greece, that looks on thee,
Nor feels as lovers oer the dust they loved;
Dull is the eye that will not weep to see
Thy walls defaced, thy mouldering shrines removed
By British hands, which it had best behovd
To guard those relics neer to be restored.
Curst be the hour when their isle they roved,
And once again thy hapless bosom gored,
And snatchd thy shrinking Gods to northern climes abhorrd!

Roderick rose from his seat and remained standing.

David Laing indicated to the man sitting with two lappets hanging from under his neck scarf. "This is the Reverend John Jamieson."

Roderick stepped towards him. The Reverend remained motionless, his hands firmly resting on top of a silver-tipped cane, his dour expression unwavering. Roderick was concerned about what the clergyman would make of the pieces, especially the Bishop. The Reverend John Jamieson appeared to be a man who could find the worst in anyone and anything.

David Laing looked towards the third chair. "And this is my dear friend Alexander Macdonald, whose love of books only matches my own."

Alexander Macdonald stood and snatched Roderick's hand with both his, he then released the hold as suddenly as he had initiated it. He sat with a theatrical flick of his coat tails as he did.

"And the William Blake?" David Laing asked him.

The man returned a despondent shake of the head. "Sothrons with deeper pockets."

David Laing rolled his eyes in sympathy.

Next was Robert Pitcairn standing to the left, the man resting on the windowsill. He was the youngest out of the group, but still double Roderick's age. A handsome face with a head of tight curly hair and a strong, square jaw. Another firm

"We will need a provenance first though," Robert Pitcairn added.

Roderick felt he had been put on the spot, that he had no choice but to say something. "My father's friend found them in a stone chamber on the Isle of Lewis. I'm afraid that's all the provenance I have at the moment." He didn't want to say anymore: he knew it would entice the argument of who owned the land from where they were discovered. The Mackenzies would have to be informed, they would then claim ownership of the pieces. With their power so great Malcolm MacLeod wouldn't stand a chance. He would end up getting nothing.

"In a stone chamber on the Isle of Lewis?" James Skene asked.

"Aye."

A thoughtful silence.

More scrutiny. "Where on the Isle of Lewis?" Robert Pitcairn asked.

Roderick remembered what Malcolm had said about the Bishop discovered later, the one left with his father in case their discoverer returned. "Near a place they call The House of The Black Women. That is all I can tell you."

More silence.

"Many like to donate their artifacts to the Society Mr Ryrie," Thomas Bruce said.

"I made a promise to my father's friend that I would sell them."

More silence.

"Would you be willing to sell part of the collection," Robert Pitcairn asked.

"Part?"

"Aye, a portion, just some of the pieces."

Roderick thought. "I would have to ask my..."

James Skene interrupted. "Your father's friend?"

Roderick nodded. This was taking longer than he had hoped. The effect of the thornapple leaves had nearly worn off,

the anxiety was beginning to creep in, as it always did. He was wondering if there was a way he could make an excuse to go outside. He would say he needed a breath of fresh air, because of his chest infection, that should be a good enough excuse. Smoke just enough to take the weariness away.

"How many objects are there altogether?" Robert Pitcairn asked.

Roderick knew he would be asked that question, he was prepared. "There are ninety-three in total." He picked up one of the round disks. "Fourteen of these." Placed it back down and picked up one of the headstones. "There are nineteen of these, some look like this." He pointed again. "Others look like these with eight sides." Roderick then picked up a Queen. "And the ones with a hand held to cheek, there are eight of these." His finger stopped at another piece. "And these men on horseback: I counted fifteen of these." He took a quick glance to the Reverend, his finger floating over the Bishop. "Those here, also fifteen," he said as it quickly passed by the clergyman. He then picked up one of the Warriors biting their shields. "And these, well four are biting their shields, nine aren't." Roderick then picked up one of the pieces with a sword resting on it's knees. "And these, there are eight of these."

"And one buckle," Robert Pitcairn added.

"Aye, one of these. That's ninety-three altogether."

"You have a good memory Ryrie," James Skene informed him.

"I cannot help but be in admiration of their workmanship sir. I have often looked at them over the past few days. Sometimes I wonder if they will suddenly come alive right in front of my eyes."

Thomas Bruce turned to David Laing. "And your thoughts Laing?" he asked. "I know where they are *not* from."

David Laing drew down his lips and plucked up one of the figures, one with a hand held to cheek. "From their attire I would say northern Europe. It's difficult to know without more

study. Could be closer to home. Maybe they are gaming pieces of some kind, only because of the smaller ones and the disks. I must say the figures confuse me somewhat."

"My thoughts also Laing," Thomas Bruce remarked. "How old would you say?"

"It is difficult to say my Lord. Could be several hundred years, maybe more, maybe less, they may even be recent. Without knowing their..." David Laing paused and took a quick glance at Roderick. "Their true history, then it is difficult to tell."

"And what game has all these pieces?" Robert Pitcairn asked, not directing the question to anyone in particular.

"They may not all be here," David Laing replied. "In the manner described how they were found it is possible some may have been mislaid."

"In the manner they were found?" Robert Pitcairn instantly picked up on, aiming his question directly at Roderick.

Roderick had to think, even he was getting confused. Out of all of those in the room he thought Robert Pitcairn the most suspicious of him, believing that all was not as it seemed.

Robert Pitcairn repeated. "In the manner they were found Mr Ryrie?"

Roderick didn't answer, he didn't know how to.

David Laing turned to look at Roderick. "You said they were found in a chamber near a place called the House of The Black Women?"

"A nunnery?" James Skene threw in.

"That I cannot confirm sir. The House of The Black Women is all I was told. Near a sand dune."

"A sand dune?" Alexander Macdonald asked.

"Aye." Questions were being thrown at Roderick from every direction. Things were starting to get strange. He didn't want to lie. "In a dune, aye sir."

Thomas Bruce cleared his throat, as if he had something important to say. "When I was in Constantinople the locals

played a game called shatranj. I believe we have a similar game over here called chess."

"Maybe there is more than one set," James Skene said.

"I've seen these sets made from ivory," Alexander Macdonald added. "It appears these could also be made from the same material."

Roderick wanted the conversation to come to an end, and swiftly. He needed to change the subject, try and get to the topic of payment. "I was hoping you might see fit to buy..." His words coming to a halt as a bellowing voice came from behind.

"You want us to hand over our hard earned cash to you, that's why you are here Ryrie, to leech money from us." It was The Reverend John Jamieson, the first time he had spoken. "Do you realise most like to make donations to the society?" he added.

Roderick had forgotten the clergyman was even there. "With respect sir, I made a promise to find a buyer for my..."

"Aye, your father's friend, the one you can't tell us anything about."

Roderick had the impression the Reverend hadn't believed anything he had said. Probably thought Malcolm MacLeod didn't exist at all, that Roderick was there for his own gain and had come by the pieces dishonestly. They may even think he was an imposter and Roderick Ryrie wasn't even his name. "Aye sir, my father's friend," he replied curtly. "My father is Captain Phineas Ryrie from the Ross-shire Buffs." Hoping that would carry some weight.

"How much!?" Robert Pitcairn suddenly asked.

Even in the harsh manner it was spoken, Roderick was relieved they had got to the subject of payment. He had played through this same scenario in his imagination, the haggling that may result, although then the atmosphere had been slightly more amicable. "How much do you..."

James Skene interrupted. "We are not an auction house Mr Ryrie."

David Laing led him to a wooden door at the end of the corridor.

As Roderick stepped in he stopped and gazed around in awe. It was as though he had entered into another world. He also knew what he was seeing at that moment was for private eyes only, beyond the sight of common folk, especially a humble clerk from a merchant's office.

The first he saw was a Celtic cross standing proud in the centre of the room, about the height of two men. It looked extremely old, as if it had been honed down by many years of outdoor existence. He couldn't help but notice the intricate carving on it was similar to that of the figures he had in his case. To the left of it was a marble statue of an armless man crouched over in a seemingly distorted and impossible position. To the right was a huge bronze bell with a coat of arms set in relief. He looked to the left and saw a glass cabinet full of clay bowls and vases, there seemed to be hundreds of them. Next to it were gold platters and bejewelled ornaments, there were rings and bracelets with the deepest blue stones, some with tiny white balls that appeared to glint with the all the colours of the rainbow. Roderick couldn't begin to imagine how much they were worth. On the walls hung paintings of different proportions and orientation, there were so many they hardly left any space between them. Most were portraits, a few landscapes, it looked like a huge jigsaw puzzle had to be solved just to fit them all up there.

"Follow me my dear fellow," David Laing said.

He took him to a long glass cabinet the height of a man's waist . Roderick stared inside as David Laing described the objects: a flint arrowhead from Skye, another carved from stone, a silver bracelet from Iona, an ancient crosier, which he informed him was from Whithorn. There were also coins galore, far too many to count.

Roderick wondered why he was being shown all this.

As they returned to the doors, David Laing turned.

Roderick was about to get his question answered.

"This is where your objects will be displayed my dear sir."

"They are not my pieces Mr Laing."

"This is where those fine figures will be on show if you were to give the Society a chance Mr Ryrie." David Laing's glare was held on him. "I can also assure you sir if you..." He paused for a moment. "I can give you a guarantee that your pieces will be on display to anyone that wishes to see them, rich and poor, old and young, man and woman, whatever their status in life may be."

Roderick felt as if he was trying to entice him. "I have a time limit Mr Laing," he told him. "Please inform me as soon as you have made your decision."

The Jeweller, the Watchmaker, the Medallist, the Antiquarian
1831

Roderick was outside the imposing entrance to the Royal Institute. He was bent over with his hands on his knees, swaying from side to side, his back pressed against one of the pillars to stop him from toppling over. He was breathing heavily, trying to force air into his lungs.

Roderick dropped the case beside his feet.

Without waiting another moment he quickly stuffed his clay pipe with thornapple leaves and after several frustrating strikes on three friction sticks he managed to get the last to spark into life. He held the tiny bowl at an angle to the flame as he drew in more of the smoke and held it in his lungs.

There he remained, leaning on the column, until his panting began to ease. A few more sucks and there was no more to burn. He looked into the bowl, just a layer of black ash remained. He

tapped the pipe against the heel of his shoe, leaving a scattering of the used embers on the ground. The remainder of the leaves he would keep for later.

Roderick picked up the case and began his journey home, to the place where he has lived with his mother for his entire life. A four room apartment on the fifth floor of a tenement block in Canongate, high enough to be away from the stench and noise coming from the streets below. The place he also once lived with his father before he packed up his bags and moved to Stornoway. Other than Roderick's meagre wages and a small allowance from his mother's family, Roderick and Margaret Pirrie had to fend for themselves. At least his father had left them a place to live, Roderick couldn't blame him for leaving, he knew how difficult his mother could be. He also knew she couldn't cope by herself.

Roderick felt trapped.

He turned left and headed down the Earthen Mound, disappointed that he hadn't succeeded in selling the small figures. He so wanted to impress his father, to be more accepted into his life. He didn't ask for much.

At the lower end of the road he passed a brute of a man whipping the hind off a stubborn mule. The man stopped with the cane held midair, glaring menacingly at Roderick. The mule also turned his head, his eyes doleful and forlorn. Roderick wanted to tell him he was not alone. He continued, passing the huge building of the Bank of Scotland. With the thornapple leaves starting to take affect he now found a spring to his step, just managing to skip to the side as three soldiers in red tunics marched past, oblivious to anyone in their path. Into Lawn Market, he passed St Giles Cathedral bustling with workman. On the other side of the road several stalls were selling fabric cut from huge rolls. Either side of him dark stone buildings loomed high above, poles protruded out of windows with recently washed clothes swaying in the wind. Roderick tipped some lavender scent into his handkerchief and kept it held it to

establishment."

"Roderick Ryrie sir."

It was then the questions came at him thick and fast, virtually the same ones he had been asked only a few hours before.

"Where were they found?"

"Further north," Roderick replied. "Where the sky is big." Decided the thornapple leaves had said that.

Forrest smiled. "Aye, although that could be anywhere but here."

Roderick smiled with him. "The parish of Uig on the Island of Lewis." He then decided to put him off the scent, the same as he had done at the Society. "Near some ruins called the House of the Black Women, deep in a souterrain."

"When were they found?"

Roderick drew down his lips and shrugged.

"*You* don't know when *you* found them?"

"Because I didn't find them."

"So who did?" Forrest asked.

Maybe this man Forrest had the same suspicions as the Reverend Jamieson and that man Pitcairn.

Roderick had to think.

"I was visiting my family in Stornoway, the person who discovered them was a friend of my father's. So I offered to bring them to Edinburgh to sell on his behalf. He has no need of them sir."

"You say near some ruins called the House of the Black Women."

"Aye,"

"How many pieces are there?"

"Ninety-three."

"Do you know what they are?"

"I am a lowly Merchant's clerk sir."

"You may trivialise yourself sir, but *please* do not misjudge me."

"Gaming pieces, so I have been told."

"What are they made from?"

"Ivory or bone...or both."

"How old are they?"

"I believe they are very old."

It was only then that the questioning changed course. That's when it came to the question Roderick was waiting for.

"How much does..." Forrest paused for a second. "Does your father's friend want for them?"

Roderick didn't have to think. Thanks to the leaves his confidence was high. "Fifty pounds," he replied without hesitation. He was surprised not to see any reaction, also relieved.

"That is a lot of money young man," Forrest said, as if it was up for negotiation. "Aye, a lot of money," he repeated softly.

"I have another party interested."

Forrest glared long and hard at him, his eyebrows plunging even deeper.

Roderick had the feeling that he had guessed who these people were.

"They are very unusual young man."

"Aye, they are that."

"I have never seen anything like these before."

Roderick didn't reply.

"And so many."

"Aye."

"I will have to take guidance before I can make you an offer."

It was not what Roderick wanted to hear. "I'm afraid I have little time sir. I am returning to see my father very soon."

"And your father's friend?"

"Aye, if he is there. If not I can leave the money with my father. You can make an offer but I will have to take the highest price before then."

"If you have one."

Roderick didn't reply.

The man thought. "Come back in six days, I will have an answer for you then."

"Six days!?"

"Aye, but you must leave some of the pieces with me."

"No!" Roderick realised how harsh it sounded. He took a deep breath and softened his tone. "I'm sorry, but that is not possible. Like I said, they do not belong to me."

"You do not trust me sir?"

"I do not know you sir." Roderick wondered if the deal was slipping away from him. "My father's friend has put his complete trust in me. I cannot break that trust under any circumstances."

Forrest stared into the case, appeared to be in the deepest concentration, his eyes skating over the contents. He picked up the Warrior, the one in a worse condition than the rest. Roderick knew the piece well, as if he had got to know each one personally. It's sword was dented in the middle, making it look bent if viewed from the front, as if its unfortunate victim had succumbed to a heavy slash of its blade. Nor did it appear as if the Warrior itself had come off lightly. Sections had been chopped away: the front and back of its helmet. A fragment from the side of its shield had also broken, the lower point also missing. His body appeared to be the recipient of a thousand slashes. Worse than that, the left eye was missing. This fighter appeared to have been in many wars; but had been in none.

"Leave this wee fellow with me. I will return it to you on that sixth day if there is no deal. If there is, and if it is one you accept, it will be mine anyway. Like I said sir, I have to take council over them. Like your father, I also have a friend."

Roderick reluctantly agreed.

The Artist, the Poet, the Collector

1831

It was the morning after Roderick's encounter with T. A. Forrest; and before that the visit to the Society of Antiquaries. Unfortunately he had to leave both establishments without success. For him it had become like a personal struggle; knowing he was doing it for someone else seemed to make the failure that much worse.

Then there was his father. How disappointed he had been when Roderick didn't make the grade into his old regiment. How would it have been possible with his affliction? His breathing wasn't improving. Even with the self-induced increase of the thornapple leaves he was struggling to keep it under control.

More importantly, Roderick knew how much difference the money would make to the lives of one family on the Island of Lewis, waiting for an eviction they knew would surely come: Roderick just hoped they would still be there if his fortune was to change.

struggle.

"Pass me the note," Roderick said.

The young man stretched out his hand as if he was afraid to enter the room. Roderick stepped over to him and saw pinched between his thumb and finger was a small envelope. He took it from him, immediately noticed a strange symbol on the front, hand drawn, what appeared to be a musical note. Roderick thought no more of it, opened it and pulled out a sheet of paper folded in half. The note was small, the top edge rough, torn from a notepad, the writing hidden from view, as though it was for his eyes only. Roderick could see the paper was of the finest quality, soft, like velvet. He unfolded it. His eyes roaming from side to side as he read.

> *MY DEAR SIR - I would be greatly indebted to yourself if I could pay you a visit at the address to whence I have dispatched this note. If I may be so bold to suggest a time of three o'clock this afternoon. If this is suitable then I would be obliged if you would inform Albert. If not, then would you be so good as to suggest an alternate time and place. My own home at 93 Princes Street would also be acceptable if you so desire. All I will say as a matter of encouragement, is that I believe you have some artifacts that may be of interest to myself, and accordingly be also beneficial to you.*

It was only when Roderick reached the end of the letter did he hold the sheet of paper as if in a trance, his mouth agape, his eyes unblinking, gazing down at the name.

> *Chas. KIRKPATRICK SHARPE*

"Charles Kirkpatrick Sharpe," he said softly, the only part of the note he read aloud.

Charles Kirkpatrick Sharpe? There was probably not one person in Edinburgh's high society who hadn't heard that name, and probably in low society too. A man who had become quite a celebrity in Edinburgh. Who had the ear of Lords and Duchesses. Whose circle of friends comprised the great and the good, including Walter Scott himself, some even say he was the author's closest confidante. He was also a man known for his writings on the occult, for his poetry and ballads, for his art, and for his collection of antiquities. He was unconventional, an eccentric, not adverse to gossip and scandal, probably creating much of it himself.

"Charles Kirkpatrick Sharpe!" his mother shrieked excitedly. "Why has *he* written to you Roddy?" Without asking, she snatched the note and began reading it herself. After several seconds. "He wants to visit you. Why in God's name does Charles Kirkpatrick Sharpe want to visit you?"

Roderick thought, he soon realised why. He looked over to the leather case sat on the table.

His mother sighed. "Not because of those little devils your father gave you to sell."

"I offered, and yes mother, probably because of those carvings, for which I have so far failed in my duty. Maybe not now though. " Roderick then looked at the young man. "I take it you are Albert?"

"Yes sir."

"And you were told to wait for an answer?"

"Yes sir. I am not to leave here without one."

Roderick stepped over to the writing desk and pulled down the flap. He dipped the quill into the inkwell and began to write.

MY KIND SIR - It would give me great pleasure to have the presence of your company at my home here in Canongate. Three o'clock this afternoon

would also be most agreeable to myself.
Your obedient servant.
RODERICK WILLIAM RYRIE

Four nervous hours had passed when there was a gentle knock at the door. Margaret Pirrie answered. His mother always answered. Roderick knew exactly who it was.

Roderick was standing in the centre of the drawing room, his hands clutched behind him, nervously twiddling his fingers, waiting to greet his guest. Everything in the entire apartment had been cleaned to an inch of its life. The fire, lit long ago, awarded the room a warm glow.

His mother was first to enter. She was followed by a man in a blue frock coat that just cleared the ground. Roderick noticed his feet were as small as a woman's as his slipper like shoes kicked out from under the coat. A white lace scarf bulged out under his chin, as though he wanted to hide anything that might reveal his advancing years. A gold watch hung from a chain around his neck, not something you would want to display around these parts Roderick thought. Nor could he fail to notice that his clothes appeared to be from a bygone age, a fashion abandoned long ago. Roderick wasn't surprised.

Charles Kirkpatrick Sharpe stepped into the room, a strongly scented handkerchief held to his nose, one Roderick could smell, even from where he stood. He handed Roderick a calling card, all that was on it was the same musical note (C Sharp) drawn onto the envelope. Following behind him like a dutiful pet was Albert, looking even more mousy than the first time.

Roderick took a step forward and held out his hand. Charles Kirkpatrick Sharpe obliged. The man's fingers were long and slender, although it surprised Roderick how firm his grip was. It was the time he kept hold of it, awkwardly long, gazing directly into Roderick's eyes as he did, the thinnest of smiles on his lips, as if he was trying to read something in Roderick.

“Please take a seat Mr Sharpe,” Roderick said, managing to slide his fingers out from his grasp, noticing the man’s hand remained as if still in hold. Roderick took a deep breath and indicated to a chair.

“Thank you, I will.” As Charles Kirkpatrick Sharpe lowered himself into the seat his attention was drawn to a book on the side table. “Ah, I see you are reading The Antiquarian?” he said with a delicate falsetto voice.

Roderick thought his voice was more like a woman’s. “Yes sir, I am,” he replied.

“Sir Walter informs me it is the book he is most proud of, and he has written so many of such distinction.”

Roderick noticed the man kept his gaze on him, hardly blinking. It made him feel uncomfortable. He didn’t know what to say, so he said nothing and took a long breath instead.

“Alas, my dearest of friends is in such poor health these days. I fear we won’t see much more from that sweet hand of his.”

“Then that will be a loss to us all Mr Sharpe.”

Charles Kirkpatrick Sharpe appeared impressed by his answer. “I’m afraid it will my dear boy, I’m afraid it will.” After a moment’s silence. “I suspect you are pondering the reason behind my visit.”

“Aye sir, I am.”

“It has been brought to my attention...” Charles Kirkpatrick Sharpe paused for a second, as if he wasn’t happy with his words. He took a deep breath. “I will go directly to the matter in hand. You have a number of small objects in your possession, that they are figures of the most exquisite carving and antiquity.”

“More like the work of the devil,” Roderick’s mother threw in.

“Please mother they are...”

Charles Kirkpatrick Sharpe interrupted by holding a hand up. “Maybe so madam.”

eyes aren't what they used to be. And I fear spectacles make a gentleman so unappealing." He continued to study the buckle. "The fastening appears to be as fresh as if it was made only yesterday."

Roderick felt as if he was trying to say something. "I believe they are of great antiquity."

"They are indeed very curious, my dear boy."

"Aye, that they are sir."

"May I ask your price?"

Roderick hesitated for a moment. If it was David Laing who informed him of the pieces then he would also have told him the price. "Fifty pounds sir."

Charles Kirkpatrick Sharpe gave no reaction. "Pray, please enlighten me of the number of pieces?"

Roderick thought about the Warrior with T. A. Forrest. "Ninety-two," he replied. He then remembered the Bishop back with his father.

"You say ninety-two?"

"Aye, ninety-two sir."

"Not ninety-three."

Roderick remembered what he had told the members of the Society. "There are ninety-two here sir."

Charles Kirkpatrick Sharpe raised the handkerchief to his nose again, as if he was wanting to hide his response.

"My dear boy, do you know there are three means by which everything can be acquired in this world?"

Roderick raised his eyebrows.

"The first is opportunity."

Roderick couldn't have disagreed. "Aye sir, opportunity."

"The second is to consider that opportunity carefully." Charles Kirkpatrick Sharpe stopped, as if for dramatic affect. "And the third my dear fellow, well, the third is not to miss that opportunity."

Roderick wondered where all this was going.

"So the price of ten pieces will be?"

Roderick was surprised by the question. "*Ten* Mr Sharpe?"

"Aye sir, ten Mr Ryrie."

Roderick had to think. Did he really want to split up the collection. If he did then he would still have to sell the rest. Would the Society or Forrest want them with ten missing. Then again, five pounds would be better than no pounds. Roderick took a step towards the writing desk. "I will have to work out a price."

"Five pounds," Charles Kirkpatrick Sharpe announced.

"Five pounds?"

"A tenth for a tenth sir."

Roderick tried to do the calculations in his head, it was right. "Which ten pieces?" he asked, expecting him to want the finest pieces.

"I believe a selection would be suitable for my needs."

Roderick thought that was acceptable, only to realise this uncovered yet another problem. "Who will choose?" he asked.

"So we have agreed on ten pieces?"

"Aye sir, ten pieces."

"For five pounds?"

"Aye sir, for five pounds."

A heavy silence followed.

"Shall I..." Roderick began, only to be interrupted again.

"I suggest Albert picks out one of the wee fellows. And if your dear charming mother is so in agreement, she will kindly liberate another piece, and so on, five each, until there are ten drawn from the case. I also suggest that neither have any knowledge of the figure they are withdrawing, that they select without looking."

"You mean blindfolded?"

"I believe averting their eyes would suffice for our needs my dear boy."

Roderick had notions of Albert's hand ferreting around for the larger pieces. "I also suggest they take the first piece they come into contact with."

"In and out my dear boy."

"Aye, in and out."

"No dilly-dallying."

"Any corner of the case, a figure from the centre if they so wish. Anywhere of their choosing sir, but no..." Roderick paused for a second. "No dilly-dallying as you put it."

Charles Kirkpatrick Sharpe beckoned Albert over to the table.

Roderick looked over to his mother. "Is that acceptable to you mother?"

She hesitated for a moment. "If it gets them out of the house."

"Only ten I'm afraid my dear lady."

"Ten is better than none Mr Sharpe," she replied.

"So be it."

So there we were: King's and Queens, Warriors and Horsemen, Bishops and the pieces from the front line, all to be exploited in a petty little game, just for the sole reason of tearing us apart, wrenching ten of us from our compatriots.

A hand plunged in, small and soft skinned, I couldn't tell if it was male or female. A Bishop was swiftly removed from the centre, one that was standing, two fingers held up in blessing. Another hand, smaller, a smattering of dirt under roughly cut nails, a woman's. It went towards the far corner. A Queen was lifted away, one holding a drinking horn. The first hand returned, towards the opposite corner, a proud Warrior removed, one of the four Kjeld the Elder had carved, the one biting his shield. The woman again. Another Bishop taken, also standing, two hands gripping his crosier. The first hand again, two fingers touched me, one either side. I was being raised up into the light and placed on the table with the other four. Four people were surrounding me, two standing further back, their gaze above us. Another Queen. Another King. A Horseman, battle worn, but ready to fight. Another Warrior. Then last of all, another Queen, who was placed by my side, the one I

remember being always beside me when Erik played those matches in Bergen.

Ten pieces had been chosen. I was one of them.

I was never to meet my compatriots again.

"So there we have it my dear boy," Charles Kirkpatrick Sharpe held his hand over his shoulder and rippled his fingers.

Albert promptly gave him the five pounds and left his hand resting on his mentor's shoulder.

Roderick gazed down at the chosen pieces, noticed none of the discs or headstones were part of the ten. He could say nothing. A gentleman's agreement had been made, one from which there could be no departure.

"We should shake hands," Charles Kirkpatrick Sharpe suggested.

Roderick accepted, hands were grasped, Charles Kirkpatrick Sharpe giving him that same lingering hold before handing the money over.

"The contract is now complete. I will need a receipt to confirm the ownership is mine."

Roderick stepped over to the writing desk.

> *On behalf of the owner, Mr Malcolm MacLeod from Penny Donald in the parish of Uig, Isle of Lewis. Whom has given me, Roderick William Ryrie authority to sell the ivory figures. I can confirm that on the 21 April 1831 the ownership of ten pieces has been transferred over to Mr Charles Kirkpatrick Sharpe of 93 Princes Street for the price of five pounds.*

Roderick handed him the slip of paper. "Might I ask what will become of them sir?" he asked.

Charles Kirkpatrick Sharpe paused, his gaze hanging on Roderick, as though he was thinking of how to answer. "I was encouraged by certain individuals to buy the entire horde, only

Eighty-two

1831

Several days had passed and there had been no word from the Society of Antiquaries or Charles Kirkpatrick Sharpe. Roderick had hardly left the house in the hope that Albert might turn up or that he might receive a note from David Laing. Time was running out, he was to return to Stornoway the following week. His only saving grace, he would have five pounds to give his father's friend. It was better than nothing.

Roderick was looking forward to getting away from the noise and stench blighting his overcrowded street. Every day it seemed to be getting louder: the clatter of the carts, the yelling of the street-traders, the arguments between the neighbours and the rent collectors. He couldn't go outside without feral children begging him for food or money, Roderick had learnt long ago not to give them anything, unless he wanted to draw out every street urchin from the alleys. The stench was becoming worse, the air was thick with it, leaving him with an unrelenting feeling of nausea. He had his own health problems to worry about. Every day he was becoming more anxious, more paranoid, his fight for breath more frequent.

He was so looking forward to returning to Lewis and smelling that sweet aroma of newly cut peat, the salty freshness of the sea air, knowing his breathing would improve to the point of not being so reliant on those thornapple leaves. It was as if they had become a perpetual habit he couldn't shake off. He had started puffing on the pipe as soon as he rose in the morning, then every few hours after that, before eventually retiring to bed. Sleep had become his only escape, if he were to have any that is. If it wasn't for his mother he would contemplate moving to the Island of Lewis permanently. She couldn't survive without him, and he didn't want to put it to the test. He also doubted his father would want him there. Even on the island he knew life wasn't easy for many of the inhabitants, how they were being forced to flee from the their homes, as Malcolm MacLeod would surely have to one day. Roderick couldn't believe how the wealthy were living in splendour while adding to the misery of people less well off. He knew how important the money would be to this crofting family.

There was only one option remaining.

Roderick walked through the door of T. A. Forrest's establishment carrying the small leather case. So not to be startled again, he instantly glanced over to the corner of the shop, saw the lectern was headless this time. He walked to the opposite wall and stared down at the craftsmen still wearing their heavy coats, their bodies hunched over desks swamped with tiny tools. How they could undertake such intricate work in this chill was beyond Roderick, it felt colder inside than it did outside. Probably had no choice he thought. One older man looked up at him, his eyes like tiny pools, his expression melancholy, it was like he hadn't even seen the stranger in the doorway. Roderick held up a hand in acknowledgement. The man continued to work on a silver ring pinched between his fingers. Roderick felt sorry for him, knowing every day he would hold precious jewels he could only dream of possessing in his wildest dreams.

"So you have returned."

Roderick spun around, Forrest was sat in the opposite corner, not appearing to be occupied. It was as if he had been there all that time, like he had become one of the artifacts.

"Aye sir, I said I would, and you have one of the figures still belonging to me."

"I take it you have not found a buyer?" Forrest asked.

"I still have several options open to me sir."

"You have not found a buyer." This time it was spoken as a statement.

Roderick decided to tell him about the ten figures in Charles Kirkpatrick Sharpe's hands. It would make no difference if he didn't buy the others; and if he did he would have to tell him anyhow. "A gentleman has taken ten from the collection."

"Taken?"

"Paid me fair money."

Forrest held his gaze on Roderick. "This gentleman did not want the entire collection?"

"Nay sir, just a selection."

"So you have separated them."

Roderick thought the man was being critical. He was annoyed, they weren't even his. "If you had bought them the first time then I wouldn't have..."

Thomas Forrest interrupted. "As I informed you at the time, I had to take council."

"Then may I enquire to the outcome of your council?" As Roderick spoke he looked around for the Warrior. It was nowhere to be seen. Not that he would be able to spot it with all the relics crammed into every free space.

"The reason for the council was to discuss how I should proceed."

"Then if you would be so good as to inform me of the outcome."

"May I see them again?"

Roderick placed the case on the lectern as he had done the time before. He flicked the latch up and the two sides sprung apart.

Without saying anything Forrest began taking the pieces out in a precise and calculated manner, leaving each one beside the case as if he was wanting to count each one in turn. When they were all out he closed the lid and pushed down the latch.

"Eighty-two," he said, as if he was confirming what Roderick had told him was true.

"Aye sir, eighty-two."

"Then it seems I have no choice but to purchase eighty-two," Thomas Andrew Forrest said.

Roderick immediately felt relief, surprise, followed by delight. "I believe I mentioned the price of fifty pounds last time we met," he said.

"Aye you did, but you have sold ten pieces since then."

Roderick was wondering if he had done the right thing splitting up the collection. He and Charles Kirkpatrick Sharpe had shaken hands on it; a gentleman's agreement not to be reneged upon. He had also been paid five pounds for them. "In that case I will only ask forty-five pounds."

"In that case I can only offer twenty."

"Twenty!" Roderick couldn't believe what he had just heard.

"Aye twenty, the collection is not whole, their value has decreased somewhat."

"I will take my leave of you sir, if you would be so kind to return the piece I left with you."

Forrest made no indication of moving.

Roderick had become mistrustful. He was given no proof that he had the Warrior. Maybe it had been a mistake leaving it with him. His breath became forced, his chest heaving. He plunged his hand into his pocket, took several thornapple leaves out, stuffed them into his mouth and started to chew. He swallowed, leaving the semiliquid lump to the side of his

Money was the first: hopefully making the journey worthwhile, although that was still uncertain.

The second reason: where he was going would be like heaven to an antiquarian such as himself: the Parthenon Marbles, the Rosetta Stone, antiquities from Egypt, from Rome, the Far East and many more places. But more importantly, hopefully soon to be forty-eight ivory figures, nineteen from the front line, fourteen round discs and one buckle.

The third reason: he would be staying with his brother and sister-in-law in Islington. His only surviving relatives. A family he hadn't seen for over seven years. After the recent death of their father, a legacy needed to be discussed.

It left him with a feeling of annoyance that he had paid a whole four pounds to sit in the cramped and crowded cabin, having to ignore the requests from the brusque gentleman sat opposite to discover what was inside the strong box Forrest was clutching. All this without the man asking the question directly. "That looks a strong lock, the contents must be important?...Is it silk lined inside?" Forrest despised elusiveness, his own discourse was always forthright. Not that he would have told him.

Another traveller was an older looking gentleman dressed in drab attire, who like Forrest, kept his own council. By the ornate chain leading to a hidden pocket watch, Forrest thought he may have been in the same profession as himself.

The other three were young, probably in their early twenties, two women and a man. Two sisters and a brother Forrest thought from their open conversation, mostly about the aunt they were to stay with in London, although they didn't sound overjoyed about it. The two women were on the same seat as Forrest, the young man sat in the middle of the two men opposite.

Forrest was sure strict rules had been put in place as to how many passengers the mail coach could carry, less than the six that were crammed in the cabin with him anyhow. His only

consolation was that he wasn't on top of the coach in the rear seats, open to the elements and having to listen to the cursing and cracks of the coachman's whip every time they got held up by a dawdling wagon.

Forrest's suffering from the nauseating sway of the coach was only broken by the hourly mail drop-offs, although only lasting for a few minutes he could relax his muscles and relieve himself if necessary. The coachman showed his impatience if anyone lingered too long. It appeared speed was of the essence as the horses tugged on their harnesses, eager to tackle the road once again. Even when sat in the cabin Forrest could feel the strain on the brakes, hoping they would hold strong whenever the coachman disembarked.

Then there were the stopovers.

First was Newcastle-on-Tyne where a drunken brawl at the Turf Hotel had woken him from a deep sleep. It appeared to have a copious amount of beggars, not that Forrest would give them anything. He had also downed several tankards of ale after noticing the rancid colour of the water. It was also a place where the horses could be stabled, fed and watered, as they were at every stopover. As he reboarded, he became aware the brusque gentleman had been replaced with an older woman, who thankfully kept her own council.

Next was York, where the plum-cakes at The George Inn were particularly good, only blighted by the pack of dogs prowling around the entrance arch as he went to stretch his legs. Fortunately the coachman came to his rescue with a long bullwhip of a cane, forcing the pack to whimper away, something he had obviously done many times before. Unfortunately Forrest never got to see the city he had heard so much about. By this time the horses had lost all their grandeur: several drools of saliva stretched down from their mouths, steam rose from their sweat covered bodies. He was glad to see two of the most ragged had been replaced with large greys, the coachmen having to swap the position of the horses to discover

the correct balance.

Then lastly, there was the relief at having warm fresh bread at the Angel Inn in Grantham, not the rock hard crusted loaves that threatened to break every tooth on the previous stops.

The entire time his thoughts were only on one thing, that the outcome would be fruitful. All indications from the correspondence with a man called Frederic Madden had indicated that it would. Forrest had also stated a price in one letter, one he told himself he would not deviate from and the return letter didn't show any sign of contradiction.

Much to Forrest's relief, the coach finally arrived at its destination at the Old Blue Boar tavern in London. It was Saturday, seven o'clock in the evening. The four backbreaking days on the road were over.

An hour later he finally arrived at his brother's house.

It was the third Monday in October, just before eight in the morning. T. A. Forrest was stood in Great Russell Street to the south of the museum. He was staring ahead, not believing what he was seeing, no one had warned him of this in the exchange of letters.

Forrest was expecting a magnificent building with towering Roman Pillars and sculptured Greek friezes. Instead it was no more than a construction site under a grey dismal sky, as if the world had been stolen of all colour. He looked to the left and saw what was once a magnificent brick house stood separate to the one they were building. It's roof and most of the top floor were missing, although rather than being erected it was in the process of being demolished. The sacrificial lamb Forrest thought.

Piles of rubble and mountains of dirt, old planks of wood and discarded bricks were strewn everywhere. He could see men with rolled up sleeves and muscular forearms, their heavy boots sinking into the earth as they pushed carts carrying huge blocks of stone, the horses precariously negotiating the wooden

boards. Other workers were in the process of cutting the stones, becoming lost in clouds of dust, the wind blowing some of it towards Forrest. Heavy industrial apparatus lay idly around, waiting their turn to be utilised, some so complex in build that Forrest had no idea what they could be used for.

Another building to his right was also in the middle of being built, a mass of thick bamboo scaffolding rose high against the huge stone facade. Lashed to it were long ladders reaching three storeys up, where another ladder to the side would take the tradesmen up to the next level, then finally to the roof.

Forrest was told to enter the east wing from the rear, which he did. With arms stretched out wide he carefully stepped along the spiderweb of planks to avoid the quagmire underneath.

He was told a man called John Doubleday would be waiting at the entrance for him. He was.

John Doubleday was a lot younger than Forrest was expecting, probably in his early thirties, smartly dressed, a strong intelligent face that looked well beyond his age. He introduced himself with a firm handshake and an unwavering stare. As they stepped inside Doubleday told him he didn't actually work for the museum, that he sometimes acted as an agent; which they had asked him to do on this day.

Forrest had made drawings and descriptions of five of the eighty-two pieces and submitted them in his letters, leaving a lot of freedom in determining a precise date for them.

John Doubleday said he had recently gifted the museum a cast of medieval seals and coins; that the members thought he would be the person best equipped to make comments on the pieces. As he spoke, Forrest couldn't help but notice he had a slight twang to his accent.

John Doubleday led him into a long magnificent room, it was the entire length of the wing and looked as if it had been built only yesterday. They continued down the centre, over the ornate inlaid floor that gave Forrest the strange feeling he was

collectables."

"And that's where you acquired them?" John Doubleday asked.

"Aye, a man entered my workshop."

"Another dealer?"

Forrest shook his head. "He works in a merchant's office."

"A merchant?"

"Aye."

"So are you saying he acquired them on his travels?" Frederic Madden said without looking towards Forrest, his eyes still ricocheting around the small figures.

"Nay sir, I am *not* saying that."

Madden released an impatient sigh. "So do you know where he acquired them?"

"He said he was visiting family in Stornoway at the time. That's when he offered to sell them for the discoverer. I assume he..."

"The discoverer?"

"Aye, he was a friend of his father."

"So this discoverer, do you know where he discovered them?"

"He said they were found on the Island of Lewis, in the parish of Uig, something about it being near the ruins known as the House of the Black Women. All I know is that it's remote and close to the sea."

"The House of the Black Women?"

"Aye."

"A nunnery?" John Doubleday enquired.

"That is all he told me."

"To break the tedium of cloistered seclusion." Madden remarked softly, as if the words were only for his ears.

"Cloistered seclusion?" John Doubleday enquired.

Madden thought for a moment, as if he hadn't heard. "They are the most exquisite carvings are they not?"

"They are sir," replied Doubleday.

"Only someone possessing the most expert skills could produce such work."

"I agree," John Doubleday kept his gaze hanging on Madden. "Are you saying it was the sisters who carved them?"

"I believe their devotion is solely for prayer Mr Doubleday. But it is my opinion..." Madden took a breath. "I have heard of a woman in Iceland that had much mastery in the carving of ivory."

"Then she is most adroit Mr Madden."

"Quite so sir...only someone with many years of schooling could produce such work, someone who has been taught from a very young age, followed by many years of service. Only then would they have reached this level of expertise."

"So not Scotland Mr Madden?"

"No, not Scotland, but I do believe..." Madden stopped.

A man with a shock of grey hair passed close by them, glancing down at the pieces as he did, as though his curiosity had got the better of him.

Forrest noticed the scorn with which Madden glared at the man.

"Henry," John Doubleday said.

"Mr Doubleday." The man replied before nodding towards Forrest, completely ignoring Madden.

Frederic Madden sighed and continued. "I believe more study is required, but if I am not mistaken Mr Doubleday these are carved for the purpose of chess-play."

'More study' were not the words Forrest wanted to hear. He continued to listen to the conversation, hoped it would divert to payment before too long.

"The Nationale Museum in Paris have pieces from a set, again, not complete as I believe these are. They are called the Charlemagne pieces. I have been fortunate to set eyes on them on my travels."

Doubleday picked up a horseman.

"That is a Knight sir, if I am not mistaken. You see, I am

also a devoted player of this game." He turned his attention back to Forrest. "Are you aware of this game called chess Mr Forrest?"

"I do not play, if that is what you are seeking, but aye, I am aware of the game." Forrest recalled something he had read in a newspaper from a few years back. "I believe there was a match played between the Edinburgh Chess Club and London Chess Club. The article caught my eye because I believe the moves were relayed by mail coach." A brazen smile came to him. "And if I am not mistaken sir, the Scottish team came out as the victors." Forrest gazed at Madden to measure his reaction. He saw none. "I have also seen single pieces said to be used for this game, but I must add, their appearance is nothing like these."

"You are correct sir," Frederic Madden said. "This is the first time I have seen pieces such as these. You say you do not play?"

"Nay sir, I do not. I fear it is far beyond me."

"If I am not mistaken, the requirements for a game are all here." He pointed to a piece. "See there, there is the King, and here is a Queen. And here a Knight as the one Doubleday is holding. And look, without question, that is a Bishop. This is interesting because there is much debate when Bishop's began to be used in chess-play. Maybe we are making history here Mr Forrest." His eyes skated around the collection of figures as though he was searching for something. He then snatched up a Warrior, staring at it for several seconds, as if he was considering his next move in a game. He then looked around the other figures, searching out any others that appeared similar. "In the process of elimination I assume these figures would be the piece known as the castle."

"A castle," John Doubleday remarked. "I'm sorry Mr Madden but the last time I saw a castle it was a fortress with battlements and..."

Madden interrupted. "As long as the players can identify it

as the piece that moves in that particular direction then you could just as well have a peanut on each corner, maybe a walnut as the King, a hazelnut as the Pawn. And I must say this fellow does look as if he is a perfect guardian for his monarch. A good choice in my opinion." Frederic Madden held the Warrior at arms length. "In that case I will call him a sentry...no!" He thought some more. "A warder, yes, I think a warder is most appropriate. Now sir, in the front we should have a row of eight pieces known as Pawns."

"The hazelnut Mr Madden."

"Correct Mr Doubleday. In my own set which is of the St George design, the Pawns are the smallest pieces." His finger drifted over to the tombstones. "I believe these pieces here will represent these." He picked one up, one with eight sides. "I have seen similar pieces from an older game from Persia, and before that from India." Frederic Madden started to count the smaller pieces. "There are nineteen." He then began counting the pieces with a sword resting across their knees. "There are six Kings, so I believe there must have been three sets in total. That means there must be several missing from the other ranks."

Forrest realised there must be a lot more in the collection than the ten Roderick Ryrie sold to his anonymous buyer. Maybe he had sold him more than the ten, maybe he had sold them to someone else, maybe some pieces had been lost before they had met.

"I believe in chess you have two different colours, one for each side. But these are all the same colour?" John Doubleday enquired.

"I have been lucky to encounter ivory pieces from the far east, where one of the sides has been stained a dark beetroot red," Frederic Madden replied. "Perhaps they have been made for another game, another reason, maybe that is why the pawns vary in size, so the design differentiates them Mr Doubleday. I see a few are significantly larger, and to win that larger piece is the objective. Perhaps a game we have no knowledge of, one

Forrest thought, he had no other commitments concerning them. "Aye, as long it is written that the collection along with their description will be returned in whole at my fancy."

"That we will do sir," John Doubleday confirmed.

"I may also seek out other buyers who wish to see them sir," Forrest said, knowing family commitments stopped him from doing so.

"Then they will be returned to you as promised," Frederic Madden confirmed.

It was a month later when Forrest returned to the British Museum, this time the meeting was held in a much less imposing room, more like an unused back office. There was also one other difference. Instead of John Doubleday there was another man who Frederic Madden introduced as Edward Hawkins, a stately looking person who was described as the Keeper of Antiquities.

A person with the rank of authority Forrest instantly thought. He looked around for the figures, realised they were nowhere to be seen. It would be hard to hide them in such a small room he thought.

It was Frederic Madden who spoke first. "We have completed our research Mr Forrest." He stopped, as if there was no more to be said.

Forrest waited.

Madden sighed, then continued. "That morning in October, when you first brought the pieces to our attention."

"Aye," Forrest strung out the word in suspicion. "How can I forget?"

"Well sir, that same afternoon the museum had another visitor. A very distinguished gentlemen indeed sir." Madden paused to study Forrest's expression. "In fact a gentleman of the greatest eminence."

Forrest wondered where this was going, also what it had to do with him.

"A gentlemen once from your hometown I believe."

"Edinburgh?" Forrest enquired as if he needed confirmation.

"Yes sir, we were very fortunate indeed to have Sir Walter Scott visit us."

"You were very fortunate sir," Forrest said and thought no more of it. Frederic Madden was just boasting about the company he keeps. "Indeed, very fortunate sir." Forrest repeated, hoping that would put an end to the conversation.

Alas, Madden continued. "He was on his way to Malta to improve on his much floundering health."

"Aye, it is with great sorrow that I have heard he is in much decline."

"It is very sad Mr Forrest. I must say his entire bearing was quite wretched."

Forrest had already voiced his regrets, so he said nothing more.

"Sir Walter knows another esteemed gentleman. Again this gentleman is from your city. His name is Charles Kirkpatrick Sharpe. I believe he is known for his collection of antiquities Mr Forrest, amongst other things."

Forrest took a quick glance at Edward Hawkins, who had said nothing so far, just stood in the same place with his arms crossed.

"I have not knowingly had the pleasure, although I have indeed heard of this gentleman sir. I believe he has a very singular bearing."

"Before Sir Walter visited here, he went to say his farewells to Mr Sharpe."

"Then he too was very fortunate."

"Sir Walter was here to peruse some manuscripts. It was only by coincidence he happened to pass the chess pieces you revealed to us. He was most anxious to study them closer. On examination he said they were virtually the same as the ten pieces his friend Mr Sharpe had in his possession." Frederic

Madden took a deep breath. "If you recall Mr Forrest, when my colleague Mr Doubleday enquired if this was the complete collection, you declared that it was."

Forrest had to think, and fast. He tried to recall the order they were displayed to him by Roderick Ryrie and what was said in their exchange of words. "As far as I am aware Mr Madden, that was the complete horde from the vendor. I neither counted the pieces or knew of any other party to another transaction."

"You did not count them?" asked Frederic Madden with a tone of disbelief.

"There are so many sir, seeing them as a collection was enough for me. Do we count the grains of sugar before a cup of tea sir, but we know it makes it so much sweeter."

On seeing Frederic Madden's unease, Edward Hawkins uncrossed his arms and finally spoke. "Having said all that sir, our studies have been favourable to you, the age and origin of the pieces are of great interest to our medieval department."

He stopped, as if allowing Forrest to say something. He didn't.

"You offered them to us at a price of one hundred guineas?" Edward Hawkins stated.

Forrest took it as a question. "Aye sir, I did, and you are correct, I did say one hundred guineas."

"At that time we were under the impression they were the complete collection."

"At that time sir, I too thought they were the complete collection."

"Nevertheless, they are not."

"Apparently."

"We will have to allow for others having some in their possession. So they are not unique to us, that is important to the Museum sir. Their rarity has been somewhat compromised."

Forrest waited, fearing the worst.

"For that reason we can only pay you the sum of eighty

pounds."

The word 'only' sounded final. Forrest had to decide whether to hold his ground or refuse the offer, which would mean him returning to Edinburgh without any reparation whatsoever. He had already laid out so much: the coach journey and the payment to his brother for his keep. He wondered what he would do if he were back at his establishment. "I will meet you halfway sir, ninety pounds."

"The British Museum does not negotiate Mr Forrest."

"Nor does Thomas Andrew Forrest, Mr Hawkins." Forrest thought for a moment. "Eighty guineas or I walk out of here with the collection in hand."

A moment's silence.

"Then eighty guineas it is sir," Edward Hawkins said.

T. A. Forrest sighed in relief.

As did Frederic Madden.

same time leaving her home to the mercy of the landlord's men. Without any means of supporting herself and her children, she had no choice but to go and travel to a land far away. News of the boat she was travelling on began to filter back to him. Thirteen died on the crossing and many more had perished after being put ashore. Malcolm never knew if she and the children were amongst them.

On top of all what was happening, Malcolm had got word from Catherine Ryrie that Phineas had fallen ill, saying her husband's time to depart this world was growing ever nearer. Malcolm left Penny Donald immediately. He arrived at Stornoway in the afternoon, the same as he had done a year earlier.

Malcolm was beginning to think that Donald and Annie Graham were correct, also his wife Agatha: while a single piece remained on the island: the suffering would also.

Phineas's eyes angled towards his friend. "Leave while you can," he told Malcolm. It was as much as he could do to utter those four words. He looked down to what Malcolm had in his hand. "Now you have the means to do so."

"I'll see it to the bitter end," Malcolm replied, not knowing when that would be, but knew it would be soon.

Malcolm was shocked to see how much Phineas's health had declined, how it had worsened since his last visit. His movements were slow and laboured, as though every small gesture took the greatest effort. His body had become skeletal, his eyes pale, his skin as dry and flaky as the scars covering the Bishop Malcolm was holding in his other hand.

"I can't feel my leg any more," Phineas had grimaced. "At least that pain has now gone," he told him, trying to force out a smile. He then tried to reassure Malcolm that he had won many battles in the past and this would be no exception.

Malcolm had seen his tray of medals, knew of his distinguished war record, but he felt this was a fight where

Phineas wouldn't come out the victor.

Roderick was also with them, sitting on the other side of the bed, crouched over with his elbows resting on the edge, as if he wanted to hold his father's hand, but didn't. In some ways Roderick was hoping his father would improve in the next few days. If not, then maybe he would still be with him when his time finally came. He feared not though. His job as a clerk at the merchant office only allowed him a week away from work, just enough time to see his ailing father, even then his employer thought he was being too generous. Roderick used this same visit to give Malcolm the thirty pounds. The five pounds from Charles Kirkpatrick Sharpe he decided to keep for himself, for expenses: he couldn't afford not to, even then he was out of pocket. He also knew how much the return journey would take out of him.

Malcolm could see that Roderick's breathing hadn't improved since the last time they met. He too was looking drawn and hollow-cheeked, his eyes sunken and bloodshot, even his speech had become slurred: a younger version of his father.

Malcolm passed the small Bishop over to Roderick, asked him to take it back to Edinburgh, sell it to the person who bought the collection in the first place "Keep the money for yourself," he told him. "I don't care, throw it over the side of the boat during the crossing if need be."

Roderick did neither.

The return journey had indeed taken it out of him.

As the days passed his seizures had become more frequent, each one more severe. Then he had his worst seizure yet. At first it felt as if he couldn't breathe; that wasn't unusual, it would soon pass he told himself. Even the thornapple leaves had no affect on this occasion. He knew his body was growing immune to them anyway, which only made him consume more. This was when his mind drifted to places he would rather not go. It had become a permanent chore; a habit that had taken over every

waking moment of his life.

In his last moments, Roderick dreamt he was laid naked on a beach, his back against the warm sand. With each wave that washed over his body a piece of him would drift away. Slowly the tide receded back to the vast ocean whence it came; and with it went Roderick Ryrie.

He died on the same day his father departed this world.

Neither knew of each other's demise.

Roderick was buried in South Leith Parish Churchyard, his father in Stornoway. Still they remain apart.

Soon after, Catherine Ryrie, along with her two sons, William and Robert, moved to be near family in Liverpool.

Malcolm would never see them again.

Catherine died aged 73 and was buried in Stornoway next to her husband. William and Robert died only two months apart from each other in 1900.

After he witnessed the continuing evictions from neighbouring villages, some having to travel many miles to settle elsewhere, only to find themselves being ejected once again; Malcolm decided to take Phineas's advice and not wait any longer. He, along with his family and the few belongings they could carry, emigrated to Australia. The thirty pounds received from Roderick for the sale of us helped pay for his passage and their settlement.

With Malcolm and his family went the secrets of our discovery.

But I know.

As do you.

So devastated was she at the loss of her only son, Margaret Pirrie left his room untouched for four years. That was until the allowance from her family ceased. Not having Roderick's salary didn't help matters either. She realised there was only one thing to do, and that was to rent out Roderick's room. For her it would be the final goodbye, as though she had wiped away his

existence from this world.

It was when she began to sort through the clothes in his closet, that she felt something in one of his coat pockets. For Margaret Pirrie it was a recurring nightmare, thinking it was the last she had seen of the figures. Roderick had even told her the remaining pieces had gone, not saying how or to whom. What was even worse, it was a Bishop, a devil in disguise as she thought. From that moment on, Roderick's mother only had one objective, the piece couldn't remain in the house any longer than necessary. Nor did she want to throw it away as the devil would curse her more than it had done already.

It suddenly came to her. She remembered those words written in the note Charles Kirkpatrick Sharpe had sent to Roderick. '*My own home at ninety-three Princes Street would also be acceptable if you so wish.*' How could she could forget that strange motive on the envelope.

The next day she dressed in her Sunday best and made the journey to Princes Street.

It was a relief to see Albert open the door, looking no different than the last time she had seen him, as if he was dressed in the same attire as someone half his age. It brought back memories from when they had picked out the small figures from the bag, five apiece, like they were Roman emperors choosing who was to be sacrificed and who wasn't.

"Do you remember me? My son Roderick sold those small figures to Mr Sharpe," she said.

Albert nodded but remained framed by the doorway.

"It's Albert isn't it?"

He nodded again.

"Is Mr Sharpe at home Albert?" she asked.

Albert moved out of the way.

She stepped past him and entered a drab hallway with walls of scuffed wood panels, a patterned threadbare rug underfoot. Albert took her up to the first floor, showed her into what she assumed was the back drawing room, just as dreary and dark as

Charles Kirkpatrick Sharpe appeared to think. "At what cost madam?"

"I only wish to remove it from my own household sir. I do not ask for recompense."

Charles Kirkpatrick Sharpe smiled. "Aye madam, I remember your resentment to these strange figures."

"With respect to a man of such distinction as yourself Mr Sharpe, but strange, nay, I can think of other words to describe them. Wicked, aye sir, I would say wicked, and evil. I believe my son would still be here if it wasn't for the cruelty they had brought onto him. His life was such a harsh one after receiving them from his father."

"That is your belief madam. I fear mine differs. They are no more than carvings." He pointed to the cabinet. "But not let us taint the air with debate. May I ask how you have come by it so late in the proceedings?"

"I have pondered that deeply sir. I found it in one of Roderick's coat pockets. Either he kept it back for himself from the first visit or he brought it back from his last time on the Island of Lewis, when he visited his ailing father. That is all I know."

Charles Kirkpatrick Sharpe indicated to Albert to take the Bishop from her. "In that case madam it will be an honour to lighten your load. In more ways than one if I am not very much mistaken." He looked up to Albert and pointed to the cabinet. "Albert will place it with the others. Now there are eleven."

The Auction Houses

1851, 1888, 2019

For another nine years I remained in Charles Kirkpatrick Sharpe's cabinet at Princes Street. There I found myself in the company of many other strange curiosities, all with gruesome tales to be told; as we informed them of ours.

The closest to us was the skull of William Duke of Queensberry, a curious sight if ever there was one. His teeth bared to the world as if in hysterical laughter, although we soon learnt there was nothing humorous about his story.

On the other side was a piece of lead from Robert the Bruce's shroud. It reminded me of the tenuous connection with us and Robert Bruce many years ago, before I was carved into the monarch I am now. I recalled how Bjarne of Bjarkoy had travelled to Bergen at Queen Isabel's request, where she instructed him to go on to Scotland to offer Norway's help to her brother Robert Bruce. Bjarne of Bjarkoy never returned from that journey; and because of that it changed our fate. But you know that already. And if he had returned? Then my journey would have been a lot different to the one I am telling now.

Every so often the doors to the cabinet would be opened and there would stand Charles Kirkpatrick Sharpe, sometimes alone, rarely with Albert, but usually in the company of others. These were mostly distinguished artisans, poets and artists, writers and scholars, men and women from the nobility, dignitaries of the highest rank.

Each time the doors were opened I noticed Charles Kirkpatrick Sharpe's carriage was becoming more slumped, his demeanor less ardent. On one showing he had a full head of dark hair. I was surprised to see on the next it had greatly thinned and become iron grey in colour. It was strange because the next time I saw him it was dark again. I can't tell you how long that period of time was; as I've said many times before, time has no effect on me. I could only guess he had started wearing a wig, like an upside down bird's nest, one that reached down to his eyebrows. I assumed it was on purpose, to cover his increasingly lined forehead. Unfortunately there was nothing he could do to hide his dropped jowls and the sagging bags under his eyes. What hadn't changed was his attire, as though he had worn those same clothes for the entire decade. Charles Kirkpatrick Sharpe was a man who refused to step away from the past. I can only guess it was the time he saw as his most fruitful, when he was at his prime in life.

Because of his deteriorating health, we all moved to a house in Drummond Street in the New Town, away from the increasingly overpopulated Princes Street. It was quieter, the air cleaner, the citizens more to his liking. Albert travelled with him.

For another ten years we were displayed in a much larger cabinet, many more artifacts began to join us. It seemed a day didn't go by without us having more company: the cap worn by Queen Mary on her escape from Lochleven Castle, a rare Cremona Violin, many notes and letters from distinguished authors and nobility, paintings by acclaimed artists. There was also an original of Edward Young's poem 'Night Thoughts'

given by Robert Burn to his lover Agnus McLehose, a lady he affectionately called Clarinda.

Strangely it was Albert who took the greatest interest in the organisation of the cabinet, although not the artifacts themselves. I think he had a flair for neatness and organisation, creating groupings and sub-divisions. It was as if he needed to do it rather than wanting to. I began to realise there was nothing he wouldn't do for Charles Kirkpatrick Sharpe, or Chas, as Albert fondly called him, even to other people, when in his presence. We were placed in the medieval section, although I feel we were not given the prominence we justly deserved. I always had this feeling that Albert wasn't much taken by us, even wanting to avoid touching us. Maybe he thought the same as others had: Agatha MacLeod, Margaret Pirrie, Donald and Annie Graham. That we had some kind of ulterior motive for being in this world, one that was not much to his liking.

Charles Kirkpatrick Sharpe died one year later, March 1851. I'm glad to say Albert was by his bedside at the time, as he had been throughout his life.

In June that same year Charles Kirkpatrick Sharpe's collection of antiquities was put to auction by Messrs C.B. Tait and T. Nisbit in their Great Room at Hanover Street in Edinburgh.

The companionship I enjoyed for so long with all the other strange and wonderful antiquities was about to be torn apart. All I hoped for was that the eleven of us would remain together. I'm glad to say we did.

The auction's catalogue described Charles Kirkpatrick Sharpe's collection as richly carved inlaid cabinets and antique chairs, a Buhl clock, with bracket, a number of curious musical instruments including a rare Cremona violin. I wondered who else would hear that beautiful sound, like a human voice. It continued: an enamelled reliquary and a triptych from Byzantine art, antique Indian and Dresden china vases. Then amongst the numerous other articles were us, described as 'the

"Lot 747 gentlemen," a bellowing male voice echoed around the room. "Shown here on my left are eleven chessmen of great antiquity. Found over fifty years ago on the Island of Lewis."

A moment's silence.

"As described in the catalogue," the auctioneer called out, staring around at the onlookers as if he was asking for everyone's attention, holding his gaze on certain individuals for slightly longer. This included a man called Francis Whelan.

"Shall we say one hundred and fifty guineas to start."

A long silence.

Francis Whelan was quietly sat in the fifth row. He knew how to remain inconspicuous, never to start bidding too early, evaluate the opposition first; and that's the way he saw the other people around him, as the opposition. Some he knew from previous sales. Some through his own research. He had evaluated their wealth, how high they might raise the stakes, like in a game of cards. Francis Whelan tried to make sure they were sat in front of him, just so he could see who was bidding, who he was up against. Sometimes it could be the faintest lowering of the head or the raise of a single finger. He had to be at his most vigilant.

Francis Whelan was a leading expert in the transaction of antiquities, known to act as an agent for several museums at auctions. He also had previous dealings with Robert Carfrae, who was a member of the Purchasing Committee and the Chair at the Society of Antiquaries of Scotland. In a recent meeting they had discussed the buying of the pieces. It was soon decided he was perfect for the job.

Francis Whelan waited for the first bid.

"Come on gentlemen," the auctioneer insisted before gazing around the room. "One hundred and twenty guineas then." He sounded impatient.

Silence.

Francis Whelan had been told by the Committee that his

limit was three hundred pounds, a sum he should not go above under any circumstances. If bidding exceeded this then the Museum would lose out yet again. Francis couldn't allow that, he had a reputation to maintain.

"We are after one hundred and twenty guineas gentlemen."

Francis noticed a slight shuffling of someone's feet sat in front, no nod of the head or a raise of the hand: he kept them in his peripheral vision.

"One hundred and twenty guineas." A slight pause. "One hundred and twenty pounds then." The auctioneer leant forward, elbows on the lectern, the wooden gavel held loosely in his fingers, as though he could drop it at any moment. "One hundred and twenty pounds," he repeated.

Francis Whelan continued to wait. It was getting close to the guide price and he knew it.

The auctioneer stood straight and raised the gavel as if he was going to slam it down without a bid being made. "One hundred guineas then." The auctioneer turned his head and spoke to one of his colleagues.

Francis Whelan was getting nervous. He had been commissioned to do a job; and that was to buy the pieces at the lowest price. His client trusted him. They couldn't complain, after all, it was only a third of his budget. Who else was waiting though. Time to find out. He stared at the auctioneer, caught his eye and gave one sharp downward nod.

"We have a bidder at one hundred guineas." The auctioneer stretched out the gavel in front of him, holding it tightly this time, as if more bids would be drawn into it. His gaze bounced around the audience. "One hundred guineas has been bid ladies and gentlemen."A short pause. "One hundred guineas." He repeated.

Francis Whelan's gaze was fixed forward, waiting for the voice of another bidder. He so much wanted to hear the slam of the gavel. A slight murmering amongst the audience made him anxious.

“One hundred guineas. Fair warning. One hundred guineas.”

Francis Whelan could feel his heart beating faster. ‘Drop the gavel’ he kept repeating in his head like it was some kind of mantra.

“One hundred guineas it is then.” The auctioneer raised the gavel, held it in the air for several seconds.

‘Now,’ thought Francis. ‘Drop it now.’

“Last warning.”

The gavel came down with a loud thud.

Francis Whelan relaxed and awarded himself a congratulatory smile: he never knew the British Museum and South Kensington Museum had abstained from the bidding.

That is not the end of our journey.

The battle scarred warrior T. A. Forrest gave to his colleague. That was sold by the colleague several year later for two pounds to a fellow antiquarian in Edinburgh. In 1964, that antiquarian’s grandson sold it to a dealer also from Edinburgh for five pounds, recording it in his stock book as ‘an antique walrus tusk Warrior chessman’. Surprisingly, because of the poor condition, no one knew about the celebrated collection of pieces it had originally belonged to.

After he died, his daughter, who knew nothing about antiquities or chess, inherited the Warrior. She kept it in a bag inside the bottom drawer of a chest in the spare room. Occasionally she would liberate it for her admiring family and friends. Still no one knew what it was. For fifty-two years this brave Warrior remained a topic of admiration in that household. For those who were without appreciation, who thought of it as a bit of old tat, the daughter would just look at them. ‘No one is perfect,’ she would say.

That was until a friend paid her a visit. A friend who happened to have a five year old grandson; and like all young grandsons of that age, he had an all consuming passion for

anything to do with dinosaurs, astonishing everyone in being able to name so many. He could tell you whether it was a Diplodocus or a Dilophosaurus, a Velociraptor or a Tyrannosaurus Rex. So, like all devoted grandmothers she took him to the National Museum of Scotland to see an exhibition called Fossil Hunters. It was about life on earth over three hundred million years ago. "Even older than me," she had told him with a smile, although her grandson wasn't so sure. So not to waste the visit, she decided to take the opportunity to see many of the other items on display. The grandson was particularly taken by eleven small ivory figures. Not so much the exquisite carving, after all, he was only five and his Transformer had just as much detail, and that had flashing lights. It was the expressions that enchanted him the most: thoughtful, angry, comical, wary, surprised, humorous, fearful, mindful, brave. The grandson didn't know which one it was. Maybe it was all of them.

I would like to say I remembered this young lad and his grandmother, but I have had so many of those bright and wondrous young eyes look at me over the last one hundred and twenty-eight years, it is difficult to remember them all. I just know it had happened.

I say once again, time has never had an affect on me.

Anyway, after her visit to the National Museum of Scotland the grandmother went to visit her friend. On being shown the piece she remarked that it was very much like those strange wee figures in the museum.

So two years later in 2018, while in London, her granddaughter decided to end all speculation and had the foresight to ask Sotheby's if it could be worth more than the five pounds her grandpa had paid for it fifty-four years previous.

"Add five noughts," they told her. "And more."

In June 2019, for nearly three quarters of a million pounds, this heavily battered and scarred Warrior was sold to an

I was not intended; and yet we survived. We were made for war but now we are at peace.

We were once no more than commodities to you, just cattle in a meat market. That was why we were separated, for your own greed.

My home is now a grand room in one of the great institutions: the same city where Roderick Ryrie and his mother Margaret Pirrie resided, where T.A Forrest, Charles Kirkpatrick Sharpe and Albert once lived. Although they have long passed, we still survive; and as you all will depart this world one day, we will remain. You have made us into something you could only achieve in your wildest dreams: we are eternal.

I am in the centre, protected by my compatriots, as I protect them, as you now protect us. Many eyes have stared at me, coveted me for what I am worth.

One of our eleven is in another room within this same great establishment. A Bishop who sits in the shadows of elaborate crosiers and sacred rings: it shares a space with others that were created to be part of what is good, but have so far failed to do so. This is the eleventh piece, the same one that was left in the souterrain close to the House of the Black Women, the one given to Charles Kirkpatrick Sharpe by Margaret Pirrie. Once returned to us; it is alone again.

A young girl stepped up to the cabinet, her eyes clear and bright, staring at us in astonishment, as you all do.

"Look at these strange people Mummy," she said.

Her mother stepped forward and began to read the display board. "The Lewis..." She stopped. " You read it darling. What does it say?"

"The Lewis chess pieces." Her eyes widened that little bit more. "Ten chess pieces, part of a large hoard buried on the Isle of Lewis and found in 1831." She stopped to focus on the back of my throne, fascinated by the two beasts biting the frame.

"What else does it say?" the mother asked.

The girl gazed back down, her eyes roaming from side to

side. "The hoard contained 93 gaming pieces in total, including four chess sets."

The girl stepped around to the front of the cabinet again, only so she could see our faces as she read, occasionally to look through the glass and stare into our eyes. She continued to read. "The pieces were probably made around 1200 in Norway. At this time, Lewis was part of the Norse-Gae..." The young girl looked up to her mother.

"Gaelic darling. Some of the people from the Isles still speak the language. It is lovely to listen to."

The girl looked down again. "...Gaelic Kingdom of the Isles, encom...encompass...encompassing islands and land along to the Isle of Man. There was a strong..." She moved her head closer to the words. "Scan..You finish it Mummy."

Her mother stepped closer. "Scandinavian influence in the region and Norway controlled the kingdom at times. Most of the pieces are made from walrus ivory, which was probably obtained in Greenland and traded back to Norway. Two of these pieces are carved from sperm-whale teeth."

And the others?

Sixty-one are in another great institution in the centre of London, along with fourteen round disks made from the surplus morse. Also that one belt buckle worn by Leif at his wedding to Birgit. Some are on a battleground of red and white, as if a war has been frozen in time, their compatriots randomly placed around it.

Six are now on the Isle of Lewis, where Malcolm Macleod and his family once lived in the village of Penny Donald. Where the Red Ghillie killed Grub. Where Neil MacLeod was captured. A King, a Queen, a Bishop, a Knight, a Warrior and one from the front line, all deserving of the great Institution they now reside in.

And that brave Warrior that had been through so much, the piece that had been battered and scarred? He has been taken

overseas to a land faraway. Alone he is displayed for the wonderment of the very few.

The other forty-nine?

Maybe one day they will surface again.

A King's Journey

&

The Lewis Pieces

That was good enough for me to choose the second variation: so 13th-15th centuries it is. To appease skeptics I decided to choose the earlier of the dates in this variation.

Next move. Where were they carved? Here we have several possible variations.

They were carved in Iceland. This is the preferred option by Frederick Madden in his 1832 analysis, 'Remarks on the ancient Chess-men found.' *It would appear most probable, therefore, that the chess-men and draught-men discovered in the Isle of Lewis, formed part of a stock of an Icelandic kaup-mann or merchant, who carried these articles to the Hebrides or Ireland for the sake of traffic; and the ship in which they were conveyed being wrecked, these figures were swept by the waves on shore, and buried beneath the sand-bank.*

Following that, Nancy Marie Brown in her 2015 book the 'Ivory Vikings,'wrote that a skilled craftswoman called Margret the Adroit had carved a walrus ivory crosier for a Bishop, the piece so skillfully executed that only someone with her skill could have carved the Lewis pieces. We also have the Siglunes piece found on Iceland, a small figure made out of herringbone that vaguely takes on the appearance of one of the Lewis Warriors. I believe more analysis is needed to make this Icelandic variation viable. Nor should it be dismissed.

We return to the 'main line'.

The pieces were carved in northern Norway, possibly the city of Nidaros, now Trondheim. It is plain to see that many carvings on the stave churches in that country are very similar to those of the thrones on the chess pieces. Morse workshops employing skilled craftsmen were known to have existed here. A fragment of a morse piece was discovered during an excavation at the ruins of St. Olav's Church in Nidaros in 1890. Unfortunately the piece itself was lost and the only evidence of its existence was a drawing and description made by its discoverer: Major Otto Krefling. Having seen the drawing myself, I can say with confidence that this is not part of the

Lewis collection, but was possibly carved at the same workshop. The piece does clearly show the Queen's hand to cheek pose. A coincidence? Ask a dozen or more morse craftsmen to carve a chess Queen in the Viking style and see how many will have the hand to cheek pose: none probably. Therefore it was possibly carved in the same workshop or the craftsman had some knowledge of the Lewis pieces.

Other pieces have also been found in Norway. For me the most convincing is a Warder found in Oland, now in the Historiska Museet in Stockholm. Another, a Knight, said to be carved in Northern Europe in the 13th century, now in the Museo Nazionale del Bargello in Florence, Italy. It has to be said that one of the most compelling finds is a piece found in Clonard in Ireland. It too has the hand to cheek pose. Another coincidence?

The next moves to analyse: by whom and why were they created in the first place? These are probably the least analysed moves in this variation.

Move one: the struggling craftsman decided to waste the next few years carving one hundred and twenty-eight very intricate pieces just because he had nothing better to do. Then to sell them down at the local market to the poor folk of Nidaros or hoping that on the off chance a passing wealthy benefactor might purchase them.

Move two: an important and rich dignitary comes along and commissions the pieces to be created. Four sets in total, a gift for a much higher ranked person or persons than himself. Possibly to enhance his own standing in society at the same time?

I know which move I would choose.

So who commissioned them and why? In my research for that period I came across a wealthy and powerful individual called Bjarne of Bjarkoy. A well travelled and interesting man who had the ear of the king and the influence to supply that amount of tusks and to authorise the creation of four shatranj

sets. Unfortunately in this 'main line' variation, Bjarne of Bjarkoy was sacrificed early in the game.

So what did Bjarne of Bjarkoy actually commission?

To answer that question; and just for a moment, we will step away from the 'main line' to explore another variation, one we will call the Chandler variation.

The Lewis pieces are described as chessmen, and yes it is difficult to argue against that: there are eight Kings and eight Queens, there are sixteen Bishops, fifteen Knights and thirteen Warriors, so we can assume one Knight and three Warriors have been lost, not surprising considering their journey. It is the 'Pawns' that throw a spanner into the works. Yes, they could be used as the front line in a chess set. But do not let us underestimate the intelligence and creativity of the Norse people at that time; as the quality of the Lewis pieces vouch for. It is possible the collection is a combination of games; hence the presence of the fourteen disks. There was a game played in that period called hnefatafl (a variant of the tafl family). I'm not going to go into the rules of the game; considering that is also under dispute. You basically need one target piece (the King?) and two armies (one 12 strong, the other 24 strong, although that changes in other variants). The pieces in those armies are of the exact same size and design, although the two armies must be distinguishable. The so called pawns from the Lewis collection could also second as pieces for hnefatafl. One pawn is noticeably larger than the others: the King? There are many with that same octagonal shape: one of the armies? There are some with intricate carvings, looking like headstones: the second army? We can only assume that many of these smaller pieces have also been lost.

I'll return to the 'main line'. So we come across one of the most important moves in the game: the creator himself? A highly skilled and experienced craftsman must have carved or overseen

the creation of the pieces: of that there is no doubt.

Other moves in that same strategy have to be analysed. Was there more than one craftsman? Many of the pieces change slightly in technique and form, as described in the excellent National Museums Scotland's publication 'The Lewis Chessmen Unmasked.' So yes, probably several craftsmen, some more skilled than others. Were some of the pieces coloured? Considering it would be difficult to play a game of chess without knowing whose side you're trying to attack. Frederick Madden wrote, *'they may have been originally stained dark red or beet-root colour, but from having been so long subject to the action of salt-water, the colouring matter, in most cases, has been discharged.'* I find his variation unclear.

I have several antique chess pieces in my possession, many are stained red. The probability they would lose all colouring, even under the most extreme circumstances, especially in the deeper recesses is very remote. If it got to that stage of discharge I'm sure the pieces would be in far worse condition (apart from some scarring, a few look as if they were made yesterday). So I chose the move that would relinquish them of all colouring; unclear, but I could find none better.

So who were these other crafts people? Many skills were passed down from elders to the younger generation; and with that, styles changed and developed. As they have with the Lewis pieces. Yes, stylistically they may be Viking, but not all Staunton sets are made in the 1850s.

The position has now become complicated, the variation unclear. The pieces are about to leave Norway. From where and when? So here I looked into several combinations. The place I chose was Bergen, the largest port for the trading of goods at that time. With the historic ties between Norway and Ireland, many merchants came from the latter. I chose the first half of the 16th century, this was when trade between the two countries was at its most productive.

So how did the pieces end up on the Isle of Lewis?

the surface.

4. *Proceedings of the Society of Antiquaries of Scotland Vol XXIII. Author unknown (maybe quoting the Rev. Alexander MacLeod), December 1888: The Head of the Bay of Uig. Chamber of dry-built stone disclosed by the washing away of a bank of sand about 15 feet deep.*

5. *New Statistical Account, Ross and Cromarty. The Rev. Alexander MacLeod, Minister at Uig. 1833: The head of the bay of Uig. In the sands.*

6. *Archaeologia Vol XXIV. Frederick Madden (quoting a newspaper from June 1831): Mealasta, Uig, Taignir collechin Dugh an Uig. No description given.*

I felt I had no choice but to included both these locations. Not at the same time, after all, this is chess.

Malcolm MacLeod lived at Penny Donald (Peighinn Dhomhnall). From an 1853 ordinance survey map this village was shown to be only a stone's throw away from Uig Bay. The earliest reference to Malcolm MacLeod was in the Proceedings of the Society of Antiquaries of Scotland Vol IV, 1860-61 written by Captain F.W.L. Thomas who was possibly quoting Donald Morrison (remember the Red Ghillie). *'Thereafter, in A.D 1831, Malcolm MacLeod, tenant of Penny Donald in Uig, found upwards of eighty of these carved relics'*. Mr Morrison died in 1834, three years after they were found, so alive during their discovery. For me, the most convincing reference to Malcolm MacLeod existence was in a pamphlet by Alistair McIntosh about Donald MacLeod's experiences concerning the clearances on the Island of Lewis: *'Penny Donald. Malcolm MacLeod (Calum Sprot) from this village found the Lewis Chessmen....Malcolm MacLeod was a neighbour of my progenitor Donald MacRitcie'*. The move not clear, but not to be dismissed.

The next move: Malcolm MacLeod passed the pieces onto Roderick Ryrie to sell in Edinburgh.

Who was Roderick Ryrie? His name has been mentioned

many times, although with every written account, the spelling varies: Ryrie, Ririe, Pirie and Pirrie. Many masters have him as a merchant, although as much as I tried, I could find no mention of Roderick Ryrie, Ririe, Pirie or Pirrie: no birth or marriage certificates, no address, no merchant's manifest; nothing. It was as though he was hiding in plain sight. That was until a member of the Stornoway Historical Society popped an email into my inbox: *we do have record of Roderick Ryrie*!

I quote: *'He was born in September 1810 to Captain Phineas Ryrie, so Captain Ryrie was the father not the son. Phineas Ryrie served with Lt John Munro, son of Rev Hugh Munro of Uig. Phineas must have maintained a friendship with the Munro family. It is my guess that Roderick was living in Edinburgh at the time. Phineas walked with a limp. He died in 1832. Through my own research a Roderick William Ryrie died in 1831 as a result of an asthma attack. There was a new minister in Uig by this time, Rev Alexander Macleod, regarded as the first of the evangelical preachers in the island. He was very critical of his predecessor whom he regarded as unspiritual. Rev Hugh Munro died in 1823.'* In all probabilities, Malcolm MacLeod from Penny Donald could have known the Rev Hugh Munro, he would have also been a very similar age to the Reverend's son John and therefore probably knew Phineas.

Next move: Malcolm MacLeod gives the pieces to Roderick Ryrie to sell in Edinburgh. The first port of call would probably be the Society of Antiquaries of Scotland. I refer to David Laing's transactions notice from 1833, *'It was proposed at the time, by a few members, to make a joint-purchase of the entire collection, and after setting aside a certain number for the Society's Museum, to apportion the others among the contributers. By some oversight or delay, this arrangement was frustrated'*.

There is no account of how Roderick Ryrie came to meet T. A. Forrest. What we do know is that Forrest did manage to

acquire eighty-two pieces for thirty pounds, quite a substantial amount in those days.

Charles Kirkpatrick Sharpe comes into play at this stage of the game. It was Dr Robert Chambers, a friend of both Walter Scott and Charles Kirkpatrick Sharpe who provides us with the best description of him, *'I feel that C.K.S. has himself become, as it were, a tradition of Edinburgh. His thin, effeminate figure, his voice pitched in alt.- his attire, as he took his daily walks on Princes Street: a long blue frock-coat, black trousers (rather wide below, and sweeping over white stockings and neat shoes), something like a web of white cambric round his neck, and a brown wig coming down to his eyebrows - had long established him as what is called a character.'*

At what stage Charles Kirkpatrick Sharpe bought ten of the figures is unclear, we just know he did. The strange thing is, out of all of his letters, of which there are many, and all well documented, not one mentions the Lewis pieces! Maybe he didn't realise the importance of them, after all his collection was vast. There is also a tenuous connection between him and T. A. Forrest. We know this through a reference made about Forrest; and not a particularly flattering one. In a letter dated 1831 he writes about a painting, *'The picture I mentioned is a very pretty one, but of course Forrest will dispose of it to anybody.'*

So how did Charles Kirkpatrick Sharpe know about the existence of the pieces for them to come into his ownership? David Laing was probably present during the original meeting with Roderick Ryrie at the Society of Antiquaries of Scotland. Again, I refer to David Laing's transactions notice from 1833. This is when I entered into the realms of possibilities and probabilities. We know Charles Kirkpatrick Sharpe was a friend of David Laing because both frequently corresponded with each other.

Charles Kirkpatrick Sharpe manages to acquire another figure, the eleventh piece, a Bishop. How this transpires is unclear, nor is it mentioned in any of his letters. This was my

excuse to make a combination of the two find locations on Lewis. The only reliable reference I could find was from Daniel Wilson, another acquaintance of Charles Kirkpatrick Sharpe, when discussing the original acquirement of the ten figures, '*The remaining one was afterwards obtained from a person residing in Lewis.*' That was it!

In the mean time, T. A. Forrest had travelled to London to secure a transaction with the British Museum. They have listed all the eighty-two pieces as being bought direct from him. This was pre-train times, one made by stagecoach, so not an easy journey by any means.

An interesting move follows. We also know from Walter Scott's own hand that he had visited the British Museum on the afternoon of 17th October: on the morning of that same day the pieces had been displayed to the museum by T. A. Forrest. Walter Scott writes: *'The morning beautiful. To-day I go to look after the transcripts in the Museum and have a card to see a set of chessmen thrown up by the sea on the coast of Scotland, which were offered to sale for. The King, Queen, Knights, etc., were in the costume of the 14th century, the substance ivory or rather the tusk of the morse, somewhat injured by the salt water in which they had been immersed for some time.*

Walter Scott was also a close friend of Charles Kirkpatrick Sharpe and in contact with him on a regular basis.

Charles Kirkpatrick Sharpe died in 1851.

Auctioneers Messrs C. B. Tait and T. Nisbett was chosen to sell his collection of antiquities in June that year. Lot 531 was bought by Albert Denison, who also goes under the title the 1st Baron Londesborough. A pamphlet titled 'Papers of the Estates of the Earls of Londesborough aptly describes what happened after. *'Albert Denison chose to live in Grimston, only coming to Londesborough for shooting. He died in 1860, his son, William Henry Forester Denison succeeded him. He inherited £2 million in stocks and shares and a yearly rental roll of £100,000, but he had been given a taste of an extravagant*

exceptional ‘Ivory Vikings’ by Nancy Marie Brown.

I would also like to thank *you*; the reader: the reason why authors put pen to paper.

Apologies to anyone I may have missed.

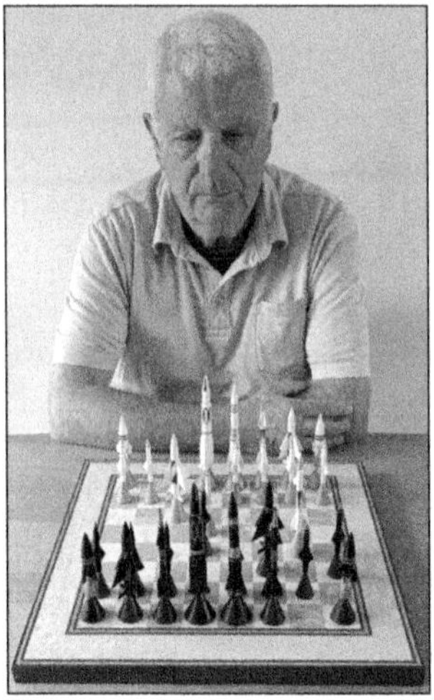

About the Author

'A King's Journey' is Tony's ninth novel. His previous genres comprise of fictional biography, humorous and political thrillers, post apocalyptic and psychological.

Back in the mid-1980's, before he had started writing novels; with his interest in collecting chess pieces and also a maker of chess sets, (his Missile Set is pictured above with author), Tony began studying the Lewis pieces. Acquiring an annual pass into the British Library, he spent much of his free time under that beautiful domed roof in the British Museum (before the internet).

Tony Boucher is also an internationally sold artist with several solo exhibitions to his name.
His works can be seen online at the SaatchiArt website.

ALSO BY
THE SAME AUTHOR

The Unfortunate Basil Albright

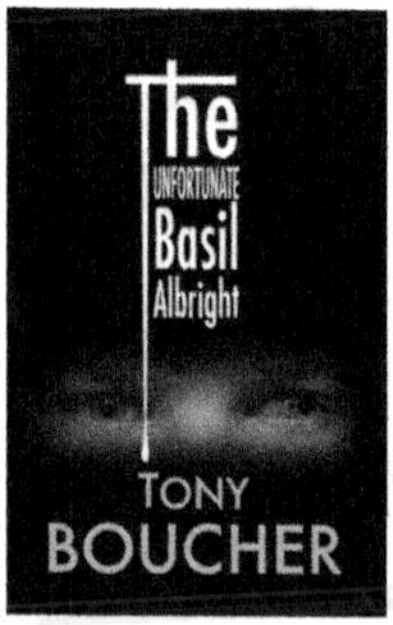

Baz's life is like a jigsaw puzzle, once connected every piece has an effect on the other, however distant. As the picture evolves his life becomes increasingly tortuous.

This is the unlikely story of Basil Albright's life from his earliest memory to the tragic consequences of his death.

A loner, a father, a one-time lover and a killer. Baz brushes shoulders with gangsters, tackles the most uninhabitable airfield of the Second World War and joins a drug-fuelled hippy commune. He questions beliefs and searches for answers. But most of all, Basil Albright is a victim of unfortunate events.

"Do you believe in the virgin birth?"
"Yes of course, I am a Christian."
"Well, you could be from a virgin birth then?"
"That's ridiculous!"
"You believed in one virgin birth, why not another?"

ANNA AND THE KNIGHT

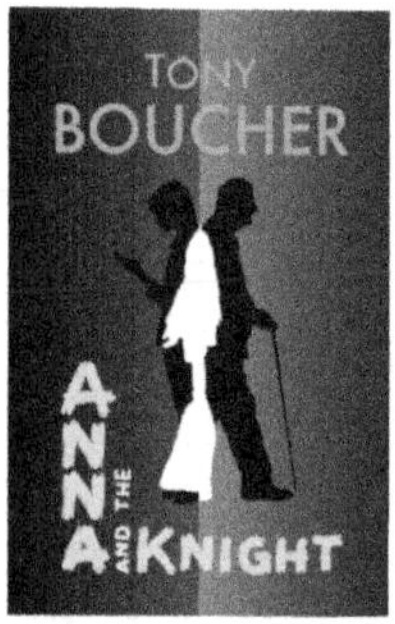

'Anna is pregnant with a cartoon rabbit and Sir James is plain old Roland Budd.

Both are on a mission to reach the site of the legendary 1970 Isle of Wight Rock Festival.'

Every Sunday lunchtime Anna is instructed to pick up Sir James at his cottage and take him back to the Dog and Duck. This is only so he can tell the unsuspecting clientele his knightly tales of crumbling bridges and unfaithful artists.

Today is different though. Today Sir James needs to scatter his wife's ashes at the place they met fifty years ago.

This is an extraordinary road story between eighteen year old Anna and the octogenarian Sir James as they travel from the village of Crendham Hook to the Isle of Wight.

The prequel to 'CLOSE'

'ALONE' MAY BE FICTION
BUT CAN IT SEE THE TRUTH?

ALONE

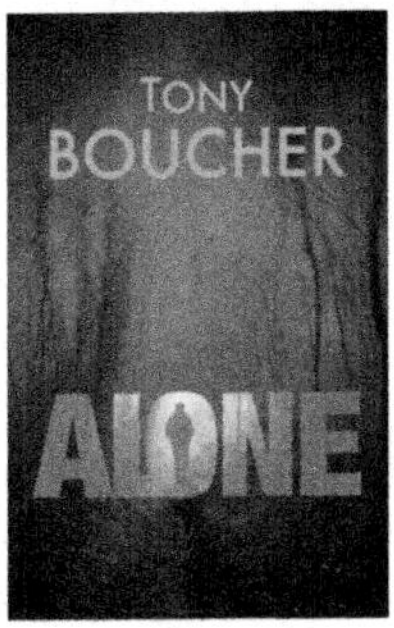

For his entire sixteen years Owen Roberts has been living a teenage boy's idyllic lifestyle, until one phone call that is, a phone call that will change it and him forever.

President Carter Ward has sanctioned the assassination of one of his agents, not realising the catastrophic results it will have on the world, or knowing this will leave one teenage boy in another country alone in this world.

Owen discovers he is not the only one who has survived, his only goal is to reach the others.

Printed in Dunstable, United Kingdom

64552414R00160